SPANISH CINEMA 1896 1983

MINISTERIO DE CULTURA
INSTITUTO DE CINE (I. C. A. A.)

SPANISH CINEMA 1896 1983

Edition under the supervision
of Augusto M. Torres.

Design: Severo Almansa and Vicente
Martínez Gadea.

Texts: Roger Mortimore,
Augusto M. Torres, Román Gubern,
Emilio Sanz de Soto, Ramón Sala,
Rosa Alvarez Berciano, Diego Galán,
César Santos Fontenla,
Equipo «Cartelera Turia», Manuel Palacio,
Emilio de la Rosa, José Antonio
Páramo and Ramón Rubio.

Translated by E. Nelson Modlin III.

Photographs: Spanish Film Library,
Augusto M. Torres, Instituto de Cine
(ICAA), Emilio Sanz de Soto and
Ramón Sala.

Published by: Editora Nacional.
Photomechanics: Progreso Gráfico, S. A.
Photocomposition: Composición Gráfica, S. A.
Printed by: Closas-Orcoyen, S. L.
Polígono Igarsa
Paracuellos del Jarama (Madrid)
ISBN: 84-505-3224-8
Depósito legal: M. 10.174-1986

MINISTERIO DE CULTURA
INSTITUTO DE CINE (I. C. A. A.)

GENERAL INDEX

PROLOGUE

Roger Mortimore

When I arrived in Madrid in September 1972 I had seen only three Spanish films, **Viridiana, El Verdugo** and **El Cochecito,** four if **Nazarin** is accounted a Spanish film; Thorold Dickinson had included these in the programmes of his seminar at the Slade Film School which I attended from 1966 to 1968. There was then in Calle de Victoria, off the Puerta del Sol, a very good and cheap Cuban restaurant called El Clarin, run by exiles from the revolution waiting for their passage to Miami. It was there that I met Paco Lucio, then working for Elias Querejeta, in April 1973. It was from Paco that I first heard of Carlos Saura, with whom he had worked on **Ana and the Wolves,** the Spanish entry at Cannes in 1973. Paco told me of another film he had just worked on for Querejeta. It had been made in a village in the province of Segovia by a friend of his called Victor Erice. It was, Paco assured me, the most beautiful film ever made in Spain.

When Rouben Mamoulian, the chairman of the jury at San Sebastian in September 1973, announced that the Golden Shell had been awarded to **The Spirit of the Beehive,** there was booing. The culprits were Spaniards. Perhaps this is a little hard to believe. But in 1973 Spaniards regarded Spanish cinema with contempt. In trendy circles the films of Saura were revered for being «subversive», but it was a state-financed «subversion». Carmen Rico-Godoy said of Erice's film in **Cambio 16:**

«There is neither plot, nor story, nor defined characters, nor suspense, nor action, nor emotions, nor feelings. The film consists of a series of very beautiful but interminable scenes in which nothing ever happens. And when something does happen it's not understood... If the cinema is a medium of communication, this film doesn't manage to communicate anything...»

The Spirit of the Beehive opened in Madrid at the Conde Duque cinema on Monday 8 October 1973. At 10 pm I finished teaching at the British Institute and took a taxi along the boulevard. I managed to get two seats in the middle of the front row of the front stalls for the 10,30 performance, the final performance on the first day being regarded then as now as the premiere. Paco Lucio had, of course, been quite right.

That autumn of 1973 I was working out my final term as an overworked and underpaid teacher of English at La Casa Inglesa, a private language school on the first floor of a house in the Plaza de Salamanca. One day Paco Lucio appeared. He told me that Saura was about to film a script called **La Prima Angelica** in the second floor flat above La Casa Inglesa. I went with Paco to deliver the script to Maria Clara Fernandez, who plays Angelica as a child. Paco told her that the film was sure to be the Spanish entry at Cannes and that she would have a trip to France. Afterwards we lunched in the garden of Las Encinas, a bar and restaurant in Calle de las Encinas. Steps

by the wall afforded a view of the derelict Sevilla studios, now long since usurped by a hypermarket.
I spent many hours during October and November watching Jose Luis Lopez Vazquez and Fernando Delgado, Luis Cuadrado peering at the light meter, Teo Escamilla hugging the camera during a dolly shot. One Saturday afternoon the technicians whistled **Greensleeves** and **Scotland the Brave,** their protest in favour of a five and a half-day week, «la semana inglesa». Geraldine Chaplin turned up from time to time. One day I sat opposite her and Saura at the long table that cast and crew lunched at upstairs at Casa Cirilo in Calle de General Pardiñas.
Next I became hooked on Spanish cinema of the Second Republic. One day in January 1974 I was having lunch in a Chinese restaurant in Calle de la Reina, around the corner from the Infantas cinema, then used by the Filmoteca, with John Reeder, pupil of Hugh Thomas and leading expatriate intellectual and bon viveur. The film to be shown at the Filmoteca at 4 o'clock was called **Patricio miró a una estrella,** made in 1934. We decided to see it as it was rare for Second Republic films to be screened.
The season of Second Republic films continued until April. I recall John and I going with Paul Preston to see a programme of Second Republic shorts that began with **Tierra sin pan,** and Paul Preston vaulting over the row in front to escape from the subsequent **Almadrabas** and tuna fishing. Only a handful of people ever turned up for these four o'clock showings. At that time, early in 1974, no Spanish critic was showing any interest in the cinema of the Second Republic. After three months I had seen twelve feature films and as many shorts. My love affair with Spanish cinema was under way. I would walk quite a few miles in the rain to see a Spanish film, any Spanish film. Attending Spanish films was how I learned Spanish (I had eight words at my command when I arrived), that and reading the subtitles on foreign films shown at the Filmoteca.
In April 1975 I interviewed Ricardo Urgoiti about his company Filmófono and the four films Bunuel «produced» for him in the Second Republic. I also interviewed Enrique Herreros, who had been in charge of Filmofono's publicity. These interviews formed the basis of an article published in the Summer 1975 number of **Sight and Sound** entitled «Buñuel, Sáenz de Heredia and Filmofono». Geraldine Chaplin was kind enough to say to Jose Luis Borau that I was «the Hugh Thomas of the Spanish cinema».
On the afternoon of Saturday 27 September 1975 three friends and I arrived early to queue for tickets for the first house of Borau's **Poachers,** which had just opened at the Amaya cinema in Paseo de General Martinez Campos. That morning there had been the execution of three presumed members of FRAP on the outskirts of a village in the foothills of the sierra near Madrid and of two members of ETA. Borau's film took on an extra dimension in the context of this repression. The queue was silent, numbed by the news.
It was widely thought that the death of Franco would usher in a glorious era of literature comparable to the Generation of 1898. This has not happened. Contemporary Spanish literature remains, with a few exceptions, all of whom made their reputations long before 1975, resolutely uninteresting. Spanish cinema, of course, does not. There is no prose fabulator to touch Manuel Gutierrez Aragon. The ending of film censorship has not produced a succession of masterpieces, but it has undoubtedly increased the intelligence of Spanish cinema.
Franco died, and Spanish cinema suddenly became of interest to foreigners. **Las Truchas** and **Las palabras de Max** shared the Golden Bear at the Berlin Festival of 1977, the year of the first democratic elections in Spain since February 1936. Spain became invaded by foreign academics, mainly American, their pockets groaning with grants, hunting for thesis material or anxious to compile an «overview» of current Spanish cinema for the fall semester.
In April 1984 I spent two weeks in Aberdeen, where I met a Swiss who told me how much he admired Saura. This would have been impossible in Franco's lifetime. this excellent book is a sign of the marvellous fact that now it is possible.

Translator's introduction

Two problems presented themselves upon translating the original manuscript. The first was the problem of English-language titles for the films mentioned throughout the book. Not a few Spanish films have been marketed all over the world and have set names in English. Even so, many of the films in this history of Spanish cinema literally have been given dozens of names in English by scriptwriters (hailing back to the not-too-distant past when some Spanish films were actually shot in English), Spanish and foreign co-producers, dubbers, subtitlers, translators at Spanish governmental agencies (both defunct and otherwise), sales groups, distributors the world over and even by critics who are «in the know». Other films, especially those made during the fifties and before that decade, perhaps have English names, but they are lost in time.
The task was virtually impossible. So I have opted for the simplest solution: to keep the original Spanish title and to add one —sometimes two— correct translations in English, even knowing that the titles of some Spanish films have been translated universally one particular way. A case in point is Carlos Saura's «Cría cuervos», known as «Cria» in practically every English-language territory. At any rate, I have always sought to explain each film's content with my translations of the titles.
The second problem was attempting to maintain each unit in the spirit in which it was written, yet with a view toward the book's final collective unity. I believe that I have done so and I am certain that the ideas and truths which were intended have been preserved in all clarity. I am delighted to have translated this vital, most necessary, and valuable work by numerous authors concerning the Spanish film world and parallel, equally rich achievements in architecture, painting, sculpture, music and literature during different and difficult political periods for Spain.

E. Nelson Modlin III

1896

1929

The shooting of Es mi hombre **(1927) by Carlos Fernández Cuenca.**

1896 1929

Augusto M. Torres

The study of this first period of the history of Spanish cinema is particularly frustrating since almost all the movies produced then have disappeared. Only a small part of these movies are still conserved and apart from being in a very poor state, they are practically impossible to see. Besides, written and spoken testimonies point to the fact that they are of very limited interest. However, they are worthy of special consideration not only for their sociological value, reflecting a new form of craftsman-like activity, but what is more important, they forge in that period the peculiarities which to a certain extent still condition film-making in Spain today.

On December 28, 1895, the day of the Holy Innocents on the Catholic calendar, the Lumière brothers present a new invention in the Indian Salon of Paris' Grand Café. They call it cinematographic and it consists of the continual projection of photographs on a canvas screen so that the sensation of movement is reproduced.

Twenty weeks later, or in 1896, one of the Lumière brothers' technicians, A. Promio, presents the new invention in Madrid. He rents and conditions a locale on the ground floor of the Hotel de Rusia, located on Carrera de San Jerónimo Street, and inaugurates it on May 15, Saint Isidro's day, as if it were one more of the many attractions commemorating the feast day of the patron saint of Madrid.

From the very first, the locale is packed by a run-of-the-mill public. They simply cannot believe their eyes and grow frightened when a train pulls into the Lyon station rushing at them.

Film arrives in Spain at a time of marked political instability. On January 3, 1874, General Pavía rides into parliament atop his horse and ends the First Republic with a violence that was only outdone 127 years afterwards.* In December of that same year, General Martínez Campos proclaims Alfonso XII king in Sagunto. A period of two-party politics based on the English style of government begins in which liberals and conservatives alternately come to power. In 1885, King Alfonso XII dies and the regency period begins which results in the loss of Spain's colonies. Cuba, Puerto Rico and the Philippines are freed from Spain's control and a time of instability begins in Morocco. Insecurity, arbitrariness and violence rule over Spain at the end of the nineteenth and at the beginning of the twentieth centuries. The privileges of the oligarchies and the powerful landowners, the poverty of the country and the very poor economic situation lead to the disasters in the colonies and in Morocco. Alfonso XIII comes to the throne in 1902, and the country's

---

* The storming of Spanish parliament by Lt. Col. Tejero in 1981.

general instability, the bad situation of the working classes and the Rif War in Africa all create a high degree of violence. In 1909, the so-called Tragic Week of Barcelona occurs, when troops who are about to embark for Africa to put down the Kabyle up-risings refuse to go.
The over-all situation in Spain produced an unemployed and illiterate public which were short on funds, but who were thrilled by the ease in which real-life conditions were created by the recent invention of cinematography. It also produced technicians ready to embark on any new venture which could possibly bring them easy cash as well as a middle-class that fears for its money and that is stingy when it comes to investing it in what is considered the least real and riskiest of businesses.
All this meant that the first film shot in Spain was made by A. Promio, the camera operator of the Lumière brothers, who presented the new invention in Spain as his entrusted mission. Noteworthy among the shorts made by Promio are: **Llegada de los toreros** (Arrival of the Bullfighters), **Maniobras de la artillería en Vicálvaro** (Artillery Maneuvers at Vicálvaro) and **Salida de las alumnas del colegio de San Luis de los Franceses** (Girls Getting out of Class at the San Luis de los Franceses School).
Wholly Spanish-made films were produced shortly afterwards in

Riña de Café (1897), by Fructuoso Gelabert.

October, 1896 by Eduardo Jimeno who shot in Zaragoza a typical movie of those filmed at that time: **Salida de misa mayor del Pilar de Zaragoza** (Leaving High Mass at the Pilar of Zaragoza Cathedral). While in France workers were filmed coming out of factories, there proliferated in Spain shorts of the faithful coming out of churches. These films toured exhibition galleries to the amazement of audiences, who tried to pick themselves out among those animated figures.
The true founder of Spanish cinema is the Catalonian, Fructuoso Gelabert, the photographer son of a Majorcan cabinet-maker. In August, 1897, he writes, produces, directs and acts in the first fictional film made in Barcelona: **Riña de café** (Café Brawl). Not happy with this first attempt and as a result of the financial impossiblity of buying a Lumière camera, he invents and builds one with which he regularly begins to work. The success of his first experience leads him to make the inevitable **Salida de la iglesia de Santa María de Sans** (Leaving the Church of Santa María de Sans). These experiences constitute a curious sub-genre which can be considered as the first truly Spanish contribution to the history of film. Also made in the Lumière style was the **Salida de los trabajadores de «La España Industrial»** (Getting Off Work in the «Industrial Spain»; 1897). Gelabert continued by

Fortunio Bonanova in Don Juan Tenorio (1921) by Ricardo de Baños.

filming his first news footage, **Visita a Barcelona de doña María Cristina y don Alfonso XIII** (María Cristina and Alfonso XIII Visiting Barcelona) and he marked up another first by exporting and selling the film to Pathé Frères. He returns to fictional film with **La Dorotea,** the first of eleven productions that he is to make between 1898 and 1906. Gelabert shows interest in sets, models and trick shots at the same time as Georges Méliès in Paris, but it is the Aragonese, Segundo de Chomón, who soon stands out in this area of film-making. An engineer from a noble family who was born in Teruel, Chomón creates the first workshop to hand-paint film in Barcelona. The French company Pathé entrusts him increasingly with greater work due to the quality of his product. Segundo de Chomón buys a camera to shoot titles and accidentally discovers the technique of superimposition, shooting frame by frame and the possibilities of doing fantastic trick shots. He uses all these advances when he shoots **El hotel eléctrico** (The Electric Hotel; 1905), showing a surprisingly new technique in film-making. He creates a world that today is practically all lost, but very influenced nonetheless by the work of Méliès. His films were very expensive and not very commercial, so he decides to accept an offer made by Pathé and goes to Paris. He skillfully uses his film tricks in shooting many pictures and begins to learn the

technique of making cartoons. In 1910, Pathé sends him to Spain, but under the condition that he make essentially Spanish films. Chomón gives up trying to make trick shots and happens to film a **zarzuela,** a form of light opera that was the most popular genre during those years. With this film he discovers what can be termed a national style of film-making which bears fruit years afterwards and which establishes a long cinematographic tradition. In 1912, he goes to Italy, where, among other things, he works as the director of photography on the big production of Giovanni Pastrone's **Cabiria** (1914), based on an idea by Gabrielle d'Annunzio. During this production, he further develops his use of the traveling shot which he had employed for the first time in France on **La vie et la passion de Jesus-Christ** (1907), by Ferdinand Zecca.
The industrial supremecy of Barcelona was made patent from the very first moment. Hispano Films, the most important production company of that time, was founded in that city in 1906. While associated with the company, Ricardo Baños directed the first version of **Don Juan Tenorio** (1908), a faithful reproduction of the theater play, and another first version of **Locura de amor** (Love Crazy; 1909). The Iris Films and Films Barcelona production companies were also created in Barcelona. For this latter company, Gelabert films **Tierra baja** (Lowland; 1907) and **María Rosa**

Josefina Tapias in *La revoltosa* **(1924) by Florián Rey.**

(1908), both based on well-known Catalonian dramatic works. During these initial years, Spanish cinema seems to be quite removed from the rich social reality existing on all sides and produces instead historical film themes based on the theatrical dramas of a late Romanticism which abound in theaters and which are staged in a badly inspired style of those grandilocuent French **films d'arte.** Many of them are directed by Ricardo de Baños as well as by Fructuoso Gelabert who has lost his early freshness to sink into this tedious style of film-making. On the eve of the First World War, Spanish cinema does not even try to mirror some of the many social and political events that are shaking the country. It has become a prolongation of the stage and has accumulated the defects of this medium, not only because of the simple filmed versions of works by Jacinto Benavente, Joaquín Dicenta, Vicente Blasco Ibáñez and Adrián Gual, but also due to the cardboard-like performances of such theater actors as Margarita Xirgú, Enrique Borrás, María Guerrero and Fernando Díaz de Mendoza. The reduced price of a ticket and the very poor economic situation of Spain soon convert cinema into the main attraction of the Spanish masses. In 1914, there are more than 900 exhibition locales throughout Spain and the annual business volume surpasses twenty million pesetas, quite a large figure for

the times. Spanish cinema hardly takes advantage of these circumstances and it is the Americans with their strong industrial drive who make the most of the enormous possibilities of the nascent Spanish market, which was and still is one of the most important in Europe.
Not only were large royalties paid for the exhibition of foreign films, but national production is subject to what is happening abroad. The small investments obtained are only sufficient to produce poorly made pictures. Film is thought of as an adventure in crafts and no one sees it in an industrial light. Developing and print laboratories soon appear and the scant number of studios constructed are small and modest. In other words, Spanish cinema has to struggle against strong foreign competition and buy machinery and film negative abroad as well. Production companies quickly appear and disappear. Generally, a theatrical success is taken advantage of to form a production company in order to write the corresponding screenplay of the work. At best, the company would make another film, but it would soon dissolve itself, regardless of whether it makes money or not. In 1914, there are seventeen production companies in Barcelona, but two years later, all have disappeared and others are in their place. The existence of the companies does not depend on economic success or failure. Investments in the film

Carmen Viance, Marina Torres, Guillermo Muñoz and José Gimeno in *Gigantes y cabezudos* **(1925) by Florián Rey.**

industry are similar to placing bets on a roulette wheel, since it is considered an adventure, not an industrial activity. Production begins in Madrid in 1915, thanks to the activities of the Perojo brothers. José dies a madman afterwards, but Benito starts his long film career as a producer, cameraman, director, screenwriter and even actor, with the screen name of Peladilla. He makes comedies that have little or no artistic quality such as **Peladilla, cochero a punto** (Peladilla, Cabby at the Ready; 1915). After working in France for several years, he returns to Spain in the mid-twenties as an important director.
In 1915, José María Codina directs **El signo de la tribu** (Sign of the Tribe), the first film production made in episodes, a widely used narrative form at that time. Within this new style of film-making, the most popular Spanish picture of these years is made, **Barcelona y sus misterios** (Barcelona and Its Mysteries; 1915), by Alberto Marro. It is a clear imitation of the American and French serials that dominate the market. The only movie with any amount of interest in this period is the co-production made with France called **Cristóbal Colón** (Christopher Columbus; 1916), but the Spanish contribution is minimal since it is directed by the American Charles Jean Dressner and the majority of the actors are French. It takes five months to make and costs one million pesetas, an unusual figure

Manuel González, Elisa Ruiz Romero, Elisa Sánchez, Faustino Bretaño, Jesús Tordesillas and Rafael Calvo in Currito de la Cruz **(1925) by Alejandro Pérez Lugin.**

Es mi hombre (**1927**) **by Carlos Fernández Cuenca.**

at a time when a film can be produced for one thousand pesetas. If the capitalists belonging to the insecure and repressive right only invest in a film as an adventure many times offering erotic angles, the governments of the timid and overwhelmed monarchy only pay attention to cinema long enough to decree absurd norms determining its activities. On the request of the governor of Barcelona, a Royal Decree of October 19, 1913, establishes film censorship. The governing class, conscious of the reigning social discontent and aware of cinema's influence over the people, takes this decision before a politically dangerous film could be made. In 1920, the governor of Barcelona prohibits film characters from resembling or having the same names of well-known persons. Millán de Prieto, the Director General of State Security, issues another ordinance in 1920 by virtue of which men have to sit apart from women in movie theaters. This ridiculous norm was meant to safeguard the moral principles of those people offended by the darkness, but was never put into effect.

On September 13, 1923, General Primo de Rivera carries out a coup by telephone and usurps power. King Alfonso XIII resigns himself to the situation. The war in Morocco takes its toll on Spain's weak economy. The dictator puts himself at the head of the army and tries to end the conflict, but it is only a stopgap measure. The period of the dictatorship, 1923-1930, meant very little for a cinema which continued to ignore society's problems, lost as it is in ponderous theatrical adaptations or films that try to catch the public eye in the coarsest way. Meanwhile, successive governments give no support to cinema.

During these years, Jacinto Benavente directs a film version of his play **Los intereses creados** (Vested Interests), but the final result of the movie is affected by the lack of film negative due to the World War. Antonio Martínez makes his debut as an actor. Later, he is to become famous with the pseudonym of Florián Rey in the first film version of **La verbena de la Paloma** (The Paloma Fair; 1920), directed by the prolific Catalonian, José Buchs. The success of the picture marks the beginning of a heyday for film versions of **zarzuelas,** one of the all-time characteristic sub-genres of Spain's cinema. Florián Rey directs the first version of **La revoltosa** (The Mischievous Girl; 1924) and another of **Gigantes y cabezudos** (Giants and Bigheads; 1925). The writer Alejandro Pérez Lugín makes a first version of his novel **La casa de la Troya** (The House of Troy; 1925), and another of **Currito de la Cruz** (1925). The future director Juan de Orduña plays the leading role in **Boy** (1925), by Benito Perojo and based on a novel by Father Coloma. All are unimaginative movies which are routinely made throughout the history of Spanish cinema.

In spite of its multiple difficulties, the craftsman-like Spanish film industry finds a profitable link with the general public that makes these questionable movies viable. Production is still considered an adventure from an economic point of view, but some directors manage to make low-budget films with a certain degree of quality. Fifty-nine feature-length films are made in 1928 when the ghost of the talkies has not yet appeared to destroy what has been patiently built up over the years.

That same year the first film societies or clubs are founded. In October, 1928, Ernesto Giménez Caballero, editor of the magazine **La gaceta literaria,** creates the **Cine-club Español** with the help of Luis Buñuel who has just made **Un chien andalou** (1928) in Paris. At the same time, José Palau and Díaz Plaza start the **Cine-club Mirador** in Barcelona. These activities represented the first and timid steps taken by Spain's intellectuals to reconcile themselves with a popular form of entertainment to which they have never paid the least amount of attention. Even so, the arrival of sound motion pictures marks a new and definitive disassociation with the world of film.

Various films produced in 1927 were noteworthy. First, there is **La hermana**

San Sulpicio (Sister San Sulpicio), by Florián Rey, the first film version of the novel by Armando Palacio Valdés and a picture which serves as the cinematographic presentation of an actress who is to become a great star, Imperio Argentina. Also made is **Una aventura de cine** (An Adventure in Film-making), by director Juan de Orduña, and based on a screenplay by Wesceslao Fernández Flórez. Another important production is **Es mi hombre** (He's My Man), by the director who would later become a critic and historian: Carlos Fernández Cuenca. The film is the first version of the play by Carlos Arniches. All these films enjoy huge box office successes and consolidate Spanish cinema. On another level and among the first Spanish experimental films that are made, of special interest are two works by Nemesio M. Sobrevilla, **Al Hollywood madrileño** (To Madrid's Hollywood; 1926) and **El sexto sentido** (Sixth Sense; 1927), although due to their nature, they are only exhibited in film clubs.

Also made in 1927 is **Las de Méndez** (Those of Méndez), by the prolific Fernando Delgado who that year makes three other films, and **Zalacaín el aventurero** (Zalacaín the Adventurer). This latter film is the first production by a new company, CIDE, which puts an important amount of money in the hands of first-timer Fernando Camacho in order to adapt the novel by Pío Baroja. The result is technically a good one and represents a small attempt to show the political in-fighting of the nineteenth century. The films has a considerable success and is bought by Metro-Goldwyn-Mayer for world-wide distribution, a rather unusual feat. Even so, as is the norm in those years, CIDE is dissolved and does not produce another picture.

Carmen Viance in El gordo de Navidad **(1929) by Fernando Delgado.**

Taking advantage of the **Primer Congreso Español de Cinematografía** (First Spanish Congress of Cinematography) in October, 1928, the **Unión cinematográfica española** (Spanish Cinematographic Union) asks the government for subsidies and legislation that would protect national film interests from strong foreign competition, the same measures being introduced in the rest of Europe. The demands made of the administration are very modest, since it is only asked, «that it be declared obligatory in all the locales of the national territory, the minimum exhibition of five Spanish films for every one hundred foreign». It is also requested, «that it be declared obligatory that for every twenty-five films which a firm imports into Spain, it acquire one Spanish film for exhibition purposes in the country where those foreign films are originally produced». The Ministry of the Economy responds to these requests and publishes the Royal Order of November 26, 1929, setting a time limit of one month for suggestions to prepare a law that

María Luz Callejo and Pedro Larrañaga in *Zalacaín el aventurero* **(1927) by Francisco Camacho.**

Fernando Fernández de Córdoba and Marina Torres in Agustina de Aragón **(1928), by Florián Rey.**

would adapt to the circumstances. Unfortunately, nothing more is done about the matter. At that time, Spanish cinema has obtained a wide acceptance among the general public, some outlets in the Latin American markets and a large annual number of productions. However, the arrival in 1929 of sound motion pictures with their greater technical complexity and their need for larger studios and investments, puts an end to a totally craftsman-like industry which is now producing an important volume of business thanks to a few.

The last successes of Spain's silent cinema are **El gordo de Navidad** (The Big Christmas Lottery; 1929), by Fernando Delgado, and especially **Agustina de Aragón** (1928) and **La aldea maldita** (The Cursed Village; 1929), by Florián Rey. **Agustina de Aragón** is the first version of a topic that in the hands of Rey and others, becomes one of the most characteristic stories of Spanish cinema. **La aldea maldita** is shortly transformed into a mythical work for the critics, finding in the picture social values and implications which only exist to a minimum degree, since it is nothing more than an old melodramatic, rural subject matter that is filmed with both human and artistic dignity.

In June, 1929, **The Jazz Singer** is premiered in Madrid. It is the first American sound motion picture, but the film is first seen without sound

since there are no movie theaters equipped with sound projection. The American talkie **The Innocents of Paris** starring Maurice Chevalier is premiered in Barcelona that same year, but only the part sung is exhibited with sound and the rest of the picture is shown silently since it is in English.
Spanish cinematography is soon faced with a curious situation. Western Electric sound equipment which quickly captures the market after an initial patents war, is very expensive and the owners of cinemas are reluctant to invest in what they consider a passing fad. So they continue to screen silent movies or close down, waiting for the sound fever to pass. Production also grinds to a halt for lack of sound equipment. From over seventy films that are made annually in Spain, production plummets to a mere five movies between 1929 and 1931. Furthermore, the films are shot in Spain without sound and are dubbed abroad due to the lack of Spanish sound studios.
Two films shot without sound and then later recorded with a sound track in the Tobias Studios in Paris were **Prim** (1930) by José Buchs, the biography of the liberal and anti-Republican Catalonian general who worked for the same cause as General Berenguer to establish the monarchy, and **Fermín Galán** (1931), by Fernando Roldán, a biography that tries to exalt freedom after the pre-Republican uprising in Jaca in 1930. Sound tracks were also layed on some of the more successful silent movies made previously such as the already cited **La aldea maldita** and **Zalacaín el aventurero.**
The arrival of sound motion pictures coincides with the great international economic depression and with the end of the dictatorship in the Spain of General Primo de Rivera, which was succeeded for a few months by that of General Berenguer. At a time when the film industry needs to invest heavily in new sound equipment for both recording and reproduction purposes and in building sound studios, the peseta is tottering, capital is being sent out of the country and investors are discouraged. So the transition from silent films to sound motion pictures is not as easy as it is in most of the major film industries around the world, but rather leads to a collapse. Talkies will have to rise from the ashes of silent movies in Spain.

1930

1936

The shooting of Patricio miró a una estrella **(1934) by José Luis Sáenz de Heredia.**

1930 1936

II REPUBLIC

Román Gubern

The introduction of talking pictures in the North American and European film industries coincided with the birth of the II Republic in Spain (1931), which ended the dictatorship of General Primo de Rivera and the ephemeral pre-democratic transitional regime led by General Berenguer. The establishment of the liberal and socially reformist regime of the II Republic took place during the world economic crisis of the capitalist system which began in 1929 and which contributed in accentuating social conflicts, therefore reinforcing the role of film-making as an instrument of ideological dissemination and of propaganda, a coveted way of controlling the political scene. This social role should also be evaluated in relation to the increase in leisure time (the reduction of the work week in the cities to forty-four hours and of the work day in the country to eight hours) and to the salary rises agreed upon in this period, measures which gave a big boost to cultural consumption and leisure time industries. On the other hand, the birth of sound motion pictures in the Spanish language had its influence on the large Spanish-speaking markets— the Spanish Peninsula and a large part of Latin America, markets that until then had been subjected to the hegemony of North American production and that now would be repudiated by the public since films were distributed in English. This new situation led to such successful Hispano-American experiments as the comedy **Boliche,** by Francisco Elías, the action of which took place in Barcelona and Buenos Aires and which starred the very popular Argentinian musical trio Irusta, Fugazot and Demare.

The first Spanish talkie was the dream-like comedy **El misterio de la Puerta del Sol** (The Puerta del Sol Mystery), shot at the end of 1929 by Francisco Elías with an acoustical recording device that was bought from the American engineer Lee De Forest. But De Forest's Phonofilm system was incompatible with the first sound equipment installed in Spanish cinemas and the film was hardly seen. This failure, symptomatic of the grave crisis experienced by Spanish cinema during the traumatic transition period from silent to sound pictures since no movie theaters were equipped for talkies, led to three alternative production formulae that depended on the sound technology of more advanced countries in the area: first, the production of sound motion pictures by Spanish companies in duly equipped German, French and English studios —from the end of 1929 to the beginning of 1931; second, after the shooting of silent movies in Spain, the recording of the sound tracks in foreign sound studios, or later, in the newly built ones in Spain, as was the

case with the noteworthy **Prim** (1930), in which director José Buchs filmed the biography of the liberal and monarchic general; and third, the emigration of professionals in order to produce films in Spanish for foreign firms, above all for American companies in Hollywood studios and those belonging to Paramount in Joinville —from 1930 to 1936. These formulae were eventually abandoned when films imported into the Spanish market were extensively dubbed in local sound studios.
It was not by accident that the first Spanish sound studios, or the Estudios Orphea, equipped with French technology, were in 1932 set up in Barcelona, capital of the most industrialized region of Spain. The project was supported by the Catalonian autonomous government which provided the building for the studios. After a professional stay in Paris, Francisco Elías, founder of the Estudios Orphea, inaugurated his installation with the production of **Pax** (1932). Only a French version was done of this film, since the financing came from that country and since it was impossible to interest a Spanish investor in the simultaneous —and cheap— preparation of a Spanish version. All the sound tracks for the Spanish films produced in Spain during 1932 and almost all those made in 1933 were recorded in these studios.
In 1933, the company moved into distribution with the creation of

Prim (1930) by José Buchs.

Orphea Films. That same year also saw the inauguration in Madrid of the new Estudios CEA (Cinematografía Española Americana), promoted by the playwright Jacinto Benavente and other monarchical writers who wanted to benefit from this new spoken medium, as well as ECESA (Estudios Cinema Español, S. A.) in Aranjuez, located south of Madrid. During the period under consideration, Spanish film production was the following:

Year	**Number of films produced**
1932	6
1933	17
1934	21
1935	37
1936	28 (until July, 1936, when the civil war began)

The shaky Spanish film industry which got underway in 1932 and which divided its production between Madrid and Barcelona, almost exactly copied the cultural models established during the silent era under the dictatorship of General Primo de Rivera. The middle-class investors in this area of the entertainment industry came from the most conservative sectors and they were both culturally wanting and economically opportunist. If during the II Republic certain products of the industry born out of culture such as books or theater received important support due to their being socially acceptable forms, cinema continued to be confined to the ghetto of what might be described as a trivial escapist spectacle and a popular way of alienation. This attitude should also be interpreted in the light of the development and the stratification of the Spanish society during the thirties. It was a proto-industrial society with vast underdeveloped rural zones, especially in the South and in Galicia, where illiteracy rates were also very high. The structure of Spain's cultural market meant that side-by-side with the production that imitated the cosmopolitan genres colonizing our screens, there persisted a local cinema dominated by ruralism, religious conservatism and aestheic autarchy.

A guiding light in the cosmopolitan cinema was Benito Perojo, who, during the years that the Spanish film industry was paralyzed, did not stop working in studios in Paris, Berlin and Hollywood, doing **double versions** in Spanish. He was the director who best assimilated the big commercial models of Euro-Yankee film-making. As was usual then, he almost always adapted novels and plays to film and he was the only director who was able to endow Spanish production with a certain international dimension, although slavishly mimetic. His comedy **Se ha fugado un preso** (A Convict Has Escaped; 1933), based on an idea by humorist Enrique Jardiel Poncela, was presented in the Venice Mostra; the success of the melodrama **El negro que tenía el alma blanca** (The Black Who Had a White Soul; 1934), an adaptation of a novel by Alberto Insúa, opened up Spanish cinema to the Argentine market; while the fortunate outcome of his **Crisis mundial** (World Crisis; 1934), did the same with the Cuban market. But he was reproached for this cosmopolitanism by the most conservative Spanish critics, who accused Perojo of being a Francophile. He certainly was not an original director, but he aspired to create a cinema that measured up to the urbane bourgeoisie, such as that dominating contemporary production in Paris or Hollywood. Although the imitation of the big American models of film-making was almost always done during these years with clumsiness, on occasions a skillful assimilation of Hollywood formulae was observed. This was the case, for example, with **Una mujer en peligro** (A Woman in Danger; 1935), by José Santugini, which competently imitated the genre of the mystery comedy formulated by Hollywood. It included the mysterious rambling house, the nocturnal storm, the disturbing intrigue and the effective expressionist effects. The cosmopolitan directors tempted by Hollywood film-making techniques were relatively few, since most of the production of the Republican period before the civil war was dominated by a mannered or rural provincialism, whose most privileged genres were the «españolada» (exaggerated portrait of Spain), the «zarzuela» (Spanish light opera) and clerical cinema. The «españolada» was really a genre which originated in France, born during the period of Romanticism with such works as **Carmen** (1845), by Merimée, which cultivated the exotic nature and the **local color** of an underdeveloped part of southern Europe. The marriage of Eugenia de Montijo, who was from Granada, with Emperor Napoleon III in 1853 further contributed to this genre, creating a pro-Spanish propagandistic atmosphere in France. This rather **picturesque** point of view was employed both in Spanish and French silent movies, even by prestigious directors or ones with artistic ambitions, producing such titles as **La fête espagnole** (1919), by Germaine Dulac, **El Dorado** (1921), by Marcel L'Herbier, or **Carmen** (1926), directed by Jacques Feyder, with Raquel Meller. Spanish film-makers willingly accepted this colonization and exaltation of a **different** Spain, that is to say, an agrarian and underdeveloped Spain dominated by religious superstitions, the Spain known for large and feudal landed estates, hunger, the cult to masculinity and for bullfighters. This stereotyped and generally reactionary genre, the pride of the pre-modern Spain of the local political bosses, was

Carmen Amaya in *María de la O* (1936)
by Francisco Elías.

continuously employed by our directors during the silent era. They continued to do so after the advent of sound motion pictures, even adding folk songs to the final result, in spite of the new and advanced political climate which ushered in the II Republic.
Even though most of the **españoladas** were set in the depressed region of Andalucia, other areas of a rural and pre-modern Spain were the backdrops for films of this type. A case in point was the rustic Aragón shown in the very famous **Nobleza baturra** (Nobility of Brute Action; 1935), by the Aragonese director Florián Rey, who became the most important advocate of this genre of film-making, polemically defending it for its **racial** merit. It was not by coincidence that the most popular stars among the Republican public were those formed in this genre such as Estrellita Castro in **Rosario la cortijera** (Rosario, The Country Girl; 1935), by León Artola, Carmen Amaya in **María de la O** (1936), by Francisco Elías, and especially Imperio Argentina in **Nobleza baturra** and **Morena Clara** (Clara the Brunette; 1936), a film that was the biggest box office hit of the time. Actress and singer Imperio Argentina, who was born in Argentina, had been discovered by Florián Rey when she was performing in Madrid's Romea Theater and contracted her to make her film debut in **La hermana San Sulpicio** (Sister San Sulpicio; 1927). Under the tutelage of Florián Rey, the actress created the peasant girl called María del Pilar in **Nobleza baturra** and the sparkling Gypsy girl Trini in Morena Clara, two anthological characters who were the perfect ways to set out a very expensive and recurrent theme in the work of Rey, the topic of blemished female honor in the old tradition of Calderón de la Barca. In **Nobleza baturra,** María del Pilar, who is the daughter of a well-to-do rural landowner, secretly loves a poor lad and is at the same time desired by a wealthy boy in whom she shows no interest. The resentful boy comes up with a stratagem which puts Pilar's sexual honor in doubt and which involves the entire town in the infamy, like the chorus of a tragedy. Finally, and thanks to the generous intervention of the priest of the town, everything is resolved and Pilar is able to marry her poor, but honest boyfriend. The film is an involuntary document of the customs, the female condition and conservative morals of an agrarian Spain exalted by Florián Rey. But it was an enormous success and in some movie theaters, the projection of the film was stopped so that some musical number could be repeated, just like in the theater.
When the Englishman George Borrow had vendicated the ethical integrity and García Lorca the aesthetic integrity of the Gypsy nature, Florián Rey in

Miguel Ligero and Imperio Argentina in Morena Clara **(1936) by Florián Rey**

(Previous page)

Manuel Luna and Juan de Orduña in Nobleza baturra **(1935) by Florián Rey.**

Morena Clara exalted the vitures attributed to the Gypsy —extroversion, warmth, ingenuity— taking advantage of the favorable populist political climate of the II Republic. In **Morena Clara,** Florián Rey stubbornly insisted on the theme of interclass love, but this time adding an interracial obstacle and reversing the asymmetrical social positions of **Nobleza baturra,** since this time he presented an unaffected Gypsy girl and a young Andalusian prosecutor of good family, who loses his initial aggressiveness and surrenders to the attractiveness of an humble girl accused of stealing some hams. Naturally, the theme of feminine honor also reappears, although this time it was not sexual honor, but rather the honesty and respectability of the protagonist, easily sullied by the fact that Trini is a Gypsy. **Morena Clara** was uniquely successful. Following a three month triumphant run after its premiere even after the outbreak of the Spanish Civil War it continued to be exhibited both on the Republican and rebel sides. The Republicans, however, withdrew it from the exhibition circuits in March, 1937, due to the belligerently pro-Francoist attitude of the director and the production company, Cifesa. During the postwar period it continued its successful run and subsequently benefited from the publicity generated by the Republican boycott. Some frankly inspired and sparkling fragments of **Morena Clara**

Charito Leonís, Miguel Ligero and Raquel Rodrigo in La verbena de la Paloma **(1935) by Benito Perojo.**

such as the court scene suggest that even the **españolada** (exaggerated portrait of Spain) with all its fallacies and myths could be redeemed with a certain amount of talent and sensitivity, virtues which did not abound among the Spanish directors of the period. This possibility was materialized in what many historians consider to be best picture of the time, the comedy about Andalusia called **La traviesa molinera** (The Mischievous Girl Miller; 1934), which was a Spanish-American coproduction (Ricardo Soriano-United Artists) directed by a former assistant to Chaplin, Harry D'Abbadie D'Arrast. The dialogue was written by Edgar Neville and was based on the plot of the folk ballad **The Miller from Arcos**— converted into **The Three Cornered Hat,** by Alarcón, starring Cuban Hilda Moreno and with the photography of Frenchman Jules Kruger. This international hotchpotch led to a film of Goyesque plasticity and solidly rooted in Spain's folk traditions. Chaplin considered it one of his favorites in spite of the fact that the American version of the film called **It Happened in Spain** was never shown on commercial circuits in the United States. A different kind of genre, although related to the **españolada** due to geographial and typological factors is the **comedia cortijera** (farm comedy), a sister style to what in Mexico is called the **comedia ranchera** (ranch comedy). Both of these styles of film-making have similar socio-cultural roots. In this latifundiary and feudatory genre, the choral action of which takes place in Andalusian **cortijos** (landed estates), a film of special interest is **El genio alegre** (The Happy Genius; 1936), a curious title directed by Fernando Delgado. The film was produced by Cifesa and was based on a text written by the Alvarez Quintero brothers. This comedy was being shot in Cordoba in July, 1936, when the Francoist coup began and General Queipo de Llano rose up in Andalusia. The lead in the picture was the actress Rosita Díaz Gimeno, a cultured woman, sensitive actress and good friend of socialist politician, Juan Negrín. In the film she played Consuelo, the cousin of a young, carefree land-owner. She finally managed to settle the fellow down with their marriage and keep the feudal property within the family. When the military rebellion began, Negrín called the actress in her hotel, and as a result, she was arrested and a court martial sentenced her to death by firing squad. She was saved at the last minute, however, by an exchange of prisoners with the other zone. The film was later finished by employing several over-the-shoulder shots with a double.

When the film was premiered after the war, the name of the actress was kept out of the titles, in spite of the fact that she appeared throughout the movie. The same thing happened to two other Republican actors, Edmundo Barbero and Anita Sevilla, who fled from Cordoba when the coup was first known.

La traviesa molinera (**1934**) **by Harry D'Abbadie D'Arrast.**

Regarding the **zarzuela,** the musical theater genre which was first shot in the silent era by Segundo de Chomón in 1910, it was introduced in the world of Republican film production due to its functionality for sound pictures and due to the comfortable use of the already mentioned **policy of adaptations,** inspired in this case by the world of contemporary popular show business. But it was also used in the new talkies to commercially compete with theatrical **zarzuela,** while at the same time, it made its presence felt in small cities and towns without theaters where only a film version of the work could be seen. Due to its freshness and handling, a noteworthy film of this genre was the version that Benito Perojo made of **La verbena de la Paloma** (The Paloma Fair; 1935), originally by Ricardo de la Vega and with music by the maestro Bretón. The local charm shown in the film came to be the equivalent of that shown by René Clair in the first sound pictures he made with Paris as a backdrop. The traveling shot of the rooftops of Madrid showing ordinary people as seen from windows and attics has the stamp of Clair when he displays Paris in **Quatorze juillet** (1932). The amusing scene of the wedding photograph which practically has no sound exhibits a

Imperio Argentina and Miguel Ligero in La hermana San Sulpicio **(1934) by Florián Rey.**

feeling for film that was evidently learned from that French director, who happened to be Perojo's friend. The effectiveness of the movie was shown when the people of Madrid were able to recognize themselves in those happy scenes of a turn of the century Madrid, a festive city deftly and openly created by Perojo in a vast scenography worthy of Lazare Meerson.

In short, what was shown on the screen was the charming and pleasant use of the common people —the leading characters are a typographer and a dressmaker's assistant— who during the years of the Republic were trying to obtain a greater say in the political affairs of the country. But since we have compared the typical Paris depicted by Clair and the typical Madrid shown by Perojo, we should speak in favor of the Spanish director's descriptive and even allusive sense of editing when showing the «verbena» or fair —the shot of the big or Ferris wheel's shadow projected on the façade of a house, a description that employs skillful editing which culminates in contrasting the amusements of the different social classes: Susana and her sister dance together in a modest flat, while in a luxury hotel, the upper-crust bourgeoisie and the army officers are holding a gala ball in a scene that was originally filmed in technicolor. No greater social information transmitted with more stylistic laconicism can be asked for.

Clerical cinema, the last important autarchic genre, was one of the ideological instruments of the rightist forces and of the Catholic church in their fight —especially true during the two-year period in which the conservatives governed the country— against the secular forces of a society which had long been submitted to ecclesiastical privileges and power. Forming part of this genre were such significant works as **El agua en el suelo** (Water on the Ground; 1934), by Eusebio Fernández Ardavín, who showed the sufferings of a young, honest priest, defamed by the freedom of expression under Republican journalistic norms (the film was banned by the Mexican laical censorship); **La Dolorosa** (The Long-Suffering Girl; 1934), a film version of the **zarzuela** by Juan José Lorente and by the maestro Serrano, directed by the Frenchman Jean Grémillon; the tear-jerking melodrama **Sor Angélica** (1934), by Francisco Gargallo; **Madre Alegría** (Mother Happiness; 1935) and **El niño de las monjas** (The Nuns' Boy; 1935), both by José Buchs; and **El cura de aldea** (The Village Priest; 1936), by Francisco Camacho.

Various of the film titles which are typified here as autarchical were produced by Cifesa (Compañía Industrial Film Española, S. A.), founded in Valencia during 1932 —even though it shot its films in studios located in Madrid and Barcelona—with a capital of three million pesetas, a considerable amount of money for those times. Initially, the company had imported and distributed North American films. In 1934 it distributed **El agua en el suelo** and the immense commercial success of this Spanish film led Florián Rey to propose that the company increase its business activities to the area of production. The first film produced is precisely **La hermana San Sulpicio** (Sister San Sulpicio; 1934), a remake of the novel by Armando Palacio Valdés and directed once again by Florián Rey with Imperio Argentina in the role of a novice who leaves her order to marry a handsome youth. Trying to imitate the industrial methods of such important producers as the German UFA, starting from its Republican years, Cifesa constituted the **industrial right** of Spanish cinema and became its most active company. Confronting it was the Madrid production company called Filmófono, the representative of the liberal, leftist and secular sectors of Republican cinema. Filmófono was one of the various activities of the industry of culture in which the Urgoiti family stood out, a family involved with newspapers such as **El Sol** and **La Voz,** the Editorial Espasa-Calpe publishing house and Unión Radio in Madrid. It was logical that sound pictures would attract the attention of engineer

Fernando de Granada and Ana María Custodio in *Don Quintín el amargao* **(1935) by Luis Marquina.**

José María Linares Rivas and Ana María Custodio in *¡Centinela alerta!* **(1936) by Jean Gremillon.**

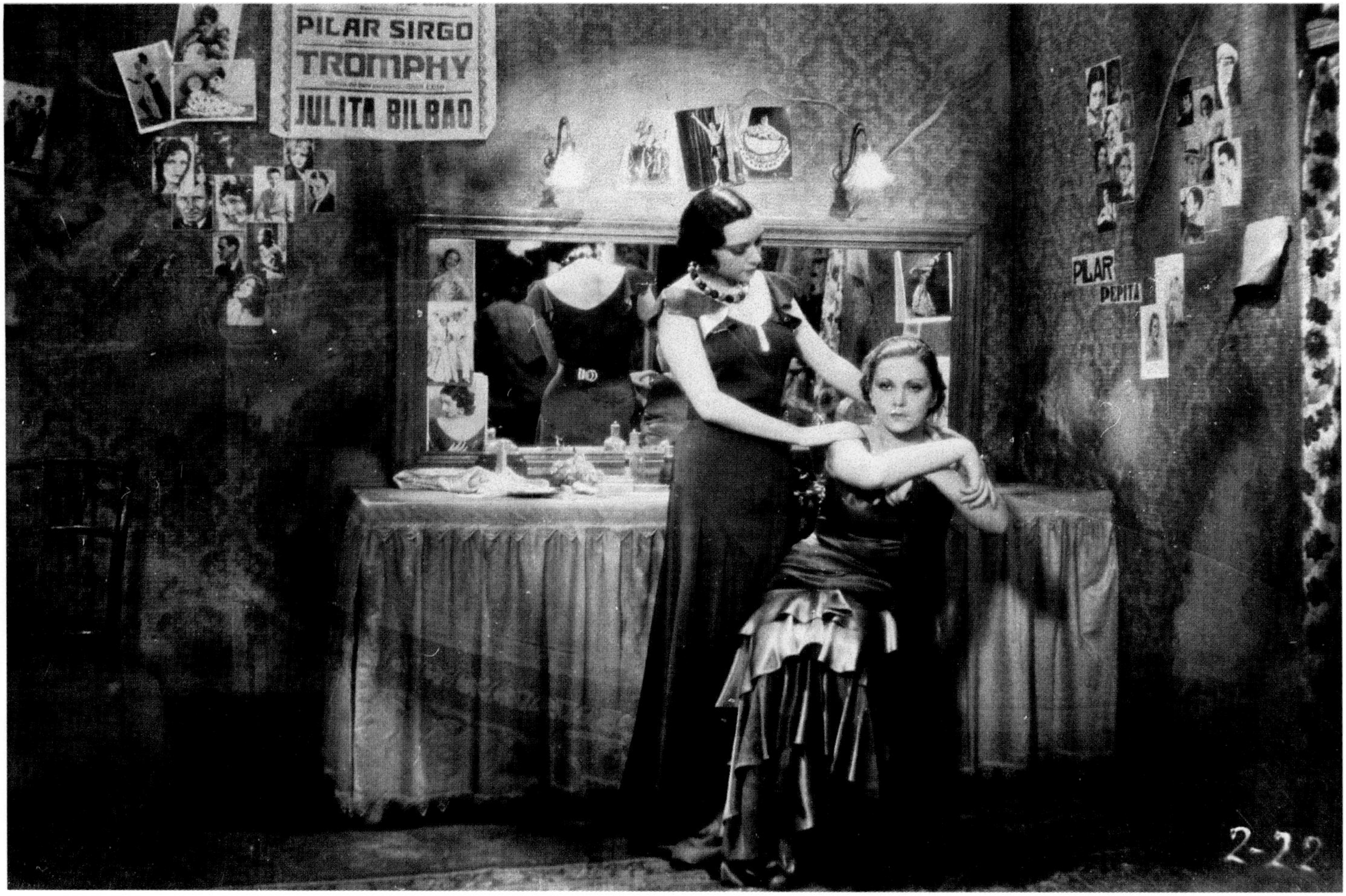

Pilar Muñoz and Porfiria Sanchiz in La hija de Juan Simón **(1935) by José Luis Sáenz de Heredia.**

Ricardo M. de Urgoiti, the inventor of a film sound system using records. He confided in his friend Luis Buñuel the direction of a film club to pre-release difficult films by Pabst, René Clair, Renoir, Dreyer, etc. which he imported for his distribution company. These films were selected from Paris by the communist film critic Juan Piqueras, the editor of the important magazine **Nuestro Cinema** (Our Cinema; 1932-35). The owner of a chain of movie theaters in Madrid and of a distribution company, Urgoiti completed the cinematographic industrial cycle by agreeing with Buñuel to produce commercial films that would be shown in his cinemas. Buñuel, who would be the executive producer of the films, contributed 150,000 pesetas to the project —half of the production cost of a film at the time. As a result, Buñuel organized a stable team of co-workers who successively made along Hollywood lines the following films: **Don Quintín el amargao** (Don Quintín the Embittered; 1935), a short comedy by Arniches and Estremera directed by the first-timer Luis Marquina; the melodrama **La hija de Juan Simón** (The Daughter of Juan Simón; 1935), begun by Nemesio S. Sobrevila and based on his own storyline, but finished by José Luis Sáenz de Heredia; the comedy **¿Quién me quiere a mí?** (Who Loves Me?; 1936), by Sáenz de Heredia; and the military comedy **¡Centinela alerta!** (Guard Alert!; 1936), by Jean Grémillon. Buñuel, as a Hollywood-style producer, always intervened to a lesser or greater extent in the direction of the films. His intervention was justified besides by the little or no professional experience of the young directors selected to make the films, with the exception of Grémillon. These films undoubtedly employed the most rank and file and commercial genres, persistently recurring to such traditionally sentimental sensationalism as that of the abandoned child or the unmarried mother, topics which could touch audiences but which heralded a professional characteristic which Buñuel would later confirm when he unreservedly threw himself into the most stereotyped genres of Mexican commercial cinema, ranging from the tear-jerker to the «ranchera» comedy. Even though the successful experience of Filmófono was cut short by the outbreak of the civil war, today it can be evaluated as a praiseworthy attempt to create in a Republican Spain where a film industry per se hardly existed, films capable of achieving a kind of harmony with the common people, the only public as a matter of fact that could contribute to the building of a true film industry through their box office demand. The liberal or progressive leanings of most of the film-makers who worked in Filmófono became evident when they went into exile abroad after the defeat of the Republic, while the rival firm, Cifesa, was converted into a prosperous bastion of Francoist cinema, the faithful servant of its watchwords, starting in 1939.

Buñuel's activity in Spanish Republican cinema has been generally underestimated since it was both intense and multidimensional. He shot the unusual and justly famous **Las Hurdes (Tierra sin pan)** (Las Hurdes—Land without Bread) around the inhospitable and underdeveloped region of Las Hurdes in 1932. The finished product displays elements of an ethnographical form of film-making, a militant cinema of social censure and the surrealist tradition, due to its hallucinatory religious imagery. Its presentation in 1933 resulted in a clash between Buñuel and Doctor Gregorio Marañón, at that time president of the Las Hurdes Society, and in the later banning of the film by the government. Buñuel would afterwards lay sound on the film in Paris in 1937 using a French off screen commentary and music by Brahms. Following this one-shot documentary experience, he dedicated himself to fomenting film club activity for the Filmófono company and, finally, to his work as executive producer for commercial films that were well-received by general audiences. When the Francoist uprising took place in 1936, he started to produce anti-fascist propaganda films. In other

María Gámez in La señorita de Trévelez **(1935)**
by Edgar Neville.

words, his experience during the Republic took in the entire range of cultural and industrial activities related to the world of film.
Before the civil war broke out, Spanish cinema had achieved a degree of competitiveness and acceptance among the Spanish public that was truly notable, in spite of strong American competition. The local star system had consolidated —Imperio Argentina, Rosita Díaz Gimeno, Antoñita Colomé, Alady, etc., and Spanish films had obtained enormous box office successes, as was the case with **Nobleza baturra, La verbena de la Paloma** and **Morena Clara.** Above all, there had arisen the names of new directors capable of changing the stereotyped genres and styles inherited from the silent era and the Euro-Yankee colonialism that had been exerted on our screens. Among these film-makers we should point to documentary directors Carlos Velo, biologist by profession, and his close collaborator Fernando G. Mantilla, both of whom were very much aware of the impact of Soviet cinema, and the documentary work of Flaherty and Joris Ivens, who would go into exile in Mexico at the end of the war.
Noteworthy among their shorts were **Almadrabas** (Tunny-fishing; 1935), an excellent and sober testimony of tunny fishing with nets in the waters of Cádiz, **La ciudad y el campo** (City and Country; 1935), about poultry keeping, and **Infinitos** (Infinites; 1935), a film based on an idea by the Belgian symbolist writer Maurice Maeterlink, who compared the structures of the sidereal world to the world of microbes, using a track of experimental music by Rodolfo Halffter.
In the field of fictional film, there was an irruption of young film-makers such as the diplomat and writer Edgar Neville, author of a sensitive adaptation of **La señorita de Trévelez** (The Young Lady from Trévelez; 1936), by Carlos Arniches, another adaptation of which would be done years later by J. A. Bardem in **Calle Mayor** (Main Street; 1956). Also making his debut during these years was José Luis Sáenz de Heredia who started his film career with **Patricio miró a una estrella** (Patricio Looked at a Star; 1934) whose plot was none other than that of the film mythomania of the leading character—Antonio Vico, who is in love with a film star. This love leads him to get a job in a studio as a worker in a storeroom, although he aspires to become an actor. **Patricio miró a una estrella** is the testimony of the frustration of large numbers of city-dwellers and the anesthetic and comforting function of cinematographic mythogeny as well as the reflection of the emergence of the local star system in Spain. The comedy by Sáenz de Heredia emerged, along with the novel **Cinematógrafo** (Cinematographer; 1936), by Andrés Carranque de los Ríos as a key to understanding what cinema represented for the Spanish postwar public. The world of film was also used as a source of inspiration to make exaggerated parodies of the classical genres of consumer features when Eduardo G. Maroto made in 1934 his shorts **Una de fieras** (One about Wild Beasts), a satire on African adventures; **Una de miedo** (One about Fear), a satire on horror films; and **Y ahora, una de ladrones** (And Now, One about Crooks), a satire on gangster films. Finally, we should mention that in this period of interesting cultural and cinematographic renewal, the debut as director of Rosario Pi, the first woman director of features in Spain. It was not by accident that she became a director at a time when feminists began to make their voices heard for the first time, when women were given the right to vote and when Victoria Kent stood out as the Director General of Penitenciary Institutions and as deputee of the **Izquierda Republicana Party.** Rosario Pi founded the Star Film production company, was a screenwriter and finally director of the curious «españolada» (exaggerated portrait of Spain) called **El gato montés** (The Wildcat; 1935), which transported the theme of **amour fou** to Andalusian settings, and later, the operetta **Molinos de viento** (Windmills; 1936).

1930

1935

Conchita Montenegro visits the makeup room of Rosita Díaz Gimeno during the shooting of Angelina o el honor de un brigadier **(1935) by Enrique Jardiel Poncela and Louis King.**

1930 1935

HOLLYWOOD

Emilio Sanz de Soto

Between 1930 and 1935, ninety-five feature films and fifteen shorts were shot in Spanish in Hollywood (1). We will omit, however, the twenty films in Spanish that Paramount made in the Parisian studios of Joinville. If we compare these figures with versions made in other languages (French, German or Italian), we can see that the supremacy of Spanish was absolute. The reason is very simple: the American producers knew that the Spanish-speaking market was much more important than any other and they acted in consequence.

All this happened at the very beginning of the sound era in pictures, and, as we have already indicated, in a very short space of time —just enough time to see the economic benefits that could be derived from dubbing.

The problem of double and triple versions of the same picture was immediately adopted and adapted by UFA in Berlin, but employing much more efficient methods. They would even use the same actress or actor in the same part in all three languages in which the film was shot (German, French and English), as was the case with the very unique Lilian Harvey and also Conrad Veidt. UFA did not seem interested in shooting films in Spanish. Several years would pass until the Nazis, who had come to power, would realize the immense popularity of Imperio Argentina in Latin America, a market which they did not dominate. They invited the actress and her husband, director Florián Rey, to shoot in Germany. At that time —the civil war was being fought in Spain— French versions were still done in studios in Berlin. As a result, we can today say that the directors of German cinema were interested in collaborating with Spain due to political reasons, but undoubtedly of greater importance were economic considerations. Thanks to **Carmen, la de Triana** (Carmen, The Girl from Triana; 1936), by Florián Rey, with Imperio Argentina assuring the film's success, German cinema was able to break into the Latin American market by using Spanish cinema.

The need to sell on the Latin American market or even on the market in Spain by making films in Spanish began in Hollywood, although its birth was at first sluggish.

Reshooting an American film, conserving its plot and its sets, and repeating scene after scene negated its creativity. The results were always a bad carbon copy of the original. Even though it might seem absurd to us today, the original films belonged to an exclusively American world, impossible to reconvert into another language by means of a Spanish, French or German film. In order to correct this initial blunder, prestigious scriptwriters, actors and actresses from the three countries already mentioned were contracted. These film-makers had no doubts about going since the contracts represented large sums of money. In the case of the versions in Spanish, even though most of the actors and actresses were Spanish, performers from Latin American countries such as Mexico or Argentina were also contracted. A chaos of accents is spoken, but it did not matter to Spanish or Latin American audiences.

The production plan for pictures made in Spanish was initially adopted by all the majors in Hollywood— Metro-Goldwyn-Mayer, Paramount, Fox, Warner Bros., Universal, Columbia, etc., and all these companies launched massive advertising campaigns in our press. In spite of this, the reaction of film critics and commentators could not have been more negative. They patriotically believed that these measures adopted in Hollywood meant nothing less than «the theft of our greatest cultural wealth: language», a theft which would hamper the normal development of talkies in Spain. Although these arguments held some weight, upon rereading those exacerbated commentaries we cannot help but smiling. Such a state of things contributed to our critics' lending an almost blind eye. They did not stop to analyze with the least amount of objectivity those Spanish films which came to us from North America. All those pictures were accused of being hybrids, completely different from what should be considered Spanish cinema. After reviewing some of these works— not all by any means but almost every one belonging to a very concrete stage in Fox's production plans, we can rediscover them today as completely Spanish and not as pictures that do not reflect Spanish culture. Later, we will analyze the reason why this phenomenon existed and why it curiously was not seen in the cinematography of any other country at that time. And I say at that time, because coproductions of today are very differently conceived.

«The truth is I don't understand the hostile reaction from certain sectors of Spanish public opinion against Spanish-speaking films that are shot in Hollywood. The patriotic feelings expressed are quite often contrary to what you might expect of them. If in California, in Hollywood, movies are made in Spanish, they should be proud of the fact. Wasn't this the land where the Spaniard Friar Junípero Serra undertook his most humanitarian work, where the architecture ranging from the far-off mission-style to the more recent Spanish-style is part of the Hispanic cultural legacy, and where today's legendary literary figures called Zorro or Ramona were created? I think it's marvelous that Spaniards are returning here, but if they have a different view I don't know the reason why.» This statement was made by Richard Blumenthal, an executive of Paramount, in the March, 1932, issue of the magazine **Cine Mundial** (World Film) which was published in New York in Spanish.

Even though the opinions of this North American film-maker are worthy of taking into account, we must recognize the fact that the films shot in Spanish during 1930 and 1931 by the majors in Hollywood were mere copies, as we have already indicated, shot scene by scene after the original versions in English. The directors of these films were unknowns, although a few, very few, made certain names for themselves as directors later on. The Spanish versions of the English scripts were entrusted to writers of merit of whom we will later speak. They in turn supervised the actresses and actors, both Spanish and Latin American, during the shooting.

What is incongruous is that double versions were not made of insignificant films, since many of these were works by prestigious directors, works that completely lost their identity when they were remade. As a way of proof, **Marido y mujer**, by David Howard and Rudolf Sieber, with Conchita Montenegro and George Lewis, is the Spanish version of **Bad Girl**, by Frank Borzage; **El código penal,** by Phil Rosen and David Selman, with María Alba and Barry Norton, is **The Criminal Code,** by Howard Hawks; **Horizontes nuevos,** by David Howard, with Carmen Guerrero and George Lewis, and

Camino del infierno, by Richard Harlan, with María Alba and Juan Torena, are respectively **The Big Trail** and **The Man Who Came Back,** both by director Raoul Walsh; **Del mismo barrio,** by David Howard, with Mona Maris and Juan Torena, is none other than **Common Clay,** by Victor Fleming; and **La llama sagrada,** by William Gann, with Elvira Morla and Martín Garralaga, is the carbon copy of **The Sacred Flame,** by Archie Mayo. Other directors were plagiarized —because it was plagiary— in various films: no less than three by the today unjustly forgotten William K. Howard: **El impostor (Scotland Yard),** by Lewis Seiler, with Juan Torena and Blanca de Castejón; **El valiente (The Valiant),** by Richard Harlan, with Juan Torena and María Calvo; and **¿Conoces a tu mujer? (Don't Bet on Women),** by David Howard. The same is true of two prestigious films by the no less unjustly forgotten George F. Hill: **The Big House,** with Wallace Beery, reconverted into **El presidio,** by Ward Wing and Edgar Neville, with Juan de Landa, José Crespo and Juana Alcañiz, as well as **Min and Bill,** with Marie Dressler and Wallace Beery, also reconverted into **La fruta amarga,** by Arthur Gregon, with Virginia Fábregas, Juan de Landa and a brief cameo appearance by Luis Buñuel as a barman.

The list of the titles we have just mentioned —very incomplete as a matter of fact— is in itself sufficiently demonstrative in proving that a remake

Juan de Landa in El presidio **(1930) by Ward Wing and Edgar Neville.**

of the same film in another language is simply impossible: a Spanish version of an unmistakably American movie cannot be done. And while talking about impossibilities, we are reminded that the renowned, super-elegant detective, Philo Vance, who was created by S. S. Van Dike and who was made famous by the actor, William Powell —even though the same role was portrayed by others, was made into a Spanish figure by Antonio Moreno, reconverting **The Benson Murder Case,** by Frank Tuttle, into **El cuerpo del delito,** by Cyril Gardner. The same thing happened with the equally famous Chinese detective Charlie Chan, the creation of Earl Derr Biggers, whose unmistakable actor, Warner Oland, made way for the almond eyes of Manuel Arbó in **Eran trece** by David Howard, a literal copy of **Charlie Chan Carries On,** by Hamilton MacFadden. But the most obvious case is without a doubt Tod Browning's **Dracula** starring Bela Lugosi, which was remade into **Drácula,** directed by George Melford and with Carlos Villarias in the leading role.

There was no treachery with the comedians, simply because they were forced to speak in Spanish. Buster Keaton came off best. His **Estrellados,** with Raquel Torres, the Spanish version of **Free and Easy,** and **De frente... marchen,** with Conchita Montenegro, idem of **Doughboys,** both conserve their original charm. The shorts of Stan

Laurel and Oliver Hardy, Harry Langdon and Charley Chase can also be favorably compared. Hearing them badly pronounce Spanish often times produced a greater hilarity in the audience. And just so that no one is left out, even the shorts of **La pandilla** (Our Gang), had their Spanish versions, probably because of the old dictum that children can learn to speak languages quickly.
Among these American films remade by Spanish-speaking screenwriters and actors, we should spotlight **El presidio**. Even though the film was directed by Ward Wing, the **set supervision** of Edgar Neville on the film is well known. As we have already mentioned, the original was called **The Big House** (1930). It was directed by George F. Hill and it featured the unforgettable performance of Wallace Beery. There was also a French version which kept the original title and a German version which was re-baptized **Menshen hinter gitter,** both of which were made by the prestigious director Paul Fejos. According to Irving Thalberg, of the three actors who redid the lead role, the Frenchman André Berley, the German Heindrich George and the Spaniard Juan de Landa, only this latter actor was able to emulate the creator of the role, Wallace Beery. In order to see if this were the case, Metro-Goldwyn-Mayer premiered in Spain all four versions to let the general public make their own comparisons.
Curiously, the euphoria of the large American production companies at the beginning of the thirties to launch films made in Spanish on the market —a euphoria which was upset in Spain by the most negative of reactions, was not a **dangerous novelty** from Hollywood as many at that time believed. It occured during the first attempts to put sound to pictures. Even before the gala night of October 6, 1927, when the sound era in film was officially ushered in with the voice of Al Jolson and by the grace of the Warner brothers —the producers of **The Jazz Singer,** even before that date Spanish had been heard from the screens of American movie theaters. On August 6, 1926, in the same cinema where **The Jazz Singer** would be premiered just one year later, the Warner brothers —especially the man really responsible, Samuel Warner— tried out a new sound system that they had patented with the name Vitaphone. And the surprise that night was not so much the premiere of a version of **Don Juan** starring John Barrymore and accompanied with the synchronization of fragments from Mozart's opera, but rather the film with a complete sound track that started off the evening. It had a Spanish title: **La fiesta** (The Party). Performing in the film were the singer Anna Case, the Herman Heller Orchestra and the chorus of the New York Metropolitan; but the ones who really stole the show that evening with their songs, dances and castanets were the members of Antonio Cansino's Spanish dance company. Cansino was a famous Sephardic «bailaor» or dancer from Seville, although he had originally come from Tetuán. He was accompanied by his children, six men and a woman, along with other relatives. The first of Antonio Cansino's family to arrive in America were his son Eduardo and his daughter Elisa. Success for both was not long in coming. The dance pair achieved enormous prestige. The father, the other sons and a relative or two were reunited with the now famous pair a few years later and they formed a select and authentic troupe of dancers. Even though Eduardo and Elisa were the main figures of the company, the one who directed the shows was Antonio Cansino, the creator and maestro of the dynasty. When putting together the dance numbers that would be filmed and synchronized in the Warner studios, Antonio Cansino wanted his seven year old granddaughter Margarita to dance some «sevillanas», accompanying herself with castanets. She was the daughter of Eduardo and a Ziegfeld dancer. No one would then imagine that it would be the first screen appearance of Rita Hayworth.
In view of the enormous successes

that the Warner brothers had in laying on sound tracks to their films by means of their Vitaphone system, William Fox quickly patented his own system which he dubbed Movietone. The first public demonstration of this patent was made on January 21, 1927, nine months before the premiere of **The Jazz Singer.** It consisted of a series of shorts with sound that were screened to complement the premiere of the still silent film **What Price Glory?,** by Raoul Walsh. These shorts were nothing more than the filming and recording of the most famous songs by Raquel Meller, who was then at the height of her career. Before Al Jolson sang **My Mammy, Mother I Still Have You** or **Dirty Hands, Dirty Face,** Raquel Meller was singing songs on the screen from her repertoire, some of which can still be heard today such as **El relicario, La violetera,** or even the song sung in the Catalan language, **El noi de la mare.** Whether by accident or not, we must recognize the fact that the Americans were responsible for both the Spanish presence at the beginning of the sound era in film and for the good idea of bringing to Hollywood a series of writers and actors and actresses of true merit. It should also be recognized that without these screenwriters and entertainers **Spanish cinema in Hollywood** would never have been made possible. This is what truly interests us, and not the error of remaking totally American films as we

Harry Crocker, Charles Chaplin and Edgar Neville. Hollywood, 1929.

have already commented.
The production company which began the exodus to Hollywood of scriptwriters and performers, not only French and German, but Spanish as well, was Metro-Goldwyn-Mayer. And this example —a bad example as far as results are concerned— was immediately followed by the other majors: Fox, Paramount, Warner Bros., etc. It is said, and it should not be doubted, that it was Edgar Neville who suggested to his friend Irving Thalberg the names of writers that he should contract. These names were not only Spanish, but some were French as well, a fact that would be recognized by Marcel Achard.
Edgar Neville (1899-1967) was a unique person, since he was an aristocrat, diplomat, novelist, playwright, film-maker and even poet and painter. During those years he was on a cultural mission in Washington, but he spent his free time, which was a great deal, in Hollywood along with his good friend Charlie Chaplin. During his vacations he supervised the Spanish versions of three films made by MGM: **El presidio** (1930) and **La fruta amarga** (1930), already mentioned, and besides, **En cada puerto un amor** (1930), a literal copy of **Way for a Sailor,** by Sam Wood. In spite of the carbon paper, the hand of Edgar Neville was very much in evidence, and later, in Spain, he would acquire his own style. That style of his was unmistakable—

refined, elegant, ironic— which impregnated both his literary and cinematographic outputs. Fifteen years after the death of Edgar Neville, the new generations of Spanish film buffs still need to rediscover in his films the signature and stamp which are natural in **auteur** films.
Thanks to Edgar Neville, the following Spaniards would come to Hollywood: Gregorio Martínez Sierra, Enrique Jardiel Poncela, José López Rubio, Eduardo Ugarte and Tono (Antonio de Lara). Joining them would be Luis Buñuel, but as he puts it in his memoirs, he was invited through the **French route** since the scandal which arose after **L'âge d'or** had not gone unnoticed by American producers. But their indifference was converted into alarm after they knew the true motives of the scandal. With the same courtesy with which he had been invited to come, he was asked to leave. Regarding the time spent in Hollywood, Luis Buñuel recalls in **Mi último respiro** (My Last Breath) how Edgar Neville presented all his Spanish companions in the house of Charlie Chaplin. As Scott Fitzgerald described it, Chaplin's home was **Spain House.**
Our country is one of forgetfulness. This is perhaps the idiosyncrasy that Spaniards are most fond of, and as Américo Castro put it, they like «interring instead of disinterring». It has always been the case, but in our own time it has been much more painful

Georgie Hale, Eduardo Ugarte, Mrs. Tono,
Edgar Neville, José López Rubio and Tono.
Hollywood, 1930.

Charles MacArthur, Noël Coward, Gregorio Martínez Sierra and Ben Hecht. Hollywood, 1933.

due to the death blow struck by the civil war. Many are the names and figures before that horrible war, who are unknown to new generations. The fact that these figures were forgotten is even more painful if you take into account that they preferred to avoid political extremism of any kind, that they preferred silence and exile to the repugnance of living under any form of totalitarianism.

One of these figures who is yet to be recovered and who occupies an important place is Gregorio Martínez Sierra (1881-1947). He was introduced to a form of literature called modernism-symbolism that was very much in line with that preached by Maurice Maeterlinck. His first book was published in 1898. He founded various influential literary magazines such as **Vida moderna** (1901), **Helios** (1903), and especially, **Renacimiento** (1907), which was later to become a publishing house. However, his most decisive influence was felt in theater, and curiously enough, not in his own work (which was not bad by any means, but too sickly sweet for our own times), but as a set designer.

F. C. Sainz de Robles rightly said that «Martínez Sierra is the best set designer ever to work in Spanish theater». He was able to become a theater director, founding the **Teatro del Arte** which would last until 1926, thanks to the profits of his work **Canción de cuna** (2), premiered in 1911 and later staged in the main theaters throughout the world. Employing his **Teatro del Arte,** which was headquartered in the Eslava Theater on Arenal Street in Madrid, he undertook a genuine scenographic revolution at the service of the best playwrights of his time. Under his direction and inspiration, he created an entire school of painters and decorators who would have a decisive influence on Spanish theater. When in 1924, Martínez Sierra takes part of his sketches and models to the **Exposition Internationale des Arts Décoratifs et Industriales Modernes** in Paris, Gaston Baty presents him as an innovator on the level of Reinhardt, Craig or Appia. The inseparable companion of Martínez Sierra, who helped him create new horizons for Spanish theater, was the great actress Catalina Bárcena. We should not forget that they ran the risk of premiering in 1920 the first work by an unknown student called Federico García Lorca The title of the work was **El maleficio de la mariposa** (The Curse of the Butterflies). All the characters were insects. The very concept of the work was ahead of its time, anticipating surrealism, but it was a failure, albeit a glorious and historic failure. Both Gregorio Martínez Sierra and Catalina Bárcena arrived in Hollywood ready to make films—something they had never done, but Spanish films, not American. The company that opened the doors to

Raoul Roulien, Catalina Bárcena and Antonio Moreno in Primavera en otoño **(1932) by Eugene J. Forde.**

them was Fox, the only major that realized that it was only possible to make films in Spanish with Spanish works and Spanish performers. Among their production plans, they decide to take special care with a series of films that are right for Catalina Bárcena and that are always done under the technical supervision of Gregorio Martínez Sierra. From 1931 to 1935 they make seven films in that delicate tone, that soft and withheld emotion established by Catalina Bárcena when she plays herself —not other people— and when she uses her very distinctive voice which film has conserved for us forever. It would have been very difficult to establish such a perfect harmony between the style of these films and the work of an actress without the contributions made by Gregorio Martínez Sierra. He provided ideas from his own works, ideas that were written for her. Martínez Sierra did not hesitate to rework these ideas or even direct her and the other actors and actresses, since the directors imposed by the studio were more technical than artistic in nature. As a result, seven films were born under an unquestionable unity of style which was not created of course by the directors whom we will now cite, but rather by the writer-actress team. These films are: **Mamá** (1931), by Benito Perojo; **Primavera en otoño** (1932), by Eugene Forde; **Una viuda**

romántica (1933), by Louis King; **Yo, tú y ella** (1933), by John Reinhardt; **La ciudad de cartón** (1933), by Louis King; **Señora casada necesita marido** (1934), by James Tinling; and **Julieta compra un hijo** (1935), by Louis King. Most of these works are based on plays written by Gregorio Martínez Sierra: **Mamá, Primavera en otoño, Una viuda romántica (Sueños de una noche de agosto), Yo, tú y ella (Mujer)** and **Julieta compra un hijo,** a work written together with Honorio Maura. The film with the most personal stamp of the seven is **La ciudad de cartón,** the original story of which was conceived for film by Martínez Sierra. It is probably one of the cleverest and at the same time subtlest satires ever shot about Hollywood. Except in the case of **Mamá,** Martínez Sierra was helped in writing the screenplays of the other six movies by one of the most prolific writers of this stage of Spanish cinema abroad: José López Rubio (1903-   ). In the five years he spent in Hollywood, José López Rubio wrote twenty screenplays. He established a record in comparison to the work carried out by fellow writers contracted by film companies. The experience undoubtedly helped him in learning the art of dialogues, which years later would consecrate him as a playwright. Even before he dedicated himself to film he had made attempts at writing works for theater with **De la noche a la mañana** (Overnight; 1929), a

Catalina Bárcena in Una viuda romántica **(1933) by Louis King.**

prize-winning play he wrote along with Eduardo Ugarte, and **La casa de naipes** (The House of Cards; 1930). It would be nineteen years later when he could return to his first and true vocation, a vocation which would lead to his entry in the Royal Academy of the Spanish Language. Among his plays, we should make special mention of **Celos del aire** (Jealous Airs), **La venda en los ojos** (Blindfolded) and **La otra orilla** (The Other Shore).

José López Rubio arrived in Hollywood along with Eduardo Ugarte (1901-1952). Eduardo Ugarte's stay in North America was brief, since he would soon return to Spain where he would found **La barraca** along with Federico García Lorca, a theater company that was one of the most serious attempts in the world at establishing a people's theater. In 1939, he went into exile in Mexico where he once again worked as a scriptwriter. Along with his friend Luis Buñuel he writes a film adaptation of a novel by Rodolfo Usigli, **Ensayo de un crimen** (Essay to Crime), which was redubbed, **La vida criminal de Archibaldo de la Cruz** (The Criminal Life of Archibaldo de la Cruz).

The work that José López Rubio and Eduardo Ugarte did together in their first contract for Metro-Goldwyn-Mayer was not very brilliant. They had to do Spanish versions of two melodramas that were originally very successful plays: **The Trial**

of Mary Dugan by Bayard Veiller and **Madame X** by Aléxandre Bisson. If the English version of the first film was used to set off the good looks and talent of Norma Shearer— and the second did the same for Ruth Chatteton, the Spanish versions, **El proceso de Mary Dugan** (1930), by Marcel de Sano, and **La mujer X** (1931), by Carlos F. Borcosque, were entrusted to the same actress: María Fernanda Ladrón de Guevara. Of greater interest is the film version that José López Rubio and Eduardo Ugarte did of their own comedy called **Totó.** It was called **Su última noche** and starred Ernesto Vilches.

José López Rubio is hired by Fox to work alone and it is with this company he does important work as a screenwriter. Even though the films he did along with Gregorio Martínez Sierra are of great consequence, we cannot help but spotlight his literary contributions and his brilliant dialogues in such films as **El último varón sobre la tierra,** by James Tinling, starring Rosita Moreno and Raoul Roulien; **¡Ojo, solteros!,** directed by John Reinhardt, with Rosita Moreno and Valentín Parera; **Granaderos del amor,** by John Reinhardt, a delightful operetta with music by William Kenell that even today conserves its charm, starring Conchita Montenegro; **Rosa de Francia,** by Gordon Wiles, a very free and improved version of the play by Eduardo Marquina and Luis Fernández

Enrique Jardiel Poncela, Gregorio Martínez Sierra and José López Rubio. Hollywood, 1932.

Ardavín, starring Rosita Díaz Gimeno in the role of Louise Isabelle of Orleans and with Rita Cansino (Rita Hayworth) as a **lady in waiting.** They tell me, although I do not know the facts, that an American who is an expert in his own cinema published in Los Angeles a very curious study on plagiaries. The work lists two scripts in Spanish by José López Rubio which it seems more or less —more than less— were transformed, without his permission it is to be deduced, into two Hollywood films. It would be of great interest to know the names of the scripts and the films.

No one doubts that Enrique Jardiel Poncela (1901-1953) was before his time. The proof is that time is bringing him back to us and not slowly, but with giant steps. Decades after our playwright described his theater productions as **theater of the implausible,** the **theater of the absurd** was born. Words really are not important here, what is are dates. His first work, **Una noche de primavera sin sueño** (A Dreamless Spring Night) is premiered in 1927. It is followed by a torrent of plays, novels and writings. Everything he touches, even film, progressively shapes and sharpens his odd personality. His is an unqualifiable, undefinable personality, but always identifiable.

It was little less than impossible that a playwright who owed so much to cinema would not be claimed by that media. Many of his works were adapted for the screen with greater or lesser fortune: **Eloísa está debajo de un almendro** (Eloísa is Beneath an Almond Tree) and **Los ladrones somos gente honrada** (We Thieves are Honest People) in Spain; **Usted tiene ojos de mujer fatal** (You've Got the Eyes of a Vamp) and **Las cinco advertencias de Satanás** (Satan's Five Warnings) in Spain and Mexico; and **Margarita, Armando y su padre** (Margarita, Armando and His Father) and **Un adulterio decente** (A Decent Adultery) in Argentina. Most of the time in these works the only thing that remained alive was that which you cannot destroy: the dialogue. Enrique Jardiel Poncela's first stay in Hollywood was between September, 1932 and May, 1933. Similar to what happened to Luis Buñuel, he practically did nothing. In order to have some fun, he appeared as an extra in two films by Gregorio Martínez Sierra and starring Catalina Bárcena: **Primavera en otoño** and **Una viuda romántica** —in this last film along with José López Rubio. Before he left and so as to justify his contract, he proposes to Fox executives an idea which seemed completely absurd, but to which they agreed, due to its low cost. The idea was revolutionary: it consisted of laying on sound to old silent film shorts with dialogues invented by him. This is how **Celuloides rancios** (Rancid Celluloids) are born. The eventual six are made in the Billancourt

José Crespo, Rosita Díaz Gimeno, Louis King and Enrique Jardiel Poncela during the shooting of Angelina o el honor de un brigadier **(1935) by Enrique Jardiel Poncela and Louis King.**

Studios in Paris. In spite of what the producers thought, they produced true amazement and jubilation in the public. Although we get away from the topic we are discussing, I believe it is interesting to point out that Jardiel Poncela repeated his «Rancid Celluloid» experiment in Spain on two different occasions: in 1938 in San Sebastián, making four shorts which he called **Celuloides cómicos** (Comic Celluloids), but this time with professional actors, and, in 1940 in Madrid, where he used an old feature-length film dating from 1914 called **La cortina verde** (The Green Curtain), by Ricardo Baños, reconverting it into **Mauricio o una víctima del vicio** (Mauricio, or a Victim of Vice), a film that was unusually hilarious.

Convinced —we return to 1933— that Hollywood would not call him back, he writes for Benito Perojo the screenplay for **Se ha fugado un preso** (A Convict has Escaped), starring Rosita Díaz Gimeno. This is the first Spanish film that was officially invited to take part in the Venice Mostra. The film surprised the public because of its subject matter and dialogues, written by Enrique Jardiel Poncela. To his amazement, not only is he contracted by Fox, but Rosita Díaz Gimeno as well.

The most important of all the Spanish films ever shot in Hollywood was born in this fashion: **Angelina o el honor de un brigadier** (Angelina, or the Honor of a Brigadier; 1935). This delightful comedy, this subtle parody, which Jardiel Poncela subtitled **Un drama de 1880** (An 1880 Drama), was a huge success when it was premiered the year before —1934— by Isabelita Garcés in Madrid's Infanta Isabel Theater. Much to the surprise of everyone, the work received a tribute from writer Eugenio D'Ors who dedicates **Tres glosas sobre una farsa** (Three Marginal Notes on a Farse) to the work. Even today we ask ourselves how the directors of Fox decided to produce a film in Spanish with all the dialogue spoken in ironic verse and dedicated to the romantic words used as fillers in poetry. The film was directed by Jardiel Poncela under the technical supervision of Louis King. The main performers were Rosita Díaz Gimeno (the unforgettable Angelina), Enrique de Rosas (the brigadier), José Crespo (Germán Valderramas), Julio Peña (the poet Rodolfo) and Andrés de Segurola (the banker). When Chaplin found out that a film had been shot that was completely unlike any other, he asked to have it screened for him, in spite of the fact that his Spanish was limited to having heard the lyrics to **La violetera** (The Violet Seller). He remarked: «I guess at a comic film, but without comedians». That was quite a guess for someone who did not know Spanish. I consider **Angelina o el honor de un brigadier** would justify in itself calling this chapter, **Spanish Cinema in**

Antonio Moreno, Raoul Roulien and Conchita Montenegro in Asegure a su mujer **(1935) by Lewis Seller.**

Hollywood. One should ask —and I most definitely do— what other films made at that time in our country equal Jardiel Poncela's movie not only in quality, but also in being essentially Spanish. I believe that **La traviesa** (The Mischievous Girl; 1934) by Jarry D'Abbadie D'Arast, and **La verbena de la Paloma** (The Paloma Fair; 1935) by Benito Perojo could equal it, but very few others.

Following such a caprice as **Angelina o el honor de un brigadier,** Jardiel Poncela had to submit himself to the rules of the game and accepts to write a script —and the dialogue, of course— for a comedy by Julio Escobar. The results could not be better. The movie was called **Asegure a su mujer** (Insure Your Wife). It was directed by Lewis Seiler, with Conchita Montenegro, Antonio Moreno and Raoul Roulien in the starring roles.

In 1935, Fox became 20th Century-Fox and months later the directors of the new company decide to restudy their production plans for films in Spanish. The majority of the contracts are cancelled. It is sad to recognize it, but a degree of quality had been reached that was at odds with profitability. This quality, however, was to be taken advantage of by Spanish production companies, especially Cifesa, which quickly contracted Gregrorio Martínez Sierra, Catalina Bárcena and Rosita Díaz Gimeno, who, along with Imperio Argentina, Florián Rey (about to

coproduce a film with France), Benito Perojo, and even Filmófono with Luis Buñuel at its head or Edgar Neville, who always worked as an independent, assured without a doubt a new Spanish cinema.

All this was brought down when on July 18, 1936, the greatest tragedy of modern-day Spain began. **The outbreak of the Spanish Civil War.** When we were about to consolidate a **new golden age,** Spanish culture is devastated. The most important names in Spanish literature, art and science go into exile. A minority remains. All that is left is broken, divided. The three years that the civil war lasted seem like three centuries. The new generations will have to rediscover what has been forbidden them, what has been hidden. Slowly names and works were joined together, the majority abroad plus the minority within, until what actually did not become **a new golden age century** was repaired as much as possible, and which was baptized by North American Hispanists as an **age of silver.** Gold was reduced to silver, a luminous silver which can still shine out.

Spanish cinema did not reach the heights of the rest of our culture at that time. Its most important works can be counted on the fingers of one hand... and you would have a couple left over. But what cannot be done—and what is too often the case—is to separate Spanish cinema from this

Rosita Díaz Gimeno and Gilbert Roland (Luis Alonso) in *La vida bohemia* **(1939) by Joseph Berne.**

(Previous page)

Antonio Moreno in *Rosa de Francia* **(1933) by Gordon Wiles.**

Greta Garbo and Antonio Moreno in *The Temptress* (1926) by Fred Niblo.

age of silver, because even though a minimal contribution was made, some, although very few of the people who were responsible for this cultural renaissance, worked in the world of film with greater or lesser fortune. I can think of Luis Buñuel, Edgar Neville, Enrique Jardiel Poncela, Eduardo Ugarte, José López Rubio, and even two actresses who went into exile: Catalina Bárcena and Rosita Díaz Gimeno.

Final note: It would not be right to close this chapter of Spanish cinema without briefly referring to the work in American films of two actress and four actors from Spain. The six took part in some of the films made in Spanish that we have referred to, but what we now want to recall —and emphasize— is their work in Hollywood films. This is a question which is part of the general framework of European contributions to United States cinema, a question which is only now being studied. It has been affirmed that until very recently, Old World influences in easily identifiable areas have not yet disappeared. These influences are part of the most varied topics and styles which define American cinema. Of course, the German-Central European influence was decisive, and was followed in importance by British, Swedish, and to a lesser extent, French cinema. Spain did not contribute any directors to Hollywood, but it did contribute subject matter, the **españolada** (or exaggerated portrait of Spain). Which Hollywood actress did not wear a mantilla at one time in her career? The long list includes Greta Garbo, Marlene Dietrich, Pola Negri, Mae Murray and Rita Hayworth. Spanish influences were also filtered through Californian and Mexican mythology, figures such as El Zorro, Ramona and the Cisco Kid.

We are going to deal with certain actors and actresses for the simple reason that they are totally forgotten and nothing has been written about them. I will do so briefly, but with the desire that one day their work is studied with the care that it deserves. Film historians tend to forget about actors and actresses, not bearing in mind that during a long period of Hollywood's history films were largely made on the basis of the star system and that both the stories and directors had to bow to its commercial dictates. Of course, this did not mean that actors or actresses did not perform in outstanding works. Among the Spanish stars, we should give pride of place to Antonio Moreno (1886, Madrid-1967, Los Angeles). In the words of de Witt Bodeen, he gave birth to the figure of the Latin lover long before Rudolph Valentino was enthroned as such. In Spain he only shot **En la tierra del sol** (In the Land of the Sun; 1927), directed by Ramón Martínez de la Riva and co-starring Elisa Ruiz Romero «Romerito» and Alfredo Hurtado Pitusín, as well as **María de la O** (1936), by Francisco Elías, along with Pastora Imperio and Carmen Amaya. But during the period of Spanish versions in Hollywood, his name headed the titles along with that of Catalina Bárcena in such films as **Primavera en otoño, La ciudad de cartón** and **Señora casada necesita marido;** with María Alba in **El cuerpo del delito** and **Los que danzan;** with Conchita Montenegro in **Asegure a su mujer;** and with Rosita Díaz Gimeno in **Rosa de Francia.**.
We want to emphasize here that his extensive American film credits represent an unusual phenomenon, a fact that has been recognized by Anglo-Saxon film historians. He was a leading man along with all the great stars of Hollywood's silent era. Here is a list of some of those figures: Mary Pickford: **So Near, Yet So Far** (1912), by D. W. Griffith, the director who discovered him; Norma Talmadge, with whom he filmed at least seven films by Van Dyke (father); Pearl White, in the film by episodes called **The House of Hate** (La casa de odio; 1918), by George B. Seitz; Gloria Swanson: **My American Wife** (Mi esposa americana; 1923), by Sam Wood; Bene Daniels: **The Exciters** (La señorita emociones; 1923), directed by Maurice Campbell; Pola Negri: **The Spanish Dancer** (La bailarina española; 1923), by Herbert Brenon; Constance Talmadge: **Learning to Love** (La que no quiso amar; 1925), by Sidney Franklin, and **Venus of Venice** (La Venus de Venecia; 1927) by Marshal Neilan; Alice Terry: **Mare Nostrum** (Mare Nostrum; 1926), by Rex Ingram; Marion Davies: **Beverly of Graustark** (Su alteza el príncipe; 1926), by Sidney Franklin; Greta Garbo: **The Temptress** (La tierra de todos; 1926), by Fred Niblo; Clara Bow: **It** (Ello, 1927), by Clarence Badger; Dorothy Gish: **Madame Pompadour** (Madame Pompadour; 1927), by Herbert Wilcox; Billie Dove: **Adoration** (Adoración; 1928), by Frank Lloyd; Colleen Moore: **Synthetic Sin** (El pecado sintético; 1928), by William A. Seiter; etc. This list is very incomplete, but it is sufficiently explicit in giving an idea of his credits and of proving him an undeniable leading man of the most important actresses of Hollywood's silent era.
After 1940, the large American production companies use him in secondary roles, almost always playing Spanish characters. Among the films he worked in, we can recall: **Seven Sinners** (Siete pecadores; 1940), directed by Tay Garnett; **The Spanish Man** (1945), by Frank Borzage; **Captain from Castile** (1947), by Henry King; **Crisis** (1950), by Richard Brooks; **Thunder Bay** (Bahía negra; 1953), by Anthony Mann; **Wings of the Hawk** (1953), by Budd Boeticher; **Saskatchewan** (Rebelión en el fuerte; 1954), by Raoul Walsh; and **The Searchers** (Centauros del desierto; 1956), by John Ford. Few actors had the same film career as Antonio Moreno in the almost half-century he worked in Hollywood. Giving him a mention is undoubtedly doing him a justice.

* * *

Conchita Montenegro (San Sebastián, 1912-...). She was discovered by Agustín de Figueroa, Marquis of Santo Floro, who gave her the leading role in **Sortilegio** (Witchcraft; 1927), a film in which this son of the Count of Romanones was, apart from producer, the director, scriptwriter and leading actor. After that first film, her career took a big international turn. According to Howard Hawks, there was never in Hollywood such a polyglot actress. She shot in direct sound—and always with a good accent— films in Spanish, French, English, Portuguese and Italian. Only Ingrid Bergman would achieve a similar record. She was hired by Metro-Goldwyn-Mayer in 1930 to make movies in Spanish, but she almost immediately started to work in the original English versions.
Conchita Montenegro was a unique case. It cannot be said that she was a great actress, but her singular personality always seemed to us enveloped in a halo of elegance, in that poetic brilliance which now that we think about it, irradiated from so many film stars. Her presence —that was it, a veritable presence— left its mark on the film industries of France, Italy and Spain. But now we will only refer to the original versions that she did in English, omitting those she shot in Spanish. We must point out that Conchita Montenegro enjoyed much more prestige outside Spain than within the country —as so often happens to Spaniards. Her films shot in English in America include: 1931, **Strangers May Kiss** (Besos al pasar), by George Fitzmaurice; **Paid to Love,** by Lewis Seiler; **Never the Twain Shall Meet** (Prohibido), by W. S. Van Dyke; and **The Cisco Kid** (El Cisco Kid), by Irving Cummings. 1932: **The Gay Caballero** (Audaz y galante), by Alfred L. Werker. 1933:

Laughing at Life (Riendo toda la vida), by Ford Beebe. 1934: **Hell in the Heaven** (El brindis de la muerte), by John Blystone, and **Handy** (Receta para la felicidad), by David Butler.

* * *

María Alba (Barcelona, 1910-...). María Casajuana is her real name. She arrived in Hollywood after winning the first prize in a photographic contest organized by Fox along with the Barcelona newspaper, **El Día Gráfico.** She was a very attractive woman and had a very sensual appearance. She was selected by Douglas Fairbanks (father) to work with him in **Mr. Robinson Crusoe** (El Robinsón moderno; 1932), by Edward Sutherland. Some of her other films were: **A Girl in Every Port** (Una novia en cada puerto; 1928), by Howard Hawks, and **Hell's Heroes** (Heroes del infierno; 1929), by William Wyler. During the sound era, she alternated films in Spanish with those in English. In 1931, she married Dave Todd who headed Fox's casting department.

* * *

And finally, we should mention three Spanish actors who worked in Hollywood. One day we should study their long film careers. Today they are three classic names of that «glorious world», as Frank Capra put it, «of character actors in American film». I am referring to Luis Alberni (Barcelona, 1885), Andrés de Segurola (Barcelona, 1879) and Fortunio Bonanova (Palma de Mallorca, 1896)

* * *

Leslie Howard and Conchita Montenegro in *Never the Twain Shall Meet* **(1931) by W. S. van Dyke.**

(Previous page)

Conchita Montenegro in *Granaderos del amor* **(1933) by John Reinhardt.**

(1) Hollywood's Spanish-language films, by Alfonso Pinto in Film in Review, Number 8, October 1973.

(2) Taking advantage of Gregorio Martínez Sierra's stay in Hollywood, Paramount bought from him the film rights of **Canción de cuna.** The screenplay was written by Marc Connolly and Frank Partos under the supervision of the author of the work. The film **Cradle Song** (1933) was well-received and established the name of Mitchell Leisen, who until that time was a set designer, as well as the great German actress Dorothea Wieck who had just arrived in the United States and whose stay was brief since she did not adapt to the work methods of the mecca of film.

1936

1939

Ernest Hemingway and Joris Ivens shooting Spanish Earth **(1937).**

1936
1939

Ramón Sala
Rosa Alvarez Berciano

As in every other area of Spanish life, the film industry was profoundly affected by the accelerated chain of political and military events which began after the unfortunate date of July 18, 1936, initiated by the uprising of part of the army. That date triggered the tremendous episode of Spanish history which was the 1936-39 Civil War.

Spanish cinema, in spite of the few or many merits which it accumulated up to that time and contrary to what has been maintained by many historians and critics, did not stop its production activities between July, 1936 and 1939, later to resume its «normal» shooting of films. The truth is that between 1936 and 1939 film activity, which had oftentimes moved off into strange directions before then, was very intense. Even though one may not know the hundreds of film shorts and not a few features that were shot during the period, it would not be right to deny they ever existed.

Film-making during the civil war forms a part of the history of Spanish cinema and it could even be said that the production methods on each of the warring sides, seen in their complexity, help in the understanding of the profound differences which resulted in the clash between the so-called «two Spains».

Spain in two

During the first days of the sedition, the military communiques were sufficiently ambiguous to try to convince the people that the self-styled **National Uprising** was being staged against the Republican government and not against the Republic itself. Many of the garrisons that rose up did so with the cry, «Long Live the Republic!» Almost immediately, however, it was seen that the passionate political and even personal phobias of Generals Mola, Queipo de Llano and Franco went much further than that, and that their fears included many more Spaniards than those who at that time made up the government. Even the hierarchy of the Spanish Catholic Church had to recognize the fact —after it had resigned itself to the idea that it had lost more than half its flock— that «Spain's war is the product of a struggle between irreconcilable ideologies: in its very origin are very serious questions of a moral and juridical, a religious and historical order» (1). The traditionally more intolerant and reactionary Spain looked back in history as has always been the case, and denying the present reality, drove in the spike by declaring a military uprising. The Spanish Earth (**La tierra española**), which inspired that lyrical film of the same title by Joris Ivens, became after that moment a land split into two very

well-delimited zones.
As a result, if until July, 1936, **one** cinematography could be spoken of, after that time it would be **two,** both of which were antagonistic in their way of going about things. The only element that they both had in common will be their almost total propagandistic slant during nearly three years of cinematographic activity, as was the case with every other artistic and cultural form of expression. But this is where the coincidences end. The cinematography from 1936 to 1939 could not help mirroring those two totally opposed conceptions of the world. While for the purely military regime which was set up by the rebels, the war was an affair that could only be resolved in the field of military tactics and equipment —which, due to the characteristics of the troops that fought on the rebel side (a professional army with a large proportion of mercenaries), it could not be fought any other way, for the Republican authorities or for the authorities of any of the political or union authorities in the governmental zone, the war had to be won on all fronts, and that meant the rearguard as well. They wanted to foment enthusiasm in defense of the legitimized power of the Republic and everything it represented: they had to overcome both the enemy forces and their own doubts. This and no other was the reason that artistic and cultural life, including that of cinema, contrasted tremendously in vitality, creative euphoria and even splendor with the colorless panorama offered in the same area by the **official** Spain of General Franco (2).
With regard to cinematography, the superiority —not only numeric— of Republican films and film-makers was so undeniable that even a historian of such pronounced Francoist sympathies as Carlos Fernández Cuenca had to give in to the evidence. «During the various months in 1937 that the Universal Exposition lasted in Paris, the pavilion of the Spanish Republic screened documentaries produced in the red zone every day. Some were very bad, but others were average and there was no lack of some that were frankly good. What did the authorities in Burgos do to counteract that intelligent and incisive propaganda?... Apart from the fact that there did not exist in 1937 any state-run organization dependent on the Burgos government that was capable of embarking on the important propagandistic mission that corresponded to film, neither did there abound enough material to offer a screening of more than a few hours. The consequences of that neglect have come down to us today, the results felt each and every day. The world only had a one-sided view of the war» (3).
A justification for the discreet film production of the Nationalist side was that the studios and laboratories remained in the Republican zone— Madrid and Barcelona. This justification is only valid with regard to the first days of the war, since Spanish film-makers supporting Franco could have easily worked in the magnificent laboratories and studios in Germany and Italy, not counting the solidarity of the nearby Portugal of Salazar. Proof of this was the regular production activities during the last stage of the war of the **Departamento Nacional de Cinematografía** (National Film Department), which coincided with the appearance of magazines specialized in commentaries demanding greater attention for film, «an unsurpassable civilizing art», «a social weapon of undeniable strength», etc. Some time would pass before these commentaries would have an effect on the Headquarters of General Franco, where only the frivolous side of film must have been seen, never as an efficient media for information and propaganda.

Republican cinema

In contrast, the film studios and laboratories stayed inactive for a very short period of time, just those first days of street fighting which stalemated the war between the rebels and the Republic's loyal forces. There was just enough time as a matter of fact for the moneyed interests of the film industry to travel to the zone which they naturally supported, the so-called **Nationalist zone.** For many youths, who until that time had only been able to theorize about film, it represented the opportunity to move on to cinematographic creation, although this happened in such special conditions. Among many other experiences, film-making in the Republican zone experienced a substantial shake-up in directors, cameramen, scriptwriters, etc. Almost from the very first days of the conflict, each political party, union organization or public opinion group had a film section more or less organized.

This was why numerous film crews were sent along with the columns of militiamen who left for the front and why they were scattered throughout the Republican zone. The political limelight achieved by the people's organizations due to their decisive influence in crushing certain isolated military units was a determining factor in shaping this unique and vital panorama of Republican cinematography.

Dawn of hope

One of these people's organizations, the **Confederación Nacional de Trabajo** (National Labour Confederation), or CNT, stood out almost immediately for its unique and almost exuberant film activity.

Its clear numerical superiority in some Republican cities, including Barcelona, and its traditional acceptance among the people who worked in the liberal arts —film, theater, magazines, etc., permitted this organization much room to move in the sector (4). The anarcho-syndicalist union was the leftist political organization that most benefited from the clashes resulting from July 18 —especially in Catalonia where it had almost 250,000 members, and it can be affirmed that it never had such a clear-cut opportunity of taking over power (5).

All this was naturally felt in the world of cinema as well. The three classical areas of film (production, distribution and exhibition) not only changed hands, but they became almost totally under the control of the anarcho-syndicalists —even though the **Unión General de Trabajadores** (General Workers Union), or UGT, shared control in certain Republican cities such as Madrid —and they also radically changed the way in which they operated.

The first step in this direction, and the most decisive as well, took place in Barcelona, the traditional bastion of the anarchists and the privileged setting for the launching of their revolutionary aspirations. In the opinion of the anarchists, these aspirations should not be put off under any circumstance, and neither should war be now used as an excuse to postpone the radical transformation of society. One of these revolutionary imperatives was that of placing the production media in the hands of the workers, or what is the same, to collectivize, socialize or confiscate them, all different ways of a basically similiar phenomenon.

One of the first sectors to be collectivized was that of public locales: movie theaters, theaters, dog tracks, etc. The first collectivizations were largely improvised by the workers in these locales. Later the entire enterprise would take on greater scope once the **Comité Económico de Cines** (Economic Committee for Cinemas) was constituted. The committee was organized under its own statutes and had control over all the box office takings of Barcelona locales, becoming a powerful concern in the world of show business. This state of affairs, coupled with the fact that the film studios and laboratories had passed into the hands of the anarcho-syndicalists as well, meant that this organization was in a position to reanimate the paralyzed film industry and even undertake projects of a somewhat utopian nature such as competing with American films for the sympathies of the public, and of course, making typically Spanish cinema using such subject matter as

that of **Luis Candelas** or **Diego Corrientes.** They had a much better chance in this latter area.
The CNT, as the rest of the political and syndical organizations of the Republican zone, dedicated a large part of its energies to the production of propaganda documentaries and news reports, but unlike the others, the anarchists assumed shall we say a much wider concept in what should have been considered **propaganda.** According to them, propagandistic activity in film should not only overcome the so-called pure situation, but should also include what they described as the **basic film,** that is to say, feature-length fiction films meant to **revolutionarily** reorganize Spanish screens. The financial support of the powerful **Comité Económico de Cines** made this production activity possible. Anarcho-syndicalist cinema did not only stand out due to its unique proposals, but also for the superior number of the titles it was responsible for: more than a hundred shorts and medium-length films. Among these films, those shot between 1936 and part of 1937 are almost exclusively dedicated to the activities of the anarcho-syndicalist militias on the different Republican fronts: its boundless enthusiasm during these first months is evident in the images and the commentary of the filmed reports (6). **Reportaje del movimiento revolucionario** (Report on the

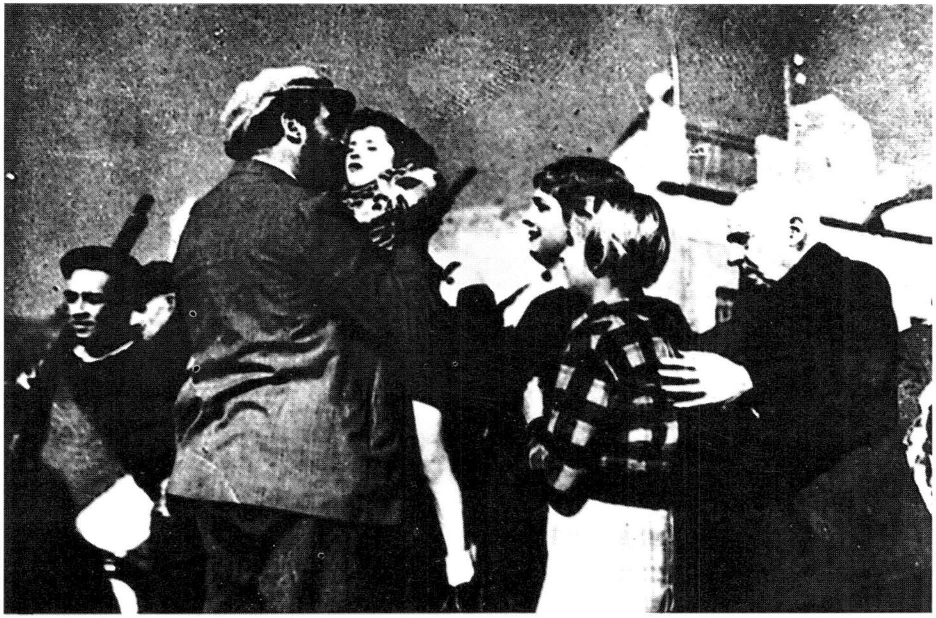

Aurora de esperanza (**1937**) **by Antonio Sau.**

Antonio Riquelme in Así venceremos **(1938).**

Revolutionary Movement), **Los aguiluchos de la FAI por tierras de Aragón** (The Eaglets of the FAI in the Lands of Aragón), **La toma de Siétamo** (The Taking of Siétamo) and **La batalla de Farlete** (The Battle of Farlete) are some of the reports made during that period. After the first months of the war, the documentaries dedicated to education and indoctrination were more frequent. The life of the libertarian communities of Aragón, the preparation of an anarchist newspaper and the training of the militias were some of the recurring topics in **Bajo el signo libertario** (Under the Sign of Libertarianism), **La silla vacía** (The Empty Chair), **20 de Noviembre** (November 20), **El acero libertario** (Libertarian Steel), **En la brecha** (In the Breach), **Alerta** (Alert) or **Prostitución** (Prostitution).

Among the main characteristics of this production, we should spotlight its spontaneity and fresh outlook, but unfortunately often at the expense of professional rigor and reflection; the triumphant and **openly** partisan tone of its commentaries; and especially, a kind of experimental zeal found in many of these works —works which instead of easily recurring to the **tried-and-true** genre of the film report or the normal documentary, moved into the field of fictionalized documentary. They were almost always improvised and did not offer a great deal of exactitude, but they showed in any case a laudable restlessness and curiosity in the film medium.

Regarding less temporal and more important production, we can say that the studios and laboratories were soon put back into working order. They had been abandoned by their owners in spite of the persistent calls made by the anarcho-syndicalists for them to return to their former positions (7). The production of **Aurora de esperanza** (Dawn of Hope) was begun, a project which the anarcho-syndicalists ambitiously called «the first attempt at social film» in our country. The Soviet films of the revolution, which at that time were being profusely distributed throughout the Republican cinemas, were assuredly the source of inspiration for the film. The rather free version of that inspiration should be pardoned since it was the film debut of Antonio Sau as both scriptwriter and director. In spite of the will and enthusiasm that were put into the project, neither the critics nor the public were very temporizing with this story about the trials and tribulations of a worker and his lady companion in the ferocious capitalist world. The film did have a few good ideas and intuitive insights, but it is totally lacking in the epic tone needed to move a public that is submerged in a heartbreaking civil war.

Almost at the same time **Barrios bajos** (Lower-class Districts) was directed by Pedro Puche, his second film. It was not very good and what he hoped would be a drama ended, much to his sorrow, in a purely absurd fashion.

These films were followed by others such as **Liberación** (Liberation), by Amichatis; **¡Nosotros somos así!** (We're Like That!), by Valentín R. González, an outlandish comedy with a little boy thrown in; **Paquete, el fotógrafo público número uno** (Paquete, Public Photographer Number One), by Ignacio F. Iquino and starring Paco Martínez Soria and Mary Santpere; and a few others that did nothing else than show up the main weakness of the CNT's production plans: film could not substantially change with the simple solution of substituting an allegedly **frivolous** story line with a would-be **social** one, and of course the CNT, or at least its **Comité de Producción Cinematográfica** (Film Production Committee) seemed to ignore the maxim that film-makers are not made overnight. «The unions, commented one auto-critical editorial of a CNT magazine, driven by their own vitality, set out to make films as someone else might make chairs or wagons. Before shooting a film, one should study cinema which has an art and a technique whose secrets require control and experience» (8).

The hardly satisfactory results of previous production activities radically changed film policies, an event which also coincided with the political decline of the anarcho-syndicalist union—

¡No quiero... no quiero! **(1937) by Francisco Elías.**

which each day found itself further from the seats of power. Disheartened by so-called **social** cinema, they decided to try a more openly commercial cinema, but not after some harsh criticism was leveled at the decision. This innovative tendency also meant a step backwards in the selection of film crews: first-time directors were rejected in favour of more experienced film-makers even though these directors might not share the CNT ideology. This time the American example, the pragmatic way mapped out by Hollywood studios, substituted the Soviet model.
A comedy was conceived to inaugurate this new production stage. It was precisely by Jacinto Benavente and was set in luxurious settings of the upper middle-class. However, it was slightly critical of this social group, and as a result, perfect for the CNT's designs: having the double purpose of entertaining, but teaching in the process. The movie was called **¡No quiero... No quiero!** (I Don't Want To!... I Don't Want To!) and it seems to have had a troubled time of it during the filming, apart from being costly. It was directed by Francisco Elías, who then was an experienced film-maker. The picture was not finished until after the war and could not be shown on Republican screens. However, it had no problem in being shown in the Francoist Spain of 1940.
In Madrid, where the CNT competed for power on a more or less equal footing with the rest of the political organizations, the anarchist films were produced along the same lines, even though fewer were made. It finished up with another **commercial** film called **Nuestro culpable** (Our Culprit), which was well-directed by Fernando Mignoni, who also wrote the script. It is a light-hearted comedy about the adventures of a likeable thief. Just like **¡No quiero... No quiero!** many people criticized the insolence of dedicating attention to a humorous topic only a short distance away from the front.

People's cinema: party discipline

As opposed to the anarchists, the communists and their allies of the moment assumed «a provisional policy of social conservatism» (9), which accented more than anything else the reconstruction of the Republican state apparatus and the creation of a wide political front that would undertake what they considered the main, and for the moment, **only** goal: to win the war. The anarchist attempts to put into practice their idea of a social revolution were logically, in view of these motives, bitingly censured if not hampered.
Another of the slogans assiduously repeated by the communists referred to unity: unity of power, unity of command, unity of the economy, etc. Socialists and Republicans also urged unity, but perhaps only the communists placed so many hopes in the beneficial results of this **unification,** which went hand-in-hand with an excessively critical attitude towards manifestations judged individualistic and counter-revolutionary, as was the case with the anarch-syndicalist collectivizations referred to above. Assuming the role of «champions of unity» (10), it was totally predictable that the communists would support the idea of a **single cinema,** in other words, one organism that would take over running film-making activities, and of course, forming part of the Republican state apparatus. It would be a «a single vertebral idea», that of an anti-fascist propaganda, one that would be opposed to a **partisan** propaganda —although obviously no one was safe from partisan politics: the difference between partisanship towards one group or another was exclusively based to a greater or lesser extent on the subtleness of the method used. Finally, the «single cinema» concept would include the rigorous control of film production, which would have to be exclusively subjected to the needs derived from the war, since, as the communists stated, «after the material elements of combat, cinema is the weapon with greatest effectiveness».
Unity, however, was never achieved, and in open contradiction to its unitary

A Soviet film advertised in its Spanish version, *La última noche*, in Madrid's Capitol cinema during the civil war.

statements —which did have great success among the military since it led to the creation of the **Ejército Popular Regular** (Regular People's Army), the communists ended up increasing the number of its insulting «cinematographic mini-republics», contributing in this way to the general dispersion of the sector with the creation of the **Film Popular** (People's Film) distribution and production group. Although this company was presented as «an anti-fascist commercial enterprise and at the service of the Republic» in order not to give up the dream of becoming the focal point for all film activities, the group's clear ideological leanings were not lost on anyone.

Existing at the same time as **Film Popular** —and before that group its direct predecessor or the **Cooperativa Obrera Cinematográfica** (Cinematographic Workers Cooperative), there were many other film units that were more or less backed by the Communist Party. Some of these units shortly afterwards were constituted into solid **cinematographic sections** with their own regular production schedules such as those belonging to the **46th «El Campesino» Division,** the **13th «Pasionaria» People's Militias Regiment,** the **International Red Aid,** the prolific **Anti-fascist Intellectual Alliance,** the **Unified Socialist Youth,** etc. All this contributed to the introduction of a vast and complex film structure, the activity and efficiency of which was well-proven by the regular publication of the weekly news bulletin **España al Día** (with its foreign versions, **Nouvelles d'Espagne** and **Spain Today**), a deed which would have been impossible in the midst of a war if it had not been for the disciplined workings of the team formed around **Film Popular.** The publication of the news bulletin became an excellent school for professionals —necessary and essential if it is considered that many of them only had theoretical training in the media, which in itself is of no little merit.

At the same time as the **Film Popular** news bulletin was published, similar organizations produced numerous news reports and documentaries, naturally referring to important questions for communist policies: the integration of the militias in the Regular Army, war industries, the military advances on the front, the maintenance of power in the Republic, etc.

Certain conclusions can be obtained from some of these reports such as **El telar** (The Loom), **Voluntarios de la libertad** (Volunteers for Freedom), **El paso del Ebro** (The Ebro Crossing), **Por la unidad hacia la victoria** (Unity in Victory) or **La mujer y la guerra** (Women and War). In general, they were made in a more exacting fashion, without running too many formal risks, an attitude which one cannot help comparing with that of the anarchists. Still another aspect of their work should be referred to: the distribution of Soviet revolutionary films throughout the Republican cinemas. The dynamic capacity of these films was only comparable to the sympathies that the Soviet Union awakened after the defection of the timid European democracies left the Republic isolated, an isolation that was mitigated by the aid provided by the Soviets. Under the pretext of screening these films, political meetings, debates and demonstrations were organized. Few people who lived in the Republican zone do not remember attending one of these sessions. Their effects among the militias due to the analogy of their personal experiences with the topics and motives of such films as **Tchapaiev** (1934), by S. and G. Vasiliev; **The Cronstadt Sailors** (1936), by Iefin Dzigan, or **Maxim's Youth** (1935), by Kosintsev and Trauberg, would fill pages and pages with commentary (11).

Spain before the world

When the Republican Minister of State, Alvarez del Vayo, stated to the League of Nations that «an international war in fact exists in Spain», he was limiting himself to giving a name to an evident situation from the first moments of the military uprising. Being aired in Spain were questions that concerned all of Europe and it was no secret to anyone that our country was becoming a testing bench for hostility among nations. Since the internationalization of the Spanish Civil War was an unavoidable fact, Republican authorities were fully aware that explaining their legitimate cause abroad could help resolve a conflict that was begun in part by the Spanish army.

With this purpose in mind, Spanish authorities prepared most of the films produced by the government's propaganda institutions. The **Subsecretariat of Propaganda** controlled all films concerning the central government, and the **Commissariat of Propaganda** everything involving the autonomous government of Catalonia—the regional government in Euzkadi, or the Basque Country, was soon forceably pushed out of Catalonian film circles and consequently produced very little since it did not have the means to do so. The Republican government wanted to palliate as much as possible the negative effects that the ignorance regarding Spanish affairs could have on foreign support for the Republic, and for this reason, authorities wanted to inform international public opinion about two fundamental points: the fascist character of the rebels and their support for the Axis powers, and the fact that the Republican government's power remained intact in the face of

attacks by the **revolutionary masses** which so frightened the European democracies, especially in view of the Soviet precedent.
In order to accomplish these goals, the medium-length film called **España 1936** (Spain 1936) was made. It traces a detailed history of events leading up to the civil war and focuses on it from a moderate point of view, avoiding allusions to burning questions, such as political plurality in the Republican zone —which led to armed clashes like those that occurred in Barcelona during May, 1937, between Catalonian communists and anarchists and the POUM. Other films were dedicated to more concrete questions such as the conservation of the national artistic patrimony, improvements in education, the care and attention given to children, etc., but always bearing in mind the need to please international public opinion by avoiding matters which might put into question the image of order, organization and harmony in the Republican zone.
The most far-reaching operation begun by the **Subsecretariat of Propaganda** was the production of **Sierra de Teruel** (Teruel Mountains), which was directed by the already prestigious author, André Malraux. The film attracted practically all the cinematographic attention possible in the governmental zone, and even though it did not fulfill its main goal of gathering support and aid for the Republican cause through

Logo of the Laya Films production company.

its exhibition all over the world (it was finished when the war had already ended), the film was a very worthy example of Republican cinema, and much more besides.
The **Commissariat of Propaganda** of the Catalonian Generalitat or regional government added to the Republican government's reasons and arguments that were sent abroad by assuring Catalonia's future role through international knowledge and acceptance. In the propagandist statements made by the Commissariat—made up mostly by men belonging to the **Esquerra Republicana,** the party of the Catalan lower middle-class—clearly laid down was the double character that the war had for Catalonia: «the struggle against the foreign invasion» and establishing itself as an autonomous nationality, making very definite its role in the war so that «in times of peace the liberties which it has conquered will be recognized» (12), as was stated by the organizer of the Commissariat, Jaume Miravitlles.
Among the many activities carried out by the Commissariat (13), cinema played a decisive role. By means of the work undertaken by its production company, Laya Films, which was directed by the versatile Joan Castanyer, the Commissariat was able to show to a greater degree the **Catalonian spirit:** its laboriousness, its peaceful nature, its loyal devotion to the defense of the Republic, etc. Films

like **Ollaires de Breda, Tapers de la Costa, El vi, L'Industria del Xampany** and **Cirerers: Agricultura,** commented on those activities considered to be the very foundations and pillars of Catalonian society, those which continued production even in the midst of a war. There were also many other films dedicated to children and schools: **Escuelas nuevas** (New Schools), **Niños felices** (Happy Children) or **Refugiados de guerra** (War Refugees); although it produced fewer films than other Republican cinematographic organizations in what could be described as newsreels on the war such as **Ofensiva en Aragón** (Offensive in Aragón) or **Bombardeo de Lérida** (Bombardment of Lérida).
By May, 1938, Laya Films had made more than a hundred film shorts including a newsreel called **Espanya al Día** (14), that was regularly produced while the war lasted. The making of newsreels began to lay the foundations of what was considered as the future of Catalonian film. More hopes were placed on this form of film-making than in other, more immediate possibilities.
In spite of these brilliant day-to-day activities, the Subsecretariat and the Commissariat were hardly able to hide the evident failure in one of their goals: the unification of the different cinematographic organizations. At the end of the war, what can be termed as cinematographic dispersion was the same or even greater than at the beginning.

International solidarity

Film-making in the Republican zone was not by any means in the hands of parties, labour unions and official propaganda institutions, although it is evident that in view of the results, these organizatons made the majority of the films shot between 1936 and 1939. There was another type of cinema which in all justice must be dealt with apart for two different reasons: firstly, because of its intrinsic cinematographic virtues, aside from its testimonial and situational value, and secondly, due to its transcendence in Europe and the Americas in explaining the Republican cause both during and after the war —to the point where through its own merits it became the almost exclusive representative of civil war cinematography.
We are talking about films shot in our country, but produced, directed or simply backed by persons who came to Spain as part of that generous movement of enthusiasm —and the last in history— which was the international solidarity with the Spanish Republic and against the advances made by fascism in our country. None of the treaties signed to perpetrate the effective isolation of the Republic (15) would prevent anti-fascists from coming to Spain from all over the world, even acting against their governments. They were driven by a clear vision of the international dimensions of the Spanish conflict. «We Americans», said one member of the Abraham Lincoln Brigade, «did not come to Spain because we had romantic or infantile notions about the war, nor did we come because we liked fanfares or festive parades. We left America silently, with no publicity, with a serious view of what was awaiting us, forced by the need to fight against the criminal invasion of Spanish soil which represented a threat to human liberty everywhere... We believe with all our hearts that the democracy attacked in Spain is the democracy attacked in all parts» (16).

L'espoir: André Malraux.

One of the persons who most untiringly dedicated himself to the fight for a Republican victory was André Malraux. A man of letters, but also of action, Malraux did prodigious work on numerous fronts. He was a pilot in a squadron formed by him and was also the Republic's unofficial ambassador to the United States and Canada. His novel **L'Espoir,** written in the months after he stopped leading the squadron into battle, recounts his experiences in Republican Spain. It was his idea to make one of the episodes of this novel into a film, giving birth to one of the most brilliant pictures

Sierra de Teruel (L'espoir; **1939**)
by André Malraux.

produced during our war: **Sierra de Teruel (L'espoir).**
The picture was one of the projects in which the Republican government placed its greatest hopes. The international prestige of Malraux would mean that a film directed by him, even though it was the first, be widely distributed throughout movie theaters in America and Europe. Since the film would have a fictional storyline, it would have a greater potential attraction than a documentary, which is normally received with more detachment.
Apart from directing the film, Malraux wrote the script (17), using part of his novel as we have already said as the basis for the screenplay. He also included in his film visible elements which referred to the lack of support and the abandoning of the Republic by the democratic nations such as the scarcity of armament and weapons which is a constant throughout the picture. These political watchwords, dictated by the need to awaken international attention in favor of the Spanish Republicans, could have become a dead weight as in so many other propagandist films if it had not been for the imagination and sensitivity of Malraux, who made a splendid film in spite of the natural limitations imposed on the production.
Unfortunately for the Republic, **Sierra de Teruel,** which went into production on July 20, 1938, had to be finished in

Sierra de Teruel (L'espoir; 1939)
by André Malraux.

Parisian studios (18) when the Republican cause was already lost. It was released years later after the Second World War had ended, and naturally outside our frontiers. After that moment, the view that many Europeans had of the Spanish Civil War was that of Malraux's. After all, part of the hopes pinned on this film were not misplaced.

The Spanish Earth

There were numerous movements of solidarity with the Republic among North American intellectuals and artists (19). Apart from obtaining funds for the Republican cause, they tried to inform the greatest number of Americans possible about the issue, a people who were enormously ignorant of European affairs —a position which was to be expected due to the huge distance between both countries and due to America's traditional absorption in its own affairs.
One of these groups supporting the Republic was **Contemporary Historians,** which brought together such names as Lilian Hellman, John Dos Passos, Archibald Macleish and Herman Shumlin. The idea to make an informative film for the American public easily came about after the group contacted the Dutch film-maker Joris Ivens, who was known both for his artful documentaries and his leftist militancy.

Tierra de España (The Spanish Earth (20) was in the initial stage of production in early 1937, and even though all the work was done by Ivens and cameraman John Fernhout, one illustrious collaborator, who many times dedicated himself to carrying around the heavy cameras, was Ernest Hemingway (21). The three were filming on the most conflictive fronts: Ciudad Universitaria, Morata de Tajuña, Jarama, etc. Shortly four months after the shooting began, Ivens returned to the United States to edit the film and print copies.
The production of **Tierra de España** was naturally conditioned by certain factors. «We never forgot the **urgency** of the job we were doing», Ivens would say. «Our task wasn't to make the best of films, but rather a good film that could be shown in the United States» (22). However, the picture made by this Dutch film-maker went far beyond that testimonial or purely informative dimension to obtain a relevant place in the history of documentary cinema.
The exhibition of the film in the United States was an obstacle race. It began well with a screening in the White House for President Roosevelt, but its distribution in the few movie theaters that agreed to show the film unleashed a furious campaign by the American right which almost resulted in a total ban on the film —something which happened in many individual states of the union. The documentary was much better received in the years following the war. Then —as now— its brilliant structure and its strange sensitivity did nothing but awaken admiration.
The promotion of the image of the Republican cause on an international scale had in Ivor Montagu one of its best allies. He was one of the film-makers who stayed in Spain the longest and who was the busiest. In September, 1936, he was in our country filming footage along the Madrid fronts for what would be his first film on the war, **The Defense of Madrid** —which had as cameraman Norman McLaren. He continued with **Testimony of Non Intervention** and **Prisoners Prove Intervention in Spain,** both dedicated to denounce the farse of a non-intervention pact among different nations which left the door open for direct military intervention by Germans and Italians. Other titles soon followed, sometimes commissioned by different people's organizations in England. Montagu not only dedicated himself to production, he also distributed Republican cinematographic material in Britain, a country whose government, which at times was scarcely able to mask its tendency to sympathize with the rebel officers, did not make too much of an effort to inform its people of Spanish affairs. This is precisely the debt which the Republic owes to this British film-maker.
Along with André Malraux, Joris Ivens and Ivor Montagu, there were other foreign film-makers who, like them, risked their lives along the Spanish fronts. We do not have enough space to talk about their work in detail. We would like to mention Herbert Kline and Henri Cartier Bresson, who in collaboration with Leo Hurwitz and Paul Strand, made two films in support of the Republic: **Return to Life** and **Heart of Spain,** both of which had their effect on American public opinion. We should also mention Roman Karmen and Boris Makaseiev, who were sent to Spain by the official Soviet newsreel production body, but who soon fell in love with Republican Spain. The images shot by both, as well as material filmed by other Republican journalists, served to give birth in 1939 to the lovely film called **Ispanija,** which was finally directed by Esther Shub.

Film in the rebel zone
Censorship

Contrasting sharply with the Republican cinematographic panorama, cinema in the zone under the control of the military rebels was considerably more insignificant. We cannot say the same, however, about the control and censorship of this cinema. It seems that censorship is inevitably present in all political systems, but in the dictatorial regime which began in 1936 it played a preponderant role that was

only be to expected.
At the moment of their insurrection, the rebel officers did not have any kind of political creed to counter that of the system they wanted to overthrow. Especially relevant were the words of Manuel Azaña, President of the Second Republic, on the first anniversary of the uprising «What is this about a war between two ideologies? I don't know the one of the adversary» Then there is the statement made by Ramón Serrano Súñer, Minister of the Interior under the first Francoist government: «The army, apart from its patriotism and its inclinations towards a state of authority, has not pronounced on any political dogma» (23). Even if the type of government that was proposed as an alternative to the Republican was not officially clear, the military rebels still had a creed that we could call reactive, of pure negativity. The political heterogeneity of the rebel zone automatically disappeared in the common anti-communist, anti-parliamentary, anti-liberal, etc., causes of the military or of any of the political groups active within its structure. The total lack of political definition and the effect of this lack in all areas, did not prevent there issuing from the Headquarters of General Franco a firm and unquestionable viewpoint announced on principle: «The spirit of criticism and of reserve is a liberal concept which has taken no

General Franco looking at a movie camera during operations in the Spanish Civil War.

roots in the field of our movement» (24). On the basis of this concise, but forceful structural principle, which denied any possibility of dissidence, Francoism was drawing up its political system.
It should not surprise us then, that rebel cinematography opened out to the world under the almost exclusive sign of censorship. Before anything else was done, the films being distributed throughout the rebel zone had to be **dignified** and **rehabilitated,** since even though no one well knew what to do with the informative and educational possibilities of film —no adequate official reaction was announced until 1938, there was an exaggerated distrust of the media's power in the hands of the enemy. The rebel officers were sure, for example, that the films and plays from the Soviet Union were the worst of scourges: «Russia, joining up with the communists over here, by means of theater and cinema with their exotic rites and customs and playing on intellectual fascination and material bribery, prepared the people's spirit for the outbreak of the revolution» (25). For others, a film like **Potemkin** had won over more new communists than a thousand speeches, which led to the conclusion that cinematography was the most dangerous propagandistic weapon. As a result, the urgent decision to submit it to a severe control was just one step away.

The official institutions entrusted with the task of watching over the **spiritual well-being** of spectators such as the policy-making bodies in Seville or La Coruña or the Censorship Board perfected their techniques during the three years the war lasted. In the ordinances announced by these institutions, apart from regulating internal workings and the amount of the quota that each user had to pay for this censorship **service** (26), very little could be found about those matters or topics that would result in censorship, except an allusion to them as being **dissolvent,** a very comfortable and multivalent description.
Such limited ideas in these matters put the Francoist cinematography on the verge of becoming a purely censorial operation. The head of national propaganda, Dionisio Ridruejo, who was then a member of the Falangists, was forbidden to see propagandist material from the Republican zone, which is highly illustrative of the fervor that was put into this activity.

Non-interrupted cinema

If in Republican Spain practically all the films made were on the initiative of political or labour union organizations and only a very small number were produced by normal production companies —showing up once again an insurmountable contrast, these traditional producers were the ones to provide the insurrectionaries with their first film footage, their first propagandistic cinema. These production companies, which were tied to big-money interests and naturally supporters of the rebel cause, did not have any other alternative than to accept as an irreparable fact that they had lost part of their patrimony, since the studios and laboratories were in the Republican zone after the initial big failure of the military uprising. But fortune —or foresight— caught two productions in Córdoba and Cádiz on July 18, 1936: **El genio alegre** (The Happy Genius), directed by Fernando Delgado, and **Asilo Naval** (Naval Asylum) directed by Tomás Alegre. Since both Andalusian cities immediately became part of the fief of General Queipo de Llano, the material being used in the shooting as well as the film team and directors helped CEA and Cifesa begin the production of war newsreels passionately in favor of the military uprising, naturally with the healthy intention of accruing good marks for the years to come.
From the very first moments, Cifesa stood out in its attempts to show «the triumphant march of the victorious troops». A total of seventeen film shorts were produced, generally dedicated to announcing and applauding the victories of the insurrectionaries such as in **Bilbao para España** (Bilbao for Spain), **Asturias para España** (Asturias for Spain), **Sevilla rescatada** (Seville Rescued), **Santander para España** (Santander for Spain), **Brigadas Navarras** (Navarran Brigades), **La gran victoria de Teruel** (The Great Victory of Teruel), etc. Its production activity can be termed as very discreet with regard to its cinematographic consequence and its propagandistic efficiency, limited to strictly observing the political directions dictated by the pertinent military institutions. Director Fernando Delgado, cameraman Alfredo Fraile and editor Eduardo García Maroto —working in Lisbon laboratories, were the authors of the films produced by Cifesa, although occasionally Mariano Ruiz Capillas or Manuel Novoa worked with this company.
CEA's participation in the war through its main representative, Rafael Salgado— and his close co-worker E. Domínguez Rodiño, was even more exciting, if possible, than Cifesa's. They directly participated by lending the generator and reflectors for the shooting of **Asilo Naval** to support the Algeciras landing. Indirectly, they participated by making important film projects such as the feature-length film, **Romancero marroquí** (The Moroccan Ballad). This movie was based on an idea by Lieutenant Colonel Beigbeder of Spain's High Commissariat in Morocco, one of the few military men with certain interests outside the armed forces. Coproduced

by the High Commissariat and CEA, it was directed by the intelligent film-maker Carlos Velo (27) and was about the generous and loyal aid given by the Moors to the Francoist cause and about their noble nature which was contrary to the theories of those who described them as blood-thirsty and barbarous persons.
Around the middle of 1938, Eduardo and Juan Ignacio Luca de Tena, José María de Ibarra, Eduardo Llosent and José María Pemán constituted a new production company called Sevilla Film, S. A. Their idea was to build large studios on the outskirts of Seville for which they had a large sum of money. They also planned to earn good marks among the military men in power by making a film that was to be called **A Madrid 682** (To Madrid 682), about the seige of the capital; but it seems that it was never made.
One man who saw the great usefulness of propagandistic film was Antonio de Obregón, the founder along with Joaquín Goyanes of **Producciones Hispánicas** at the beginning of 1936. The lack of money and equipment, however, necessarily limited the number of their projects. One of them, perhaps the only one, was **Marcha triunfal** (Triumphant March), which it seems was wholly given over to the capture of the northern cities, including Bilbao. According to Fernández Cuenca, this film's publicity announced it as one of the three best war documentaries in the rebel zone along with **La gran victoria de Teruel** and **España heroica** (Heroic Spain).

A party cinema?

Apart from the film production of private companies and that of the first official institution, the National Department of Cinematography, activity was also carried out by the two groups with greatest political support among those which actively took part in the uprising: the **Falange Española y de las JONS** (Spanish Falange), and the **Comunión Tradicionalista** (Traditionalist Communion).
The **Requeté** (Carlist forces) cinema hardly had time to flourish, since it was limited by its chronic lack of material means and the shadow which the Falangist group threw over it, especially since the Falangists were the undeniable masters of Press and Propaganda during almost the entire war. It should not be forgotten that among its members and sympathizers, the Falange had the majority of the intellectuals who remained in the rebel zone, and therefore was more prepared to undertake these tasks. Besides, the concession of Press and Propaganda to the Falangists doubly favored its members: on the one hand, along with their natural coarseness—and for their **coming out in society,** it was very useful for them to have the support of the florid and shrill rhetoric of the fascists, good for showing off and for exhibiting themselves as the only ones capable of stirring up the masses; and on the other, the concession of this area of power, which was evidently not given much importance by the General Headquarters of General Franco, relieved it of having to concede other areas considered of greater importance. We could say that the local color was created by the Falange, while General Franco continued to take over the power and to put it at his exclusive service.
Until April, 1937, the date on which the **Partido Unico** (Single Party) is created and the time when political heterogeneity in the rebel zone is suppressed with the stroke of a pen—even though this is only officially the case, the **Falange Española y de las JONS** had its own Press and Propaganda Department, the one which showed the most notable activity. During almost all this time, it was headed by Vicente Cadenas, while Antonio Calvache together with the sporadic help of Ricardo Gutiérrez, Cecilio Paniagua, Ricardo Torres and Mariano Ruiz Capillas, organized an improvised film section. The section made few of its own films due to its lack of economic independence, and perhaps for this same reason, it frequently

worked in collaboration with private producers as is shown by Calvache's work for Producciones Hispánicas, Ufilms and Films Patria in **Marcha triunfal, Derrumbamiento del ejército rojo** (The Collapse of the Red Army) and **¡¡Madrid!! Cerco y bombardeamiento** (Madrid! Siege and Bombardment). Political unification meant that the Falange's Press and Propaganda Department was promoted to become a national body, which paradoxically did not mean that it lost any of its autonomy. As a matter of fact, it even seemed to be reinforced, probably due to the necessary concessions that had to be made by the military men in power, the result of the strong Falangist opposition to the Unification (28). On the other hand, the Falange, stripped of its more radical elements and swelled by all sorts of opportunists since the beginning of the war, «only from time to time took out the box of national syndicalist thunder» (29).

Placed at the head of the Press and Propaganda Department of the **Falange Española y de las JONS** —but now **Tradicionalista** as well— was the effervescent priest from Pamplona, Fermín Yzurdiaga, «the most rhetorical and sugar-sweet of the disciples that Eugenio d'Ors has ever endured», in the opinion of Dionisio Ridruejo (30). His predecessor, Vicente Cadenas, a supporter of Hedilla and a fervent opponent of the solitary ascent of General Franco, had fled to France as a result of the Unification. Due to his excessive and uncontrollable moods, Yzurdiaga would later be removed from his tasks in Press and Propaganda. For the moment, the priest from Pamplona named a council— or rather he was given the list to name, including some of the persons that would later inherit the institution: Dionisio Ridruejo, José Antonio Giménez Arnáu, Eladio Esparza, García Valdecasas, etc. In order to continue with the unitary fiction, a Carlist or two was included on the council, such as Esparza.

The cinematographic activity of this **new** Falange not only was much more considerable, but the subject matter of its films underwent a substantial change: from the more or less partisan propaganda of its beginnings, it moved on to a purely Francoist propaganda. Although Falangist leaders would frequently appear in a leading role in these films, none of these pictures were ever lacking in the obligatory reference to the **Caudillo** (leader) by showing him in one of those military parades, a clumsy imitation of their Italian equivalents, or by mentioning him with one of those well-known panegyrics such as «the direct heir of the Catholic Monarchs». There were also no lack of references to the Unification and its alleged beneficial effects. Of course, the traditional Falangist demagogy made all this possible without any sense of tradition whatsoever. As the historian Stanley G. Payne said, the Falange would just the same preach unity and sacrifice as social justice and economic reform. All of this can be seen in such films as **Estampas del frente y de la retaguardia** (Pictures of the Front and the Rearguard), **Frente de Vizcaya** (Vizcayan Front) and **18 de Julio** (July 18) —where with fantastic cheek, the bombing of Guernica is blamed on **dynamiters** and **incendiaries,** or in other words, Asturian miners, **La guerra por la paz** (The War for Peace) or **España azul** (Blue Spain). These films also shared the characteristic rhetorical vanity of Falangist theorists with profuse and nostalgic allusions to the Empire, the Catholic Monarchs, Carlos V, etc.

Precisely while thinking about Spain's lost empire, the Latin American Section of the **FET y de las JONS** was born. Almost immediately the section became very industrious and was made up by Joaquín Martínez Arboleya, who had taken part in the making of some of the previously mentioned film reports, Antonio Solano and Juan Patous. Practically at the time it was formed, an improvised team was constituted to accompany Falangist Augusto Atalaya on a mission to Latin America from the rebel Spain. Setting itself up in Argentina, the team would start preparing the edition of an Intercontinental Newsreel especially designed for South American countries.

In general, its tone is more **rabid** and the appearance of leaders of the Falange is surrounded with greater pomp, from which we can deduce that perhaps distance eliminated **caution.**

The National Department of Cinematography

The final chapter of **national** cinema has been the best remembered with the passing of time.
We are referring to the National Department of Cinematography, created well into 1938 by the institutionalizing inertia which had as its goal «to convert the Uprising into a political concern». From the outset, the Press and Propaganda services were taken over by the imposing Ministry of the Interior, which was headed by Ramón Serrano Súñer, who in turn named as director of Propaganda an old hand in these matters, Dionisio Ridruejo. It would be erroneous to think, however, that all this new apparatus would produce any substantial change. The reality of the situation is that the façade had become more complicated, while inside work went on in a similar fashion. The Falange, in the person of Dionisio Ridruejo, continued to head Propaganda as had always happened. Now, the only difference consisted in the substitution of the always excessive and sometimes bubbling Fermín Yzurdiaga with Ridruejo, who, as Ernesto Giménez Caballero (Falangist theorist and a unique person if ever there was one) would say that being a radical Falangist and without feeling anything for Francoism, it helped him to triumph more than any decided Francoist, but without knowing it.
What is undeniable is that the National Department of Cinematography, at whose head Ridruejo placed the versatile and enterprising Manuel Augusto García Viñolas, quickly distinguished itself for the regular production of newsreels —the **Noticiario Español,** film reports and documentaries, including some of the best ever made in the rebel cinema. To be absolutely fair, this was not so much due to the institutional complication of this film section as to the initiative and constant work of García Viñolas and the team he soon surrounded himself with: Antonio de Obregón, Carlos Martínez Barbeito, José Manuel Goyanes, Joaquín Reig, José Luis Sáenz de Heredia, Enrique Gaertner, Alfredo Fraile, etc.
Upon the projection of the first documentaries made by the National Department of Cinematography, García Viñolas received the enormous personal satisfaction of attracting the attention and interest of the authorities in Burgos which earned him a decoration from General Franco himself, although he received very little new equipment or money. In spite of its late creation, the National Department of Cinematography put together a total of nineteen **Noticiario Español** newsreels as well as various film reports and documentaries, some of which were made by García Viñolas such as **Llegada a la patria** (Arrival in the Fatherland) or **Prisioneros de guerra** (Prisioners of War), others by Edgar Neville such as **La Ciudad Universitaria** (University City) or **Vivan los hombres libres** (Long Live Free Men), and finally, the majority put together from material filmed by different operators of the Department such as **18 de julio** or **La batalla del Ebro** (The Battle for the Ebro).
The success obtained inside the country was not correspondent abroad. Fernández Cuenca says that the screening of this material in foreign countries had little effect «since there were too few titles which, besides, arrived too late, when the government of the Republic or the revolutionary parties and organizations had saturated the world with its tendencious cinema, but which nevertheless had an impressive effectiveness» (31). All of which only goes to show again, if we do not bear in mind the tendencious partisanship of Fernández Cuenca, that a true abyss existed between one cinema and the other.

Typically Spanish actions in Berlin

We have seen that if for the success

Concha Catalá, Miguel Ligero and Estrellita Castro in Suspiros de España **(1938) by Benito Perojo.**

(Following page)

Estrellita Castro in El barbero de Sevilla **(1938) by Benito Perojo.**

of the rebel cause the support of the Axis powers was decisive, its cinematography was no less indebted. Since Germany and Italy both had at that time important film industries, these two countries more than made up for anything that their Spanish allies lacked. We must remember that the studios and laboratories stayed in the zone under Republican control, and not counting on the invaluable aid from Portugal, politically and geographically very close to the rebels.

Even so, it was Germany that maintained the most consistent and continued film cooperation with the Spain of General Franco, cooperation which of course was not free from calculation. It produced, for example, various documentaries on the Spanish Civil War, even though the majority were dedicated to the honor and glory of the Condor Legion and its movements on the different Spanish fronts, where the German war machine tried out new techniques.

The common interests of both countries took definite shape when Hispano-Film Produktion was formed at the beginning of 1938. The promotor of Spanish interests in the society was Norberto Soliño, the former chief of Cifesa's offices in Cuba. For German cinema, which was trying to expand, the company represented an opportunity to break into the Latin American markets through Spain. The films made would be completely

Imperio Argentina in Carmen, la de Triana **(1938) by Florián Rey.**

(Following page)
España heroica **(1938).**

Spanish when it came to the director, actors and screenplay, but German in financing and later control. Hispano-Film Produktion produced throughout 1938 and part of 1939 five feature-length films, three of which were directed by Benito Perojo: **El Barbero de Sevilla** (The Barber of Seville), **Suspiros de España** (Sighs from Spain) and **Mariquilla Terremoto,** and as one can see, all about topics that foreigners have always considered typically Spanish. The two others were made by Florián Rey: **Carmen, la de Triana** (Carmen, The Girl from Triana) and **La canción de Aixa** (Aixa's Song). In these films, Cifesa's normal cast were practically all there, playing their **familiar** roles to test lady luck again. The difference was that now the Andalusian patios were impeccably reproduced not in Spanish, but Berlin studios. In Nazi Germany, amidst German film crews, Imperio Argentina and Estrellita Castro moved the trains of their dance costumes in front of the cameras. To conclude, we should say that thanks to this Spanish-German production company, the rebels had their own epic filmed in one of the pictures which propagandistically produced the greatest repercussions. It was called **España Heroica** (Heroic Spain) and started out as an ambitious project by Joaquín Reig, who stayed out the entire war in Berlin laboratories editing the material shot in Spain. Even the Ministry of Propaganda of the

España 1936 (**1937**).

Third Reich headed by Goebbels had a hand in making the film. The Germans realized that their allies would have an opportunity to receive a kind of international hearing with a film that showed the causes **justifying** the **glorious Crusade.** They were partly successful since **España Heroica** which Reig directed with a German film crew had a greater propagandistic effect than the rest of the films produced in the rebel zone.

(1) Collective letter from the Spanish Episcopate published in July, 1937. It is a highly intructive document if one is interested in the role played by the Spanish Catholic Church on the side of the insurrectionist officers, whom they undoubtedly favored from the very first moment.
(2) The man who was also the chief of propaganda in the **National** zone recognized this sharp contrast. Says Dionisio Ridruejo: «At first sight, it was seen that the Republican propaganda measures had been very superior to ours and their intellectual assistance much more extensive, valuable and organized» —in **Casi unas memorias,** published by Planeta, 1976, page 167. His opinion was shared by the German ambassador in Madrid in 1936: «The comparative strength on both sides regarding morale and propaganda is equally won by the side of the government (Republican)»— document included in **La guerra de España en sus documentos,** by Fernando Díaz-Plaja, Plaza y Janés, Barcelona, 1975, page 75.
(3) **La guerra de España y el cine,** Editora Nacional, Madrid, 1972, page 244.
(4) In the Catalonian CNT, a Public Spectacles Union (SUEP) had been operating since 1930. If it had a large number of members, they were mostly non-qualified. On the other hand, the strength of the other union in the sector, the General Workers Union (UGT), was much less: it was not until June 30, 1936 until they would organize their Regional Federation of Public Spectacles.
(5) It seems that the president of the Catalonian Generalitat, Luis Companys, put in the hands of

the labour union the institution which he presided, which, apart from showing the political skill of Companys, shows the important role played by CNT-FAI in the fights which put down the initial military rebellion.
(6) This enthusiasm caused problems for the Republican government, like what happened with **Reportaje del movimiento revolucionario** (Report on the Revolutionary Movement), by Mateo Santos, which shows the forceably emotional and tense moments in the days immediately following the initial victory over the insurrectionaries. The scenes in the film, quite often plain to see, were repeatedly shown by the insurrectionaries, who, lacking their own material, saw in this film an occasion to palpably prove their thesis regarding the political activities of the Republican government, pointing up the **barbarity** and the **red hordes.**
(7) «Film producers can work today under exactly the same conditions as before the revolutionary event», it was said, not without a certain amount of naîveté, in the bulletin put out by the CNT-FAI on September 23, 1936. The calls to private producers were repeated, but even the most near-sighted individual could see that conditions had radically changed.
(8) **Espectáculo,** III, Barcelona.
(9) Raymond Carr in **España,** 1808-1939, Ediciones Ariel, Barcelona, 1970, page 633.
(10) Several authours have written about the high moral cost of the unconditional search for unity, some of them blaming the communists and their policies for the lack of enthusiasm and solidarity seen in the last months between the soldiers and the Republican population.
(11) When the Soviet Union stopped sending aid to the Republic after the first moments of the war and after it signed the Non Intervention Pact, it also decreased the favor it dispensed to these films. On the other hand, when contradictions between communists and anarchists became more accute, this latter group tried to prevent the exclusive exhibition of what it considered to be completely communist propaganda films.
(12) **Mi revista,** number 36, Barcelona, 1937.
(13) The Commissariat, which opened offices in a large number of European and American cities, frenetically went about its different activities which included: a photographic series on bombardments, art exhibitions, the publishing of brochures, books and magazines, informative bulletins, etc., placing it among the bodies which had the most complex and richest of experiences.
(14) At its beginnings, the Noticiario was coproduced by Laya Films and Film Popular, but with time, each one of these production groups edited it on its own.
(15) On August 15, 1936, and on the initiative of the governments of 29 countries including France, England, Germany, Italy and the Soviet Union, the Non Intervention Treaty was signed. It was to prevent intervention in Spanish affairs. Even though it was very effective in putting obstacles in the way of granting aid to the Republic —the Soviet Union was affected by this, it was unable to prevent what was an evident fact during the entire war: military intervention from Germany and Italy. The United States was also quick to adopt a similar norm: the Arms Embargo Law which went into effect on January 6, 1937.
(16) **La guerra de España en sus documentos,** already cited.
(17) With the invaluable collaboration of writer Max Aub.
(18) The cooperation of French producer Edouard Corniglion-Molinier resolved the film's financial problems in the end.
(19) A large part of the Spanish star system of that time was vetoed in the **Nationalist** Spain due to their manifest pro-Republican sympathies. Their films were screened, but their names were not included in the credits.
(20) Before coming to Spain to shoot, Ivens left **Spain in Flames** prepared for exhibition, a montage with material shot by Republican cameramen.
(21) All Hemingway's modesty did have its compensation. Ivens excellent relations with Republican authorities gave the writer the opportunity to go closer to areas where events were in the making. The writer said later that with the camera over his shoulder, he crossed over to places where by normal means he would have never been able to reach. The commentary of the film was jointly written by Ivens and Hemingway.
(22) **The Camera and I,** Seven Seas Book, England, 1969.
(23) **Entre Hendaya y Gibraltar,** Editorial Epesa, Madrid, 1947.
(24) A speech by Franco given on July 18, 1938, on the second anniversary of the **Uprising.**
(25) Collective letter from the Spanish Episcopate, cited above.
(26) For more information on the matter, see **La censura (Función política y ordenamiento jurídico bajo el franquismo, 1936-1975),** Román Gubern, Ediciones Península, Barcelona, 1981.
(27) At the end of the film, Carlos Velo, whose political sympathies lay with the Republicans, was able to flee to the governmental zone when he was traveling to Berlin to edit his film.
(28) The Unification policies involved severe repressive measures including imprisonment and not a few death sentences such as the one handed down to the Falangist leader Manuel Hedilla, although it was later commuted.
(29) **Falange. Historia del fascismo español,** Ediciones del Ruedo Ibérico, 1965, page 145.
(30) Idem, page 116.
(31) Idem, page 243.

1940
1950

The set of El bailarín y el trabajador **(1936) by Luis Marquina.**

1940 1950

1939: It is not the year which marks the end of a war, but the year that starts the beginning of a victory. And over the laurels of that victory, Francisco Franco Bahamonde sets up his camps. It is no longer a general who governs us, it is a generalissimo. According to the dictionary of the Spanish Royal Academy, a generalissimo is «the chief who commands the military state in peace and in war with authority over all the other generals in the army». Let us forget what is said in this Spanish dictionary. Our case is different. Here he commanded all Spaniards. The nation —at last— was a huge barracks at his orders. To the surprise of some in Spain and of the world (20th century), he considered himself generalissimo «by the grace of God». He governed from the heights and the persons who wanted to merit his favors had to raise their faces and supplications to him. A new Eucharist had been born. The war was a crusade, the dead the martyrs; but there were the blind who did not want to see the miracle that had been worked. They were shocked when they found out that the new religious pictures were made with Falangists in the Nazi salute, levitating towards heaven with robust eagle's wings and flaming swords in their hands. Of course, a long time ago and for much less, such spectacles were declared heretical. Not now. A dawn of a new day had come to Spain and daily **te deums** of thanksgiving were raised. God was with the victors and the devil with the vanquished, and the person who did not believe such stories had best keep his mouth shut. The hour of silence had arrived. Silenced like the dead were hundreds of thousands of incredulous Spaniards. All this happened so far above in the heights that those down below had to do their best to survive. There was hunger and there was misery. Roguery sprang up and so did robbery, but «Oh blessing of the new times!», such actions were not sinful, only sex was nauseous.

* * *

The stairway which led to power was long and narrow, but all that was needed was to feign faith or to really have it —it takes all sorts— until a helping hand permits you to steal, half-and-half, of course, like good brothers, like good companions. There were the eternal birds of ill omen who loathed these miracles. They pleaded problems of conscience, of an old-fashioned conscience. They did not know how to be up with the times. They say that driven by need, some fearfully drew near the stairway of power in search of others as old-fashioned as themselves and at times they found them, although this hardly happened. They were just creating problems for themselves. They

Emilio Sanz de Soto

did not realize that the world that they lived in was no longer horizontal, but vertical, and that you had to climb and climb to reap the benefits. These unbelievers did not understand that everything that happened was the result of a war which had produced a million dead; that what had been imposed was a dictatorship, even though this word did not figure in its rites; that they, the victors, considered themselves the saviours of the fatherland; and that the saviour of the saviours was up above, ready to make everything and everybody follow his saintly will with a firm hand.

In such circumstances, a new cinema came to light in Spain. This cinema was extremely new, since it had nothing to do with that made in the Second Republic. That abandoned and solitary cinema had to win over its public and become popular. It did so. Of course, anyone who says public, says the people. In the new Spain of orders and command, it was decided from **up above** to protect cinema with surprising generosity. The truth of it is that no one was deceived. In order to receive generous aid, one had to make the cinema that was demanded, not silently, but to the letter of the law. As if it were an examination, it was obligatory to climb the stairway of power and first present the script for classification, and then later, the film. It was not easy to guess at what was understood as «the exaltation of racial or educational values of our moral or political principles». That is why many were surprised to see that during those first postwar years, no truly Falangist pictures were made. The truth is they were never made, then or ever. Furthermore, the few that at that time dared present films about the tragedy that Spain had just suffered, encountered unexpected official reactions. Edgar Neville was criticized because at the end of his **Frente de Madrid** (Madrid Front; 1939), a Nationalist and a Republican, both of whom were wounded, embraced each other. The scene had to be cut and the dialogue changed. Even more surprising was the case of **Rojo y negro** (Red and Black; 1941), by director Carlos Arévalo, a film which had received the advice of none other than José María Alfaro and which only a few days before its release was banned. It seems that the amorous relations between a Falangist girl and a militiaman in wartime Madrid simply could not be tolerated, in spite of the fact that the girl was murdered and the militiaman was delivered from his erroneous beliefs, also dying at the hands of his fellows. Even more inexplicable was the refusal to give an exhibition license to the film **El crucero «Baleares»** (The Baleares Cruiser; 1940), by Enrique del Campo, due to its low technical quality. This phenomenon led the majority to avoid purely political cinema and move into the field of patriotic exaltation or patriotic jingoism, into History —with a capital letter, but told as a melodrama, and finally, into religious-like film. Even so, the refuge of good literature, or at least, films made on the basis of non-dangerous literature, was the type that produced the best results as we shall later explain.

This is how an imposed cinema was born. Sometimes the public accepted it and other times they rejected it, but the producer did not care one way or the other; all he was interested in was obtaining from the state the prebends that he had earned. In other words, he had to be on good terms with the **official commissions,** and especially, with the body that classified films, since this depended on the number of import licenses for foreign films that he would be assigned. It may seem incredible, but just by selling these licenses he could cover all his production costs and even make a tidy profit. Then, too, there was the direct— or vertical— dependency on the SNE (National Entertainment Union), which was the body that could grant up to 40 % of the film's total budget. That is why there was a tendency to make super-productions which were oftentimes deceiving. And, of course, there were the awards which carried cash prizes that were annually distributed by the same body.

The producers, as a result, planned their films with the almost exclusive

Alfredo Mayo and Raúl Cancio in *Raza* (1941) by José Luis Sáenz de Heredia.

goal of coming to good terms with state criteria. These demands created a series of directors who knew how to mold themselves to the established norms, eventually becoming **official directors,** while others were excluded from this privilege. The director who best knew how to adapt to the role that the state asked of cinema was José Luis Sáenz de Heredia, probably because he truly believed in the new ritual of **Franco's Spain.**

I insist that it was not easy to guess at the ritual, because ritual was asked and even required in the new Spanish cinema of the postwar era. Above the Falange and above the Catholic Church, the two powers which existed back then, there was another, superior power which always knew what was not wanted. Sometimes this power could be cruel and that is why it took an indescribable effort to guess at what was really required, since it was kept secret and was not likely to be shown. I am referring, of course, to the ambiguity of General Franco. This ambiguity was creating—engendering— an imprecision, a confusion which disconcerted not only close advisors, but very concrete areas of Spanish life during those years. However, unexpectedly cinema was to receive an example of Franco's wishes in the shape of a script signed under a pseudonym. The film was called **Raza** (Race; 1941), scripted by **Jaime de Andrade** and produced by the **Consejo**

de la Hispanidad (Hispanidad Council). The director of such an important endeavour could be none other than José Luis Sáenz de Heredia, cousin of the founder of the Falange. Neither Hitler nor Mussolini, both of whom were interested in cinema as a weapon of control and propaganda, had ever gone so far with their sophisms as to write a screenplay and to hide the name of the true author. What General Franco was unaware of is that **Raza** with time would take on a decisive importance when trying to obtain a deeper understanding of all his frustrations. More than a film, it is an X-ray: from the family he would have liked to have had, to the character—even physical qualities— of José Churruca, the role played by Alfredo Mayo. In this connection, the film goes way beyond any cinematographic considerations or merits —which it does have from time to time— to become a work of incalculable psycho-analytical value. What is significant in **Raza** is not so much what General Franco wanted to hide, since he hides nothing, but what much to his own sorrow he leaves transparent. If the image we have today when looking into the mirror of the screen is very different from that which in his day he originally wanted to give us, we are convinced that just by writing the screenplay for **Raza,** General Franco fell into the sublimation trap. As Rainer Maria Rilke once wrote, «When sincere, sublimation always reveals to us the other side of the coin, the hidden side».

I wanted to head this brief history of Spanish cinema in the first decade of postwar Spain by putting the film **Raza** in first place, alone and well apart from the rest. This is not only due to the fact that the author of the screenplay is General Franco, although this has a lot to do with it, but because this film contains all the moral, religious and patriotic principles that the **Caudillo** (leader) would have liked to have seen in **his cinema,** and that when they appeared, except on very rare occasions, they were common, if not decidedly vulgar. The only director who opened up new roads and doors in this directed and controlled cinema was José Luis Sáenz de Heredia, albeit more intuitively than in a studied fashion. His innate sense of honor saved him, apart from his work, from the rejection which could be expected from future generations. At a later moment, we will talk about his films.

It is only left to be said that there are two decisive works for the better understanding of **Raza:** the excellent book by Román Gubern called **Raza: un ensueño del general Franco** and the no less excellent montage film titled **Raza: el espíritu de Franco** (Race: The Spirit of Franco; 1977) by Gonzalo Herralde.

The return of the recognized artists

1) Florián Rey: As is known, he obtains huge successes in both Spain and Latin America with **La hermana San Sulpicio** (Sister San Sulpicio; 1934), **Nobleza baturra** (Nobility of Brute Action; 1935) and **Morena Clara** (Clara the Brunette; 1936), films which all starred his wife at that time, Imperio Argentina, undoubtedly Spain's greatest **star.** Once I wrote something about this actress that I would like to repeat: «Without her, something would have been lacking in Spanish cinema: the knowledge that a simple smile can sometimes illuminate an entire screen. The miracle seems simple, but it was was a simplicity so hard to accomplish that it would be difficult for another, similar miracle to come our way again». The enormous success of the director and his star who conquered the entire Latin American market, until then under the absolute dominion of North America, did not leave the other European film industries indifferent as might be expected. Suddenly, the eyes of millions of new spectators turned towards Spain. The first country to seriously think about working with our country was France, providing the idea for a big production starring Imperio Argentina as both actress and singer. The work selected was none other than the well-known operetta by Jean Gilbert called **La casta Susana** (The Chaste Susana). Everything was

prepared to go into production when the civil war broke out. The project was called off and Imperio Argentina and Florián Rey left for the United States. What France was unable to bring off, Germany did when it offered the two film-makers the possibility of shooting films in Spanish in the Berlin studios. The project offered to them was nothing less than a script written by Goebbels himself: a biography of Lola Montes. With his Aragonese stubbornness, Florián Rey rejected the screenplay and offered to do a typically Spanish version of Carmen by Prosper de Mérimée. There was a clash of opinion, since according to the heads of the German cinema at that time, the Nazi cinema, such a work was an exaltation of the Gypsy race. Finally, the obstinacy of Florián Rey overcame his hosts' doubts and **Carmen, la de Triana** (Carmen, The Girl from Triana; 1938) was born. It represented a new success for Imperio Argentina, who, to the surprise of everyone, shot the German version, including the songs. **Carmen, la de Triana** was first premiered in the rebel zone and later, once the civil war had ended, throughout the rest of Spain. Cifesa believed that the times had not changed and hurried to bring back its director Florián Rey, but not its star, since the marriage between Rey and Imperio Argentina had fallen apart. A wrong decision was made, however, in choosing story and star. The Spanish public did not have the heart to see the drama of **La Dolores** (1939), by José Feliú y Codina, nor for that matter Conchita Piquer, an excellent stage singer of «tonadillas» (a kind of popular song of the time). She was no substitute for the magical presence of Imperio Argentina on the screen. Florián Rey, who was conscious of the fact that times had changed, tried to bring himself up to date, but he had difficulty in doing so. The same thing happened to all the directors of his generation. We will study this problem later. Even so, in the decade of the history of Spanish cinema that we are now dealing with, Rey continues to shoot important films.

He again films **La aldea maldita** (The Cursed Village; 1942), which, even though it does not achieve the same naked strength of the silent version, possibly because far greater technical means were used in this second one, it is a work of great beauty. The film is able to avoid the dangers of an excessive aesthetic beauty. What is always evident in the film is the skilful hand of a director who is more, very much more than run-of-the-mill. He obtained a medal in the Mostra of Venice in 1942. Both versions, with and without sound, merit a place in the history of Spanish cinema.

The year afterwards he goes from Pedraza de la Sierra to the Ansó Valley where he shoots **Orosia** (1943), which undoubtedly would have been his greatest film if he had not been forced to tone it down in fear of the censorship which existed then. The entire end of the film, in which Orosia almost shamelessly forces a confession from her husband on their wedding night that he was the murderer of her lover, the only man she ever truly loved, needed a heartrending tone which at that time was impossible to put in a movie. In spite of that, the film contained a peasant-like truth about it, not very much in keeping with Spanish cinema at that moment. A less important picture than the last two cited, but full of the fresh and authentic qualities found in Andalusia, was **Brindis a Manolete** (Toast to Manolete; 1948). We must, then, acknowledge the fact that no other Spanish director was able to approach the various popular moods and feelings from the time of such films as **Nobleza baturra** or **Morena Clara**— pictures truly made for the gallery— to that of **La aldea maldita** and **Orosia**— more transcendental in their popular outlook— with the mastery of Florián Rey.

2) Benito Perojo: The greatest virtue of this director was his efficiency, but an efficiency which was not exempt from a certain brilliancy that did not become a style because he simply was not interested in moving in that direction. His work in the silent era in which he made his debut at the early age of eighteen conserved a quality

which was not always given the recognition that it deserved and which Jean Renoir considered essential for the film director: that of an **animator.** And that is what Benito Perojo was, an **animator.** There were never what can be termed dead periods in his pictures and his characters seemed, at least to us, as if they were infected with the enthusiasm of the director. He very easily moulded himself to any topic. That is why many considered him to be a director with an ill-defined personality. If we observe his work from a purely cinematographic point of view, it can instantly be divined that his is an ability to adjust both simply and instinctively between the image and the content. He knew how to tell a story, which is saying a great deal. When the victory burst out, Benito Perojo found that his film **Nuestra Natacha** (Our Natacha; 1936), just finished when the civil war broke out, was to be banned by censorship. Between both of these very sad dates, he had shot in Germany **El barbero de Sevilla** (The Barber of Seville; 1938), **Suspiros de España** (Sighs from Spain; 1938) and **Mariquilla Terremoto** (1938). Just as Florián Rey's **Carmen, la de Triana,** all these films were conceived for the Latin American market. Thanks to these completely Spanish films, both Germany and Italy were able to produce films like those made in the II Spanish Republic. Seen today, it is difficult to believe they were shot in

Julio Peña and Rafael Calvo in Marianela **(1940)**
by Benito Perojo.

foreign studios. Of course, when the Second World War erupted, both fascist countries lost the Latin American market. The above-mentioned films by Benito Perojo were exclusively designed to serve as a distraction and amuse audiences, which they were certainly able to do.

Once back in Spain, he has the good idea of adapting for film the novel by Benito Pérez Galdós called **Marianela** (1940) and of giving the leading role to an actress who had never before appeared on the screen, Mary Carrillo. Just like Galdós, Perojo dwells on the main subject of the film without falling into the melodramatic trap. The characters seem to fit in perfectly with the mining atmosphere. The characterization that Mary Carrillo gives Marianela truly amazes us. According to many, this is the best film by Benito Perojo. One might continue to think that the best is **La verbena de la Paloma** (The Paloma Fair; 1935), but this film would undoubtedly come a close second. The film itself has a great deal to offer, but curiously, it is not typical of the way its director goes about doing things in his work. **Marianela** is given a prize in the Mostra of Venice in 1941.

Later, after being contracted to make a comical farce called **Héroe a la fuerza** (Hero of Necessity; 1941), Benito Perojo is offered another, but much more important contract: **Goyescas**

Ana Mariscal and Jesús Tordesillas in *La florista de la reina* **(1940) by Eusebio Fernández Ardavín.**

(1942), with Imperio Argentina in the starring role. Super-productions, and this film was one of them, are always difficult to bring under control. However, he was not intimidated by the magnitude of the task at hand. Quite to the contrary, he was able to set off the set designs by Sigfrido Burmann —much better than on other occasions, or perfectly incorporate the beautiful models not only designed by Julio Laffite for Imperio Argentina, but also those of Manuel Comba for the rest of the cast. He also did a perfect job of integrating Enrique Granados' music with Regino Sainz de la Maza as guitar soloist and with Madrid's Philharmonic and Symphony Orchestras to the popular «tonadilla» songs of the time or to the choreography of Vicente Escudero, etc. He is able to achieve the best possible with Imperio Argentina playing one of her greatest roles and with Michel Kelber doing excellent camera work. Benito Perojo's magnificent film obtains a **Copa** in the Mostra of Venice in 1942.

Perojo, however, was not very comfortable in postwar Madrid. He recognizes the fact that the heroic films which are imposed on him do not fit in at all well with his temperament. Upon receiving a proposal to shoot a film in Argentina, he immediately accepts and leaves Spain.

3) Eusebio Fernández Ardavín is a discreet director in the noble sense of

the word, who gives his films a deft and refined charm which is not normal in our cinema. Every time he was forced to climb up on the throne of his films and exaggerate them, as was the fashion with films made in the forties, he failed. This was the case with **El abanderado** (The Standard Bearer; 1943) and of course with **El doncel de la reina** (The Queen's Page; 1944-46). To the contrary, he was very successful in evoking the atmosphere at the turn of the century, but without ever touching on the melodramatic or falling into the puerile trap like so many other directors of those years, who, due to the more vulgar nature of their films, were much more successful with the public.
Some of the films directed by Eusebio Fernández Ardavín resist the passage of time without becoming in the least bit ridiculous, precisely because of those virtues already mentioned. He possessed, as we have already pointed out, a way of evoking things. Every time he was able to transmit what he wanted to say in soft tones he hit right on, as what happened when he directed **La florista de la reina** (The Queen's Florist; 1940) and **La rueda de la vida** (The Wheel of Life; 1946). Even with such a religious topic as the biography of Father Manjón called **Forja de almas** (The Forge of Souls; 1943), his cinematography was devoid of great emphasis or of theatricality, softening the film with humanity and tenderness. He was able to bring out in the great actor who played Father Manjón, Alberto Romea, a performance full of ingenuity and life. There was no extravagance in his portrayal whatsoever. Both in **La rueda de la vida** and **Forja de almas** he invaded the screen with a miracle of grace, charm and freshness which was the inimitable actress, Antoñita Colomé. She was all intuition, all truth, which no one was able to take advantage of fully. Films that Eusebio Fernández Ardavín made which should be remembered include: **Unos pasos de mujer** (The Steps Taken by a Woman; 1941) based on a short novel by Wenceslao Fernández Flórez, and **Neutralidad** (Neutrality; 1949), which was made on the verge of his retirement from the world of film.
Finishing with **the return of the recognized artists,** we will recall Fernando Delgado and José Buchs.
4) Fernando Delgado: A director who did not recover in talkies the freshness he had achieved in silent cinema such as in **Las de Méndez** (Those of Méndez; 1927) or **¡Viva Madrid, que es mi pueblo!** (Long Live Madrid, Which Is My Town!; 1928). In spite of this fact, he insisted on, tried out and explored more popular subjects —without a doubt the area he was best, but he was not able to stamp them with the personality he gave his earlier films. He is obviously prematurely tired and old. It is true that a film that assuredly would have allowed him to make up for lost time remained unfinished due to the outbreak of the civil war: **El genio alegre** (The Happy Genius; 1936-39). When Cifesa asked him to finish it as best he could, forcing him to use doubles —almost always with their backs to the camera— in order to substitute the actor and actresses who had gone into exile (Edmundo Barbero, Anita Sevilla and Rosita Díaz Gimeno, who miraculously escaped death), Fernando Delgado accepted this disagreeable task out of loyalty to the production company. Upon seeing the film again, we must acknowledge that the studio scenes —which were the ones shot in 1936— do not lack their special charm. Conscious of the fact that the veteran director had paid them a great favor, Cifesa chose him to direct a very ambitious and high budget film: **La gitanilla** (The Little Gypsy Girl; 1940), based on one of Cervantes' Exemplary Novels. What could have marked a great come-back for Fernando Delgado came to nothing when the role of **Preciosa** was given to Estrellita Castro and **Don Juan de Cárcamo** to Juan de Orduña. Curiously enough, the same error would be committed three years later in another, equally ambitious film, **La maja del capote** (The Pretty Girl of the Cape; 1943), when the leading role would be given again to Estrellita Castro, a very popular actress, but very limited in her acting abilities. In the decade of the forties, which was the last of his life,

Fernando Delgado only made one good picture: **Fortunato** (1941), which included one of the great performances among the many of the career of that extraordinary actor called Antonio Vico, who has only been given roles worthy of him on very few occasions.
5) José Buchs: Everything said about Fernando Delgado can be applied to José Buchs, one of Spain's most important directors during the silent era, but who just barely saved himself from mediocrity during the era of sound pictures. And while we are remembering titles, only two spring to mind as being any good: **Un caballero famoso** (A Famous Gentleman; 1942) and **Aventuras de don Juan de Mairena** (The Adventures of Don Juan de Mairena; 1947).

* * *

As we previously pointed out, none of these veteran directors were able to mould themselves to the new atmosphere forced upon Spain after the victory of General Franco. Curiously, they did not belong to the political left. But in a country where changes had been made, these changes would also shake —it was a genuine quake— the world of film. It was more than a generational problem; it was a total change, which uniformly affected people of very different ideologies, but who had known a

La malquerida (1940) by **José López Rubio.**

world of liberties that were suddenly and strictly denied them. The fact that their very way of understanding and living life had changed, was another, and the change of mentality which was being demanded came too late. They opted to admit defeat, even though at first they had thought themselves the victors. These statements can also be applied to the generation which we will now study.

The other «Generation of 1927»

Under this epigraph, whose title is none other than the one selected by José López Rubio for his entry speech in the Royal Academy of the Language, are included five names. Even though as film-makers they have nothing in common, apparently as literary figures they all belong, to a greater or lesser degree, as epigones to the **Generation of 27,** a movement which must be considered in a wider sense and not limited to the great poets who formed part of the movement. These five names had the privilege, and privilege it was, to move about in one of the most civilized worlds ever produced by Spanish culture. None of them bore the name of a Federico García Lorca, a Salvador Dalí or a Luis Buñuel. They moved in different circles when they were young. If at the end of the civil war they remained in Spain as members of

the winning side, time and their works have shown us that it was almost impossible for them to give up their liberal convictions. Some pretended more, others pretended less, some abandoned their principles more, others less, but they had to fend for themselves in an atmosphere —that of Franco— whose strictness and provincialism suffocated them. They escaped from asphyxiation by using humor, cosmopolitanism and by using «half words» or cryptic language.
Even though it is a little late —because many have died, the youth of today have brought them together again with their companions who went into exile in an attempt to forget, to undo forever, those «two Spains» on which a horrible war would have such tragic consequences. We will see that except for one, these five names did not contribute to Spanish cinema what might have been hoped from them. Did the circumstances have an influence? It is little less than impossible to deny it, but one might also think that in spite of such adversities, a Luis Buñuel —the great film-maker of the **Generation of 27**— was able to open his **way** in such a narrow-minded film industry as that of Mexico, and in Spain, on another level, Edgar Neville would do the same.
Since we are exclusively talking about Spanish cinema in the decade of the forties, we must talk about five names. They are in alphabetical order and not

Maria Brú in *Pepe Conde* (1941)
by José López Rubio.

Fernando Fernán Gómez and Rafael Romero Marchent in *La mies es mucha* (1948) by José Luis Sáenz de Heredia.

necessarily in order of importance: José López Rubio, Luis Marquina, Edgar Neville, Antonio de Obregón and Claudio de la Torre.

1) José López Rubio: It is enough to cast a glance over the titles of the films —six features and three shorts— that José López Rubio contributed to Spanish cinema to be assured that a greater artistic concern could have been demanded of precisely this man. Of course, they are works that were contracted out and that in other hands probably would have produced more vulgar results, but his only merit in directing them was exactly that, saving them from vulgarity. What represents a great deal for our cinema is really very little for a man who would later write plays of such great scope, and who before, in Hollywood, wrote very original, funny and sophisticated screenplays which here were made conspicuous for their absence. Probably the postwar years were not the most adequate for his artistic temperament. It is evident that he had to bow to the requirements and demands of the moment. He shot his corresponding historical film: **Eugenia de Montijo** (1944) to save, they say, the honor of the empress, which had been compromised by the image given her in the film **Suez** (1938), by Allan Dwan. He also filmed his corresponding historical film: **Alhucemas** (1947), which, it should be recognized, was one of the best of the genre. The

El último husar (1940) by Luis Marquina.

rest were an adaptation of **La malquerida** (The Disliked Woman; 1940), which was written by Jacinto Benavente and which was rather cardboard-like, and a few works, the best as a matter of fact, which were at the service of the comicality of Miguel Ligero: **Pepe Conde** (1941), **El crimen de Pepe Conde** (Pepe Conde's Crime; 1946), **Sucedió en Damasco** (It Happened in Damascus; 1942), which was an adaptation of the **zarzuela** (Spanish light opera) called **El asombro de Damasco** with music by Pablo de Luna, and one delightful short entitled **A la lima y al limón** (To the Lime and to the Lemon; 1941). And that is all. If it were any director it might even seem an acceptable list of credits to us, but since it is that of José López Rubio, we must describe it as not far-reaching at all.

2) Luis Marquina: It is difficult to grasp and what is more, to define the style of Luis Marquina. In the works which really belong to him, **which are the minority,** he appears to us as the antithesis of Spanish cinema in the forties, both emphatic and pompous. Everything about him was reserve and discretion. Let us say his work showed a timid man. I do not know if he was, but it does seem to be the case. His shyness was not lacking in a certain amount of elegance, an attitude which one should always be thankful for, especially in our film industry. Another factor lacking is a narrative sparkle that

can be found among true directors, a factor which curiously was one of the characteristics of his second and best film shot during the II Republic, called **El bailarín y el trabajador** (The Dancer and the Worker; 1936).
As was the case with many of his generation, postwar Spain had a disorientating influence. It was not the world that they had dreamed of, no matter how far on the right a man was situated. It could not be identified with for that matter, by leftist intellectuals, the majority of whom had gone into exile. If on the one hand in his youth he had been a friend of Salvador Dalí and had known different avant-garde movements, on the other, he was the son of Eduardo Marquina, one of the most conservative playwrights that one could imagine. He walked a sure road between «two waters», running with the hares and hunting with the hounds. Film for him was suggested and admired. Formally revolutionary film was never undertaken by this director. His is a work of an essentially classical stamp, classically pure and cold.
In 1940, he shoots in Italy the double version of **El último húsar** / **Amore di ussaro,** which was undoubtedly the best Spanish film of those made in that country during the years of fascist film cooperation. The script was written by Antonio de Obregón. It was a difficult screenplay to direct due to the fact that the thread of the story— and never has the word thread been

Guillermo Marín, Isabel de Pomés and Antonio Casal in La torre de los siete jorobados **(1944) by Edgar Neville.**

(Previous page)

Fernando Freire de Andrade, Alfredo Mayo and Manuel Luna in Malvaloca **(1942) by Luis Marquina.**

better used— hardly existed at all. The film really tried to ridicule the world of around 1900 by means of the clichés of an operetta. Everything had to be shaded, subtle and sheer. The film was so successful in this respect that not only the general public, but the critics did not comprehend what was going on. In order to achieve such a task, Luis Marquina used the refinement of such a unique actress as Conchita Montenegro.
Among the films that he would shoot in Spain until 1950, we will only look at a few titles. It is surprising how he dealt with a typically Andalusian theme by Serafín and Joaquín Alvarez Quintero, a theme so well-known and scenically played out as **Malváloca.** His **Malvaloca** (Hollyhock; 1942) did not even touch on the cheap «Andalusianisms» or the easygoing castanets. Almost as if he were walking on tiptoe, almost as if he were talking to the actors on the quiet, he achieves a serene and very deep film, which even today conserves its charm and the charm of a pair of performers who were then in the midst of their youth: Amparo Rivelles and Alfredo Mayo.
Also worth remembering are **Noche fantástica** (Fantastic Night; 1943) and **El capitán Veneno** (Captain Venom; 1950), based on a novel by Pedro Antonio de Alarcón, our cinematographic novelist by antonomasia, and in which an understanding is always evident

between the intelligent and cultured director and the main actor, the excellent actor who has these same qualities: Fernando Fernán Gómez.
3) Edgar Neville. We ask ourselves how it was possible that one of our most personal and intelligent film-makers passed little better than unnoticed in front of the nearsighted gazes of our critics. It is difficult to answer that question due to the evident superiority today seen in his films if we compare them to those which in their day received the applause of the critics and official recompense. But if we delve deeper into this superiority, we will find that his film-making technique is of a deceiving flippancy. The irony which characterizes all his work is not easy to understand. It provokes smiles, never laughter. It does not let itself get trapped. It insinuates more than it says, but it never tries to hide. In Edgar Neville's films everything is simple. However, appearances are deceptive. Behind his popular themes, almost farcical in their outlook, coupled with characters and little characters who are only sketchily drawn, he tells us stories that could almost be real, but in which we soon guess at the hand of illusionist, who teaches us the other face of reality, avoiding any sort of moral. Good-natured because he is skeptical, incredulous because he is civilized, ironic because he is a humanist, this **bon vivant** aristocrat is not easy to classify. His own background, the background of his time, contributes to this confusion. Upon remaining in Spain after the victory of General Franco, this **little daddy's boy of the Republic,** as Ramón Gómez de la Serna defined him, certainly did not sell himself to anyone since he had more than enough money of his own. Even so, his image could not help becoming somewhat disfigured for the younger generations. When we finally try to remake and recover our own contemporary culture that was undone, destroyed by a horrible civil war, we see the figure of Edgar Neville reappear as a friend of José Ortega y Gasset, Federico García Lorca and even more recently, Jacques Lacan. This is why curiosity for this man is born, especially for his work as a film-maker, since our cinema does not exactly have plenty of civilized directors. Julio Pérez Perucha sets about revising all his films, ordering and classifying them. The surprise is not long in coming. Edgar Neville is revealed as the antipode of vulgarity, of pretentiousness or of being the bore. In other words, he is hailed as being the opposite of a large part of Spanish cinema. But this praise was too late in coming, because Edgar Neville had died. His tragedy was that he created a very personal style of film-making in those postwar years, turning his back on what was then done, asked and prized. The critics

Rafael Durán and Conchita Montes in La vida en un hilo **(1945) by Edgar Neville.**

(Previous page)
Alicia Romay in Domingo de carnaval **(1945) by Edgar Neville.**

Manuel Luna, Antonia Plana and José Franco in El crimen de la calle de Bordadores **(1946) by Edgar Neville.**

normally recognized the quality of his scripts, but at the same time calling him an inept director. Today we are in a position to affirm that his self-confident way of directing evokes the name of Jean Renoir in more ways than one.

Let us recall some of his films. The most unclassifiable and probably the most personal is **La torre de los siete jorobados** (The Tower of the Seven Hunchbacks; 1944). The significant and the insignificant, the fantastic and the realistic play hide-and-seek in an ancient synagogue hidden underground in the old part of Madrid, the secret redoubt of a group of hunchbacks who counterfeit coins. The leading character of the film is guided to that place by a one-eyed ghost— who wears an eye patch and who likes to tell jokes— in order to save the niece of a very strange individual. The story, which is based on a novel by Emilio Carrére, allows Edgar Neville to play with his ironic poetry, the key to his entire work, in juggling two apparently incompatible concepts: the realism of Madrid's «sainete» or one-act farce with the unrealism of German film expressionism. The result, of course, is very unusual, while all the time he tells it with the improbable transparency of a children's story. If one were to classify Spanish cinema, **La torre de los siete jorobados** would probably be included as one of its most beautiful pictures.

Domingo de Carnaval (Shrove Sunday; 1945) is a film that can be stylistically linked to **La torre de los siete jorobados.** In both pictures the action takes place in a turn-of-the-century Madrid. The real and the farcical are also present in this movie which narrates the murder of an old lady money-lender and the search for her murderer. We are confronted with an unreal and fantastic world of the absurd carnival atmosphere created by painter José Gutiérrez Solana. We should not forget that Edgar Neville was one of the discoverers of the genius of this painter.
One of his fundamental works is **La vida en un hilo** (Life Hanging from a Thread; 1945). It tells the story of what was and what could have been, due to a dirty trick played by destiny, which, in spite of what we might suppose, is never presented to us in a transcendental fashion, but rather hidden beneath the almost imperceptible play of circumstances. Far from philosophizing in the same way as not a few of the great masters in the history of cinematographic comedy, Edgar Neville makes and unmakes a tangle in the plot of his film, employing the elegance of a poet and the wisdom of a juggler. **La vida en un hilo** is an exceptional work within its genre.
We must also mention **El crimen de la calle de Bordadores** (Crime on Bordadores Street; 1946) and **El señor Esteve** (Mister Esteve; 1948), based on **L'auca del señor Esteve,** by Santiago Rusiñol, as well as two shorts: **Verbena** (Fair; 1940) and **La Parrala** (1941).
Edgar Neville's credits allow us to end these brief commentaries on his work within the decade of the forties with his very significant film called **El último caballo** (The Last Horse; 1950).
It has been said and written that the influence of new Italian realism—neorealism has always existed— arrived in Spain with two works; **Surcos** (Furrows; 1951), by Nieves Conde, and **Esa pareja feliz** (That Happy Couple; 1951), by Berlanga and Bardem. This is quite an arbitrary assertion since one year before, Edgar Neville's **El último caballo** appeared on Spanish screens. The film is neorealistic, although it is a neorealism that does not copy anyone, since it is filtered through the unmistakable personality of its director. The plot of this film tells the thousand and one adventures of a soldier, who after getting out of the armed forces, buys the horse he rode in his regiment, since the regiment is about to be motorized and since the horse would be sold to die in a bullring. Much to his sadness and surprise, he finds that there is no place for such a noble animal in the capital city, in Madrid. The viscissitudes of the ex-soldier and his horse acquire an unsuspected human element and the film ends as a song to nature, long before ecology became such a worrisome issue in our modern-day society. It would be unjust to mention **El último caballo** without referring to the exceptional acting work of both Fernando Fernán Gómez and José Luis Ozores.
Edgar Neville's work is very much **auteur** film. It really is not that important whether we agree with this definition or not. By using the term we can better understand the importance of this film-maker —the author of the screenplays of all the films he directed— who was discovered after his time, but who holds an unquestionable and outstanding place in the **History of Spanish Cinema.**
An inseparable part of Edgar Neville's work is the cultured and refined actress named Conchita Montes, who is always able to transmit or play that double game (making the easy, difficult and the difficult, easy) which so characterizes the film of such a peculiar individual.
4) Antonio de Obregón: With his first film called **Mi vida en tus manos** (My Life in Your Hands; 1943), he seemed to want to bring literature to such a commonplace cinema as ours. His intentions were good ones and even opportune, but they soon came to nothing when it was seen that in his later films he had practically no cinematographic feeling. The abyss separating cinema from literature led to his downfall.
(5) Claudio de la Torre: Another could

have been. This figure from the **Generation of 27,** who today is unjustly forgotten, was in many ways a precursor, but an elegantly reserved, silent precursor. Among his novels we will recall **En la vida del señor Alegre,** the winner of the 1924 National Literary Prize, which received tremendous praise from Pedro Salinas. Among his plays is a work of notable avant-garde importance called **Tic-Tac** (1930). Always interested in film-making, he works in Paramount's Joinville Studios between 1930 and 1933, the years in which several versions were made of the same film. There he filmed in 1931 a totally French film with story and dialogue by Yves Mirande titled **Pour vivre heureux** in which the performance of an unknown actress called Simone Simon did not go unnoticed. The film received both public and critical acclaim. Everything augured well for his first production in Spanish cinema, a cinema which was very much at another level of quality.
Unfortunately, things did not work out that way. **Primer amor** (First Love; 1941), based on a work by Ivan Turgenev, **La blanca paloma** (The White Dove; 1942) and **Misterio en la marisma** (Mystery on the Marsh; 1943) were three films totally pale and lifeless, offering no cinematographic brilliancy. After he made these pictures, he returned to the world of literature, to the world of theater. It is sad that a person with his cultural stock of knowledge did not make a better showing as a director.

The new recognized artists

The Spanish cinema which was officially born after the civil war, after the victory of General Franco, has absolutely nothing to do with the cinema made under the II Spanish Republic. They are diametrically opposed both in content and form. Let us say that they belonged to two different countries. This discrepancy is not casual at all. It represents the reality of a situation that new generations will have trouble understanding. From a popular cinema (when it was good) and a common cinema (when it was bad), Spain violently jumps to an imposed cinema where of course everything that is political predominates. What is most revealing is that in this new cinema a new social class appears which is none other than that of the victors. This change in classes —going from the common people to the bourgeosie— can be considered fundamental in understanding the cinematographic phenomenon as a reflection of the social phenomenon. Of course, not all the films show us this change in the same degree, but the important ones of this period of our cinema do reflect this change, films that are none other than those which received the official prizes. More than prizes, however, today they seem to have been decorated with military honors.
The change from the former regime to the new regime was so radical that by natural law new directors had to appear, since the veterans, the recognized film-makers were incapable of modifying their creative registers. They later showed this to be the case.
The man who really pointed the way for Spanish cinema to follow was José Luis Sáenz de Heredia, first cousin of José Antonio Primo de Rivera. The figure of the man seen and analyzed today shows us a person who was much less inclined to take reprisals than what was common during those sad years. He always acknowledged the fact, which in itself was not usual then, that his life was saved in the Republican zone thanks to the intervention of Luis Buñuel.
Sáenz de Heredia was the director whom General Franco entrusted with the job of making **Raza,** and the dictator was lucky, since his script in the hands of another would have become ridiculous. There was no such danger with Sáenz de Heredia since his very Spanish sense of humor —or better said, his wit and charm— kept him from coming out with all those grandiloquent phrases that his companions were inclined to make.

In this new controlled cinema, able to clip the wings of the most prudent of directors, Sáenz de Heredia was laying down his law with worthy films of a more than acceptable technical quality. What was especially good about these films was that they had characters of flesh and blood, which at that time was surprising. It is something for which we should be thankful.
He was undoubtedly the most noteworthy of our **official directors.** This term can have for us a pejorative sense, but due to the fact that it answers to an unquestionable reality during those years, I do not believe that it could offend a person who always acknowledged and accepted Francoism.
Alongside José Luis Sáenz de Heredia we should place two other directors: Antonio Román and Rafael Gil.
All three of these men were recognized directors after their first films. All three were the representatives of the changeover, the representatives of new Spanish cinema under Francoism. All three monopolized the official rewards.
Setting ideology to one side, we must ask ourselves, how is it that three directors who began with some promising works, ended up making films that we assume they were ashamed of? Is it a sign of decadency that these three directors mirrored the decadency of Francoism? Whatever the case and although they may have been surprised at this statement, we would have wished them a better outcome for their work.
1) José Luis Sáenz de Heredia: We believe that the career of Sáenz de Heredia would have been a very different one if he had not had the luck, or rather the misfortune, of coinciding with the advent of Francoism. By temperament he seemed meant for a more direct cinema, more than just comedy, comical farces. This genre was done badly in Spain, but he would have been able to do it well. He gave signs of knowing how to make this cinema, but not enough to create a style. As a matter of fact, his film-making lacks a style that could define it. Through his work, like winks, appear a desire for breathing space and open air, but always suffocating in transcendental questions. Probably this was not a totally unconscious reaction in him, but what cannot be doubted is that he needed this freedom. We are referring, and this should not be forgotten, to the decade of the forties.
In his first film, **Patricio miró a una estrella** (Patricio Looked at a Star; 1934), he shows us that he already dominates the grotesque element, giving it a human touch within the great Spanish tradition of the farce as a style. He again shows this aspect of his work in **A mí no me mire usted** (Don't Look at Me; 1941). Both Antonio Vico in the former film and Valeriano León in the second, are two persons who are perfectly sketched in the dangerous art of being the dauber. The times, however, demanded and even required him to take more transcendental roads, or apparently anyway. He comes off with flying colors in the uneasy task of making **Raza** (Race; 1941), a film that today would lend itself to rejection, if not laughter, but given its treatment, which is that of Sáenz de Heredia's and not General Franco's, the public can view it as a very revealing document of other times, since it is —as we have already pointed out, an unconscious X-ray of the **Caudillo.**
It is surprising, and I believe that this says a great deal in his favor, that far from taking advantage of the fact that he made **Franco's film,** he waits for two years before finding a topic that he likes and elects the novel by Pedro Antonio de Alarcón in order to make **El escándalo** (The Scandal; 1943). In this film he hides his own way of being so as to return to the film the very style of the original author. And he does it. As is known, the work by Alarcón fluctuates between two tendencies: the last breaths of Romanticism with the appearance of a literature of manners, and even with realism. Using this topic to its best advantage is easy, but giving this topic the tone it deserves is quite difficult. It requires a constant equilibrium between emphasis and reflection. By using his common sense —one of his

Mercedes Vecino and Armando Calvo in El escándalo (1943) by José Luis Sáenz de Heredia.

virtues— more than by inspiration— as was said back then, Sáenz de Heredia achieves a film that when judged today only has a few small details for effect that are not needed.
Undoubtedly he has a place of honor in the history of our cinema, but not that place of honor which was given him back then.
His work has been overrated, but we should not mistakenly underrate this film. Every detail of the picture is controlled —actors, photography (Michel Kelber), sets (Luis Santamaría)—by a director who knows what he wants. Despite the wounds that time might inflict on this picture, **El escándalo** still conserves the willful strength of its director.
Following the heavy burden of **El escándalo,** Sáenz de Heredia returns to himself with **El destino se disculpa** (Destiny Says It's Sorry; 1944), based on a story by Wenceslao Fernández Flórez. In respect to the Galician writer, he keeps alive its humor in detriment to the farcical aspect, which is the one he knows how to work with. In spite of this, the film conserves its freshness, but— Who would have said it back then?— it simply cannot be compared to the great works of Edgar Neville.
In Sáenz de Heredia the occupation prevails, while in Neville, creativity. But since our cinema does not have plenty of intelligent films, and this one is, we

must put **El destino se disculpa** in the place it deserves. It does not receive high marks, but it passes with merit. **Mariona Rebull** (1946) is probably the best film that Sáenz de Heredia ever made. It is impeccably done. At moments he shows human nature to a greater extent than the novel on which it is based, a work by Ignacio Agustí. There is no affectation whatsoever. The characters are able to dominate the reality of their situations and their surroundings.

This is a virture which even in his last and unfortunate films, the immense humanity of this director is revealed to us. **Las aguas bajan negras** (The Water Flows Black; 1947), **La mies es mucha** (That's a Lot of Corn; 1948) and **Don Juan** (1950) close the cycle of films that Sáenz de Heredia made in this decade. These films should not be belittled, but we continue to think that this director never was totally true to himself. We are sure that he would have been, although probably in a lesser tone, if he had written his own scripts, if he had been sincere with himself without fearing to laugh at life and if he did not feel at times the **bearer of eternal values.**

2) Antonio Román: If this director had continued along the very personal and very brilliant lines which he established when he first started out, he today would be one of the decisive men in the history of our cinema. Both those delicate lines went astray and, in spite of praiseworthy attempts to recover them, he would never again recover the inspiration of his youth. And I say inspiration since at twenty-four years of age he makes two film shorts, something so lacking in Spanish cinema, called **Canto de emigración** (Emigration Song; 1935) and **La ciudad encantada** (The Enchanted City; 1935), and he does not employ the usual reflections in the water or the poems of Rubén Darío as a way of commentary. After the civil war he shoots a decorous patriotic film called **Escuadrilla** (Squadron; 1941), with which he makes a name for himself in the new regime, starting off as a film director with enough prestige to select his own subjects and to have sufficient technical means and money at his disposal.

Rafael Durán and Fernando Fernán Gómez in El destino se disculpa **(1944) by José Luis Sáenz de Heredia.**

The year after he surprises everyone with a film that has nothing to do with the embroidery of our cinema: **Boda en el infierno** (Wedding in Hell; 1942). The truth is that the topic was the most conventional imaginable and was not lacking in a very elemental political moral.

We will not tell the story line since it is totally ridiculous and would make it little less than impossible to dedicate any praise to this picture. However, there pulsates in the film an atmosphere which is totally infrequent in Spanish cinema, and not simply because the action takes place outside our borders. That is not it at all. What surprises us is the climate of refinement which envelops the entire film, to the point that we forget the absurd plot and we submerge ourselves in the interior, not exterior beauty of its images. It is unquestionably a sign of a true cinematographic creator. In that same year, or 1942, he shoots **Intriga** (Intrigue), a very unusual work that is also enveloped in a very refined atmosphere. The film is based on an account by Wenceslao Fernández Flórez. The story line is the following: a body appears in the dining room of a house and a police inspector takes over the case, suspecting the daughter of the owner of the house and the butler of having committed the crime. When the inspector goes to question the butler, he finds him dead as well. Days later, the girl whom he suspects is kidnapped and enclosed in a Latin American embassy. She is able to escape. The boyfriend of the girl under suspicion decides to play the detective and following up his first clue, goes to a **Fat Men's Club** where he discovers a dead servant, who really is not dead and who is the chief of police of the Latin American republic. Later, the body of the lady owner of the house turns up and when a grandfather clock is opened, her dead husband falls out. Tremendous pressure is brought to bear to clear up these mysteries. He finally points in a certain direction and

Conchita Montenegro in Boda en el infierno **(1942) by Antonio Román.**

when all the actors turn their heads, out walks the director of the film who is accused by all of being the one to blame for the whole mess. Needless to say that the picture was not a success at all among the public. The critics did not know what to say. Decades would pass before Luis Buñuel would casually discover the film on a Spanish-speaking channel in the United States. He was so enthusiastic about **Intriga** that he later wrote, «It is the best Spanish picture that I've ever seen». **La casa de la lluvia** (The House of Rain; 1943) is also based on a story by Wenceslao Fernández Flórez. The picture is conceived and directed as no other film that was shot either then or today. The action takes place in a Galician country manor, shrouded in a downpour and in an atmosphere of occult sciences and hypnotism.
Without achieving the perfection of **Intriga,** it is a film in which the hand of a director-creator is in evidence.
If Antonio Román had continued down the same road, he would today be one of our greatest directors, but he had to pay due respect to the subjects which were then in vogue (historic and patriotic), otherwise his film career would have ended.
He curiously did a good job when he was forced to inflate his films into super-productions, resulting in **Lola Montes** (1944) and **Los últimos de Filipinas** (The Last from the Philippines; 1945), without a doubt our best

historic film and our best patriotic film. The elegance radiated in **Lola Montes** (a film which has nothing in common with the later masterwork of Max Ophuls) has not been surpassed in Spanish film of yesterday and today. The set designs by Francisco Escriña and Antonio Simont, the sketches for the costumes by painters José Caballero and Juan Antonio Morales and the dresses by Cristóbal Balenciaga created for Conchita Montenegro in her last and greatest cinematographic appearance, were all elements that were controlled by Antonio Román in his film. The resulting picture was far above the tastes of the public and of the critics, since they did not possess the necessary cultural or aesthetic levels to appreciate the high degree of civilization obtained in this film.
Los últimos de Filipinas could be more easily understood and appreciated by the general public. It was an enormous success. It narrates the well-known story of Captain Las Moreras who belonged to the Baler garrison on the Philippine Islands. He was able to resist in a church of the town close to a year after the Spanish-American war had ended. The screenplay for the film was cleverly written by Antonio Román along with Enrique Llovet and Pedro de Juan. The action of the film moves right along, something that was very difficult to achieve due to the reduced space in which the director had to work. Antonio Román naturally obtained the

Lola Montes (1944) by **Antonio Román.**

first prize from the regime's show business union for **Los últimos de Filipinas.** Anyone then would have foretold that his career would be assured and that he would only have to dedicate himself to historic-patriotic or religious film. But it did not turn out that way. It was all downhill after this film. What is sad is that he decides to shoot important works such as **Fuenteovejuna** (1947), by Lope de Vega, or **El amor brujo** (Bewitched Love; 1949), by Gregorio Martínez Sierra and Manuel de Falla, but both films got away from him. He is partially successful with his **La vida encadenada** (The Chained Life; 1948). Later would come isolated achievements —I can think of **Los clarines del miedo** (The Bugles of Fear; 1958), but he would never again recover the refined atmosphere of his first films. Spanish film lost just after his birth a possible director-creator. A person who only knows his work after 1945 would have difficulty believing this statement. And that is what is so sad.

3) Rafael Gil: It is not easy to define a director like Rafael Gil due to the fact that since 1941, the year in which he made his first feature, down to our own days, he has not stopped making films of the most varied stories and styles, and to reduce all these films— like some do— in trying to describe a director's trade or main area of interest, seems too easy to me, too elemental.

Probably the most personal style of this director can be seen in the decade of the forties, but what can also be divined is a continuous change in topics, according to trends and circumstances, always trying to obtain the official recompense. In just these ten years he obtains fourteen prizes from Franco's vertical trade union, very much a **record.**

Just as what happened to José Luis Sáenz de Heredia and Antonio Román, but to a much lesser degree, he begins by trying a personal style of film-making and ends up with the most absolute impersonality. It is as if he were slowly losing all interest in his work until he finally converts it into a way to **make a living,** just like any other. Although in Rafael Gil's case, he could have made for a better life by doing things better. He was not lacking experience in his trade. Why did he end up shooting commonplace films when he could have made very acceptable pictures? It is quite a common phenomenon in the history of cinema to lower one's sights instead of raising them higher. It is said, although this is debatable, that the film industry itself forces the professional to do so. However, there are cases such as that of Luis Buñuel, who, just as old age begins to set in, starts to raise his sights. Whatever the case, an abyss exists between Rafael Gil's beginnings and his film-making today. At first he was seen as a restless film-maker, who sought interesting topics —never his own, topics that he shot a little coldly, but with greater strength than some of the directors of his generation.

In his first movie, **El hombre que se quiso matar** (The Man Who Wanted to Kill Himself; 1941), based, as was the tradition in those years, on a story by Wenceslao Fernández Flórez, Rafael Gil comes off as a director who is capable of telling a story, and not a commonplace story at that. The hopes placed in him are completely fulfilled in his next two films: **Viaje sin destino** (A Trip without Destination; 1942) and **Huella de luz** (A Sign of Light; 1943). **Viaje sin destino** is based on a very suggestive story by José Santugini and tells the story of a travel agency that organizes a trip on which the passengers do not know where they will be going. With the pretext of a breakdown, the bus stops in front of a mansion that is falling into ruins. The passengers wring their hands for several hours until they realize that everything has been schemed by the travel agency.

The investigation later turns up both dramatic and comic situations. Rafael Gil develops the plot with surprising skill and has the good idea of shooting a sequence with film techniques used at the beginning of the century, which is very much a confession of his love for cinematography.

Huella de luz, which is also based on a story by Wenceslao Fernández Flórez,

Antonio Casal and Rosita Yarza in *El hombre que se quiso matar* **(1941) by Rafael Gil.**

Alberto Romea and Fuensanta Lorente in Viaje sin destino (1942) by Rafael Gil.

is probably the most sincere and delicate film made by a director, who, throughout his long career, has unfortunately not been faithful to these two virtues. It tells the story of a modest employee of a large textile company, who, upon fainting from evident lack of nutrition, is invited by the owner of the company to a luxurious spa in which he owns stocks. There he gets to know the daughter of a wealthy businessman and falls in love with her, at the same time pretending to be a rich man himself. The young man happens to find out about a swindle that his girlfriend's father plans to pull on his boss and protector. He immediately informs him of the planned swindle and the story has a happy outcome. Even today, the film has an unquestionable charm. Even though it is a lesser work, it is held up by a director who then was considered to be greater than he was. During the years that followed, the order of things was inverted: the works grew in importance while the director diminished.

He later makes **Eloísa está debajo de un almendro** (Eloísa is Underneath an Almond Tree; 1943), in which he does not achieve the delirious and poetic tone demanded by Enrique Jardiel Poncela's work, and **Lecciones de buen amor** (Lessons in Good Love; 1943), an outmoded work by Jacinto Benavente which he was unable to give new life.

Antonio Casal and Isabel de Pomés in
Huella de luz (1943) by Rafael Gil.

Amparo Rivelles in *El clavo* (1944) by Rafael Gil.

From 1944 to 1947, Rafael Gil enters into a dangerous period of **epoch cinema.** The success obtained by Sáenz de Heredia with **El escándalo** —and when we speak of success, we mean both public and official— made many of Spain's directors turn to the past, not the historic, but rather the literary past, since it was impossible to film stories of greater scope, as most contemporary ones were prohibited. The novelist selected is Pedro Antonio de Alarcón, not, of course, a Benito Pérez Galdós or others.

Even so, Rafael Gil does not obtain his greatest successes with Alarcón in this period of his cinema. Both **El clavo** (The Nail; 1944) and **La pródiga** (The Prodigy; 1946) have not well resisted the passage of time, while **El fantasma y doña Juanita** (The Ghost and Doña Juanita; 1944), by José María Pemán, and **La fe** (Faith; 1947), by Armando Palacio Valdés, have many of their qualities still intact.

Among the rest of his ostentatious, pompous and big-budget productions, we can say that the impossible task of filming **Don Quijote de la Mancha** (Don Quixote of La Mancha; 1947), written by Cervantes, only resulted in a few shots that may be remembered, while the rest of his films taken as whole, although grandiloquent and rhetorical, are not all that ridiculous, as can be seen in **Reina Santa** (Holy Queen; 1946).

Much more interesting are two films

based on the stories and dialogues of Miguel Mihura: **La calle sin sol** (The Sunless Street; 1948) and **Una mujer cualquiera** (Just Any Woman; 1949). **La calle sin sol** is concretely one of the best films by Rafael Gil. Both the adaptation of Vicente Blasco Ibáñez' **Mare Nostrum** (1948) and Jacinto Benavente's **La noche del sábado** (Saturday Night; 1950), both of which were done for María Félix, turned out to be icy, since the coldness of the Mexican actress vied with that of Rafael Gil, who was becoming a manufacturer of films based on just about anything. Resolution in one's occupation is often unadvisable.

Rafael Rivelles, Sara Montiel and Julia Caba Alba in *Don Quijote de la Mancha* **(1947) by Rafael Gil.**

Obligatory intermission

At a time when films were shot with an eye to their classification and the official prizes they could receive, it was not an easy task to appease both the authorities and the general public. Even so, by the middle of the forties it became obvious that what the state authorities wanted was not a political cinema, but a patriotic, not a historical cinema, but an anecdotical, and not a religious cinema, but a catechistical one. The intellectual level of the state authorities was not very high and our producers and directors were able to sigh in relief. The inspection to which they had to submit their films was not as difficult as was first suspected.

These factors contributed to one of the saddest episodes of our film history. A personalized work did not matter at all. What is more, anything intellectual was viewed with suspicion by **those upstairs.** These authorities wanted harangues for the barracks and Sunday sermons to choke them up with emotion. If these messages were to be presented in luxury, that is to say, if they were super-productions, so much the better. Our cinema had to leave off from being rickety. What was imposed was grandeur, and the grander the film, the better. Needless to say that the production company that best understood these watchwords was Cifesa. It contributed to making films which, unfortunately for our cinema, produced an enthusiastic response from the public.
I ask myself if such a desolate panorama did not contribute to the downfall of the majority of the directors we have just cited. For these directors, it meant lowering themselves to a level that must have shamed them. Some of them did so and they became finished as directors. Others— and this is very significant— did what was asked of them and found that these films fitted in perfectly with their temperaments. For them, the sublime was the presumptuous, the luxurious was the pretentious... and a sum of calamities.
The time of the mediocre directors had arrived, even though they did not

consider themselves as such. They thought that they were inspired and looked towards the heights with faces full of emotion. Finally they would be able to make great films.
This is how Juan de Orduña became a recognized director. Never has any director been more sincere in making insincere films. With remarkable inspiration —they say he cried while making his films, he inflated the melodramatic to incredible limits. This director set no limits on himself when it came to transmitting his emotions. He gave himself totally to his films. The degree of affectation, ingenuity and mannerism was so delirious that he left both believers and the profane open-mouthed. Juan de Orduña believed in what he was doing while others saw in him a false game, for everything was truth, no matter how ridiculous and shameful the work might be. Those who worked with Cecil B. De Mille say that he was convinced that his films were all masterworks. Well, the same thing was true of Juan de Orduña. When it comes time to judge his films, this blindness —to give it a name— produces a certain amount of tenderness in us. Destroying these films is the equivalent of destroying their author. When faced with the atrocious bad taste of such famous films as **Locura de amor** (Love Crazy; 1948), **Pequeñeces** (Little Things; 1949) or **Agustina de Aragón** (1950), we prefer to remain silent, especially since this bad taste is very Spanish in nature —although every country has its own. One film that probably has a few saving graces is **Ella, él y sus millones** (Hers, His and the Millions; 1944).
Another director who was less inspired, fortunately for him, was Luis Lucia, but he also knew how to add fuel to Cifesa's fire when it was necessary. If the art of making films is above all a business —a factor that one should very much respect, directors like Juan de Orduña and Luis Lucia are always in urgent demand. What they do, they do well in their own way. In all the different arts, there are scales of value. Every artist must be measured according to his or her scale. I suspect that Luis Lucia never claimed that he was deceiving anyone, he put himself at the orders of the producers and that was the end of it.

Rescuing from oblivion

After taking a look at the loud-mouthed and shrill cinema, I believe it just to recall those directors who tried to make a personalized cinema with discretion, even though they were not always successful due to the many imperatives with which they had to struggle.
First of all, we would like to spotlight Jerónimo Mihura, who, with the always valuable help of his brother Miguel as screenwriter, makes a series of films where —Oh miracle of our cinema!— vulgarity was conspicuous due to its absence. Among these films is a masterwork of humor: **Mi adorado Juan** (My Adorable Juan; 1949). It is the story of a young lady from high society who spends her time stealing dogs and who marries a simple man, a nature lover, the opposite of his dedicated father, a famous physiologist. It is a work which still does not occupy the place which it merits within our cinema. The script was so good that later Miguel Mihura would convert it into one of his most famous theatrical comedies.
Noteworthy among the films that Jerónimo Mihura did along with his brother are: **Castillo de naipes** (House of Cards; 1943), **Confidencia** (Confidence; 1947), **Vidas confusas** (Confused Lives; 1947), **Siempre vuelven de madrugada** (They Always Return at Dawn; 1948) and **El señorito Octavio** (Young Master Octavio; 1950), this last work based on the novel by Armando Palacio Valdés. He also makes **El camino de Babel** (The Road to Babel; 1944), with a story line by José Luis Sáenz de Heredia. All these works should be revised, since the discovery of **Mi adorado Juan** is not made casually.
Another director who should be rescued from oblivion is Arturo Ruiz Castillo. This intellectual, a film lover from his youth, artistic director of **Biblioteca Nueva** and a collaborator of

Juan de Landa, Conrado San Martín and Luis Pérez de León in *Mi adorado Juan* (1949) by Jerónimo Mihura.

the **La barraca** theater company, which was created by Federico García Lorca, after making numerous shorts, valiantly moves into the world of commercial cinema by shooting in 1946 an adaptation of **Las inquietudes de Shanti Andía** (The Worries of Shanti Andía), by Pío Baroja. One might have thought back then that a director with a considerable cultural background had made a hopeful start in our cinema. It certainly was the case, but he had no other choice than to follow the imperatives set down by governmental and political orders if he wanted to keep on shooting films. Without a doubt, Ruiz Castillo and a few others of his generation would have been able to make a very different kind of cinema, with much more quality, if they had lived at another time. What is abject is that the official subject matter got the better of him. He made the religious film, **La manigua sin Dios** (The Godless Brushland; 1948), the patriotic film, **El santuario no se rinde** (The Sanctuary Refuses to Surrender; 1949), and the historic film, **Catalina de Inglaterra** (Catalina of England; 1951). The last two films are not without a certain amount of quality and can be considered among the best that were made in their genre.

New graduates

Springing up during these years are new directors in which can be seen, more for what they say than for their films, an innovative zeal which was very much needed by our cinema. The obstacles that they had to overcome were enormous. More than just showing that theirs was a personal work, they tried to prove that they knew how to direct. There is no doubt whatsoever that they prove it. Their first pictures can be deceiving when trying to evaluate the evolution of these directors. The exception is José Antonio Nieves Conde, who later gave us two films that already occupy important places in the history of Spanish cinema: **Surcos** (Furrows; 1951) and **El inquilino** (The Tenant; 1959). Among his first four films, there is one in particular, the second, which is unique and much better than the one which would bring him fame, or **Balarrasa** (Hothead; 1950). I am referring to **Angustia** (Anguish; 1947). If this film had been done with greater aloofness and more humor, its story line would have stolen a march on **La vida criminal de Archibaldo de la Cruz** (The Criminal Life of Archibaldo de la Cruz; 1955), by Luis Buñuel. The previous warning of anguish for someone who is dreaming about committing some crimes which later do happen without his being able to avoid them, greatly recalls the film that the Aragonese director was to make years later. The tone of the picture is different, of course, but Nieves Conde's film still conserves a disturbing mystery, which, if it had been shrouded in poetics, would today be a unique work. Despite this fact, it merits an important place among the credits of this no less important director. **Llegada la noche** (Nightfall; 1949), based on an idea by Hans Rothe, also has a climate of inexplicable mystery. Even though it is not exactly an uninteresting work, it does not attain the perfection of **Angustia.**

Antonio del Amo has the same restless attitude of his fellow «graduate», Nieves Conde, but his films are simply not on the same level. The fact that his best picture is **Día tras día** (Day After Day; 1951) makes us suspect that the scripts by Manuel Mur-Oti acted as a burden on his first films. There are works that are partially successful, moments which show an instinct for film, but his work taken as a whole makes us guess that he felt forced to submit form to content, and that is why a resulting affectation invalidates many of his first films. The most revealing example of what I am saying is **El huésped de las tinieblas** (The Guest of Darkness; 1948), an alleged biography of Gustavo Adolfo Bécquer, as pretentious as it is empty. Of greater interest is his first film, **Cuatro mujeres** (Four Women; 1947). The fact that the praiseworthy attempt of Antonio del Amo to search for a style ended at the service of Joselito, the child singer, is a very sad note. But

in no other art do circumstances play such an important part as in cinema. In the first films made by Francisco Rovera Beleta there was more instinct than reflection and what then could have seemed a defect ended up later a virtue. That is the reason he should be remembered for his later works **Expreso de Andalucía** (Andalusian Express; 1956), **Los tarantos** (1963) and **El amor brujo** (Bewitched Love; 1967), and not for his first babblings. At the opposite pole is Julio Salvador, another director with instinct. His **Apartado de Correos 1.001** (Post Office Box 1,001; 1950) filled us with a hope that later slowly died. This is perhaps why we ask ourselves today whether this good film was not due in part to the script of Antonio Isasi and Julio Coll.
And finally, we should point to the particular case of Manuel Mur-Oti who burst onto the Spanish film scene with **Un hombre va por el camino** (A Man Goes down the Road; 1949). The picture, which has a conventional plot, can deceive the viewer since most of it is filmed in the open and benefits from the always efficient photography of Manuel Berenguer. When first premiered it was overrated since it was different from the film that was made at that time in Spain. Over the years, the many defects in the work of Mur-Oti have hardly let us see the few virtues it offers.

Ana Mariscal and Fernando Nogueras in Un hombre va por el camino (**1950**) **by Manuel Mur-Oti.**

A unique case

Until very recently, the work of Carlos Serrano de Osma was so difficult if not impossible to pigeonhole that the experts on Spanish film skipped over it, but at the same time feeling a kind of remorse that they were committing an injustice. It was this remorse that led to a revision of his films, a revision that left everyone surprised, not because of the perfections —there were many, but because it is absolutely unthinkable in the Spanish postwar years that someone dared to make films that had nothing to do with the general film-making trend.
One man who rediscovered him, Julio Pérez Perucha, writes in a book dedicated to Serrano de Osma, «A radical and refractory film-maker, not standing on ceremony and with a kind of frenzy that was both haughty and suicidal in the dominant cinema of the time, Serrano de Osma saw his career burn out at the beginning of the fifties. His case is that of a forceful opponent within Francoist cinema to its most generalized and mediocre habits, a fight that would end in a relative failure. But the testimony of his attitudes is seen today in a collection of exemplary and valuable films, situated among the most irrepressible antipodes of the cinema of that time».
The film-making technique of Carlos Serrano de Osma is experimental, not in the generalized sense that is

Lola Flores and Manolo Caracol in *Embrujo* (1947) by Carlos Serrano de Osma.

normally given to this word, but rather in a much more particular sense, much more personalized. Before beginning each one of his pictures, he seriously considered the **film's staging,** as if he were searching for the language that he was going to express himself with, as if he were searching for a part of himself. This is how his films should be understood and seen, in the same way that today we read certain books or look at certain paintings. The style is that of experimentation, or, if you prefer, the inverse of experimentation. What is dramatic about a director like Carlos Serrano de Osma, and of many others with different film-making concepts, is that we will always remain with the doubt as to where they would have evolved, since they really only had a chance to begin. We are referring to a type of director who is continually evolving. The conditioning factors of cinema, and we repeat this yet again, have no equivalents in other art forms. In other words, the case of Serrano de Osma is universal and is not particular to Spain. Even so, the man who was able to direct four films in the middle of the forties and within the very narrow limits of our cinematography has left us perplexed. These were the films: **Abel Sánchez** (1946), based on the work of Miguel de Unamuno; **Embrujo** (Bewitchment; 1947), **La sirena negra** (The Black Siren; 1947), based on the work of Emilia Pardo de Bazán, and **La sombra**

iluminada (The Illuminated Shadow; 1948). Each one of these films has its own aesthetic, but each has its common denominator as well, a constant sense of searching. Today, they occupy a **corner** of Spanish cinema, and I well say **corner** because it is a place apart for a unique name: **Carlos Serrano de Osma.**

The hodgepodge

We are going to try to include in this section a varied group of directors hailing from Spanish cinema of the forties. Omitting their names would be an injustice, but none of them deserve any special attention.
First of all, we will remember Manuel Augusto García Viñolas, whose influence during this period is more political than artistic. An important Falangist, he founded the National Department of Cinematography in the midst of the civil war. In 1941, he makes the documentary, **Boda en Castilla** (Wedding in Castile), which receives a prize in the Mostra of Venice, as well as a feature-length film of absolutely no interest called **A los pies de usted** (At Your Feet; 1945). Regarding his work with José María Leitao De Barros, we will speak of it later while studying the work of this Portuguese director.
Gonzalo Delgrás: He is worth remembering for the acceptance among the Spanish public of his sugary comedies done in the **white telephone** style of fascist Italy. The most acceptable were **La tonta del bote** (The Dizzy Broad; 1939), **Un marido a precio fijo** (A Husband at a Fixed Price; 1942) and **La boda de Quinita Flores** (The Wedding of Quinita Flores; 1943). We would prefer not to speak about his dramas.
Ignacio F. Iquino: Prolific producer and director, who groups in his extensive credits from the most ephemeral to intuitive qualities that are more mimetic than creative, in which one can guess at possibilities that were never realized. In the period we are studying, the following films were given prizes: **Una sombra en la ventana** (A Shadow In the Window; 1944), **El obstáculo** (The Obstacle; 1945), **Aquel viejo molino** (That Old Mill; 1946), **Noche sin cielo** (A Skyless Night; 1947) and **Brigada criminal** (Criminal Brigade; 1950).
Ricardo Gascón: His best film and not devoid of a certain amount of interest is **Don Juan de Serralonga** (1948), based on a work by Víctor Balaguer. By way of courtesy, we will mention another film called **La niña de Luzmela** (The Girl from Luzmela; 1949), based on the novel by Concha Espina.
Enrique Gómez: He became known after the success of **Viento de siglos** (Wind of Centuries; 1945), which is rather hopeful in a way. He never shoots what can be termed a finished product, but two films that never become vulgar are **Extraño amanecer** (Strange Dawn; 1947) and **El ẏerdugo** (The Hangman; 1947), based on a story by Balzac.
Sabino A. Micón: Well-known film commentator and critic during the years of the Republic (writing for **El Imparcial** and **Ahora**), he shoots in 1944 his only sound picture, **Paraíso sin Eva** (Paradise without Eve), which can be described as both spontaneous and funny.
Eduardo G. Maroto: This irregular director has an unforgettable film among his credits called **La hija del penal** (Daughter of the Penitentiary; 1935), although a large part of it had to do with the dialogues by Miguel Mihura. Viewed alone, his image becomes much more vulgar. However, we asks ourselves if this vulgarity does not give his film a certain personal stamp. Among the films from this period, we should spotlight **Mi fantástica esposa** (My Fantastic Wife; 1943) and **La otra sombra** (The Other Shadow; 1948).

One of a kind

We will try to rescue from oblivion five pictures which, as isolated and solitary cases, run the risk of not being included in any section, either because they are the only works ever made by the director or because the director never again makes a similar quality film. They should all be cited at the hour of recalling Spanish cinema in the forties. We will mention them in the chronological order in which they were made.

1. **Un bigote para dos** (A Moustache for Two; 1940), by Tono (Antonio de Lara) and Miguel Mihura. Just as Enrique Jardiel Poncela invented his **Celuloides rancios** (Rancid Celluloides), so did the film-makers of his same generation and style, Tono and Mihura, create a similar picture with an old film from the German silent era, reediting it and dubbing it with absurd diologues. The result was an incredibly funny film. Unfortunately, they did not repeat the experiment, for in spite of its unquestionable revolutionary and avant-garde appeal, it would have meant working with a genre that is not appreciated by a part of the Spanish public, accustomed to seeing this type of humor thanks to the weekly magazine **La Codorniz,** created by these two men.

2. **Espronceda** (1945), by Fernán (Fernando Alonso Casares). In spite of fitting in perfectly with the films of the time and in particular with those recalling the Romantic period, which had such a significant effect in the forties, this film has a style which is not of this period of film-making in Spain, since it has a soft tone about it and the picture seems to hold back. It is not even close to being melodramatic and is not given to gesticulations. The set designs do not even feel burdensome, since the tulles are done in the Max Ophuls fashion. It can definitely be said that this film is elegant. Due to the fact that the other two films made by Fernán do not have the charm of **Espronceda,** we ask ourselves if the quality of the film is not due to the decisive influence of the photography of Cecilio Paniagua, the set decorations by Francisco Escriña, Pierre Schild and Juan Antonio Simont, and the superb costume designs by Víctor María Cortezo. It would be useless to point out that the unquestionable qualities of true cinematographic science of aesthetics found in **Espronceda** were recognized by only a few and this unusual film was thrown into the trunk of forgotten items while others of its genre were hailed as masterworks. What masterworks of ridiculousness and pretentiousness!

3. **Dulcinea** (1946), by Luis Arroyo. Hardly without any money at all, without saying a word, Luis Arroyo obtained a film version of the work by Gaston Baty —beautifully translated into Spanish by Huberto Pérez de la Osa, that was very superior to the picture that Vicente Escrivá was to direct fifteen years later, a picture that was highly touted as a super-production. It is a lesser work, but our cinema was and still is very much in need of lesser works like this one. Furthermore, its lesser tone fits in perfectly with the intimacy required by the subject. Probably it was an isolated success since Luis Arroyo never again did anything similar. It can be seen that he is very close to the story and the character, which was given an excellent interpretation by his sister, Ana Mariscal. It is a work that should be rescued from oblivion and from the burnings.

4. **La honradez de la cerradura** (The Integrity of the Lock; 1950), by Luis Escobar. Based on a work by Jacinto Benavente, a splendid screenplay was done by the director, Luis Escobar. The first film experience by the man who was Spain's best theater director in the postwar years could not have been more fortunate. One might have expected a good example of filmed theater, but it is pure film. The atmosphere obtained is that of a realism which surprises the viewer, since few times has the old part of Madrid been shown to us so correctly, in a climate of etchings, but one of delicate beauty. The characters are alive and their dialogue sounds true-to-life. It is a charming film that is unfortunately much better than the second and last made by Luis Escobar: **La canción de la Malibrán** (Malibrán's Song). If he had continued down the road marked by the evident skills shown in **La honradez de la cerradura,** our great theater director would have also undoubtedly become a great film

director. Either he did not want to dedicate himself to film or he was not able to, since this was the closed-off reserve of arrivistes who lacked both talent and culture, although this is less true today. The lead in this film was done by a man who would later become one of our greatest international stars: Francisco Rabal.

5. **La corona negra** (The Black Crown; 1950), by Luis Saslavski. Although its spirit cannot be considered a Spanish film, its production most definitely is. It is surprising how a film like this can be found in our cinema. Even though it is very much on the fringe, its qualities are coming to the fore as time goes by. It is slowly becoming a rarity, but a rarity of quality. Based on a story line by Jean Cocteau, and scripted by Charles de Peyret Chappuis and with dialogues by Miguel Mihura, the film conserves the spirit (although some take the opposite view) of the author of **Le sang d'un poète.** The story of a woman who recovers her memory at the same time as she recovers her destiny, a story in which real and imaginary worlds are confused and in which the omnipresent image of death is always hovering nearby, is like the work of Cocteau in its conception. This fidelity would never have been possible without the collaboration of the director, Luis Saslavski, a man who knew perfectly the literary world which he describes and who converts it into a film world of tremendous quality. Probably it has one or two dream sequences too many, for the whole is the work of an inconsistent director, who, when he does hit the mark, becomes the true creator of his films. The fact that **La corona negra** is a Spanish film —since its producer is Spanish— should fill us with satisfaction and we should not analyze it as a rare bird of our cinema. All the film industries in the world have been able to take advantage of foreign formulae, at least when they came their way. One other observation: this is one of the best films ever made by actress María Félix, and the most forgotten.

Foreigners in Spain

The Second World War forced a few European film-makers to seek refuge in Spain. The blindness or simply the ignorance of the leaders of our film industry prevented them from taking advantage of this circumstance, except in a few, very concrete cases. They were almost always film-makers who fled from their own countries and who tried to make names for themselves after going to a lot of trouble. The reverse was never true. Except in the case of Ladislao Vajda, their work here was only provisional. Not all were fleeing from fascism, some came looking for it. We will only cite names, not ideologies.

Two especially important figures arrived in Spain at the beginning of the forties: Leni Riefenstahl and Abel Gance.

The creator of **Olympische Spiele** (Olympia; 1936) filmed here the location shots for her **Tiefland,** in which she also performed and which after four years of work remained unfinished. When the allied troops, concretely the French, arrived in the Tyrol, she was arrested and the negative of this film was confiscated. It was not until 1954 according to some, and 1958, according to others, that the material would be revealed. **Tiefland** (Lowland) is the adaptation of the opera by Eugène Albert based on the work by Angel Guimerá, **Terra Baixa.** During her stay in Spain, Leni Riefenstahl was very warmly received by the Falange.

The creator of **Napoleon** began to shoot in Spain a film about the famous bullfighter, Manolete. The bullfighter himself was the star, but because of economic problems, it was interrupted after two weeks of production. The screenplay was by Eduardo Marquina and his son Luis Marquina was to be the technical advisor to Abel Gance. The title of the film was **Sol y sombra de Manolete** (Sun and Shade of Manolete; 1944-1945).

Víctor Tourjanski —he is also known by the name of Viktor or Wratyslaw— was a Russian director who made films on an international scale. During the thirties, he made a big name for himself. He directed the most famous actors and actresses of his own country, and those of Germany, France and Italy. He is one of the European directors with the biggest credit list to his name. His work deserves to be studied. In Spain he made **Si te hubieses casado conmigo** (If You Had Married Me; 1948) with the actress Amparo Rivelles.

Fédor Ozep is another Russian director who made films in many different countries. He directed some of the classics of European cinema. In Russia he made **Ziemeia v. Plenu** (1927); in Germany, **Der Lebende Leichnam** (1929) and **Der Möder Dimitri Karamazoff** (1931); in France, **Amok** (1934) and **La dame de Pique** (1937); and in Italy, **La principessa Tarakanova** (1938). He died immediately after arriving in Hollywood in 1948. In our country he shot **Cero en conducta** (Bad Marks for Conduct; 1943-1946) under the assumed name of Pedro Otzoup.

Julien Duvivier is a French director who made such well known works as **La bandera** (The Flag) and **Pepe-Le-Moko** in France, and **Tales of Manhattan** (Seis destinos; 1937) and **Flesh and Fantasy** (Al margen de la vida; 1946) in the United States. In Spain he made **Jack el negro** (Black Jack; 1950).

Pierre Caron, another French director who made numerous vaudevilles, also shot in our country.

Max Neufeld was an Austrian director who specialized in making double and triple versions due to his knowledge of languages. I do not believe that there is another director with a list of credits similar to Neufeld's. Apart from shooting in his own country, he made films in Germany, Czechoslovakia, Hungary, Holland, France, Italy and Spain. He always made light comedies or musical comedies that were not badly done. In the Cinecittá studios in Rome he made the double Italian-Spanish version of **Fortuna/Lluvia de milliones** (Raining Millions; 1940). Later, in Spain, he would make another double version called **Madrid de mis sueños/Buongiorno Madrid!** (Madrid of My Dreams; 1942), with María Mercader. That same year he makes a completely Spanish film called **Idilio en Mallorca** (Romance in Majorca) with Antoñita Colomé.

Richard Bush is a practically unknown director who shot **Sarasate** (1941) in the CEA studios. Alfredo Mayo played the leading role of the eminent Navarran violinist and singer Margarita Carosio did the role of Adelina Patti.

Six different Italian directors film during these years in Spain. Apart from Fernando Mignoni, the director who had the closest ties with Spanish cinema, we will cite: Flavio Calzavara, Gian Carlo Capelli, Ferruchio Cerio and especially Primo Zeglio who did **Fiebre** (Fever; 1943) with Mary Carrillo and Raffaello Matarazzo, **Dora la espía** (Dora the Spy; 1943) with Francesca Bertini, and **Empezó en boda** (It Began as a Wedding) with Sara Montiel and Fernando Fernán Gómez.

And finally there was the Mexican Fernando de Fuentes who made **Jalisco canta en Sevilla** (Jalisco Sings in Seville; 1948); two Argentinians, León Klimoswski with **La guitarra de Gardel** (Gardel's Guitar; 1949) and Luis Saslavski with **La corona negra** —a film to which we have already referred; and two Portuguese, Arturo Duarte with **El huésped del cuarto número 13** (The Guest in Room Number 13; 1946) and José María Leitao de Barros, who, with his **Inés de Castro** (1944) and with the supervision of Manuel Augusto García Viñolas, achieves one of the best historical films in Spanish cinema.

Ladislao Vajda

This Hungarian director, son of the eminent screenwriter Lászlo Vajda, is considered a Spanish director by just about everyone, not only because he became a nationalized citizen, but because his most important pictures were made in Spain and dealt with very Spanish topics —in spite of the fact that he shot films in Hungary, Britain, France Italy, Germany, Switzerland and even a Spanish-Portuguese coproduction. From the time of his first picture in Spain, **Se vende un palacio** (A Palace is for Sale; 1943), which can be described as a light comedy, Vajda was seen as a director who was very sure of himself. The ones who say he was sure, also said he was skilfull. He showed himself much better than all the other foreign directors who made totally Spanish films. His way of creating sets and of directing actors seemed completely in keeping with a Spanish director. His ability to assimilate, of picking up nuances surprised people back then and continued to surprise them throughout his career.

After that first film he shot **Doce lunas de miel** (Twelve Honeymoons; 1943), **Te quiero para mí** (I Want You for Me; 1944), **El testamento del Virrey** (The Will of the Viceroy; 1944) and **Cinco lobitos** (Five Little Wolves; 1945), all of which were comedies. To tell the truth, they were much lighter, much snappier than those made by our own directors. This was his style. He was unhurried, assuring himself a prestige that years later would allow him to shoot big-budget films that would launch Spanish cinema into foreign markets. But this Ladislao Vajda will be dealt with in another chapter.

Epilogue

After this incomplete panorama of our film production from 1940 to 1950, it is seen —I believe— that, in spite of the burden of the Francoist regime, controlling and directing our cinema by means of an iron will state protection, behind the backs of the public, through loans made by the «vertical» trade unions, with import licenses and official prizes, there was always a crack through which one could escape in order not to make a film that was a reaction to a feeling of suffocation— that kind of film would come later. However, there was the opportunity to make one's voice heard by means of apparently lesser works, very much on the fringe and not the beneficiary of state aid.

The so-called greater works were the ones that made their voices heard. They were included in patriotic cinema (and jingoist cinema): **Raza, Escuadrilla, Harka, ¡A mí la legión!** (I Like the Legion!), **Alhucemas, Los últimos de Filipinas, El santuario no se rinde,** etc.; historical cinema (anecdotal and jingoist, too): **El abanderado, Doña María la Brava, El doncel de la reina, El tambor de Bruch** (The Bruch Drum), **Eugenia de Montijo, Inés de Castro,** etc.; religious cinema (and sometimes historical): **La mies es mucha, Misión blanca** (White Mission), **La manigua sin Dios, Reina Santa, El capitán de Loyola,** etc.; and the escapist cinema going back to the nineteenth century: **El escándalo, El clavo, La pródiga, Espronceda, El huésped de las tinieblas** (Gustavo Adolfo Bécquer), **Noche de estreno** (Opening Night; José Zorrilla), **Sarasate, La canción de la Malibrán, El marqués de Salamanca** (The Marquess of Salamanca), etc. But below this cinema, not above —films that were both bad and good as we have pointed out, were voices that were heard with a lesser intensity, but not lesser in quality. When tallying up, they seem to us to be the best. As the reader has seen, we have given special attention and affection to these pictures. Time is the factor which definitely establishes a scale of values. Throughout history, states have continually made mistakes while trying to impose ideas. Man in his weakness is always the stronger. This great hope is made known to us not so much by looking forward in time, but by looking backwards.

Final note: On February 18, 1947, the **Instituto de Investigaciones y Experiencias Cinematográficas** (so that we understand each other better: the **Film School**) was created. Times would change, but the state of course, was unaware of this. States have always ignored this fact.

1950
1961

Viridiana (1961) by Luis Buñuel.

1950 1961

Diego Galán

At the beginning of the fifties, the regime of General Franco made every effort to come to terms with the reigning situation in Europe after the allied victory. It was no longer possible to maintain that diplomatic obstinacy which considered the international blockade of Spain meritorious nor, for that matter, to continue living with one's back turned to the world. As a result, while Spain prepared for entry into UNESCO, for the signing of accords with the United States and for the approval of a concordat with the Vatican that would make official the real power of the Catholic Church, some changes tried to harmonize the preservation of the old autarchic structures with the democratic demands of the age.

In 1951, for example, the Ministry of Information and Tourism was created for a double purpose: on the one hand, to control the expressions of increasing opposition to the regime which could even be found among a good part of the people who contributed to Franco's victory in the civil war, and on the other hand, to offer foreign countries a more open view of Spanish life in order to attract economic aid and tourists. It was an insurmountable contradiction that had a clear repercussion on the world of Spanish cinema which was then directly dependent on that ministry. In order to better understand the situation, the doubts of the director, Julio Coll, should be cited. He did not know which of the ministry's dictates he should follow: the one that forbade him the use of bikinis in his films because their use was immoral or the one that proposed that he should use them precisely to foment the Spanish tourist industry.

The case of «Surcos»

Such a contradiction was found in all aspects of Spanish cinema and even contributed to a small scandal. The Director General of Cinematography who first occupied the post in the new ministerial organization, an Air Force colonel who worked in the Legal Corps, José María García Escudero, was the first victim of the impossible dissimulating purpose of the regime. A film buff who had already been a critic, García Escudero believed that the **new** times were represented by his moderate liberal leanings, and with that illusion in mind, he opted to economically protect with official prizes a film made by a director who supported the Hedilla tendency within the Falange, José Antonio Nieves Conde, a director who for the first time showed some of the postwar disasters within Spanish cinema. Seen today, **Surcos** (Furrows) may seem insufficient due to the timid way in which problems are focused and due to its Christian hopes, but in 1951 it amounted to a criticism of the real situation in Spain which had come about after the civil war. It was, then, part of a reply from a certain non-conformist right.

Surcos narrates the story a family of peasants who emigrate to Madrid, the capital of the country, in order to improve their fortunes. Misfortune, however, soon descends upon them, since on the road they find the world of the black market. Life was not as they imagined, and finally they decide to return to their small village. Before they make their decision, **Surcos** had shown an atmosphere of hunger and unemployment, something which had never been done in Spanish film of the forties.

García Escudero's basic problem was having wanted to give official protection to **Surcos,** in spite of the fact that the ecclesiastical censorship had classified the film as **gravely dangerous,** and to deny protection to a film which had already been granted all sorts of official blessings. The film in question was no less than **Alba de América** (America's Dawn; 1951) by Juan de Orduña, a super-production made by Cifesa which told the story of the discovery of America by Christopher Columbus from a Spanish propagandistic point of view. This film had been shot on the initiative of the country's officialdom as an attempted reply to the British production **Christopher Columbus** (1949) which starred Fredric March and which was directed by David MacDonald. The film had been banned in Spain, since, among other things, it told of the miserable last years of Columbus' life. **Alba de América,** on the other hand, played up the virtues of the Catholic Monarchs, Ferdinand and Isabella, who had helped the discoverer make his first trip. The film also maintained the religious spirit which had become normal in Spain's postwar cinema: it insisted on the positive social role which the Catholic Church exercised over Spanish society. According to the official version, it was not tolerable that such a patriotic and expensive film should be shoved off into a corner while its place was given to such an ungrateful and black film as **Surcos.**.

García Escudero had to quickly leave the Department of Cinematography and it would be many years before he would return to the post. Meanwhile, everything he had tried to do fell apart and **Alba de América** obtained all the official aid, while **Surcos** was forgotten in the drawer of **damned** films and it would only be later when it would begin to obtain unofficial prizes.

Controversy at this point was irreversible. When **Surcos** appeared before the censors, strikes sprang up in Barcelona, Bilbao and San Sabastián and in student circles a contrast was seen between the official culture and the ideas of those who had not fought in the civil war. University magazines

José Prada, María Francés, María Asquerino and Marisa de Leza in *Surcos* (1951) by José Antonio Nieves Conde.

and publications began to deal with another type of culture.

Bardem and Berlanga

Logically, **Surcos** was not an isolated case. Other fims that were different from the official cinema began to surface timidly at the same time. Among them, a picture that should obviously be cited is **Esa pareja feliz** (That Happy Couple; 1951), which was jointly directed by Juan Antonio Bardem and Luis García Berlanga, both of whom had graduated together from the **Instituto de Investigaciones y Experiencias Cinematográficas** (Cinema Research and Experiences Institute), or IIEC. The two young men had enrolled in the film school when it was inaugurated in 1947.
Esa pareja feliz was also refused economic aid in the Ministry of Information and Tourism and it was only premiered two years later. When it was exhibited, it was shown under bad conditions and the general public did not support the film, even though it was one of the most important pictures that Spanish cinema had produced until that time. It was logical that the film did not interest the defenders of the new Francoism since its bitterness did nothing to recommend it to the local public and its sordidness made it unapt for foreign sales.

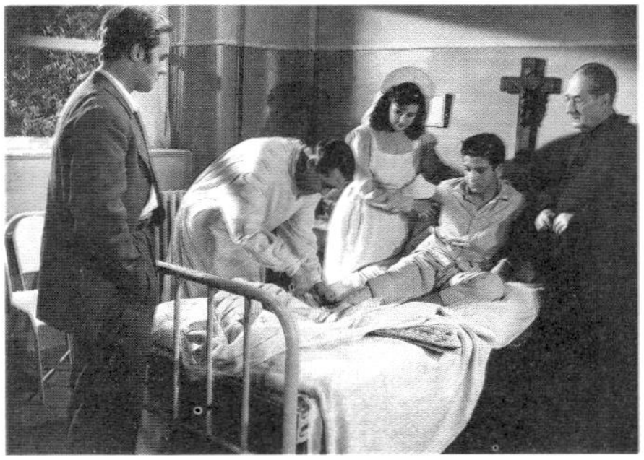

Mario Berriatúa, Manuel Zarzo and José Prada in Día tras día **(1951) by Antonio del Amo.**

(Previous page)

Antonio Vilar, Alberto Romea, Amparo Rivelles and José Suárez in Alba de América **(1951) by Juan de Orduña.**

Although the film contained both humor and tenderness, **Esa pareja feliz** hid a biting vision of a working-class neighborhood in which a young couple dreams of bettering their future. Everything is mediocre: the apartment block's common patio, that humiliating half-hunger, correspondence courses, films running all day at the local cinema, the empire of radio, roguishness, dreams and love. It was the first film made by a new generation, and as can be expected, it judged the very type of film-making it was rebelling against. The first sequence precisely takes place during the shooting of an **historical** film in which the actress of the moment, who is playing the role of the medieval queen of the moment, grotesquely falls from the merlon of a castle and the studio workers —among whom is the leading man— do not catch her in time. Later, the film would poke fun at theater and specifically **zarzuela** (Spanish light opera), the genre which General Franco liked so much.
As their marriage slowly ends in failure, although paradoxically they win «the happy couple» contest, the film shows the bitterness of a social class which had not been shown in film. It is precisely this documentary aspect, which would later be picked up by other directors, that is the best that the film has to offer today. When speaking about **Surcos** or **Esa pareja feliz,** titles to which should be added

Día tras día (Day after Day; 1951), by Antonio del Amo, Italian neorealism should be referred to. Despite the fact that it reached Spain later than other countries, it had an important effect on a large number of the film-makers who refused to observe the guidelines set down by state aid or protectionism or by tradition. Upon taking cameras out into the streets and telling stories set in the outskirts of major urban centers, Spanish cinema acquired an unusual aesthetic concept. The rest of the country's film production, which consisted of the real nucleus of the pictures shot in Spain, remained attentive to the moral principles set down by the censors and the genres of proven profitability. Other types of exceptions, such as those films by Catalonian studios which dabbled in the detective genre or those that were made by Edgar Neville on his own did not change the reality of the day-by-day situation of Spanish cinema.

The new censorship

The traditional production companies preferentially worked in two areas in the immediate postwar years: religious and folkloric film. The first area, which had acquired special importance in war pictures, was **adapted** to the new political circumstances promoted by the Catholic Church as a result of the concordat, and the second, in which melodramas or comedies used songs as illustrations, generally were set in Andalusia. Spanish authorities wanted to propose a nationalistic solution in showing all of Spain as a cliché, and to a certain extent, to reply to the incipient Spanish neorealism by offering an idyllic glimpse of the same characters.
Religious cinema really began to filter its way into all genres, and soon the «folks» would become nuns or priests and would appear in the comedies watching over the outcome of the story line and giving their advice as to the road that should be followed. Much of this form of film-making inherited the high-flown character of the **historic** genre and when the folkloric films changed their tone by using a more commonplace language, it represented the tombstone of morality which ferociously crushed them. Spanish cinema had changed in some of its forms, but the spirit of 1939 was still very much alive.
The Minister of Information and Tourism, who had ousted José María García Escudero after the **Surcos scandal,** was a man who so firmly believed in his religious convictions that he did not hesitate in announcing that the work of his ministry was to **obtain souls for heaven.** As proof of this mission, Gabriel Arias Salgado reformed the censorship norms and created a new system of economic aid for Spanish cinema.
Until then, censorship had not explained the reason for its severity. It just banned or put fines on films without its motives being known by film-makers. Starting in March, 1952, it was known that the censors examined films from three fundamental angles: the moral, the one referring to a picture's «good customs» or respectability, and the political and social angle.
On the other hand, the substantial reform of the economic protection system placed very much in first place the own particular tastes of the minister or his close helpers, so that only those films which were liked could hope to obtain substantial monetary aid. The new classification was structured in three categories: films of National Interest, 1 A, 1 B, 2 A, 2 B and 3, the aid corresponding to different percentages of the film's total production cost. Fifty percent of the total budget was given back to the producer if the film was declared of National Interest; 40 % if it was classified as 1 A; 35 % for a 1 B classification; 30 % for a 2 A classification; 25 % for a 2 B classification; and no protection whatsoever if it was classified in the third category. The criteria in establishing these classifications were naturally capricious.
It is logical that the producers thought long and hard about what type of film

would interest Mr. Arias Salgado and his close helpers, and how they could inflate the theoretical production cost of each film so that the partial aid given by the ministry would cover the complete cost and more besides. They cared very little about whether their films would be a success or a failure with the public. When the **important** films were premiered, they had already been amortized.
It is certain that the new norms regarding economic aid were the result of the crafty ways that had been developed by the previous system by means of which import licenses circulated on the black market and sold for a good price to the distributors of foreign films. But it is no less certain that these measures put Spanish consumer cinema to sleep, a cinema that was self-censured due to money.
This is not only the reason for the Tridentine character of the **commercial** films of the time, but also for the mixture of genres and characters that were already cited, making Andalusians out of priests and nuns, devout believers out of the «folks» and asexuals out of men. A patriotic or moral watchword could jump out from any corner of a film.
It was also the reason that Spain began to make **double versions.** What the censor prohibited for exhibition inside the country was absolutely necessary for its hypothetical sale

Gerard Tichy, Manolo Morán, Eduardo Fajardo and Fernando Fernán Gómez in *Balarrasa* (1950) by José Antonio Nieves Conde.

abroad. Passionate kisses were filmed for the foreign market and tender smiles for Spanish spectators. These years marked the beginning of a tradition that would not be given up by our cinema until very recently, after the death of General Franco: double versions were almost inevitable, since otherwise it would be impossible to sell a film outside Spain and propagate tourist slogans.

Religious cinema

If we have spotlighted the genre of so-called **religious cinema** as one of the most important during the first years of the fifties, it is not so much to exaggerate, but rather to show that the spirit of these pictures went beyond that of any other genre, making their moral qualities coincide with those of the most conservative sector of the Catholic Church. At any rate, many films had a priest as a leading character, placing them in working-class atmospheres —in a way reforming the bitterness of the neorealist films, in upper classes of society, in faraway **missions,** in times gone by or in the midst of the recent civil war. Military cinema had given way to religious cinema.
Among others, the following films emphasized the heroic military conduct of priests who fought in favor of the insurrectionists: **Balarrasa** (1950), by J.

A. Nieves Conde; **Cerca del cielo** (Close to the Sky; 1951), by Domingo Viladomat, and **El frente infinito** (The Infinite Front; 1956), by Pedro Lazaga, a film that put a priest in the leading role. **Balarrasa,** which was the film that Nieves Conde made immediately before his controversial **Surcos,** was the very beginning of this cycle of films and it was an enormous commercial success. And producers could not complain of good box office takings after receiving official aid. The film narrated the story of a lieutenant who, tormented by the death of a companion in his same trench, decides to become a priest. His family, however, leads a dissipated life, but by example and courage, he leads them back to lawfulness and respectability. The film is not, of course, comparable to **Surcos,** but it does give an idea of the atmosphere lived in by an economically well-off social class and evidence of a black market can be seen. Later, José Antonio Nieves Conde would direct **El inquilino** (The Tenant; 1957) in which he would denounce the slowness or corruption of the bureaucracy when it came to the lack of housing. He employed a much more critical tone than in **Surcos,** progressively giving his films more social commitment and clarity. Naturally, **El inquilino** was held back by the censors who did not allow its release until the story had a happy ending and the tormented married couple who were the stars in the film obtained an excellent flat built under official protection. **Balarrasa's** references to the civil war were no more than indirect, because in the civil melodrama which occupies the central part of the anecdote, a moral message was expounded. This did not prevent other films from specializing in a civil war atmosphere or from showing a priest freely circulating about on the screen. In any case, there were films that frequently tried to teach the theories held by the Catholic Church. For example, **La señora de Fátima** (The Lady of Fatima; 1951), by Rafael Gil, included a speech by the Virgin Mary in which she claimed that there would be a new world war if mankind did not turn its eyes to her **so that Russia would convert. La mies es mucha** (That's a Lot of Corn; 1949) by José Luis Sáenz de Heredia and **Molokai** (1959) by Luis Lucia exalted the figure of the missionary; **De mujer a mujer** (Woman to Woman; 1950) by Lucia, **El padre Pitillo** (Father Pitillo; 1954) by Juan de Orduña, **La hermana Alegría** (Sister Alegría; 1954) by Lucia, and **Un día perdido** (A Day Lost; 1954) by José María Forqué, showed how a priest could take part in all aspects of everyday life, and in these cases, by helping to recompose the family with the illegitimate off-spring; **Cerca de la ciudad** (Near the City; 1952) by Lucia explained how charity was the only way to resolve the misery of others, following a young priest as he works in a shanty town; **La guerra de Dios** (God's War; 1953) by Gil, **Sor Intrépida** (1952) by Gil, **El Judas** (1952) by Ignacio F. Iquino, **El beso de Judas** (The Judas Kiss; 1954) by Gil, and **El pórtico de la Gloria** (Portico of Glory; 1953) by Rafael J. Salvia, were among the many films that insisted on the existence of a moral code inspired by Catholic doctrines, capable of resolving any wrong. Similar films were also made in other countries as a result of the tense cold war atmosphere, although their outlook was slightly different.

Children's cinema

The priest film that was the most successful among the Spanish public was undoubtedly **Marcelino, pan y vino** (Marcelino, Bread and Wine) which was directed by the exiled Hungarian film-maker Ladislao Vajda in 1955. Vajda made several other estimable works that were excellently done. The story was a simple melodrama that was resolved by the surprise of a miracle that stirred up emotion in audiences from many different countries. A six year old orphan is taken in by a convent of friars where he grows up in solitude, inventing a talkative friendship with Manuel, a nonexistent boy. When Marcelino discovers an abandoned image of

Juanjo Menéndez, Pablito Calvo and Juan Calvo in *Marcelino, pan y vino* (1954) by Ladislav Vajda.

Christ in the attic, he begins another invented friendship, every day giving him bread and wine. But the Christ, which has really consumed what has been brought him, takes pity on the innocence of the little boy and carries him to heaven to the surprise of the friars, who, filled by emotion with the miracle, can no longer be distinguished as individual personalities. Until then, each friar embodied a different character, from the emotionless grouch to the sentimental and timid individual. Little delicate clashes would spring up between them, contributing to the humor in the film.

Marcelino, pan y vino created its own school. After that moment, numerous child actors and actresses appeared and disappeared on the Spanish screens, all trying to emulate Pablito Calvo, the successful little actor who was to appear in other productions by Ladislao Vajda such as **Mi tío Jacinto** (Uncle Jacinto; 1956) and **Un ángel pasó por Brooklyn** (An Angel Came Through Brooklyn; 1957), more interesting than the first picture, although less of a success among Spanish audiences. Later, Pablito Calvo would appear in the films of numerous directors until he gave up working in cinema in 1964.

The sentimental comedies in which children contributed the necessary tenderness and humor, were quickly illustrated with music, so that the folkloric genre would soon become more ambitious. Joselito was the first child songbird of this cycle. In 1956, he starred in **El pequeño ruiseñor** (The Small Nightingale), a title that would soon be followed by similar ones: **Saeta del ruiseñor** (The «Saeta» of the Nightingale; 1957), **El ruiseñor de las cumbres** (The Nightingale of the Heights; 1958) and **Escucha mi canción** (Listen to My Song; 1958). Joselito's characteristic voice was soon known in Latin America and Europe, where his films were enjoyed with the same enthusiasm as in Spain.

Generally, the stories were very schematic in which an orphan boy or the son of poor parents would triumph in the world of song. The spectators were not very choosey since they received with identical enthusiasm the appearance of another child's voice, that of the little girl called Marisol, whose films seriously competed with those of other countries on the Spanish market. The plots of her films were naturally very similar to those of Joselito, but Marisol's true talent has helped her over the years to become an excellent actress, although not prolific.

Along with Joselito and Marisol, other child songbirds began to appear (Rocío Dúrcal, Pili and Mili, Estrellita, Maleni Castro, Ana Belén, etc.), although this did not mean that **dramatic** child actors and actresses had disappeared. Miguelito Gil could be seen in **Recluta con niño** (Recruit with a Son; 1955), by Pedro L. Ramírez, or in **Un traje blanco** (A White Suit; 1956), by Rafael Gil, which told the story of a little boy who had an accident while secretly working in order to buy himself a suit for his first communion. Another example was Pepito Moratalla in **El golfo que vio una estrella** (An Urchin Who Saw a Star; 1956), by Ignacio F. Iquino, in which some poor children write a letter to God renouncing their Christmas presents so that He might be able to cure their mother. The letter is read by some employees at the post office and the children receive gifts that they had never dreamed of.

In any case, the **musicals** were the films that had the greatest repercussion in the cinema which had child stars. This was logically the case, since the folkloric genre was at that time, one of the areas with the greatest popular impact. The demand for these consumer films offered work opportunities to directors with very different aesthetic aspirations.

Noteworthy among these directors is Antonio del Amo. Even though he specialized in making films with Joselito—he did eight in all, he was a curious defender of a certain **qualité** with the parallel critical description of different social atmospheres: **Cuatro mujeres** (Four Women; 1947), **El huésped de las tinieblas** (The Guest of Darkness; 1948) and **Sierra maldita** (The Cursed Sierra; 1954). Antonio del Amo also became interested in the neorealistic attempts of the young new directors and in that same dramatic line he shot **Día tras día** (Day after Day; 1951) the same year **Surcos** and **Esa pareja feliz** were made. The leading role were that of a traditional priest who, from the screen, spoke to the spectators, explaining to them the conduct of the uprooted boys who make up the rest of the characters. **Día tras día** is a kind of dramatic documentary which studies the life of working-class neighborhoods on the outskirts of Madrid and some of the social reasons for delinquency. The morals that were put over suffocated the film, but expressive possibilities were seen in the director that he would once again employ in **Sierra maldita**. Even so, it was the films Antonio del Amo made with Joselito that established his career as a frustrated one. Together with the pictures of the boy singer, this director made a few folkloric films that played up some of his stars.

Folkloric cinema

Undoubtedly, the dancers and singers who were the leads in the folkloric pictures became Spain's most popular stars. They frequently appeared in pictures, their songs were heard on radio stations (still very much a basic part of the Spanish social life), and they performed before the public live. Perhaps more fundamental was the fact that this folkloric cinema, which was not exactly a musical cinema, since comedies or melodramas were interrupted by songs, was already an important tradition in Spanish cinema. All that need be done is to go back to the times of Imperio Argentina, who had made some of the biggest hits in previous decades, or to look at the perennial attempts to transform any well-known singer into a bearable actress, in order to understand that the folkoric was not a genre which sprang up during the postwar period. This does not mean that the genre did not undergo important changes during that time. To cite one example, **La hermana San Sulpicio** (Sister San Sulpicio), a novel by Armando Palacio Valdés, which was adapted for film in the silent era (1927), and again in a second, sound picture in which Imperio Argentina marked up one of her first big successes, was adapted twice more in 1952 and 1971, both times directed by Luis Lucia. The delightful and gentle anti-clerical tone which Florián Rey used in the first two films was transformed in the fifties into a new recitation of respect owed to the Catholic Church and the correct way to establish amorous relationships with decency. The folkloric cinema, which should have responded to farcical comedies and comedies of manners, also became impregnated with watchwords and examples.
This kind of cinema was preferentially set in Andalusia, aesthetically deforming the situation that existed in that region of Spain, and transforming misery into something that bordered on the picturesque. The so-called cute young women who starred in these films resolved their problems by means of a kind of legal and playful dishonesty after they were not given some implacable chastisement if they had sinned in love. Never was the reason for their economic condition discussed, nor for that matter, did they ever ask about the reasons behind the imposition of recent or ancestral customs from which they suffered. If they emigrated to some other country, it was to forget a platonic, yet passionate love or to honor a fabulous contract from some multi-national magnate.
It was also frequent for folkloric cinema to have male stars. Men dreamed of success just as much as women singers did. Modest fishermen, street salesmen, taxi drivers or children from convents were transformed into well-known figures in the world of song —**El pescador de coplas** (The Fisherman of Songs; 1953) by Antonio del Amo; in great bullfighters— **Brindis al cielo** (A Dedication to the Heavens; 1953) by José Buchs; or even in priests— **El pórtico de la Gloria** (Portico of Glory; 1953) by Rafael J. Salvia. They copied women's cinema trying to achieve the same degree of optimism, because even if they did not become

successful —**El rey de la carretera** (The King of the Road; 1954), by Juan Fortuny— they aways managed to be happy in the end. At any rate, being able to sing was a consolation.
Three women stood out from the rest. Lola Flores came from the decade of the forties. Her very special personality, both strong and aggressive, gave true character to her roles, although they were many times limited by the plot. One film that stands out in Lola Flores' credits is an unusual work called **Embrujo** (Bewitched; 1947), by Carlos Serrano de Osma. The public practically wanted to burn their seats in the movie theaters where it was shown, since the director's telluric conception of the work, his fascination for what was being done in the avant-garde, did not correspond to the demands of the genre. Serrano de Osma, a director who made few works, is an imaginative film-maker who deserves to be studied in depth. Carmen Sevilla tried to make the Andalusian woman more sophisticated in her roles by eliminating her fiery spirit and forwardness, while Paquita Rico, the third «folk» woman of the decade, was perfect for the role of the girl without problems, confronting on the screen her commonplace love adventures with a certain degree of vivaciousness. It goes without saying that they were not good actresses. All three of them showed this to be the case in **El balcón de la luna** (The Moon's Balcony; 1962), by Luis Saslavski. They tried to join forces when they had already gone into their decline.
Since folkloric cinema just as religious cinema filtered its way into a large part of Spanish film production, it is not easy to point to typical or specific titles of the genre. It was so normal for characters in Spanish cinema to stop the action in order to intone Andalusian songs —we already saw that this was also normal in films starring **child prodigies** — that soon any Spanish film was contemptuously called an **españolada.** Folkloric cinema wanted to propose a nice way of seeing life that would contrast with the increasing university protests and their reflection in the bitter neorealist chronicles. In a way, this cinema wanted to look to the future and forget the black aspects of the past. Made along these same lines were the **rose** comedies which became popular at the end of the fifties.
They substituted the optimism of the underdeveloped folkloric cinema with the ideas of Spain's new middle class. The spectators who saw these films, did so with less enthusiasm than when they viewed foreign productions, either because all those moral harangues began to bore them or because the truly interesting films were made with little money. Spaniards opted for foreign cinema, even with the suspicion that the censors had mutilated these films. This distrust towards a film's integrity should be emphasized. Regarding Spanish pictures, one could have greater confidence that they were shown in their entirety, because ever since 1953 the previous censorship of scripts had been ordered. The Ministry of Information and Tourism could partially or totally ban films in pre-production by refusing to issue them the necessary **shooting permit.** Even though this did not eliminate the possibility of the censor making more cuts once the film was completed, the scripts were marked by governmental criteria even before the first day of shooting.
With respect to foreign films, apart from cutting out photograms or entire sequences, the dubbing could vary in certain aspects from the original plot. Numerous cases became known, but we should cite here the famous example of **Mogambo** (1953), the American film by director John Ford. Spanish censorship made Grace Kelly and Donald Sinden brother and sister instead of a married couple in order to hide the fact that she was commiting adultery. However, the **sinful** tone of the film became more evident when it was insinuated that the former husband, now brother, was jealous of his sister, thus creating a relationship of incest that Ford had never planned.

Félix Fernández, Luis Pérez de León, Manolo Morán, Elvira Quintillá and Nicolás Perchicot in *Bienvenido, Mr. Marshall* (1952) by Luis García Berlanga.

«Bienvenido, Mr. Marshall»

There were some notable exceptions in folkloric cinema in which the quality of the research surpassed the more trite aspects of the film —**Duende y misterio del flamenco** (The Spirit and Mystery of Flamenco; 1952), by Edgar Neville— or in which the skill of the director was able to transform it into a new social document. This is the case of **Bienvenido, Mr. Marshall** (Welcome, Mr. Marshall; 1952), the film which Bardem and Berlanga prepared together after the experience of **Esa pareja feliz.** They accepted the offer of a producer who asked them to make a film that would set off the looks and talent of a new «folk» actress, Lolita Sevilla, the sister of the now famous Carmen. The film was finally directed by Berlanga alone, ending a relationship that the two film-makers had maintained since the beginning of their careers. After that, each of these directors would go his separate way, although never in the opposite direction.

Bienvenido, Mr. Marshall showed, as a comedy, a panorama of the miserable life led by some Spanish towns, very concretely in the light of their hope that economic aid from the United States would be the panacea for all their problems and frustrations. In 1952, the year in which the film is produced, the Marshall Plan is being introduced all over Europe. Spain was not included in this plan, although

Josette Arnó, José Luis López Vázquez and Antonio Riquelme in Novio a la vista **(1953) by Luis García Berlanga.**

(Previous page)

Lucía Bosé and Alberto Closas in Muerte de un ciclista **(1955) by J. A. Bardem.**

other accords were signed with the United States. Fortunately, they were not agreed upon until after the film had been made, otherwise it might never have been produced.
In the small and imaginary Castilian town of Villar del Río the townsfolk are awaiting the arrival of the ambassadors of the Marshall Plan. Hoping to better win their favor, the locals dress up as Andalusians, even transforming the houses of their village into colorful Sevillian streets. Each of the peasants dreams of the gift that he will ask of the Yankees, but the Americans completely miss Villar del Río, leaving the inhabitants with their lost hopes and even poorer, because now they will have to pay the expense of dressing up the town. The **great star of Andalusian song,** who was played by Lolita Sevilla, became a mere character in the episode, a simple illustration.
It was logical that a director like Berlanga would not be interested in traditional folkloric cinema. He belonged to a group of film-makers, who, either with crudeness or tenderness, dealt with the true dimensions of the reality of the situation. When **Bienvenido, Mr. Marshall** received a special jury prize in the 1953 Cannes Film Festival, it represented an important event for Spanish cinema and meant recognition for its director. Years later, when Bardem was also awarded a prize in this French film festival for **Muerte de un ciclista** the importance of this new Spanish cinema could not be denied by the ministry, although this did not prevent it from carefully keeping watch over the scripts that were presented not only by these two film-makers, but also those of the other members of their generation.
Novio a la vista (Boyfriend in Sight; 1953), the next film by Berlanga, was manipulated by the censors in order to eliminate any reference to the military profession of its absurd characters. **Muerte de un ciclista** suffered a moralizing change of its ending. **El inquilino,** by José Antonio Nieves Conde, as has already been pointed out, also had its outcome transformed. What was worse, however, were the regular bannings of their scripts. All of these film-makers wrote screenplays that were never filmed.

The Salamanca Conversations

In light of this situation, the **Objetivo** magazine, which was outspoken in its defense of neorealism in the latest Spanish films and on whose editorial staff were Juan Antonio Bardem and Ricardo Muñoz Suay —who was to play a transcendental role not only in this but other important moments in Spanish cinema— convoked, along with the Film Society of the University of Salamanca, the so-called **National Conversations** on the future of Spanish cinema. The call to hold these talks was signed by Muñoz Suay who stated that «the problem of Spanish cinema is that it does not have any problems, that it does not bear witness to our time» and concluded with an optimistic, «Spanish cinema is dead. Long live Spanish cinema!».
Turning up in Salamanca were intellectuals and film-makers of different political leanings, from clandestine communists to card-carrying Falangists or liberal Catholics, such as the ex-Director General of Cinematography, José María García Escudero, who strongly supported the **Conversations,** since, all things considered, no other reforms would be proposed other than the ones he wanted to push through as head of cinematography —years later, when he would again occupy the same post, he would put into practice some of the formulae agreed upon in the **Salamanca Conversations.**
Juan Antonio Bardem synthesized in a now famous pentagram the situation of cinema:
«Spanish cinema is:
— politically ineffectual
— socially false
— intellectually the worst
— aesthetically nonexistent
— industrially weak.»
The conclusions reached after several days of conversations began by pointing out that it was necessary to make a cinema «that reflects the

situation of the Spaniard, his conflicts and the reality of the past and especially that in our own times». Also demanded was that «the state formulate and undertake a policy suitable with its principles», that «economic aid be given to a cinema of artistic quality or of national interest», that «inaccessible topics and questions be clearly defined and that there be sufficient room in order to give Spanish cinema the possibilities to deal with important topics».
Regarding this last question, the conclusions call for the need for censorship not to distinguish between national and foreign cinema, they request that moral censorship only be exerted by the teaching body of the Catholic Church —hoping that contacts with children would make for more tolerance— and they asked for the obligation that no official body later be given the option to change the report of the censors, which in itself indicated that such a practice existed.
The Conference's ideas regarding the necessary legal ordering of Spanish cinema, work contracts, coproductions, film journalism, the monopoly of the official state newsreel NO-DO, the granting of scholarships and the quality of the professors in the IIEC were still valid until very recently, and in some respects, they are still pertinent today.
The support that these **Conversations** gave to the incipient Spanish social cinema had its logical repercussions in university circles and among intellectuals and artists from different areas of Spanish culture. The success of some of these social pictures in film festivals also attracted the attention of a number of foreign film critics, thus increasing its possibilities of further existence. The Ministry of Information and Tourism, however, continued to put obstacles in the way of this cinema. When Berlanga tried to shoot a parody of religious devotion called **Los jueves, milagro** (Miracles Every Thursday; 1957), the implacable arm of censorship fell upon him. He was forced to change half the film according to a script that one of the censors, Father Garáu, helped him write.
Spanish cinema did not have long to wait. Absolutely none of the legal ordinances were changed and the timid requests made by delegates to the **Salamanca Conversations** just put on record how grave the situation of cinema in Spain really was.
Besides, it would not be long —only until February, 1957— before a reshuffle in the cabinet would take place in order to better repress the student protests (resulting from the creation of a united platform among all democratic forces, or the FUDE), to arrest the clandestine communists (once that party had given up its plan for a **national reconciliation**) and to better put down the strikes which sprang up in the Basque Country, Navarre, Catalonia and Madrid. That new resolve was already hardening during the **Salamanca Conversations.**

Sara Montiel

One event did superficially change the penury of Spanish cinema. It was the appearance of a new singing star called Sara Montiel in **El último cuplé** (The Last Song; 1957) by Juan de Orduña. She was a beautiful woman who had taken her first steps in the world of film during the forties —in the famous **Locura de amor** (Love Crazy; 1948), for example, she played the role of the perfidious Moorish princess— but hardly with any fortune. She emigrated to Mexico, and from there, to the United States, where she married the director Anthony Mann. She would soon divorce him and later return to work in Spanish cinema. During those years in Hollywood, however, Sara Montiel was to do important roles in several films— **Veracruz** (1954) by Robert Aldrich, **Dos pasiones y un amor;** (**Serenade;** 1955) by Antony Mann and **Yuma** (**Run of the Arrows;** 1957) by Samuel Fuller—and was to return to Spain with a certain popularity.
El último cuplé was an unpretentious film and even its own producers had little confidence in it. But surprisingly, it was a huge box office success, making

Sara Montiel the best known star in Spanish cinema, only comparable to the popularity of Imperio Argentina years before. The reason for the film's success was twofold. On the one hand, Sara Montiel did not specialize in Andalusian songs, but rather in old «cuplés», or music hall songs, which awakened a nostalgia in the adult audiences and which, in any case, broke the molds of Spanish **musical** cinema. On the other hand, the music hall songs she performed were about naughty love stories with ingenious double meanings which no modern-day song-writer could copy, giving Sara Montiel a kind of exhibitionism, a generous and brilliant eroticism which would make her the first woman of Spanish cinema with a sexual capacity. Even though this exhibition of her temptations was always punished, leading the character down the road to redemption —she could suffer an accident on the Titanic, see how a young man dies after she has hidden her past, die herself as the result of an attempt to defend the man she loves because he is the husband of her own daughter, end up going into a convent fleeing from the world, suffer from tuberculosis, etc.— Sara Montiel, with that ambivalent way of hers, would show that sex was possible.

None of the films that she starred in are worth any more attention. They coincide with movements or films made by other stars in under-developed countries. She was not a good actress and no better singer, but she stirred up the interest of different publics with that new erotic touch of hers if one looks back over those old melodramatic serials. Her films initiated a brief flurry of films with other singers of music hall songs. They tried to imitate her success, but they were not able to do so. Sara Montiel was really the exception. Only some of the Italian **maggloratas** could indirectly compete with her —Silvana Pampanini, Gina Lollobrigida or Sophia Loren. They were the only ones who could totally or only partially upset the sexual serenity of Spanish spectators. Briggite Bardot was forbidden.

Years later and at a time when she hardly had any work, Juan Antonio Bardem made a new version of **Cómicos** (Comedians; 1953), with Sara Montiel. **Cómicos** was the first film that Bardem had made alone after **Esa pareja feliz. Varietés** (1971), however, did not have the same fresh qualities as Bardem's original film about the poverty of postwar traveling actors, nor for that matter did it help Sara Montiel in the impossible task of developing her nonexistent acting talent. At any rate, this footnote is a way of showing that the myth of this star, born at the end of the fifties, was still alive until very recently.

At the same time as Montiel's first box office success in Spain, there arose another type of cinema which morally contrasted with her sensual offers, a cinema which only proposed a platonic relationship in any amorous adventure. This cycle in Spanish cinema showed the anguish of innocent young maidens who hoped to find the man of their life. The so-called **rose comedy**— which also had its first bit success, **Las chicas de la Cruz Roja** (The Red Cross Girls; 1958) by Rafael J. Salvia— is a phenomenon that has come down to our own days, searching in different social classes for the ideal settings to narrate the same sort of story. The smallest conflicts of couples in love could be found, as in the case of the above mentioned film, among taxi drivers, mechanics, football players or university students. **Muchachas de azul** (Blue Girls; 1957), by Pedro Lazaga, speaks of the flirtations of the girl employees of big department stores; **Historias de la feria** (Fair Stories; 1957), by Francisco Rovira Beleta, told of the comings and goings of a group of fairsmen and women; **Las aeroguapas** (The Aero-Cuties; 1957), by Eduardo Manzanos, situates the same story in the midst of air line stewardesses; **Quince bajo la lona** (Fifteen below the Canvas; 1958), by Agustín Navarro, does so in military barracks; **Luna de verano** (Summer Moon; 1958), by Pedro Lazaga, sought refuge for the same story in the summer courses offered to foreign university students; **Parque de Madrid**

(Madrid Park; 1959), by Enrique Cahen Salaberry, totally took place in the gardens of Madrid's Retiro park; **Ya tenemos coche** (We've Now Got a Car; 1959), by Julio Salvador, was based on the purchase of a first utility car; etc.

Independently of the success or failure of these films, various critics have decided to evaluate them in terms of their reflection of apparent changes in Spanish society. It is certain that the sequences of these films invariably contain parallel information about the new type of economic and social life that could be found in Spain. The optimism of its conclusions, however, does not hide the evidence of a kind of still latent squalor, because even though the **rose comedies** wanted to disassociate themselves from cinema previously made in Spain, they were still impregnated by their consequences. At the same time that these films **modernized** Spanish cinematography, there continued to exist at their side those pictures which prolonged the previously mentioned types of cinema.

Historical-sentimental cinema had a new success with **¿Dónde vas, Alfonso XII?** (Where Are You Going, Alfonso XII?; 1958), by Luis César Amadori; political cinema with **Rapsodia de sangre** (Rhapsody in Blood; 1957), by Antonio Isasi, where the 1956 repression in Hungary was tendentiously criticized; religious cinema with **Molokay** (1959),

Concha López Silva, José Luis López Vázquez and Mary Carrillo in *El pisito* **(1958) by Marco Ferreri and I. M. Ferry.**

97

by Luis Lucia, in which the biography of the life of Father Damián was given, a missionary who voluntarily worked among lepers; or folkloric cinema with **María de la O** (1957), by Ramón Torrado, which repeated the old success of Republican cinema. Nothing has substantially changed for the moment.

The tenderness of angry young people

Testimonial film, which the **Salamanca Conversations** had defended to the hilt, continued to exist, but with great difficulties. Even directors on the liberal right insisted on including a certain amount of reality in their films. José Antonio Nieves Conde attempted this in **El inquilino** (The Tenant; 1957) when he narrates the difficulties of finding a worthy flat. The censors, however, force him to reshoot the end of the film, so that the married couple finds a flat subsidized by the state.
Francisco Rovira Beleta, an estimable yet contradictory director, made a similar attempt in **Hay un camino a la derecha** (There's a Road on the Right; 1953), a melodrama which is set in the port of Barcelona. The same was tried by Luis Escobar in **La honradez de la cerradura** (The Integrity of a Lock; 1950), Julio Coll in **Distrito quinto** (Fifth District; 1957) and **Un vaso de whisky** (A Glass of Whisky; 1958), and even

Nino Manfredi and Angel Alvarez in El verdugo **(1964) by Luis García Berlanga.**

(Previous page)

José Luis López Vázquez, José Isbert and José Alvarez «Lepe» in El cochecito **(1960) by Marco Ferreri.**

by the actress Ana Mariscal in **Segundo López** (1952) in her second film as a director when she showed Madrid's shanty towns.
At any rate, it was with the appearance of **El pisito** (The Little Flat; 1958), which was the first film directed by the Italian Marco Ferreri and which dealt with the problem of finding a dwelling, when critical cinema in Spain reached a new level, leaving behind a more mannered approach in order to achieve a black humor. This type of cinema would result in the best films made by Berlanga and directly or indirectly, numerous other directors would try their luck in this genre with greater or lesser success.
El pisito tells of a young couple who are in love, but who put off their wedding until they can find a flat where they can live. The man marries an old woman who owns an apartment so that when she dies he can marry his young fiancé. However, the old woman, who is very enthusiastic about her young husband, never dies. This rather **black** view of Spanish life and its traditional problem of finding a place to live and which was dealt with by Berlanga in his masterwork. **El verdugo** (The Executioner; 1963), was again retold by Ferreri in **El cochecito** (The Little Car; 1960). The film shows the misery and solitude of old people when it narrates the story of one of them, a person who likes to go to the countryside with his disabled friends

Los golfos (**1959**) **by Carlos Saura.**

in an old jalopy.
The biting humor of this film was initiated with the screenwriter, Rafael Azcona, who since then, has worked with Marco Ferreri in many of his films, and who has worked with Luis García Berlanga ever since he was called on to write the script for **Plácido** (1961). Azcona laughed at everything around him, probing into the reasons that so much cultural poverty existed and revealing the Third World character of a large part of the Spanish institutions. Disrespectful and corrosive, he was able to infect all the directors with whom he worked with that acid tone, that dispairing and comic way in which he sees life.
Another important film, **Los golfos** (The Scoundrels; 1959), the first of those directed by Carlos Saura, also contained black humor, although it would be years later when Saura also worked with Rafael Azcona in some of his best scripts such as **El jardín de las delicias** (The Garden of Delights; 1970) and **La prima Angélica** (Cousin Angélica; 1973) that he laterally connected with that point of view.
In **Los golfos,** Saura studied the validity of neorealism, making a kind of dramaticized documentary about other **olvidados** (forgotten ones), about other **vitelloni,** but without the sweetening aspects of the Italian genre. In France, the **nouvelle vague** was in its early stages, and even though this movement was unknown in Spain, it is

undeniable that a similar need for change was springing up in every country, but with different names. **Los golfos** officially represented Spain in the 1960 Cannes Film Festival, although at the same time the Ministry of Information and Tourism gave it a negative classification of 2 B, which prevented it from recovering the economic investment that had been made and which kept the film from being premiered in acceptable conditions. The censors also mutilated about ten minutes of **Los golfos** which left it incomplete in some of its basic aspects. **El pisito** encountered the same fate, a fact that clearly shows the closed ideas of a regime that gave very bad classifications to two of the best Spanish films of the decade.

«Viridiana»

The 1960 Cannes Film Festival was also an historic occasion since it brought together Spanish film-makers and Luis Buñuel, whose basic work was unknown in the cinema of his own country. Carlos Saura and Luis Buñuel began a cordial friendship which eventually led to the possibility of the exiled film-maker returning to Spain in order to shoot a film. Buñuel had not made a film involving Spain since 1932, when he shot **Las Hurdes (Tierra sin pan)** (Las Hurdes —Land without Bread).

Buñuel accepted the offer and wrote the screenplay for **Viridiana** (1961), with the blessings of the Ministry of Information and Tourism which saw the film as an opportunity to foment its policy of creating a good image abroad. The screenplay was received with amiability, although substantial reforms were demanded: the outcome planned by Buñuel in which the former novice, Viridiana (Silvia Pinal), was transformed into the lover of her cousin (Francisco Rabal), had to be changed. Buñuel then thought up a new final sequence —Viridiana playing cards with her cousin and his mistress. His first intentions were extended and enriched, representing a delightful contradiction involving the censors who prefered a **menage a trois** to a more orthodox relationship.
Produced by UNINCI, the company which had contributed to making some of the best Spanish cinema of those years and which was directed by Juan Antonio Bardem and Ricardo Muñoz Suay, among others, the film was selected to participate in the 1961 Cannes Film Festival.
For the first time in the history of Spanish cinema, **Viridiana** received the Golden Palm, which was personally picked up on stage by the Director General of Cinematography and Theater, José Muñoz Fontán, bestowing on the award his official benedictions. The tragedy began the day afterwards when the Vatican newspaper, **L'Osservatore Romano** published a criticism of the film accusing it of blasphemy and of being anti-Christian, undoubtedly a very serious situation for a government such as that of Spain which professed to the Catholic faith. General Franco decided to depose Muñoz Fontán from his ministerial post and ban **Viridiana** not only from public exhibition, but prohibited the name from ever being pronounced in public. The official documentation regarding its production even disappeared. Fortunately, the film had been coproduced with Mexico and a negative had been deposited in Paris in order to conclude the editing process by dates required by the Cannes Festival. From that time on, **Viridiana** was seen throughout the world as a Mexican film, but it was not premiered in Spain until seventeen years later, after General Franco had died, significantly on the very day on which the communist party was legalized. The troubles springing from the **Viridiana** scandal perhaps affected the health of the Minister of Information and Tourism, Gabriel Arias Salgado, who died a short time afterwards from a heart attack. But this did not affect the decision to close the UNINCI company. Many of its projects remained locked in the desks of the film-makers who had recently graduated from the Cinema Research and Experiences Institute. It was a logical ending for a difficult decade.

1 9 6 2

1 9 6 7

The shooting of Los farsantes **(1963) by Mario Camus.**

1962 1967

César Santos Fontela

The quinquennium, or rather, the six year period from 1962 to 1967 is one of the best defined in the recent history of Spanish cinema. It is a period which opens and closes when José María García Escudero takes over and leaves the office of Director General of Cinematography. It is a period marked by the birth, the growth and practically the death of **Nuevo Cine Español** (New Spanish Cinema), by the increasing importance of the **Escuela Oficial de Cine** (Official Film School), closely linked to that new movement, and by the new censorship and protectionist norms which came to light during those years.

Ever since Spain joined the United Nations in 1955, a more or less clearly expressed idea was formed that the regime should give at least an appearance of liberalism, even in the economic field, so that it could seem like the European democracies. The 1957 change of government resulted in the **technocrat** cabinet, in which twelve of the eighteen ministerial portfolios were given to other politicians. Also observed was the rising influence of the members of **Opus Dei,** a political-religious association, which would definitively make its power felt in the following cabinet reshuffle of 1962. This is when things began to change. Regarding the film industry and the Ministry on which it directly depended, or the Ministry of Information and Tourism —currently called Culture, no great change was noted. Arias Salgado is one of the six ministers who continues in his post. Even in 1961, when the **affaire Viridiana** broke out as the result of the Cannes Film Festival and when many thought that the minister's ten year stay in office would end, the whole affair was resolved by the dismissal of the Director General of Cinematography, Muñoz Fontán. It was only in 1962, after eleven years in office, when Arias Salgado steps down to make way for Fraga Iribarne currently —1984— the chief of the opposition in Spanish parliament to the socialist government and at that time a man who came from a university atmosphere, where he was a full Professor of Political Law. Only a few days after his appointment, Fraga named García Escudero as Director General of Cinematography, a post he had held for a few months about ten years before. García Escudero's appointment is received with joy in all the sectors of the Spanish film industry, especially in the most advanced areas. The new Director General of Cinematography had participated in the Salamanca Conversations of 1955, the conclusions of which continued to be valid seven years later, or at least, it seemed that way. He was not of an opposition by any means. But apart from his faithfulness to the regime headed by General Franco, his membership in the army and his belief in the guiding light of the second Vatican Council, he is a man with liberal ideas and a good will that has rarely been put in question. He is essential in understanding part, if not all of the period we are now going to study since his decisions were the basis for everything that happened. In other words, the history of these years is made **from up above** and as a consequence, certain political sectors have refused to see anything of interest in the period for the mere fact that Spanish cinema was guided from seats of power. Although this may be deniable, what really existed during the years of García Escudero was a double game in which both sides that played were to a greater or lesser extent conscientious and responsible when it came to the rules. That is, while the authorities played the card of liberalism for the outside world to see and while they gave fewer liberties than promised, the different sectors inside the profession took advantage of the more favorable circumstances to make a freer cinema, less dependent on commercial interests in order to produce as far as possible more personal pictures. They were times of what might be described as **possibilism,** or the activity which meant taking the greatest possible advantage of every chance at freedom given by the **apertura** (a political opening up). It meant more promises than anything else for the professionals in the film business, while for the authorities, it meant giving as little as possible so as to win over to their side people who until then had been in the opposition. In summary, no one was fooling anyone else, although it was pretended that the opposite was true. The fact is that coupled with its virtues, defects and inadequacies, Spanish cinema lived during those years a time which we might consider of excessive optimism and elation. The films of the period were worthy of interest, and the results were moderately postive.

It was obvious that the films made for the domestic market did not have outlets abroad, either on commercial circuits or in film festivals. García Escudero, who had denounced the problems of Spanish cinema in a **Historia de cien palabras** (History of a Hundred Words), which ranged from cinema's beginnings to the year 1954, would write twelve years later, a **Nueva historia** (New History), which would say the following: «The figures say, not I, what Spanish cinema is today. Those two names in 1954 —Bardem and Berlanga— have increased to become a legion of young directors. These film-makers have represented us in international festivals and are producing an ambitious cinema which is no longer an adventure, but a serious possibility. At the same time, a radical reform of the system of protection for another, founded on the returns of the pictures themselves, will produce a cinema for the public and will create strong production companies, capable of venturing out on foreign markets. The true battle of Spanish cinema will be fought by them, but at least for the first time we are preparing to win it.» Later, in an article by the magazine **Film Ideal,** in which this **Nueva historia** was published, García Escudero himself would develop his ideas point by point, line by line. If his arguments were not always irrefutable, one could say they were totally sound. But the time has come to deal with the matter in stages, beginning with what was happening in the **Escuela Oficial de Cine** (Official Film School), which at the time when García Escudero took over office of Director General of Cinematography was still called the **Cinema Research and Experiences Institute.**

The Official Film School

Created in 1947 and little less than dependent on the **School of Industrial Engineers** since it was headquartered in its faculty building, the **Cinema Research and Experiences Institute** became known as the **Escuela Oficial de Cine** (Official Film School) after 1962. It had its moment of splendour —designed to promote Spanish cinema abroad— when in 1960 its director at that time, José Luis Sáenz de Heredia —the director of the film **Raza** (Race; 1941) with a screenplay by Francisco Franco, decided to open the academic year with a public ceremony in the **Palacio de la Música,** one of the most prestigious cinemas in Madrid, exhibiting the pictures which had been made by students who had graduated in previous classes at the school. It should be said in all fairness that the impression caused by the films, and especially, **Habitación de alquiler** (Room for Rent; 1960), by Miguel Picazo, was excellent. The following year, when the same pictures were presented in the **First Film School Colloquies,** held in the San Sebastian Film Festival, the Spanish films had nothing to envy of those made in other film schools. A kind of halo was created around the Official Film School which was not totally unjustified since during those years the students who studied and taught in its classrooms would form the pillars of what would later be the best Spanish cinema. In spite of a lack of proper teaching materials and not the best of curriculums, certain interesting exercises were carried out that sometimes produced surprising results. Today, they may seem somewhat old because of their subject matter and even because of style, but they still have an undeniable quality as final products. It was logical then, that in their plans to rennovate Spanish cinema, García Escudero and his team included the school. They gave it greater support, although sometimes they played up its possibilities in excess of what it really offered. One of the first concerns of the new Director General of Cinematography would be to provide what was then the **Institute** with new installations, and from a legislative point of view. to grant the graduates, or rather, the producers who made films with them, new privileges such as the concession of the **Special Interest** category to their films so that they would be elegible for state aid. But this will be spoken of later. Two years after having been appointed Director General of Cinematography and in statements made inaugurating the 1964-1965 course of studies, García Escudero took stock of what had been done by the students of the school ever since his appointment. He said that while in the first thirteen classes of the school only four directors which had graduated as such joined the profession, in the last two classes twelve did so. What is undoubtedly certain is that not all of these new directors were from the last two classes, but this is not excessively important either. What is important is that the graduates were finding greater opportunities to enter into the world of commercial cinema, even though difficulties still existed. Even so, this cause for optimism will not last for long, since at the conclusion of García Escudero's mandate at the end of 1967, the school would begin to fall apart, and not long afterwards, it would disappear altogether. It would be replaced, if one could say that, by the «image» or cinema area of study in the **Faculty of Informational Sciences,** which had recently been created. Ending our study of the Official Film School, it should be pointed out that there existed the areas of Direction, Production, Screenwriting, Acting and Sound and that some of the more interesting of Spain's directors who studied there included Luis García Berlanga, Bardem—although he never graduated, José Luis Borau, Carlos Saura and Gutiérrez Aragón.

Bardem and Berlanga

Before beginning to study the new directors who would make up the members of the **New Spanish Cinema,** one should ask what happened to the most important —if not the only— representatives of Spanish cinema until that time (although we do not include Buñuel whose activities were interrupted in Spain after **Viridiana** was made in 1961). For Bardem, this period is not precisely the easiest or the most glorious. In 1962 he went to Argentina to shoot **Los inocentes** (The Innocents), a film that the Spanish censors did not authorize for Spain, although on his return from Latin

America, he does make, under the new censorship norms, **Nunca pasa nada** (Nothing Ever Happens; 1963). **Los inocentes** is not one of the best films by this director, due in part to the fact that he had to transfer its action to a distant and different country.
Regarding **Nunca pasa nada,** which was well-received in the Mostra of Venice, it represents a return to the provincialism and the style of **Calle Mayor** (Main Street; 1956), which was unquestionably his best film. **Nunca pasa nada** was hailed by many as a recovery, while others described it as hardly being original. He had better luck with **Los pianos mecánicos** (Player Pianos; 1965), an adaptation of the novel by the Frenchman Henri-Francois Rey and a film that was shot in coproduction with France, starring such international figures as Melina Mercouri, James Mason and Hardy Kruger. The incidents which interrupted the shooting on more than one occasion did not help the final result, although the picture was a solid commercial success, at least in Spain, due in part to its **daring** subject matter. Bardem would not make another film in the period we are now studying.
Berlanga had better luck, although like Bardem, he had to emigrate to Argentina in order to shoot one of his films called **La boutique** (1967), precisely at the end of García Escudero's stay in office which only goes to show that the political

Manuel Alexandre, José Calvo, José Suárez, Luis Peña and Alfonso Godá in Calle Mayor **(1956) by J. A. Bardem.**

Julia Gutiérrez Caba and Jean-Pierre Cassel in *Nunca pasa nada* (1963) by J. A. Bardem.

opening up of the censorship norms were not as great as had been said, a fact which Berlanga had found out in his previous film, **El verdugo** (The Executioner; 1963), which not only suffered considerable cuts by the censors —even more significant if the length of the film is taken into consideration, but was also little less than a diplomatic incident during the holding of the Mostra of Venice. **El verdugo** is undoubtedly one of the best pictures by this director. In a screenplay that Berlanga wrote with Azcona, a man with whom he regularly worked ever since the picture **Plácido** (1961), he constructs a cruel farce involving the death sentence when the story is told of a poor and unemployed man, who, after marrying the daughter of an executioner, finds that he is about to follow in the footsteps of his father-in-law. Nino Manfredi did an excellent job in the main role of the film, while Emma Pennella and José Isbert did splendid supporting performances. There was also a very good cast of secondary actors and actresses which this director has always known how to choose and to work with so well. Before **El verdugo** and during the same period, Berlanga had shot **La muerte y el leñador** (Death and the Woodcutter) as one of the episodes which formed part of the collective film **Las cuatro verdades** (The Four Truths; 1962), which was made in coproduction with several countries

Elvira Quintillá and Casen in *Placido* (1961) by Luis García Berlanga.

and in which its star, Hardy Kruger, failed to do a good job, or to be more exact, the German actor failed in his attempt to physically portray his character. With respect to **La boutique,** the film that was shot in Argentina, the same thing happened to Berlanga as to Bardem when he transferred the action of the picture to another country and tried to use actors who were not the best for the roles. The result was a hybrid product, not excessively stimulating.

Coproductions

Coproductions were a particular concern during this period. Begun in the previous decade, the phenomenon increased to what can be considered excessive limits, especially since the majority of these pictures were inferior products which only hoped to take advantage of the protectionist measures of two or more countries. Frequently, Spanish participation in these films was reduced to providing sun, landscapes and a more or less **distinguished** group of extras and actors for one-liners. This was the case of the numerous spaghetti westerns that were preferably shot in Almería, where stunt teams were created and where mock-up towns of the American far west were used time and time again. In other cases, supposedly Spanish films were made under the pretext of producing a more saleable product on international markets, since a more easily recognizeable fare had less chances of success. But these **disguised** pictures —that were not truly international in scope— were very impersonal and were unrecognizable as a national product. These years also saw the rise and fall of the Bronston Empire. The American producer who shot a film in Spain called **El capitán Jones** (John Paul Jones; 1959), by John Farrow and with less than a minimum participation of Spanish actors and technicians, would later make such films as **Rey de Reyes** (King of Kings; 1961) by Nicholas Ray and **El Cid** (The Cid; 1961) by director Anthony Mann. When García Escudero became Director General of Cinematography, Bronston became very important on the Spanish film scene taking over the only studios in relatively good condition and making in Spain films in which local participation was little less than symbolic such as **55 días en Pekin** (55 Days in Peking; 1962), directed by Nicolas Ray and **La caída del Imperio Romano** (The Fall of the Roman Empire; 1963), by Anthony Mann. This last film would almost become prophetic as a title, since it marked the beginning of **the fall of the Bronston Empire.** The end would definitively come with **El fabuloso mundo del Circo** (The Great Circus; 1964), which was both an artistic and financial failure in spite of its spectacular scenes and a cast headed by John Wayne, Rita Hayworth and Claudia Cardinale, under the direction of Henry Hathaway. Following this film, the studios and sets which had been constructed by Bronston crumbled, just like his empire. The result of the venture is a fabulous debt which possibly still has not been paid. On the other hand, Bronston was awarded the Cross of Isabella the Catholic Queen, one of the highest decorations that can by given by the Spanish government, and he in turn, as a way of saying thank you for the **laissez faire** situation which he had enjoyed, made two political propaganda documentaries, one of which was **El valle de la paz** (The Valley of Peace; 1961), which had the Valley of the Fallen civil war monument outside Madrid as a topic and Andrew Marton as director. But the **Bronston case,** even though the most spectacular and representative, was not by any means the only one. More or less real coproductions with more or less minority Spanish participation reached figures during the 1962-67 period that surpassed totally Spanish productions. In 1966, there were 97 coproductions made for the 67 totally Spanish films made, while the figure was 70 to 55 in 1967. The situation led to an impoverishment of Spanish cinema and to a sale at a low price of its talents —even though at prices that were above those that local cinema was prepared to pay, collaborating with the **enemy** in its own territory.

The new censorship.

Before we analyze the **New Spanish Cinema,** let us take a look at the new norms of censorship which in part make these films possible, or at least viable. It should be pointed out that such norms mainly benefited foreign film, since one of its first results was to lift a ban on titles which of course were already ready to be released. Meanwhile, Spanish films had to keep on passing through the previous censorship of scripts and later through that of the completed film, meaning that they arrived late and in unfavorable circumstances to compete with the so-called **frozen** product, if it can be given a name. It should also be pointed out that not only the modest but grotesque liberties which these norms instituted, by presuming that everything was allowed which was not prohibited, at the time were well-received —at least in the beginning and in principle— by all sectors, including the professionals in the industry and the most politically advanced circles in Spain. They were **something** in view of the previous **nothing.** At least they constituted an attempt at codification, although in reality they oscillated between casuistical and vague generalities, perfect for the censors to interpret as they liked. It would be best to lay out here the text of these norms, even though it will not be the complete

text, so as to better understand the cinema which developed as a result. The following was said:
«1. Each film will be judged not only by its shots and individual scenes, but also as a whole in terms of the totality of its content and according to the characteristics of the different cinematographic genres and styles. If a film in its entirety is considered seriously dangerous, it will be banned before (final) authorization until alterations and supressions are made that substantially modify it.
»2. Evil can be represented as a simple fact or as the element of a dramatic conflict, but never as justifiable or attractive, nor for that matter in such a way as to awaken sympathy or a desire to imitate it.
»3. The representation of circumstances which can humanly explain a morally reproachable conduct will be done so in such a way so as not to seem objectively justified to the spectator.
»4. The film must logically lead to a condemnation of evil, considering it at least as an attempt against the principles of a natural moral, but it is not necessary that this condemnation be explicitly shown on the screen if there are sufficient elements to believe that it takes place in the conscience of the spectator.
»5. The condemnation of evil is not always sufficiently assured with a disapprobation in the last shots (of a film) or in an accidental or marginal way; nor does it necessarily require the repentance of the evil-doer nor his human or external failure. It is advisable that evil is offset by good during the development of the plot.
»6. There is no reason to ban the presentation of individual or social blights, nor for that matter to avoid unrest in the spectator by showing the degradation or suffering of others, if it is done obeying the principles of an honorable criticism and does not go against what is established in these norms.
»7. There is no reason to prohibit a film which limits itself to showing true problems, even though not providing a complete solution, but it should be done in such a way as not to prejudge an inacceptable conclusion according to these norms.»
Along with these **general norms,** there followed those **of application,** which are really a series of prohibitions casuistically listed, such as the following:
«I. Prohibited will be:
»1. The justification of suicide.
»2. The justification of homicide resulting from compassion.
»3. The justification of revenge and duels. Their representation will not be excluded as simple events in relation with social customs of certain periods (in the past) or places, provided that an objective or general justification is avoided.
»4. The justification of divorce as an institution, adultery, illicit sexual relations, prostitution, or in general, everything that offends the familiar institution or the family.
»5. The justification of abortion or of contraceptive measures.
»II. Prohibited will be:
»1. The presentation of sexual perversions as the central part of the plot and even with a secondary character, except if in this last case it is required in order to develop the action and has a clear and predominant moral consequence.
»2. The representation of drug addiction or alcoholism in a plainly inductive fashion.
»3. The presentation of crime in such a way that, due to its excessively detailed character, constitutes the spreading of criminal means and procedures.
»III. Prohibited will be those images and scenes which could provoke base passions in the normal spectator and the allusions made in such a way as to be more suggestive than the presentation of the fact.
»IV. Respected will be the intimacy of conjugal love, prohibiting images and scenes which offend it.
»V. Prohibited will be images and scenes of brutality and cruelty towards people and animals, and those of terror presented in a morbose or unjustified way in relation to the characteristics of the plot or of the

corresponding cinematographic genre, and, in general, those which offend the dignity of a person.
»IX. Prohibited will be the colloquial expressions in scenes or shots of an intimate nature which would offend the most elemental norms of good taste.
»VII. Prohibited will be:
»1. The disrespectful representation of religious beliefs and practices.
»2. The disparaging and outrageous presentation of political ideologies and everything that offends in any way the institutions and ceremonies that require honorable and respectful treatment. Regarding the representation of the characters, it must be made sufficiently clear to the spectators the distinction between the conduct of the characters and what they represent.
»3. The tendentious falsifying of facts, people and historical settings.
»VIII. Prohibited will be those pictures which advocate hatred between peoples, races or social classes and which defend as a general principle division and clashes between men in a moral and social order.
»XI. Prohibited will be anything that offends:
»1. The Catholic Church, its dogma, its moral and its cult.
»2. The fundamental principles of the state, national dignity and the country's domestic or foreign security.
»3. The person of the Chief of State.
»X. When the accumulation of scenes or shots, which in themselves are not grave, creates due to reiteration a lascivious, brutal, crude or morbid atmosphere, the picture will be prohibited.
»XI. When the pictures will be exclusively exhibited before minority publics, the aforementioned norms will be given a wider interpretation in accordance with the degree of these audiences' presumable preparation. Blasphemous, pornographic and subversive pictures will be prohibited for all publics.»
As one can see, carefully reading the above text with a minimally restrictive interpretation, everything, absolutely everything could be prohibited under the norms considered politically more openhanded. The norms give a wide scope of subjective action to the censors, leaving in their hands something that is as undefinable as the criteria of **good taste.** After all these years, it is little less than shocking that in 1963 these norms could have been received with joy, and little less than miraculous that under them, one could speak of a liberty of expression for new film-makers. A liberty that supposedly would allow these directors to do what they would **not have been allowed to say** before. Although it would have been difficult to say any great things with these new norms either! This is what happened, although it would not take many long to find out the trap into which they had fallen. Upon admitting a series of prohibitions, even casuistically listed, they were accepting the very act of being able to prohibit. Even so, it must be acknowledged that in many cases, **possibilism** was played on both sides, giving the norms a relatively wider interpretation, otherwise, it would have been a definitive bolted door to any attempt at liberalization.

The new protection

Regarding the innovations in the cinema protection system established by the state, apart from increasing the exhibition quota from one Spanish day of Spanish film for every four days of foreign, to a one-to-three ratio, an automatic protection system was established whereby each film would receive fifteen percent of its gross box office take during the six first years of exhibition. Also, an imperfect, but necessary box office control system was established.
What would really benefit the **New Spanish Cinema** are the ordinances that would create the qualification of **Special Interest** that the **Film Appraisal and Censorship Board** —the successor of the previous **Qualification Board**— will grant bearing in mind the eventual «guarantees of quality... relevant moral, social, educational or political values», and, in any case that «help the incorporation into a professional career

of the graduates of the Official Film School». This qualification would carry with it an advance in money —a million pesetas at that time— towards the general subsidy of fifteen percent, although this advance could be raised to a maximum of fifty percent of the estimated cost of the film, but in no case could it exceed five million pesetas. In addition to this, the General Directorate of Cinematography made itself a jointly liable guarantor of the medium-term loans that were granted by the **Banco de Crédito Industrial,** up to a total of one million pesetas. And finally, there was one last subsidy that included not excessively clear percentages which corresponds to films of an international interest and which are successively presented in film festivals.
All of these measures will logically open the doors to a type of film-making which is not the commercial kind that had been predominantly made until then. These films, at least in theory, had export potential. At least they could be presented in international film festivals along with the works that the still prestigious Bardem and Berlanga practically were sending systematically.

New Spanish cinema, year by year

Now is the moment after studying the birth and development of the period in which García Escudero was Director General of Cinematography to look at the very essence of the **New Spanish Cinema,** a cinema that distinguishes and was the consequence of these years. For many, neither a stylistic nor a generational unity can be seen in this cinema. If the former is to a certain extent true —although not in an absolute sense, the latter is less so. In fact, the immense majority of the directors that make up the **New Spanish Cinema** have lived independently of each other from the exact date of its birth. In the classrooms of the **Official Film School** they have seen —or refused to see— the same pictures, and have read —or refused to read— the same books. One can then speak of a generation. With regard to style, if one cannot speak of a unity in the strict sense of the word, one can speak **roughly** of a style that oscillates between the neorealistic formulae to the newest discoveries such as the French **nouvelle vague,** while the subject matter, more than being attributed to a social realism, can be ascribed to a critical realism, but always within the limitations set by the norms which were mentioned above. In summary, one can speak of a realistic cinema, but anchored in an intimist lake, since epic cinema was inconceivable in the circumstances in which Spain of that time was living, being driven to despair more than despairing, and as a result, passably pessimistic. This definition, of course, is not applicable to each and every one of the pictures of the movement in question —if one can speak of a movement although I believe this to be the case, but at any rate, each one of the films included in the movement have at least two or three of the characteristics mentioned.
Regarding the exact time when **New Spanish Cinema** began, it can be said that its characteristics appeared before the time of its **official** birth with the first feature-length and fictional film by Carlos Saura called **Los golfos** (The Scoundrels; 1959), a chronicle of uprooted young people which had more to do with the novels of that time, especially with **El Jarama,** by Sánchez Ferlosio, than with the later films of Saura —with the exception of the recent **Deprisa, deprisa** (Hurry, Hurry; 1980). **Los golfos** would establish the foundations of what would later come. Some people, however, have cited **Surcos** (Furrows; 1951) as the precedent for **New Spanish Cinema,** the first clear example of the neorealistic influence in Spanish cinema. In any case, it would be excessive to say this. Due to generational reasons, it would be more logical to point to Saura's film, which, successfully presented in the Cannes Film Festival, would only be premiered in Spain two years later and even so, missing parts that were cut out by the censors. In 1962, when García Escudero took over his post, we find

Félix Fernández, Angel Alvarez, Agustín González, Xan-das-Bolas, Juanjo Menéndez and José Orjas in Cuando estalló la paz (Los que no fuimos a la guerra; **1962**) **by Julio Diamante.**

two films that one way or another could be attributed to the movement: **Los que no fuimos a la guerra** (Those of Us Who Didn't Go to War) by Julio Diamante, previously called **Cuando estalló la paz** (When Peace Broke Out), but changed by the censors, and **Noche de verano** (Summer Night) by Jorge Grau, a picture in which the later famous Elías Querejeta was first to work in production. Neither of the two films can be openly included in the concept of **New Spanish Cinema.** The picture by Diamante was the adaptation of a story by Wenceslao Fernández Flórez, a humorist whose works have often been converted into films. The action of the picture would take place in the immediate past and was done as a farce with the screenplay by Diamante himself. The second film, whose screenplay was also partially written by its director, was a work marked more by the influence of Italian cinema, a fact that is totally logical if it is born in mind that Grau had been educated in the **Centro Sperimentale di Cinematografia** in Rome, and particularly influenced by Antonioni. More than a film dealing with customs or manners, it is a moral chronicle with characters coming from the different social classes of Barcelona and who celebrate the **night of Saint John.** The film is well put together and the direction of the actors—outstanding among with are María Cuadra and Francisco Rabal— is much

better than what was then normal in Spanish cinema. On the other hand, the very philosophy of the picture can be put in question. But this is something which normally occurs in Grau's films and does nothing to lessen their interest.
It is in 1963 when the effects of the new film policies are really noticed, even before the appearance of the new censorship norms, and of course before the ordinances are approved that will change the face of official protectionism. At least eight directors, practically all from the **Official Film School,** made their first films that year, and one of them, Mario Camus, immediately makes his second in 1963 as well. Beginning then with Mario Camus, we can say that his case is not only atypical for having made two films in the same year, but because both of these pictures were produced by Ignacio F. Iquino, a man who never stood out for his intellectual interests and who played, like the good businessman he is, the card of the **new cinema,** although he would rapidly leave the game. Camus' two films were **Los farsantes** (The Actors) and **Young Sánchez.** The first picture, which reached the Spanish public after numerous changes and cuts, is the more interesting of the two works. It tells of the comings and goings of a travelling theater company during the days of forced inactivity during Holy Week, a period during which at that time all public spectacles and performances were forbidden.
Presumably shot with modest means, the film had a particular strength and was at times distressing. A noteworthy performance was done by Margarita Lozano, then a young actress who would later do several leading roles in Italy. Regarding **Young Sánchez** it was an adaption by Ignacio Aldecoa, a writer which Camus admired a great deal and who was a personal friend until his death. The picture is set in the world of amateur boxing. **Young Sánchez** was an unusually strong film for the time, and perhaps for this reason, did not receive the success it deserved. Julián Mateos did a good job in the leading role. The photography of Víctor Monreal is excellent in the black-and-white contrasts.
Following **Los golfos,** Saura changes his outlook. **Llanto por un bandido** (Lament for a Bandit; 1963) is a super-production with an international billing including Francisco Rabal, Lea Massari and Lino Ventura. It is shot in color and a lot of money was put into the film, although not as much as had been thought —or promised— initially. It is the story of highwaymen of the last century, but treated as a Spanish western. The film, which was not too well received at the time, has its points of interest. One of these points is the treatment given the story which developed from a screenplay written

Margarita Lozano in *Los farsantes* **(1963) by Mario Camus.**

Lea Massari and Francisco Rabal in Llanto por un bandido **(1963) by Carlos Saura.**

by Saura and Mario Camus. Far from being a commonplace plot, it was very much based on popular tradition. There are very beautiful moments in the film, both intimist and violent. The picture also offered a superb photography by Juan Julio Baena who knew how to show the grandiose qualities of the natural settings.

Other films of the same type, although not in chronological, or, of course, in order of their importance, were the following:

Del rosa al amarillo (From Rose to Yellow; 1963), by Manuel Summers, is divided into two parts. The first shows us a pre-adolescent, almost child-like love, while the second tells of another between an old man and a woman who both reside in an asylum. Before entering the world of film, Summers was, and still is, a well-known graphic humorist. As his exercise in the Official Film School, he was one of the few students who elected humor as a medium. In his first film, which was both an enormous critical and financial success, he presented his characters from a tragi-comic point of view, specially in the second part of his film. He wonderfully directs non-professional actors and actresses, at least then, since the leads in the first episode would continue making films. His first film was among the two or three best that he ever made. He is one of the few members of the **New Spanish Cinema** with a large number of

Pedro Díaz del Corral and Cristina Galbó
in Del rosa al amarillo (1963)
by Manuel Summers.

films to his credit, continuously making them over a long period of time. In order to do so, however, he has often had to make weighty commercial concessions.

Another interesting first film in 1963 is **El buen amor** (Good Love), by Francisco Regueiro, another humorist —although in this case both graphic and literary— who entered into film. The film tells of an **escapade** that two young students make to Toledo. The students are played by Simón Andreu and Marta del Val. When coming into contact with the old stones of the Imperial City and in view of the sensation of freedom which their trip gives them alone and far from home, they take a new look at their love and their situation. The picture makes excellent observations at times, has an atypical note of humor and is well performed by the two stars. Even though he has had his ups and downs, Regueiro has enjoyed a continuous career, alternating his work in cinema with that in television. Some of his most important works have been the relatively recent films called **Duerme, duerme, mi amor** (Sleep, Sleep, My Love; 1974) and **Las bodas de Blanca** (Blanca's Weddings; 1975).

Anton Eceiza, who began co-directing a couple of documentaries with Querejeta and producing along with him some of his first films, began as a feature-length director with **El próximo otoño** (Next Autumn; 1963), after having done work as a critic in **Nuestro**

Simón Andreu and Marta del Val in *El buen amor* (1963) by Francisco Regueiro.

Cine. The film is perhaps excessively **programmatic,** adapting itself too much to the eventual need of the times, focusing as a result, on what we could call **thesis cinema.** Eceiza would direct three more films in Spain and would later do two more in Mexico, although they have never reached Europe.

The case of Juan G. Atienza is a curious one. A prestigious screenwriter, he made **Los dinamiteros** (The Dynamiters; 1963), a delightful story starring the more than veteran Sara García, José Isbert and Carlo Pisacane. It was not badly received either by the critics or the public, but it seems he voluntarily left the world of feature films to dedicate himself to documentaries, especially to shorts relating to occultism, science fiction and parapsychology.

The same thing happened with Jesús Fernández Santos, although he went on to dedicate himself to literature basically. One of the best Spanish novelists, he only made one film called **Llegar a más** (Succeeding in Life; 1963), starring Manuel San Francisco and María José Alfonso. The story is about a young couple who want to climb out of the situation of mediocrity in which they live, but they are unsuccessful. In wanting to justly show mediocrity, the film falls into the same trap. Even though its good intentions were, and still are, undeniable, the film leaves a great deal to be desired.

Another first film was **Nuevas amistades**

(New Friendships; 1963), by Ramón Comás. It was an **illustration** more than an **adaptation** of the novel by Juan García Hortelano which was just a **scandalous** success. The film was about an obscure story of a clandestine abortion in the midst of well-to-do and carefree young people. Excessively faithful to the estimable literary original, the film was hardly personal at all. Not only that, but the limitations the censors imposed on the film over the novel, deprived it of the **attraction** of that which is forbidden. Many of the actors and actresses who appeared in the film disappeared from Spain's film panorama shortly afterwards and even though their collective performance was not brilliant, it was adequate.
Regarding **Se necesita chico** (Boy Wanted; 1963), by Antonio Mercero, it was to a certain extent a bigger version of his graduate thesis, **Trotín Troteras** (1962). Unlike the **original,** it did not receive the public's favor and the director left cinema, only to return from time to time. He basically dedicates himself to television, a medium in which he has obtained innumerable successes, both for his television films such as **La cabina** (The Telephone Booth; 1975) and for such series as **Verano azul** (Blue Summer; 1982).
Finally, the last interesting debut of the year was that of Francisco Prosper. His **Confidencias de un marido** (Secrets of a Husband; 1963) was a more than acceptable comedy, including good acting and an average job of direction, but Prosper preferred after the experience to work in his second speciality, or decoration. He is still considered to be one of the most important Spanish experts in **special effects.**

Javier Cebrián in Se necesita un chico **(1963) by Antonio Mercero.**

As can be seen, of these almost ten new directors, a few left cinema after a first attempt. Except for Summers and Camus, none of them would make films the year afterwards. Some acted the way they did independently of how their films were received, while others left cinema due precisely to the reception of their films. What is certain is that apart from Summers' picture, none of the others were huge commercial successes. The distributors did not believe in **New Cinema** and they released the films on the market without enthusiasm, which in turn led the exhibitors to give these films the worst possible dates and took them off their screens at the slightest sign of a weak economic showing. This phenomenon continued to happen with all the first time directors, whose work lacked to a large extent that necessary power of communication.
In 1964, one of the most atypical men of Spanish cinema, the neither new nor old hand, José Luis Borau, made his debut with feature length films after having made commercial shorts and after having been a professor at the **Official Film School.** His two features

were both **genre** films, a western and a police story called **Brandy** (1964) and **Crimen de doble filo** (A Double-edged Crime; 1965). Both of these pictures, especially the second, are well made, but they do nothing to announce the man who ten years later would direct **Furtivos** (Poachers; 1975), one of the best films recently made in Spain. Disheartened because he could not do what he wanted, Borau preferred to create an advertising production company so that once he could achieve his economic independence, he would make his own films including, apart from those already cited, **Hay que matar a B** (B Must Die; 1974) and **La Sabina** (1979), as well as **Río abajo** (On the Line; 1984), which he just finished shooting in the United States and which is about wetbacks or clandestine Mexican workers.
The critic and theoretician, Román Gubern, without a doubt the most important of Spain's writers on films, and the self-taught Vicente Aranda, joined forces to produce and direct **Brillante porvenir** (Brilliant Future; 1964), a social drama which it should be said, had better intentions than results. Even so, it does have a couple of excellent scenes and a good handling of the actors and actresses, among which Serena Vergano stands out, the **muse** of the **Barcelona School,** a movement which we will talk about later on.
Jorge Grau enters into the arena again with **El espontáneo** (The Spontaneous Bullfighter; 1964), a film about a city boy, more concretely a bellhop at a hotel, who, fed up with the life he is leading, one day decides to join in a bullfight in order to call attention to himself. The story is well told, and Luis Ferrín does an excellent job as the star, especially considering that he is not a professional actor.
Summers returns to make **La niña de luto** (The Girl in Mourning; 1964), a satire of the almost medieval customs which were still observed in certain parts of Andalusia when a family went into mourning. Using black humor, Summers tells us a story of love, or, if you prefer, a lack of love, which fact irritated more than one spectator. This is probably the reason that the film, excellent in many ways, was not as successful as the previous picture, even though his former film was more difficult to put across.
Regarding **El rapto de T.T.** (The Kidnapping of T.T.; 1964), by José Luis Viloria and the screenplay of which was co-written by Regueiro, it was a madcap comedy that did not achieve its aims, despite the fact that it had some very funny scenes. It was shown in very bad conditions and when it was seen, its passing was uneventful.
Los felices 60 (The Happy Sixties; 1963) was the first feature by the Catalonian director Jaime Camino, previously the author of some very interesting documentaries. The film was a love story set in the midst of an egoistic and a merciless middle-class. Today his bitter humor and perhaps his pedantic dialogues may seem old-fashioned, but at the time it was released the film, the photography of which is very tailored, caused a certain sensation. Starring in the film were the French critic, Jacques Doniol-Valcroza and the Russian actress residing in Spain, Yelena Samarina.
The third film by Camus is based on a screenplay he wrote along with Carlos Saura. It is a semi-police film called **Muere una mujer** (A Woman Dies; 1964). Heading the cast is the important actor Alberto Closas, and even though it was not a big success, it did achieve exhibition and box office levels that were far superior to his first two films. Sure of himself, after that moment Camus would begin the career of an excellent narrator, whose films would frequently reach the meritous level of his scripts. His pictures are well told and are done with a laudable economy. He also excellently directs actors and actresses.
Diamante also shot another film called **Tiempo de amor** (Time for Love; 1964), based on a script that he wrote together with his wife Elena Sáez. It is composed of three episodes which take place in different atmospheres and social levels. Each of the episodes are of a different quality, although their level of sincerity is appreciable.
Especially standing out among the excellent performances in the three

María José Alfonso and Alfredo Landa in
La niña de luto (1964) by Manuel Summers.

Mariloli Cobos, Carlos Sánchez and Aurora Bautista in *La tía Tula* (1964) by Miguel Picazo.

episodes are Julián Mateos and Lina Canalejas.

The film that really towers above the rest of those made in 1964 is another by a first timer. The film is **La tía Tula** (Aunt Tula) and is directed by Miguel Picazo who based it on the novel by Miguel de Unamuno. It is about the life in small provincial cities and the story centers on a woman who, after the death of her sister, goes to live with her brother-in-law and son in order to care for them. She becomes horribly frightened of a love for the father that grows as a result of her affection for the son. The complexes and frustrations of the female lead, the cruelty of the people who surround her and the mediocrity of the provincial way of life are very well put over. Aurora Bautista does an excellent job in the title role, and there is a brief, but well-defined scene involving José María Prada. Given a prize at the San Sebastián Film Festival, **La tía Tula** has become a model work within **New Spanish Cinema.** In spite of the success obtained by the film, Picazo saw his following film, **Oscuros sueños de agosto** (Obscure August Dreams; 1967) massacred by the censors. After the catastrophe, he retired to work in television, where only from time to time does he come out with an interesting work. It took years for him to be able to direct one of his most beloved projects, **Los claros motivos del deseo** (The Clear Motives of Desire; 1976).

Fewer first time films were made in 1965, but it is the year in which it is seen who among the new directors will remain in the profession and who will go on to other things. Mario Camus is definitely established and makes two more films, one of relative interest. **La visita que no tocó el timbre** (The Visitor Who Did Not Ring the Doorbell) is the adaption of a successful theater comedy which really only set off the stars of the film, Alberto Closas, José Luis López Vázquez and Laura Valenzuela. The other film is of undeniable interest. **Con el viento solano** (With the East Wind) is the film version of a novel by Aldecoa about the world of the **quinquis,** a particular type of delinquent that comes from the very fringe of Spanish society. The picture marked the return to film after many years of a person who in her day was the mother of the lead in the film, portrayed by Antonio Gades. Presented in the Cannes Film Festival, the picture was not well understood. There is strength in the different scenes and they deal with questions that are not normally seen on Spanish screens, but the film can be viewed as a transcendent melodrama.

Summers, Eceiza, Grau and Regueiro all directed films again. The first made a picture that can be described as interesting, although there is nothing about it that can be debated. It is called **El juego de la Oca** (Snakes and Ladders; 1965), a story of a triangle that is dealt with **Spanish-style.** Just like Camus' film, it disoriented spectators in the Cannes Film Festival where it was presented. The second director, or Eceiza, made a film that was on a different register than the realism which he showed in his first picture. He adapted a novel by Gonzalo Suárez, one of the most original and imaginative writers of the younger generations of that time, a writer who would later become a director as well. **De cuerpo presente** (Laid Out; 1965) is a fantasy, an imitation to a certain extent of American gangster films, stuffed with symbolistic truffles and resolved with imagination. Symbolism and imagination are also present in **Acteón** (Actaeon; 1965), by Jorge Grau, a revisitation of the Greek myth, but in modern times. If the film seems pedantic at moments, especially due to its dialogue, it contains beautiful shots and a sharp intellectual focus.

In 1965, Francisco Regueiro, whose first film was a commercial flop, embarks on a greater adventure. **Amador** (Lover) is a coproduction with France. An important actor heads the cast, while the leading actress is the prestigious Amparo Soler Leal. The story is about a murderer of women who is redeemed by love when it is too late. He does so throughout an irregular script in which together with excellent moments, there abound dead points. The film was presented in the

Critic's Week in the Cannes Film Festival and its reception was only so-so. Producer Emiliano Piedra, who until that time had only promoted commercial ventures into film, contracts Orson Welles to make **Campanadas a medianoche** (Falstaff; 1965), with almost all Spanish capital. It is a passionate and pathetic Shakespearian fresco centering on the figure of Falstaff, which the director himself plays, popping up amidst the different texts of the British playwright that can be found in the film. It is one of the most beautiful pictures ever made by this director, and also one of the saddest. A double prize-winner in the Cannes Film Festival, it has an international cast in which actor Fernando Rey has the most relevant role among the Spaniards.

Among the first time directors, Jesús Yagüe stands out with a praiseworthy attempt to make a light, aesthetic and pop cinema. The picture, however, suffered from the film's low budget and from the adverse reception it was given when it was premiered in the San Sebastian Festival, a place where it never should have been presented. The title of the film is **Megatón** (Megaton; 1965) and starring in it were the Micky y los Tonys singing group. With regard to Julio Diamante, he makes **El arte de vivir** (The Art of Living; 1965), an acid comedy about the frustrations of a young couple. But for the film itself and what it represents, the most important film of the year is perhaps **Nueve cartas a Berta** (Nine Letters to Berta), the first by Basilio Martín Patino, the man who got the **Salamanca Conversations** going in 1955. The picture is divided into nine chapters, as many as the letters written by its young male lead, a student in the internationally known university city of Salamanca. He is writing to a girl, the daughter of an exile, whom he got to know —and fell in love with— on his first trip abroad. In each one of the letters or chapters, a basic aspect of coexistence in a provincial city is dealt with. There is more than one excellent moment in the film and the whole is filled with an air of sincerity which is both convincing and moving. The film starred Emilio Gutiérrez Caba, the youngest of the members of an illustrious dynasty of actors and actresses. The majority of the critics considered the film as a model for the cinema that **should** and **could** have been made at the time. It was also successful with the public.

Maurice Ronet in Amador **(1965) by Francisco Regueiro.**

(Following page)

Emilio Gutiérrez Caba in Nueve cartas a Berta **(1965) by Basilio Martín Patino.**

Special mention should be made of **La caza** (The Hunt; 1965), by Carlos Saura. Given a prize in the Berlin Film Festival, it began to open the doors of the international market for quality Spanish films. The story is about four men who belong to different generations and who also see life differently. During a hunting party, they are dragged into a spiral of violence in which they will be both the victims and executioners.

José María Prada, Alfredo Mayo, Emilio Gutiérrez Caba and Ismael Merlo in La caza **(1965) by Carlos Saura.**

Made with a laudable economy of means, the superb black-and-white shots by Luis Cuadrado (a director of photography who died prematurely and who made a good part of the most important Spanish cinema produced during those years) were able to perfectly convey the tension and anguish of a desperate situation that Saura used to the utmost advantage. The four main actors in the film were Alfredo Mayo, Ismael Merlo, José María Prada and Emilio Gutiérrez Caba.

1966 is distinguished for the appearance not of a distinct, but an opposed phenomenon to the happenings of the **New Spanish Cinema.** Vicente Aranda, who along with Román Gubern had directed **Brillante porvenir,** a film that was clearly part of that movement, made a second picture alone called **Fata Morgana** which marked the birth of the **Barcelona School.** This second movement would consolidate the year afterwards, and even though it did not last very long, it unleashed passionate arguments. **Fata Morgana,** the same as **De cuerpo presente** the year before, is an adaptation of a story by Gonzalo Suárez and is shot from a radically different point of view than the cinema in Madrid. Apart from being what can be described as a science fiction film, although an everyday science fiction, found in its scenes is a sophistication which springs from the immediate

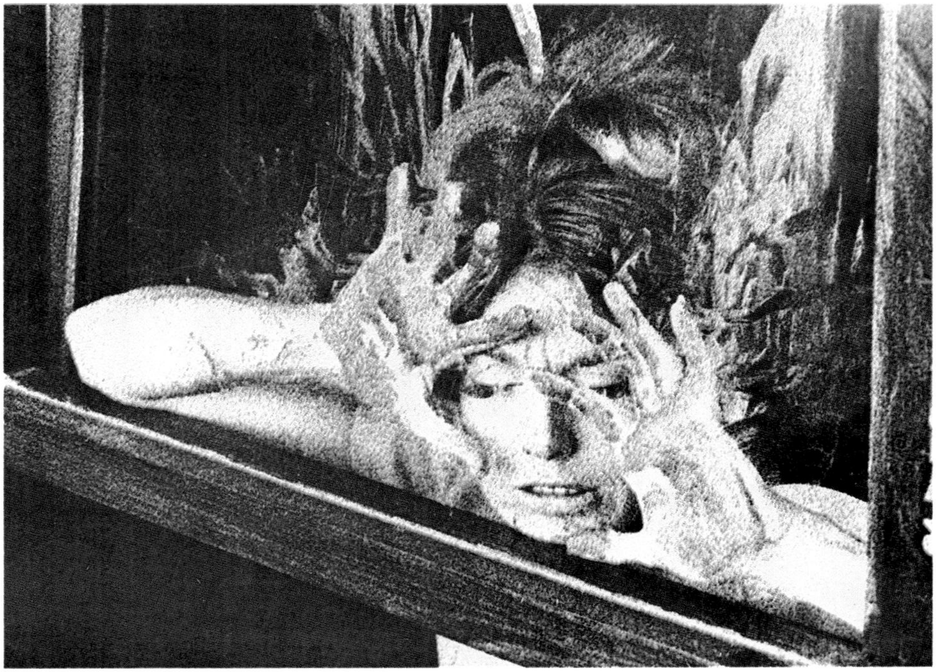

Teresa Gimpera in *Fata Morgana* **(1966) by Vicente Aranda.**

realism, almost naturalist in its outlook, of the other films in the **New Spanish Cinema. Fata Morgana** is above all, cinema of imagination and of fantasy, even though it never loses touch with reality. The star of the film, Teresa Gimpera, a model who was making her first steps in the industry, would become one of the most sought after actresses in Spanish cinema in years to come, both in commercial and creative cinema. Presented in the Critics' Week in the Cannes Film Festival, it would be received with interest and applause by the international critics.

Grau also shoots **Una historia de amor** (A Love Story; 1966) in Barcelona, although the film would not be built on the postulates of the School, which would be developed later. As the title implies, it is a love story. The action revolves around three characters —two sisters of the husband of one of them— during the days before the wife is about to give birth. The younger sister has come to take care of her and it is Christmastime. Teresa Gimpera plays the pregnant sister and Serena Vergano the younger lead. The latter actress obtained the best actress award in the San Sebastian Film Festival for her performance. The entire atmosphere of the film is excellent and so is the direction of the actresses.

Also shot in Barcelona is **El último sábado** (The Last Saturday; 1966), an excessively forgotten film by Pedro Balañá. It is about the life —and death— of a young man of humble descent who is obsessed by motorcycles and women. The film is very well made and credible. Julián Mateos' performance as the lead is excellent.

Jacques Perrin in La busca **(1966) by Angelino Fons.**

Returning to Madrid, while Mario Camus makes a picture for the greater glory of the singer Rafael called **Cuando tú no estás** (When You Aren't There; 1966) —a picture that was deftly done, Antón Eceiza loses his way with a melodramatic film about the love of a flamenco dancer and a woman from the so-called «good society». The film is called **El último encuentro** (The Last Encounter; 1966) and stars Antonio Gades. Yaqüe tries a similar theme in **Los flamencos** (1966), a picture without mistakes that did not merit its failure, apart from the fact that it was a long time in being released. Among the first time directors, Raúl Peña does an interesting job with **Los amores difíciles** (Difficult Loves; 1966), a story of intertwined loves and starring the sister of the director, Julia Peña, among others.

The director who would really be the object of attention is Angelino Fons, who made an adaptation of **La busca** (The Search; 1966), a trilogy by the great novelist Pío Baroja in which the problems of a country boy who arrives in the big city are analyzed. A well-written screenplay, which is faithful to the original text only in spirit, brings the problems presented in the film into a modern light, while a carefully created atmosphere which is not lacking in inspiration, gives the film an unusual **finish** for Spanish cinema. The lead in the film, Jacques Perrin, was given a prize for his performance in the Mostra of Venice, and in the big cast, especially noteworthy is Emma Penella. Another of the most notable films of the year is **Juguetes rotos** (Broken Toys; 1965), a film which Manuel Summers must have produced himself. People who were famous in a more or less recent past are interviewed in the picture, while at the same time, and using them as examples, the picture reflects on failure and its possible causes or injustices. It is perhaps the best film made by this director. The fact that it was a failure at the box office conditioned to a large extent his later career, making him give in to the compromises of commercial cinema except in a few cases that will be analyzed later.

1967 is the last under the aegis of García Escudero. At the end of that year he would be dismissed from office, and with him would disappear the General Directorate of Cinematography. It would be replaced by an ambiguous General Directorate of Popular Culture which would be headed by the brother-in-law of Culture Minister Fraga, Carlos Robles Piquer. Picazo, as has already been pointed out, failed with his second film called **Oscuros sueños de agosto,** while

Juguetes rotos (1966) by Manuel Summers.

Regueiro makes a plausible melodrama in **Si volvemos a vernos** (Smashing-Up; 1967). It tells the difficult relationship of a Spanish woman **with a past** who is married to a black officer who works in the American air base of Torrejón de Ardoz. A noteworthy acting job was done by Esperanza Roy, an actress who had come from the world of musicals. Her dramatic performance is simply excellent. To a certain extent, Saura breaks with his former film-making techniques and lays the foundations for his future style with **Peppermint frappé** (1967). It is a secretive and mysterious film with enormous imaginative strength and an excellent formal resolution. Just like **La caza,** it will be produced by Elías Querejeta, a man who is not only responsible for a large part of the **New Spanish Cinema,** but the new cinema that is generally done in Spain.

What stands out in this last **official** year of the movement in question is not the films which are part of it, but the ones that are done in Barcelona with another perspective. If **Fata Morgana** is considered the first link in the chain, **Dante no es únicamente severo** (Dante Is Not Only Strict; 1967), by Joaquín Jordá and Jacinto Esteva, will be considered the film manifesto. Meanwhile, the manifesto of the **Barcelona School** has been explicitly announced in the following statement by Joaquín Jordá, one of its «theoreticians», and published in the specialized **Nuestro Cine** magazine:

«1) Self-financing and a cooperative production system.
»2) Team work with a constant interchanging of functions.
»3) Preponderantly formal concern towards the field of the image's structure and the narrative structure.
»4) Experimental and avant-garde character.
»5) Subjectivity within the limits allowed by the censors in dealing with the subjects.
»6) Characters and situations different from those of the cinema in Madrid.
»7) Use, within trade union limits, of non-professionals.
»8) Production not considering distribution, since it is non-desirable, forced by the circumstances and the narrow-mindedness of the majority of the distributors.
»9) Except in certain cases, a non-academic and non-professional education.»

As one can see, if the **New Spanish Cinema** in a strict sense came about as a result of opposition to commercial cinema of the time, the **Barcelona School** movement was born out of a clash of a group of Catalonian film-makers with the basic ideas of a cinema that was being done in the country's capital. They were especially concerned about **contenutismo** (continuity), since the defenders of the **Barcelona School** were interested in a more imaginative and **modern** cinema. They claimed that the other cinema was a heavy burden to bear —due to the limitations imposed by censorhip— if one is interested in free creation. The practical results of this theoretical position will be titles such as the already mentioned **Dante no es únicamente severo, Cada vez que...** (Each Time...; 1967) by Carlos Durán, **No contéis con los dedos** (Don't Count with Your Fingers; 1967) by Pere Portabella, or **Ditirambo** (Dithyramb; 1967) by Gonzalo Suárez. All these directors bet on originality, even though obtained through provocation, and aspire to knock down a more or less traditional view of classical narrative cinema by means of excessive subtlety in the shots, twisted dialogues, a humor bordering on surrealism and self-satisfaction.
Dante no es únicamente severo, as has already been pointed out, is the representative film of the movement and is set in an artificial world of high-fashion models and idle intellectuals with no specific jobs. Its scenes are beautiful and at times extraordinarily suggestive, although at others they irritate the viewer— undoubtedly the makers of the film were seeking to irritate. More restrained is **Cada vez que...,** a love story between young people, which paraphrases a line by Brigitte Bardot, «Each time I fall in love I think it's for always». With regard to **No contéis con los dedos,** it is undoubtedly the most serious experimental work of these films, as will be the future films by Suárez. **Ditirambo** is a free version of the novel written by the director himself. It is a police fantasy about a very beautiful woman which represented the film debut of a now popular actress called Charo López. Serena Vergano and the model Romy would become the **muses** of the movement in question, regularly or sporadically performing in these films. They represented a type of woman which was radically different from those seen in Madrid cinema. Jacinto Esteva and his production company called Filmscontacto would also represent to a lesser degree for the **Barcelona School** what Elías Querejeta did for Madrid cinema. After the boom of **New Spanish Cinema,** Querejeta would continue to be one of the most coherent producers in the country to whom is owed almost all of Saura's films as well as those of the most important Spanish directors including Manuel Gutiérrez Aragón, Jaime Chávarri and Emilio Martínez-Lázaro. It is certain that the Barcelona movement burnt itself out quickly, practically after the ruin of Filmscontacto, but some of its directors, who had already broken off from the movement, such as Aranda and Suárez, continue to make films, albeit at their own relatively slow

pace. The others moved into other areas, some related to film. It is also certain that the films of the **Barcelona School** were not widely seen throughout Spain, nor for that matter outside the country except in a few film festivals. The same phenomenon occured with Madrid cinema, although to a lesser extent. The critical success of the **New Spanish Cinema** did not reflect an automatic box office success, except in a few cases. In both cases, this new form of cinema was generally rejected by the large distribution companies —mostly the representatives of the majors, although there were exceptions. The films that were well-received and even given prizes in festivals were passed over. This was precisely the main argument used against these films in certain sectors. One person even said that they were «films without public which had not found an author». In addition to this, the most liberal political sectors denied that what they had to say was valid or sincere since they were fomented by the authorities. The magazine **Nuestro Cine,** considered at that time to be on the left, reproached itself for having been used as a springboard for the **New Spanish Cinema,** and as a result, for having played the government's game. To a certain extent this could have been true, but it did not invalidate in any case the words of praise it had pronounced in its pages, pages that were equally open to the defenders of the **Barcelona School.** With the perspective that only the passage of time gives, it can today be said that the cinema of the quinquennium —or the six year period— which we have dealt with could be judged insufficient as a cinema that breaks with the past and it is not in more than one case an absolutely personal cinema. But this did not prevent it from being of historical interest. Many of its works have resisted unscathed the passage of time and the political and cultural circumstances witnessed by the country. All this is independent of the fact that the majority of the directors of that period who continue to work today have given up the assumptions of that **New Spanish Cinema,** which was just one stage more —possibly a necessary one— in the development of the Spanish film industry.

1967

1975

Lucia Bosé, Pere Mortabella and Luis Cuadrado in the shooting of *Nocturno 29* (1969) by Pere Portabella.

1967 1975

Augusto M. Torres

On August 19, 1964, the **new norms for the development of cinematography** appeared. They represent one more area of the **Economic Development Plan** with which the new ministerial team appointed by General Franco in July, 1962 can prop up the unsteady national economy. These norms generate a type of film-making which is called the **New Spanish Cinema,** created by Manuel Fraga Iribarne, at that time Minister of Information and Tourism, and implemented by José María García Escudero, Director General of Cinematography. It is practically produced by the state, since the budgets of the films are amortized by the subsidies which they receive. It also represents Spain in the international festivals and even wins a few prizes, but it has great difficulties in reaching national audiences. To a large extent, these **new norms** meant that two different types of films were made at the same time: **a low-quality,** but very commercial product designed for the domestic market, and other, higher-quality films that made little money in local cinemas, but were aimed at publicizing the other face of Spain abroad.

The **New Cinema** that the state subsidized, but which is strictly controlled by a double political and economic censorship, logically constitutes the cinema that the state is interested in making. For this reason, the criticisms that these films would level at society are either limited, or more directly, inexistent.

After the constant struggle against the administration by **opposition** screenwriters, directors and producers, if one of these pictures goes beyond the filters established by the state it will be cut for exhibition on the domestic market. However, the authorities may allow it to be shown in a more complete version to fulfill its propaganda mission.

All this confirms the inoperativeness of the famous conclusions reached in the **Salamanca Conversations** of May, 1955. Requested at the time was a censorship code, a new protection system, a federation of film societies, state aid to the **Instituto de Investigaciones y Experiencias Cinematográficas** (Cinema Research and Experiences Institute), and an end to the NO-DO newsreel monopoly. With the exception of this last point, everything was obtained, especially the measure which made the subsidies dependent on the box office takings. But the truth is that each day Spanish cinema enjoys less freedom and is more dependent on state interests.

This situation leads some directors who make their debut during the period to try new formulae in order to make a personal type of film that would be unaffected by the censorship. These attempts, which logically turn out to be Utopian when they run head on into the harsh reality of things, can be reduced to two large groups. To a large extent they are the result of the world economic optimism characteristic of the sixties, although, like always, they are reduced to the level of Spain's very poor situation. The first is the so-called **Barcelona School,** a movement which establishes itself in the second half of the sixties and which enjoys very good support from publicity, but it soon falls to pieces due to the state's inflexibility and the public's incomprehension. The second, very different group, almost opposed to the first, bases itself on the possibility of working in 16 mm., but due to its fragile aesthetic viewpoints and its poor economic foundations, together with the inaccessible bureaucratic machinery of the administration, this group does not obtain any positive results.

The **Barcelona School** endeavors to make a different cinema with a certain industrial viability, trying to avoid the systems of state control. As its name indicates, the movement appears in Barcelona and is constituted by a group of directors who would never admit to such a name. The solvency of the movement is based on the wealth of some of its members. The most important films of the group are made without official economic support and without having previously presented the scripts to the censors, but at no time do they break out of the circle of state control. The statement defining the movement, which was pronounced in a press conference in the 1967 Pésaro Festival by Joaquín Jordá, is the following: «Since we can't make Victor Hugo, we will make Mallarmé». This phrase was later publicized rather widely.

Serena Vergano in Dante no es unicamente severo **(1967) by Joaquín Jordá and Jacinto Esteva Grewe.**

The first films made by the **Barcelona School** are: **Fata Morgana** (1965) by Vicente Aranda, **Dante no es únicamente severo** (Dante Is Not Only Strict; 1967) by Jacinto Esteva and Joaquín Jordá, **Noches de vino tinto** (Nights of Red Wine; 1966) by José María Nunes, **Ditirambo** (Dithyramb; 1967) by Gonzalo Suárez, and **Cada vez que...** (Each Time...; 1967) by Carlos Durán. Seen in these pictures is something which could be described as fantastic realism. It represents an interesting stylistic novelty and is in contrast to the critical realism which Madrid film-makers try to do. Both the economic and aesthetic limitations of these works, their weak repercussion both in Spain and abroad and the rapid disbanding of the group soon reduces the **Barcelona School** to a few directors who try to combine a different aesthetic within a similar commercial concept. They live and work in Barcelona, but they have never been able to escape from state manipulations.

Also in the middle of the sixties there appear all over Spain little unconnected groups which make 16 mm. films in an artisan-like fashion,

not proposing to create any great economic or aesthetic productions by any means. They are mainly interested in not being controlled by any of the state mechanisms and in not joining their forces. Weighing heavily upon them, however, is a terrible kind of economic censorship which makes their jobs technically deficient and extremely limited in scope, forcing them later to disappear. Due to their birth outside state control, these films do not have legal existence, do not enjoy any type of subsidy and cannot be screened publically. The impossibility of screening these pictures even in film societies prevents them from amortizing their small budgets and soon they are not made anymore.
Even though the general norms of Spanish cinema have nothing to do with the film of this format which is produced at this period all over the world, the Spanish 16 mm. films peak in a small way during 1967 and 1968. The focal points which have appeared in Barcelona, Madrid, Santander, Valencia and Zaragoza are consolidated and various medium- and feature-length films are produced. Later, work stops in this area and the groups disband, except in the cases where they acquire a marked political nature and go on to directly depend on clandestine political parties. The films of this short-lived movement soon disappear, films mythicized in certain specialized magazines, but which are only known in small circles and in a few foreign film festivals which are interested in **new cinema.**
To the extent that their directors have continued to work in diverse areas of the film industry, the most characteristic 16 mm. films shot during these years are: **El crimen de la pirindola** (The Spinning Top Crime; 1964) by Adolfo Arrieta, **Ditirambo vela por nosotros** (Dithyramb Watches Over Us; 1966) by Gonzalo Suárez, **Circunstancias del milagro** (Circumstances for the Miracle; 1967) by Emilio Martínez-Lázaro, **Querido Abraham** (Dear Abraham; 1967) by Alfonso Ungría, and **La mano de madera** (The Wooden Hand; 1968) by A. M. Torres, along with other works by Julián Marcos and Lorenzo Soler. The economic precariousness and the resulting bad technical conditions of these films, together with the disappearance of the copies over the years, have given them a certain air of lost ghosts of the past.
More casually than premeditated, the most important members of the **Barcelona School** and the groups which work in 16 mm., meet up with the students of Madrid's **Official Film School** during the First International Film School Talks held in Sitges from October 1-6, 1967, under the presidency of Carlos Fernández Cuenca. The discontent of the **Barcelona School** and the 16 mm. directors, who by that time have

Charo López and Gonzalo Suárez in *Ditirambo* (1967) by Gonzalo Suárez.

grown very conscious of the inviability of their aims, is coupled with the unrest of the students of the **Official Film School,** who see their future threatened by the same controls which are strangling the rest of the industry. These problems lead to a series of conclusions in the Talks, providing possible solutions for Spanish cinema. However, these solutions are considered highly dangerous by Carlos Fernández Cuenca who calls on units of the Civil Guard to prevent them from being made known. As a result, the closing dinner of the Talks in the Calípolis Hotel is converted into a clash between film-makers and members of the Civil Guard which ends in the temporary custody of some of the people present and the confiscation of the conclusions. In later years, these Film Talks would become dedicated to horror films, and still later, would include fantasy films as well.
The conclusions of the First International Film School Talks, which were only published in a few specialized foreign magazines, since their divulgation was banned in Spain, are:
«1. Advocated is the creation of an independent and free cinema, free of any industrial, political or bureaucratic structure.
»The following conditions are indispensable:
»**a)** Free access to the profession with the following implications:

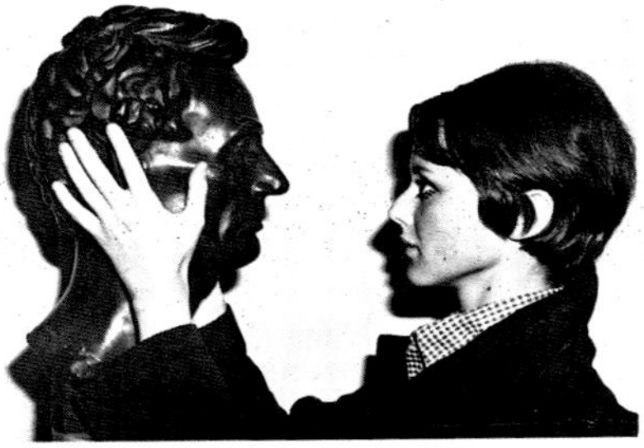

Susana Olmo in Querido Abraham **(1969) by Alfonso Ungría.**

»**b)** The elimination of the **Sindicato Nacional del Espectáculo** (National Syndicalist Show Business Union) and the creation of a union based on democratic principles.
»**c)** The elimination of shooting permits or any other kind of secondary permits.
»**d)** Freedom of expression not subject to government controls or direct or indirect administrative restrictions.
»**e)** Elimination of previous censorship or censorship when the film is completed and ready for exhibition.
»**f)** The elimination of the Special Interest category (of classification) and any other kind of subsidy which acts as a mechanism of control, handing over powers (that affect Spanish cinema) to the Democratic Union.
»**g)** The control of production, distribution and exhibition mechanisms by the Democratic Union.
»**h)** All means of professional training and education should be in the hands of the Democratic Union which would imply the transformation of the current structure of the Official Film School.
»In this new School, the students will be full members of the Democratic Union.
»2. The following points have been agreed upon:
»**a)** Continue holding these Talks in succesive years.
»**b)** Inform all Centers of what transpired in the Talks and the conclusions drawn up.

»**c)** Organize the next Talks in a democratic and effective way as well as nominating the different pertinent committees.»

On January 12, 1967, the creation of **Art** and **Special** cinemas is authorized. The conditions set for these cinemas is that the total seating arrangement not exceed 500, that they only be opened in towns of more than 50,000 inhabitants, and, in view of the new exhibition quota established only a few months before, that for every three days of foreign films seen in a subtitled version —given special treatment by the censors, there will be one day of Spanish films that have already been classified of **special interest.** Several foreign films are distributed on this reduced, yet completely controlled channel of exhibition. These films would include Roman Polanski's **Repulsion** (Repulsión; 1965) and Joseph Losey's **The Servant** (El sirviente; 1963). They were enormous successes since they included subject matter which was above the ceiling of permissiveness normally established by the censors. Even so, this level would soon be brought down to previous limits. Also distributed in these cinemas are the most interesting Spanish films made during these years, but their economic chances were hurt due to the fact that their potential audience was much more restricted. The situation would reach such an extreme that sometime

Sonia Bruno and Rodolfo Beban in La boutique **(1967) by Luis García Berlanga.**

afterwards, the measure would be abolished due to the bad effects it had on quality Spanish productions.

A cycle is completed with this new ministerial order that creates the **Art** and **Special** cinemas. Films are controlled by means of censorship and the concession of subsidies by the Ministry of Information and Tourism. The men who make the films are controlled by means of the **Official Film School,** while the spectators are controlled by means of the **Art** and **Special** cinemas. Since the machinery works perfectly and has all the pieces in their place, as a result of the economic measures which will end in the new devaluation of the peseta, on November 17, 1967, the General Directorate of Cinematography disappears as such and its functions are temporarily taken over by another department. The event marks the end of the incipient **apertura,** or political opening up, which characterizes the first years of Manuel Fraga Iribarne as head of the Ministry of Information and Tourism.

In another respect, 1967 is one of the most productive years of Spanish cinema, at least in the area of the number of films actually made. A total of 138 were produced, 48 totally Spanish pictures and 90 coproductions. These high production figures are due to the number of false coproductions which characterize these years and which was the result of the new film legislation. Thanks to these norms, foreign films with a minimal Spanish technical or artistic participation are able to obtain Spanish nationality and completely benefit from all the subsidies which totally Spanish pictures enjoy. Among these false coproductions are a large number of spaghetti westerns and espionage films done James Bond-style that are made in coproduction with Italy and that lack any interest whatsoever. The only coproductions which cannot be included in this general tendency include **Volver a vivir** (Living Again), by Mario Camus, that was made with Italy and that starred Raf Vallone and Lea Massari, skilfully telling the love story of a middle-aged football coach, and **La boutique,** by Luis García Berlanga, which was shot in Argentina due to problems with the censors. **La boutique** had an unfortunate cast and due to what can be described as a lack of connections with the realities of Spain, it does not turn out to be a credible film. Berlanga wrote the screenplay along with Rafael Azcona and it is the story of a man who is destroyed by a woman.

Standing out among the low-quality commercial films is **El amor brujo** (Bewitched Love), by Francisco Rovira Beleta. It was an ambitious, yet unsuccessful adaptation to Spanish ballet of Manuel de Falla's work. The film starred Antonio Gades and La Polaca. Other pictures which also stand out and which include a high degree of realism include **La piel quemada** (Burnt Skin), by Josep María Forn, dealing with the problem of the «charnegos» or non-natives of Catalonia; **Las salvajes en Puente San Gil** (The Savages on San Gil Bridge) by Antoni Ribas, based on the play by Martín Recuerda; and **Si volvemos a vernos** (Smashing-Up), by Francisco Regueiro, regarding the relations between a prostitute and an American soldier stationed in the Torrejón air base. Another film which assumes a slightly different line since it focuses on characters who live in an insane asylum is **Oscuros sueños de agosto** (Obscure August Dreams), by Miguel Picazo.

Rossana Yanni and Emma Penella in *Fortunata y Jacinta* **(1969) by Angelino Fons.**

In all the cinema offering a certain amount of interest during this last stage of the dictatorship, a constant struggle between their directors and the censors can be seen. However, it is precisely in these highly realistic films where the impossibility of this struggle can be glimpsed. The directors and screenwriters would automatically censor themselves when starting a film project so that the potential outcome of their pictures is affected, while on the other hand, the censors would cut and change what they liked. The result is much altered from the original idea. Film production falls in 1968. There are 48 totally Spanish films and 69 coproductions produced, making a total of 117. In 1969, these figures

Francisco Viader and Francisco Rabal in Después del diluvio **(1968) by Jacinto Esteva Grewe.**

would later increase to 74 national productions and 49 coproductions, totalling 123 films. However, the same production formulae and controls are employed. The vast majority of the production is dedicated to spaghetti westerns and awful imitations of James Bond pictures, although horror films will soon begin to open their way in the market. Of course, the Spanish-style comedies are still made, becoming a sub-genre with very well-defined characteristics such as the noteworthy **No somos de piedra** (We're Only Flesh and Blood; 1968), by Manuel Summers. From time to time there do appear thought out and well directed commercial productions such as **Las Vegas 500 millones** (500 Million in Las Vegas; 1968), by Antonio Isasi, an action film with an international cast; **La residencia** (The Residence; 1969), by Narciso Ibáñez Serrador, a horror film with a big budget; or **Fortunata y Jacinta** (1969), by Angelino Fons, a well-prepared and cared for adaptation of the novel by Benito Pérez Galdós. Meanwhile, there are unsuccessful production and direction attempts with such films as **El hueso** (The Bone; 1968) and **El cronicón** (The Short Chronicle; 1969), both made by Antonio Giménez-Rico in the area of comedy; **El último día de la guerra** (The Last Day of the War; 1969) by J. A. Bardem, in the genre of war films; and **Tuset Street** (1968), begun by Jorge Grau and finished by Luis Marquina

Mark Stevens and Manuela Vargas in *España otra vez* (1968) by Jaime Camino.

due to disagreements with the star, Sara Montiel; **Palabras de amor** (Words of Love; 1969) by Antoni Ribas, and **Un, dos, tres..., al escondite inglés** (One, Two, Three... Playing at English Hide-an-seek; 1969) by Iván Zulueta, both in the musical genre.

While the directors of 16 mm. films stop working in view of the impossibility of their risky ventures, the **Barcelona School** fire off their best and last shots. Both in **Después del diluvio** (After the Flood; 1968), by Jacinto Esteva, and **Nocturno 29** (Nocturnal 29; 1968), by Pere Portabella, violence, symbolism and some interesting aesthetic experiments bordering on surrealism are skilfully combined in an attempt to find new formulae to explain the evils of Spanish society. Those film-makers who support extreme realism again hit their heads against the wall of self-censorship and state censorship when they begin their projects. The clearest case is that of Jaime Camino both in **España otra vez** (Spain Again; 1968) when he tries to criticize the current situation of Spain as seen through the eyes of an American who fought in the Spanish Civil War in the International Brigades—criticism that almost becomes praise, and in **Un invierno en Mallorca** (A Winter in Mallorca; 1969), when he tries to give a somber view of Spain as seen through the love of Chopin and George Sand in the Balearic Islands.

In the midst of so much desolation,

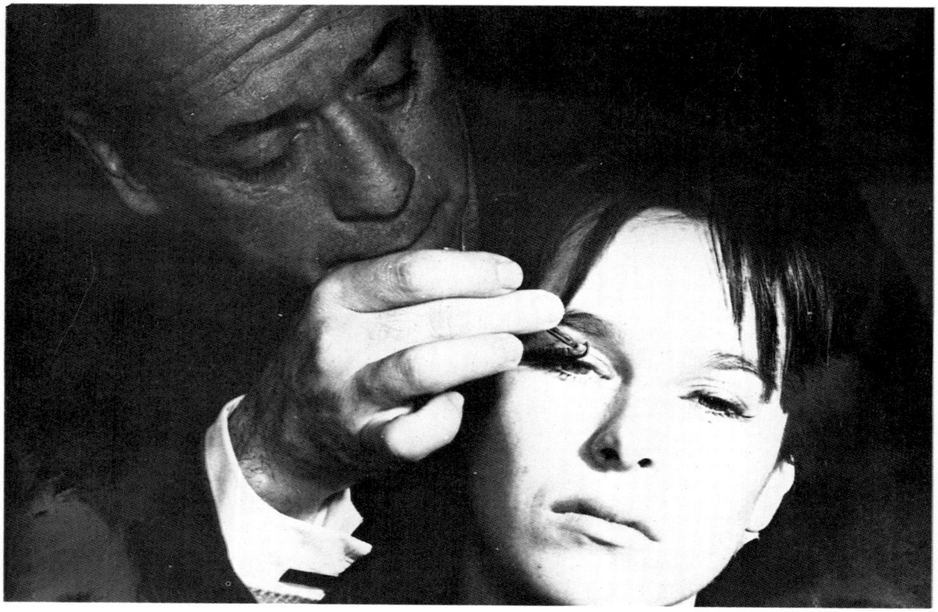

José Luis López Vázquez and Geraldine Chaplin in *Peppermint frappé* (1967) by Carlos Saura.

(Following page)

Per Oscarsson and Geraldine Chaplin in *La madriguera* (1969) by Carlos Saura.

the only direction that seems valid is that taken by Carlos Saura as director, Geraldine Chaplin as actress and Elías Querejeta as producer in **Peppermint frappé** (1967), **Stres es tres, tres** (Stress Is Three; 1968) and **La madriguera** (The Den; 1969). Even though the second is not all that successful and the first is the best of the trilogy, they represent a form of analysis of the Spanish middle-class couple which is not destroyed by the censors, they make possible the creation of works of interest, and especially, they are fairly well received both in Spain and abroad. A problem arises when Elías Querejeta tries to follow this same line or direction of film-making on a different level with other film-makers. He fails both in **Las secretas intenciones** (Secret Intentions; 1969), by Antón Eceiza, and **Los desafíos** (Challenges; 1969), by Claudio Guerín, José Luis Egea and Víctor Erice. Other directors also try to head in this direction of film-making such as Basilio Martín Patino in **Del amor y otras soledades** (On Love and Other Solitudes; 1969). Of special interest are three films which cannot be included in this general tendency. The first is **Ama lur** (1968), by Néstor Basterrechea and Fernando Larruquert, a simple documentary about the Basque country, but which could be considered the first Basque feature. Then there is **El extraño caso del Dr. Fausto** (The Strange Case of Dr. Faustus; 1969), by

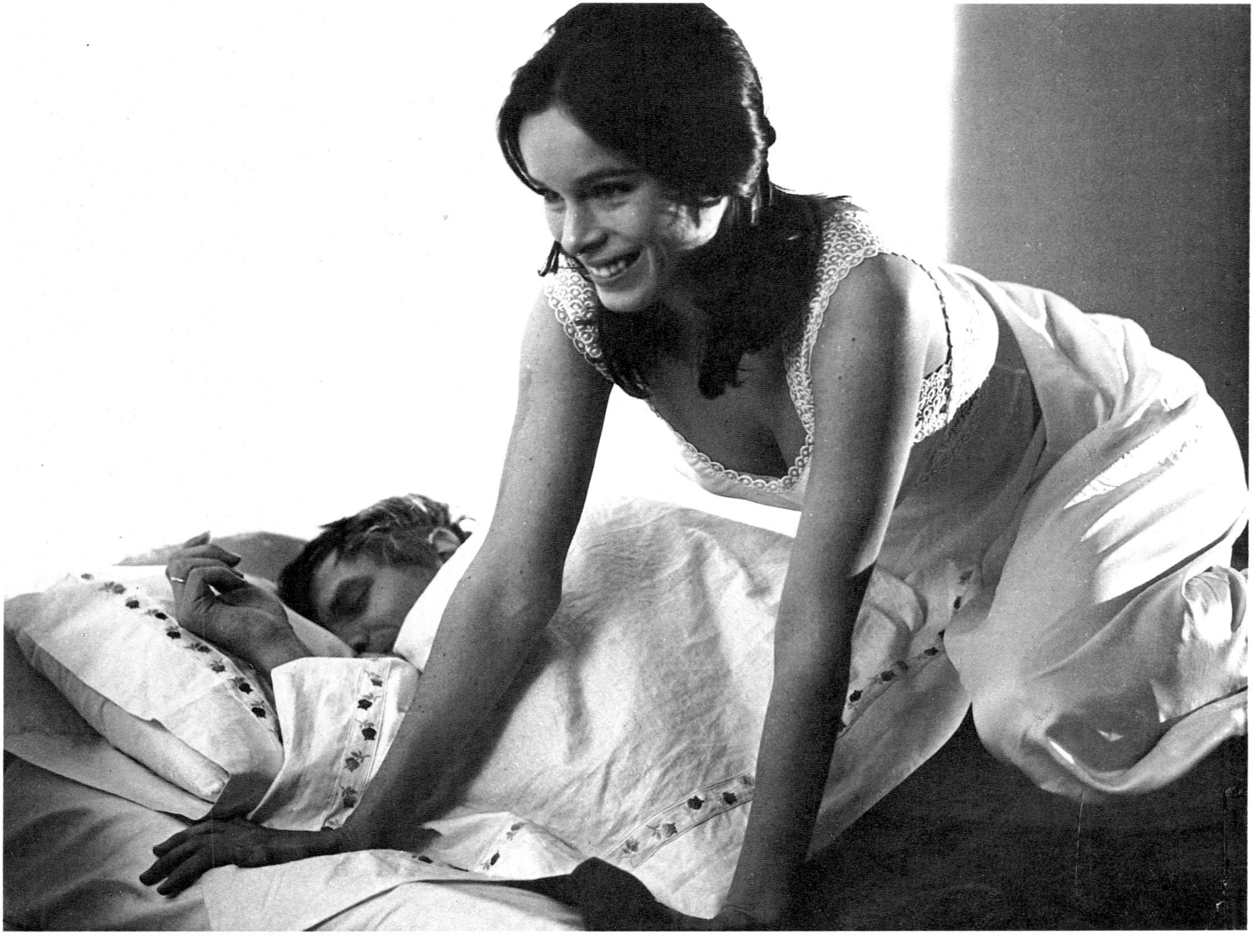

Gonzalo Suárez, a desperate and failed attempt by this writer to find a film equivalent to his passionate novelistic style. Finally, there is **Las crueles** (The Cruel Women; 1969), by Vicente Aranda, one of the most important figures of the **Barcelona School.** The picture is based on a story by Gonzalo Suárez and tries to find a middle ground between experimentalism and commercialism.

The immense financial scandal produced by a company called Matesa, leads General Franco to appoint a new government on October 29, 1969. Influenced by Admiral Carrero Blanco, vice-premier of the previous government and personal advisor from the forties, the new cabinet is made up by men of Opus Dei and the portfolio of Information and Tourism is given to Alfredo Sánchez Bella. While in the rest of Europe at the beginning of the seventies there is a liberalization of customs which in the area of film means the practical disappearance of censorship, in Spain not only does the timid liberalization of the sixties come to an end, but the whole system falls back on the obscurantism characteristic of the period in which Gabriel Arias Salgado is the Minister of Information and Tourism.

Coupled to this problem is the fact that at the beginning of 1970 when the average cost of a picture totals eight million pesetas, the state is thirteen months behind in the payments of subsidies to producers and owes them 230 million pesetas. The situation arises after the former ministerial team headed by Manuel Fraga Iribarne decides that each film must receive subsidies amounting to fifteen percent of its gross box office take. Authorities in the Ministry of Information and Tourism at that time are more interested in the percentage given in other European countries than in the real amount they have available for this purpose. The figures of the **Film Protection Fund** (the pool used to provide the subsidies) had never been very clear and money had never been sought to put them into the black. These two facts led to **Asociación Sindical de Directores y Realizadores Españoles de Cinematografía** (Spanish Directors's Association), or ASDREC, to convoke an extraordinary assembly for November 23, 1969, but the meeting was banned by the president of the **Sindicato Nacional del Espectáculo** (National Show Business Union). However, the assembly was finally held in the midst of tremendous expectation on March 16 and 17, 1970, when the administration's debts with the Spanish film industry amounted to 300 million pesetas and when the state-owned Banco de Crédito Industrial had frozen its policy of loans to producers as a result of the Matesa financial scandal.

Apart from the conclusions reached in the assembly, the members of ASDREC

Jean-Louis Trintignant and Haydée Politoff in *Las secretas intenciones* **(1969) by Antón Eceiza.**

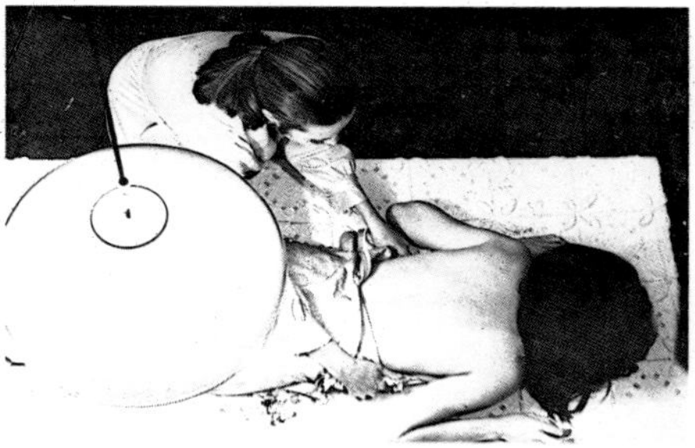

Capucine and Judy Matheson in *Las crueles* **(1969) by Vicente Aranda.**

requested that the administration do away with the obligatory screening of the NO-DO newsreel in commercial cinemas, eliminate the shooting permit issued by the Ministry of Information and Tourism, ban the dubbing of foreign films into Spanish, undertake an efficient box office control by establishing the obligatory use of vending machines, pay the subsidies punctually and suppress the **Special Interest** category. Regarding censorship, the assembly approved the following first points:

«1. The total establishment of the full right to freedom of expression in accordance with Article XIX of the **Declaration of Human Rights,** and, as a result, freedom of expression in film production.

»2. The elimination of cinematographic censorship. Any possible criminal responsibilities resulting from the films will be judged according to the existing Spanish penal code.

»3. In order to try to put into effect the general principles approved under titles 1 and 2, the extraordinary general assembly of ASDREC agrees to constitute a committee that will demand while the current situation exists:

»**a)** The elimination of the previous censorship of scripts.

»**b)** The ending of discrimination between Spanish and foreign film.

»**c)** The ending of censorship

Teresa Gimpera in *El extraño caso del doctor Fausto* **(1969) by Gonzalo Suárez.**

discrimination between commercial films and **art** films.

»**d)** The modification of the make-up of the current Censorship Board, admitting a majority of representatives from the film industry (producers, directors, actors, technicians, etc.) democratically elected by their respective professional groups.

»**4)** Freedom of expression and film exploitation for the different languages and cultures of Spain.»

Meanwhile, the situation of the industry is generally the same. A group of new directors again makes films in an absolutely personal fashion, generally in 16 mm. and behind the back of the administration, but when it comes to obtaining the necessary exhibition licenses to show their work to the public, they are confronted with insurmountable problems both in the area of censorship and in labour, since their plots, production and work methods are totally different from those normally employed. The following directors are not able to legalize their films: Ricardo Franco with his **El desastre de Annual** (The Annual Disaster; 1970), Paulino Viota and his **Contactos** (Contacts; 1970), the architect Ricardo Boffil who directs **Esquizo** (Schizo; 1970), or Pere Portabella with his **Cuadecuc** (1970). Only Alfonso Ungría is able to legalize **El hombre oculto** (The Hidden Man; 1970). This film is a huge critical success when it represents Spain in the

Teresa Gimpera in Aoom **(1970) by Gonzalo Suárez.**

(Following page)

Catherine Deneuve in Tristana **(1970) by Luis Buñuel.**

Mostra of Venice, and some time later it is timidly released in Spain. Although these five films, along with the experimental and unknown **Aoom** (1970), by Gonzalo Suárez, constitute a homogeneous block in which experimentation is mixed with the exposition of some problems affecting Spain seen from very different points of view, they really have very little or nothing to do with the rest of the cinema that is being done in the country and did not have the least repercussion in Spain.

As a result of all these economic problems, the annual number of films produced falls again in 1970. The total of 105 is divided between 58 completely national productions and 47 coproductions. Among these latter films, there are three of special importance. First of all, there is an old project by Luis Buñuel based on one of Benito Pérez Galdós' lesser novels. The film would mark Buñuel's returning to work in Spain after the multiple problems he had with **Viridiana** (1961), a film which was still banned and which did not legally exist. It had never been released in the country. The censors of the time totally prohibited the script, but when Fraga Iribarne found out that Buñuel planned to shoot it in Portugal, he personally authorizes the script without any changes and the production gets underway. The resulting film called **Tristana** is a coproduction with France

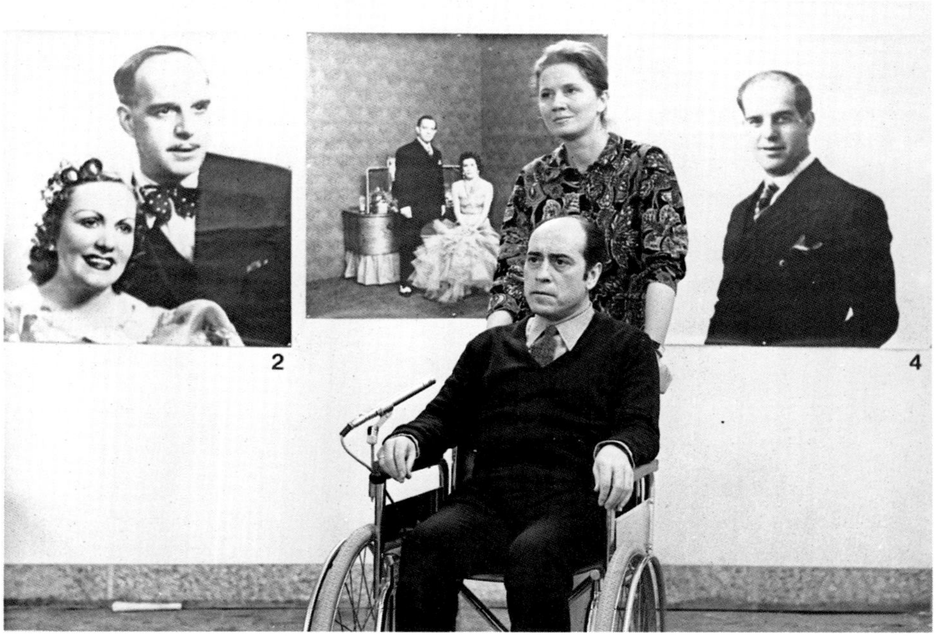

Francisco Pierrá, Amparo Martí, Charo Soriano, Margarita O'Wisledo and José Luis López Vázquez in *El jardín de las delicias* (1970) by Carlos Saura.

and stars Catherine Deneuve and Fernando Rey. It is among Buñuel's greatest works and it was a success all over the world. The second is a coproduction with Brazil directed by the then **enfant terrible** of Latin America, Glauber Rocha, and with which the **Barcelona School** tries to make inroads on the international market after failing in their attempts in Spain. **Cabezas cortadas** (Beheaded) is a critical fantasy on Latin American dictatorships, but it is a failed attempt and marks the end of the ascending career of Rocha and the **Barcelona School** as well. Finally, **No desearás al vecino del quinto** (Thou Shall Not Lust After Thy Neighbor on the Fifth Floor), by Ramón Fernández, and done in coproduction with Italy, becomes the prototype Spanish-style comedy and is a resounding success.
Standing out among the rest of the films produced are three very different pictures which have serious difficulties with the censors. **La respuesta** (The Reply), by Josep María Forn, is an adaptation of a work by Manuel de Pedrolo shot two years before with the title of **La contestación** (The Answer), but was only authorized for exhibition with another title, multiple cuts and the total mutilation of the idea it wanted to put across regarding the revolutionary events in May, 1968, in France. **¡Vivan los novios!** (Long Live the Bride and Groom) is a macabre satire about the married couple which opens

up an entire new way of film-making in the work of Luis García Berlanga, another film that was scripted along with Rafael Azcona. Finally, there is **El jardín de las delicias** (The Garden of Delights), the script of which was also written along with Azcona. The film is about the workings of Spain's middle class. The censorship under Sánchez Bella, prohibited the release of the picture for several months until it was finally given authorization after several cuts were made.
During this period, the decomposition process of the **Official Film School** is accelerated thanks to the skilfull work of Juan Julio Baena, who had been appointed by Sánchez Bella to carry out the mission. Appearing in 1947 under the wing of Madrid's School of Industrial Engineers is the **Cinema Research and Experiences Institute,** the school where all Spain's youth interested in film studied and shot their first meters of film. Due to the fact that a large proportion of Spain's most important directors studied in its classrooms, Fraga Iribarne renames it the **Official Film School** and puts it under his control. In his attempt to destroy all forms of culture that are uncomfortable for the regime, Fraga's successor, Sánchez Bella, is able to strike it a death blow at the end of the sixties and it agonizes until it finally disappears at the beginning of the seventies.
During these year, the Franco

Nuria Torray and José Luis López Vázquez in El bosque del lobo **(1970) by Pedro Olea.**

government has another serious incident with another major American production company. The first took place some years before when the government tried to prevent the shooting and world distribution of Fred Zinnemann's **Behold a Pale Horse** (Y llegó el día de la venganza; 1964). It was unsuccessful in its attempts and as a result, it decides to close down Columbia's operations in Spain for two years and prevents its films from being distributed by other distributors. The second incident takes place when the Spanish government finds out that United Artists has begun a production regarding the situation in the Americas during the times of Spain's colonization. Once again the Franco's regime threatens to close the Spanish market to an American major, but this time for good. This blackmail forces United Artists to change the Spanish flag into a Portuguese, while the setting is switched to Portugal's former colonies. The title is also changed from a Spanish **Quemada** to a Portuguese **Queimada.** Italian director Gilo Pontecorvo's **Queimada** (1970) starring Marlon Brando was later premiered in Spain and passed unnoticed.
During the month of December, 1970, the country is rocked by the **Burgos trials.** A military court martial in that Castilian city decides on death sentences for six members of the Basque terrorist organization, ETA. Thanks to the strong pressure brought

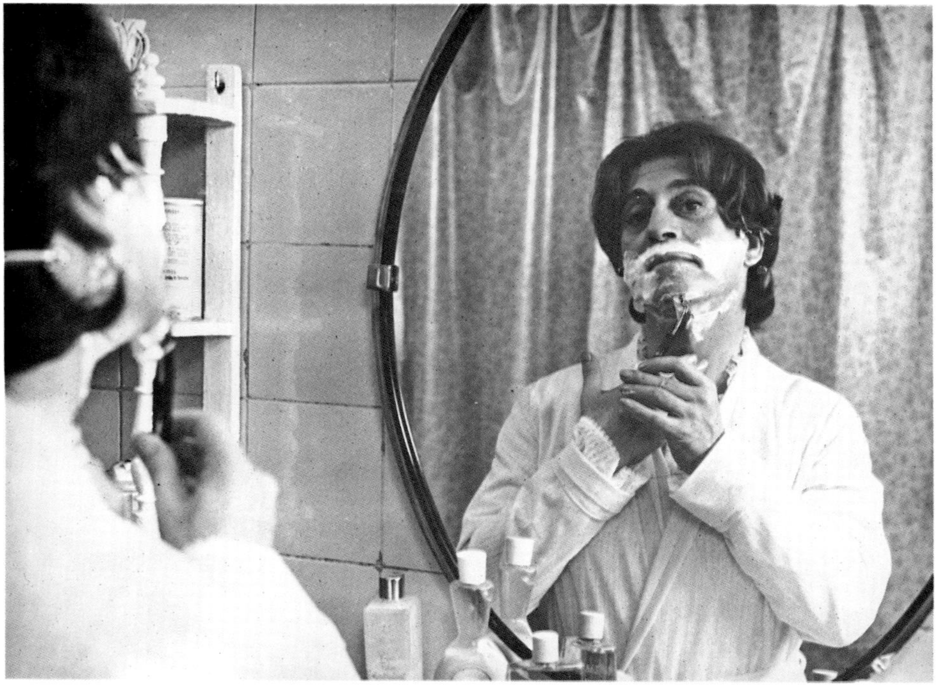

José Luis López Vázquez in *Mi querida señorita* **(1971) by Jaime de Armiñán.**

to bear by world public opinion and the interest shown in the case by important figures, General Franco finally consents to commute the sentences.
In March, 1971, the economic situation of Spain's producers is so bad that new legislation is passed to help them out. The decision reached by Spain's film authorities is a stupid one, since it reduces the fifteen percent in subsidies that had previously been granted over and above the gross box office takings of Spanish films. Due to its logical unpopularity, it has a very short life and even before the law it put into effect, loans are sought to cover the 400 million pesetas which at that time the administration owes to producers.
The government also begins to consider ways of systematically increasing the total amount deposited in the **Film Protection Fund.**
Production logically falls again in 1971 and only 96 films are made: 45 totally Spanish films and 51 coproductions. The industrial situation continues to be very bad, although a a few productions do have some success. Noteworthy among these films are **Españolas en París** (Spanish Women in Paris; 1970) by Roberto Bodegas, and **Adiós, cigüeña, adiós** (Good-bye, Stork; 1970) by Manuel Summers, in the area of dramatic comedy; **Cántico** (Canticle; 1978) by Jorge Grau; **Helena y Fernanda** (Helena and Fernanda; 1970) by Julio Diamante, and **El techo de cristal** (The Glass Ceiling; 1971) by

Andrés Mejuto in *Tirarse al monte* **(1971) by Alfonso Ungría.**

Eloy de la Iglesia, among the dramatic productions; while in the area of coproductions there are **La casa de las palomas** (The Dove House; 1971) by Claudio Guerín, and **Goya** (1970) by Nino Quevedo. However, the most interesting films of the period are **El bosque del lobo** (The Wolf's Forest; 1970) by Pedro Olea, and **Mi querida señorita** (My Dear Young Miss; 1971) by Jaime de Armiñán, which show unusual aspects of Spanish life. Still other films have problems with the censorship which in some cases prevent them from being released. Among the last films of the **Barcelona School** is one by Carlos Durán called **Liberxina 70** (1971), the title of which is changed to **Liberxina 90.** The film is banned from exhibition and it is never released, even though parts of it are cut out. Another film which is never released is the 16 mm. picture by Alfonso Ungría called **Tirarse al monte** (Take to the Hills; 1971). The film was never shown to the Spanish public due to the individual actions taken by the censors and the producers. Only **Canciones para después de una guerra** (Songs for After a War; 1971), by Basilio M. Patiño, an interesting montage film about postwar Spain remains prohibited until after the death of General Franco, and in 1976 it is released to tremendous critical and public acclaim.

Even though no solution has been found for the producers' problem with

the administration, the loss of money in the sector hits its lowest point. During 1972, the number of films produced slightly increases and a total of 103 films are made, 52 completely Spanish productions and 51 coproductions.
The huge national and international success of **Tristana** (1970), by Luis Buñuel, leads to a revival of adaptations of classics from Spanish literature after a period in which they had been forgotten by the industry. Angelino Fons directs **Marianela** (1972), a film based on the novel by Pérez Galdós; Rafael Gil shoots **Nada menos que todo un hombre** (Nothing Less Than Every Bit of a Man; 1971), based on a story by Miguel de Unamuno, **La duda** (The Doubt; 1972), based on Galdós **El abuelo,** and **La guerrilla** (The Guerrilla Fighter; 1972), which was a novel by Azorín; Adolfo Marsillach makes **Flor de santidad** (Flower of Saintliness; 1972), which was scripted from the work by Valle Inclán; and even a coproduction is shot with Mexico on Miguel de Cervantes' Don Quixote of La Mancha which is called **Don Quijote cabalga de nuevo** (Don Quixote Rides Again; 1972), directed by Roberto Gavaldón and starring Fernando Fernán Gómez as Don Quixote and Cantinflas as Sancho Panza. Compared with Buñuel's brilliant work, all the rest are mere opportune adaptations, made without imagination and clumsily. As can be expected, they leave no mark on the Spanish film scene.
Numerous horror films are produced and soon make a figure out of Paul Naschy, the artistic name of Jacinto Molina. As an actor, screenwriter, director and producer he makes pictures of little importance although he does become known in international circles for his work in the genre. The horror filmes made during this period range from very poor fare to personal works of enormous interest. The irregular works include **Morbo** (Disease; 1972), by Gonzalo Suárez; **Ceremonia sangrienta** (Bloody Ceremony; 1972) and **Pena de muerte** (Death Sentence; 1972) by Jorge Grau; **Nadie oyó gritar** (No One Heard the Scream; 1972) by Eloy de la Iglesia, and **Vera, un cuento cruel** (Vera, a Cruel Story; 1972) by Josefina Molina. However, there are more interesting works such as **Umbráculo** (Latticework Shed; 1971), by Pere Portabella, a curious work which ran parallel to **El conde Drácula** (Count Dracula; 1970), the experimental nature of which and the fact that it is shot in 16 mm. made it impossible to distribute, even though it stars Christopher Lee; **La casa sin fronteras** (The House Without Frontiers; 1972) by Pedro Olea, a confusing and impossible pastiche on the Opus Dei; and **La novia ensangrentada** (The Bloody Bride; 1972), by Vicente Aranda, an interesting adaptation of **Carmila,** by Sheridad Le Fanu, a film that was seriously mutilated by the censorship.

Canciones para después de una guerra (**1971**) **by Basilio Martín Patino.**

(Following page)

Ana Torrent and Isabel Tellería in El espíritu de la colmena (**1973**) **by Víctor Erice.**

Towering above all these films is **El espíritu de la colmena** (The Spirit of the Beehive; 1973), by Víctor Erice, one of the few masterworks of this period.
The original idea was to make a Frankenstein, but the director is able to remold the great American tradition of making fantasy film in order to create a most unusual work, very Spanish in its outlook and extraordinarily beautiful, a picture that shows the harsh life of Castile during the forties.
In the field of comedy there are three different and unsuccessful attempts to vary the normal format: **Corazón solitario** (Lonely Heart; 1972) by Francisto Betriu; **El love feroz** (The Fierce «Love»/Wolf; 1972) by José Luis García Sánchez, and **No es bueno que el hombre esté solo** (A Man Shouldn't be Alone; 1972) by Pedro Olea. The big successes of the season are **Un verano para matar** (Summertime Killer; 1972) by Antonio Isasi, which is another example of the action films with international appeal that this director makes; **Experiencia prematrimonial** (Premarital Experience; 1972) by Pedro Masó, which thanks to the attractiveness of Ornella Mutti and the erotic nature of the story of a university couple, awakens the interests of audiences who have been deprived of sexual attractions in film; and **El niño es nuestro** (The Baby Is Ours; 1972), by Manuel Summers, the second part of **Adiós, cigüeña, adiós** in which the eroticism of adolescents also plays an important part. These two latter films were extraordinarily popular.
Meanwhile, a large group of new directors which come from specialized film magazines and the Official Film School are able to make their way into the world of film through a new door, through directing medium-length films. All these pictures are basically similar in that they are done on a shoestring, produced by the directors themselves, and are fictional. The new directors shoot these films in 16 mm. and try to carry out their work with freedom and with an innovative spirit. Some of these medium-length films also try to compete in unfair circumstances with the NO-DO newsreels, which exhibitors are forced to show in their cinemas and which are rented out at ridiculous prices. Even though the quality of these pictures is only so-so —they are done with few technical means— they are attractive to the public precisely because they are not documentaries. The most representative of these medium-length pictures are **Semejante a Pedro** (Like Pedro; 1969) by Francesc Bellmunt, **Estado de sitio** (Martial Law; 1969) by Jaime Chávarri, **¿Qué se puede hacer con una chica?** (What Can You Do with a Girl?; 1969) by Antonio Drove, **El último día de la humanidad** (The Last Day of Humanity; 1969) by Manuel Gutiérrez Aragón, and **Amo a mi cama rica** (I Love My Wonderful Bed; 1970) by Emilio Martínez-Lázaro.
The administration continues to put off the payment of subsidies and Spanish producers are now owed some 500 million pesetas which means that the number of films annually produced continues to fall. The big hit of the 1972-73 season is **Last Tango in Paris** (El último tango en París; 1972), directed by Bernardo Bertolucci. Since the film is banned in Spain and is famed to be an erotic work, **Last Tango in Paris** attracts a number of Spaniards to southern France where the film is shown with subtitles in Spanish. **Time** magazine quipped that between January and June, 1973, some 110,000 people saw the film in Perpignan, a small border city consisting of some 100,000 inhabitants. This case gives an idea of the disproportion between the levels of censorship in Spain and in the rest of Europe. The phenomenon of this film is not an isolated case either, since travel agencies organize weekend excursions to French cities just over the border in order to see pictures that are banned in Spain. The so-called «film weekends» allow Spanish viewers to see at reasonable prices pictures that are banned in Spain, but that are freely distributed in France. At one stage, the popularity of these films is so great that every week advertisements are taken out in Spain announcing the programing in France, but the time comes when even these advertisements are banned. The phenomenon also leads to comic

by-products in Spain such as the film, **Lo verde empieza en los Pirineos** (Eroticism Begins at the Pyrenees; 1973), by Vicente Escrivá.
Another of the normal practices of these years to fight against censorship is to make **double versions.** Due to the impossibility of exporting completely out-of-date films with respect to those made in the rest of Europe, it becomes a custom in Spain to make one comfortable version for the censorship in Spain and another in which the kisses are more passionate and in which there are naked women, so as to better sell them abroad.
One curious case was reported in Santiago de Compostela when a cinema mistakenly shows a version meant for export purposes of **Las melancólicas** (The Melancholic Women; 1972), by Rafael Moreno Alba. The city turned out **en masse** and busses were chartered in nearby towns to see the picture.
When Admiral Carrero Blanco is appointed prime minister on June 12, 1973, there is a cabinet reshuffle and a member of Opus Dei, Fernando de Liñán y Zofío, takes over the portfolio of Information and Tourism. Even though he only has a brief stay in office, since on December 20, 1973, Admiral Carrero Blanco is killed in a terrorist attack carried out by the Basque terrorist organization, ETA, changes are made in the ministry Mr. de Liñán y Zofío heads.

Burgess Meredith in Hay que matar a B (1974) **by José Luis Borau.**

In the area of film, the new minister begins to pay off the existing debt with Spain's producers, meaning that the fall in annual production figures hits bottom. As a result, 73 total Spanish films are made in 1973, while 45 coproductions are produced, bringing the total to 118. With the exception of the fascinating **El espíritu de la colmena,** by Víctor Erice, and the controversial **La prima Angélica** (Cousin Angélica), by Carlos Saura, it is one of the least interesting years production-wise in the last stage of the dictatorship. Only four frustrated attempts at direction stand out: **Hay que matar a B** (B Must Die) by José Luis Borau, **La loba y la paloma** (The Wolf and the Dove), by Gonzalo Suárez, as well as **Los viajes escolares** (School Trips) and **Habla, mudita** (Speak, Mute Girl), the first and promising films made by Jaime Chávarri and Manuel Gutiérrez Aragón, respectively. There are a few uninteresting horror films such as **La campana del infierno** (Hell's Chime) during the shooting of which its director, Claudio Guerin, dies, as well as **Una gota de sangre para morir amando** (A Drop of Blood to Die Loving), by Eloy de la Iglesia. There are also several comedies which do not live up to their own aspirations such as **Vida conyugal sana** (A Healthy Married Life), by Roberto Bodegas; **Tocata y fuga de Lolita** (Lolita's Toccata and Fugue/Elopement), by Antonio Drove,

Jorge Rigaud, Bruce Robinson, Fabián Conde, Maribel Martín, Guillermina Mota, Lucía Bosé and María Francés in Los viajes escolares (1973) **by Jaime Chávarri.**

and **Los nuevos españoles** (The New Spaniards), by Roberto Bodegas, within a movement that might be called the **third way.**

On January 5, 1974, General Franco appoints Carlos Arias Navarro as prime minister to prepare a program for the immediate future. On February 12 of that same year, Arias Navarro would read before the **Cortes** or Spanish parliament his awkward program of political reforms and on December 21, 1974, the **Juridical Statute to the Right of Political Association** would be enacted, the first step towards legalizing political parties. The falseness and ineffectiveness of this new political **apertura** or political opening up, would be shown with the appointment of Pío Cabanillas as Minister of Information and Tourism and his rapid dismissal on September 24, 1974, for having been too liberal in his policies.

Pío Cabanillas' brief stint as minister paves the way for the premier of the controversial **La prima Angélica** (1973), by Carlos Saura. The same film was an enormous success at the Cannes Film Festival. **La prima Angélica** would mark the completion of the trilogy that Saura along with screenwriter Rafael Azcona dedicated to the socio-political situation of Spain at that time that was begun with **El jardín de las delicias** (The Garden of Delights; 1970) and continued with **Ana y los lobos** (Ana and the Wolves; 1972). In spite of the fact that it had to resort to an excess

José Luis López Vázquez in *La prima Angélica* (1973) by Carlos Saura.

of symbols to get through the fine sieve of the censors, each one of these three pictures is more successful than the last and confirms Saura as an important national and international director. The view that **La prima Angélica** gives of the Spanish Civil War and the satire which it sometimes dumps on a Falangist awakens tremendous controversy. The film was almost banned, but once it is premiered, **La prima Angélica** immediately becomes a huge success, even though several bombs are placed in the cinemas where it is exhibited. Due to the deterioration in relations between the Catholic Church and the state, characterizing the last years of the dictatorship, some films are made based on amorous relations between priests and women. There are two complementary types of film, both products of the same opportunism in taking advantage of a passing fad, but which are more successful than the norm. Due to their greater quality, the first type are those pictures which are set at the beginning of the century and are based on classic works from Spanish literature. These include **Pepita Jiménez** (1974) by Rafael Moreno Alba, **La regenta** (The Regent; 1974) by Gonzalo Suárez, and **Tormento** (Torment; 1974) by Pedro Olea, based respectively on the works by Juan Valera, Leopoldo Alas and Benito Pérez Galdós. The other type of films all have modern settings. These pictures

José María Prada and Fernando Fernán Gómez in *Ana y los lobos* (1972) by Carlos Saura.

have original screenplays and are uninteresting: **Tu Dios y mi infierno** (Your God and My Hell; 1974) by Rafael Romero Marchent, **Un hombre como los demás** (A Man Like the Rest; 1974) by Pedro Masó, and **¡Ya soy mujer!** (I'm Now a Woman; 1975) by Manuel Summers, which is the greatest success, since it appeals to the Spanish public's interest in the goings-on of adolescents and the later fad of seeing nudity on the screen.

In cinema, the results of Arias Navarro's timid liberalization is echoed in the greater tolerance for erotic scenes which during the seventies had led to a large percentage of the foreign films premiered in Spain. In the area of national production, new censorship norms are passed which revoke the code established in 1963. These norms are also announced as a sign of what was to come in a new **Film Law** that is never passed. Enacted on February 19, 1975, the main novelty of these norms over the old censorship code can be found in Article IX which reads: «Nudity will be admitted if it is required by the total unity of the film and it will be rejected when it is presented with the intention of awakening passions in the normal spectator or when it is considered pornography.»

The measure permits the appearance of nudity on the screen, and as a result, opens the way for the exhibition of some of the foreign films that were

Fernando Fernán Gómez and Ana Belén in El amor del capitán Brando (1974) by Jaime de Armiñán.

banned during the last few years for this reason. The more conflictive foreign pictures are only authorized in the dying **Art** and **Special** cinemas, which now scarcely have material to distribute after their initial success. At the same time, a new kind of production springs up, the only purpose of which —contrary to the new censorship norms— is to show a timid and fleeting scene with nudity. The only virtue of these new films is that they vary the normal formulae for making comedies —in which the lead is always running after women— which inundated the Spanish market since the end of the sixties. There continues to exist a strict ban on serious erotic questions, and political and social problems continue to be inaccessable, while the most recent foreign films seen in Spain include cuts by the censors and in some cases, they are even banned.

For Spanish cinema, this slight **liberalization** will mean that after ten years of box office statistics being recorded, the money earned by Spanish pictures will surpass that taken in by foreign films for the first time ever. The phenomenon is due to the existence of a type of production which includes slightly more audacious subject matter which is mixed with some trifling nude scenes. This happens with such films as **El amor del capitán Brando** (The Love of Captain Brando; 1974) by Jaime de Armiñán,

José Luis Borau in *Furtivos* (1975) by José Luis Borau.

Pim, pam, pum... ¡fuego! (Ready, Aim... Fire!; 1975) by Pedro Olea, **La joven casada** (The Young Married Woman; 1975) and **Los pájaros de Baden-Baden** (The Birds of Baden-Baden; 1975) by Mario Camus, and **La trastienda** (The Back Room; 1975) by Jorge Grau. The most successful production and the one that clearly shows Spain's poor relations with the rest of the world—very characteristic of the last months of Franco's dictatorship, is **Las adolescentes** (The Adolescents; 1975) by Pedro Masó. The film tells the story of a group of young Spanish girls who go to London to learn English, but they are raped and used as models in pornographic films.

On August 27, 1975, a Decree Law is passed that includes measures against terrorism and one month later three members of the FRAP terrorist organization and two members of ETA are shot, despite an international campaign against the decision and the pressure brought to bear by important world figures. These events force the breaking off of diplomatic relations and the recalling of many ambassadors Finally, during the most chaotic moments, General Franco dies tranquilly in his bed on November 20, surrounded by his friends and relatives and knowing that he had **left the situation well in hand.** The end of almost forty years of a strict censorship that was imposed by the will of an uncultured man is marked in

Ana Torrent and Geraldine Chaplin in *Cría cuervos* (1975) by Carlos Saura.

cinema by two outstanding films. The two pictures are finally premiered following months of a censorship ban, one before Franco's death and one after. Both films are big national and international successes. The first is **Furtivos** (Poachers; 1975), by José Luis Borau, a perfectly directed rural drama which resumes the last moments of the dictatorship. The second is **Cría cuervos** (Raising Ravens; 1975), by Carlos Saura, a film that narrates the awakening of a girl who lives in a house full of military officers and marked by a stigma of death. The screenplay is the first that Saura writes alone and **Cría Cuervos** is one of his most praiseworthy films.

1975

1983

Manuel Gutiérrez Aragón preparing a shot for *Demonios en el jardín* **(1982).**

1975 1983

Equipo «Cartelera Turia»

The latest period of Spanish cinema starts during the last year of the life of the dictator, Franco, continues during the so-called transitional years, keeps on going through the successive governments of the much debated **Unión de Centro Democrático** (Democratic Center Union) and culminates after the socialists (Spanish Workers Socialist Party) democratically take over power in the country.

It is a period filled with transformations and conflicts, a period in which Spanish society begins to know and fully develop its desire for freedom and its political and social rights.

In the area of Spanish cinema, the period offers data and certain socio-political aspects that should be considered.

They can be divided into two areas. First, there are those aspects of the long-awaited normalization process: the distribution of key foreign films that were banned by Francoist censors, the disappearance of paranoic censors, the eruption and participation on the production scene of Spain's new autonomous governments, the changes and bettering of the country's film laws, etc. Secondly, there are those aspects which contribute to the worsening of the economic and social crises in the film industry: the agreements with television, the appearance and boom of the video market, etc. These problems raise a series of questions and are open to different solutions, which, at the time of writing these lines, are still in the process of being discussed and implemented. Although in many cases we find important titles of films that are straddled between two significant periods of recent Spanish cinema, we have found it convenient to divide the various periods chronologically. Logically, the beginnings and endings of these periods will be established in purely conventional ways and will be susceptible to numerous reflections.

The last year of Francoism (1975)

Despite the fact that the film industry had chipped away at and had taken advantage of an ever-so-slight slackening of the censorship reins, only in the sadly famous scenes containing nudity and a few cunningly framed allusions or **symbols** referring to Spain's current situation or its history could its effects be found in a cinema that has been long gagged. One of the most noteworthy films of that year is **Furtivos** (Poachers), directed by José Luis Borau and starring Ovidi Montllor, Alicia Sánchez and Lola Gaos. The film shows the sordid relations of dependency and domination in Spanish society —civil guardsmen, politicians, delinquents, poachers, etc., and it has serious problems with the censors. However, it wins the main prize in the San Sebastian Film Festival and the risks taken by the picture's producer —Mr. Borau himself—and the distributor —José Esteban Alenda— were amply rewarded by a tremendous financial success at the box office. Two years after the explosive and scandalous premier of **La prima Angélica** (Cousin Angélica; 1973), Carlos Saura directs a more intimate film, conveying his own particular anxieties through the relations between children and adults and employing as a backdrop a social class and society in crisis. The film is called **Cría cuervos** (Raising Ravens) and stars Ana Torrent, the charming girl of **El espíritu de la colmena** (The Spirit of the Beehive), the highly acclaimed picture by Víctor Erice. Director Jaime Camino makes **Las largas vacaciones del 36** (The Long Vacation of 36), an interesting and big-budget film which is clearly situated on the frontier between the two periods. On the one hand, Camino's film includes the influences of Saura set in a civil war atmosphere as well as the so-called **third way.** On the other hand, it anticipates what will be a big tendency in post-Francoist cinema and that of democratic Spain: the **new** chronicle of the fascist uprising in 1936 and the war among Spaniards. The picture tells the story of the last days of a group of friends and family members who are vacationing together on the eve of July 18, 1936, the day when the civil war began. It is a solid form of film-making which takes a truthful look at the events. It is directed towards a large cross-section of the Spanish public and is at the same level as some interesting Italian and French films which have dealt with similar situations. Not only that, but **Las largas vacaciones del 36** is a considerable success.

José Luis Gómez in Pascual Duarte **(1975) by Ricardo Franco.**

Ricardo Franco, who until 1975 only had made a few features on the very fringe of the industry such as **El desastre de Annual** (The Annual Disaster; 1970), directs an Elías Querejeta production called **Pascual Duarte** which is based on a novel by Camilo José Cela. The film stars the great theater actor, José Luis Gómez, who at that time begins a very suggestive film career. The film is a sober chronicle of the harsh realities of Extremadura before the civil war and it wins an important prize in the Cannes Film Festival. Another first timer is Bernardo Fernández, who directs a black-and-white feature called **Contra la pared** (Backed to the Wall). The picture is made with almost total unconcern for commercial conventionalisms and it is hardly distributed.

The rest of the productions which stand out among Spanish cinema are clearly made with an eye to a quick and advantageous return on the investment. The remainder of the so-called **third way** is represented by **La mujer es cosa de hombres** (A Woman Is Meant for Men), a comedy by Jesús Yagüe, and to a certain extent, **¡Jo, papá!** (Gee, Papa!), by Jaime de Armiñán. Neither of these two films would rival the success of the previous pictures made by these two directors. However, one veteran who would carry

Angela Molina and Ismael Merlo in *Las largas vacaciones del 36* (1975) by Jaime Camino.

off yet another big success is Manuel Summers with his **¡Ya soy mujer!** (I'm Now a Woman!), a comedy about the sexual awakenings of an adolescent. The film is very much in line with the nudity found in a big percentage of the productions of the time. Nudity can also be seen in **El poder del deseo** (The Power of Desire) by Juan Antonio Bardem, **La adúltera** (The Adulteress) by Roberto Bodegas, **La Carmen** (A Girl Called Carmen) by Julio Diamante, **La querida** (The Mistress) by Fernando Fernán Gómez, or the enormously successful, **La trastienda** (The Back Room) by Jorge Grau. All these films are made by directors who have seen better times. Superficially similar to Jaime Camino's **Las largas vacaciones del 36** are two **retro** films that take a commercial look at times gone by: **No quiero perder la honra** (I Don't Want To Lose My Honor), a comedy by Eugenio Martín which is set during the years of black marketing in Spain, and **Pim, pam, pum... ¡fuego!** (Ready, Aim... Fire!), a melodrama by Pedro Olea which was done with a large budget, referring to the two sides of Spain and making the bad guy out of the opportunist who is on the winning side in the civil war. Among the films made by veteran film-makers, who are always prepared to seek easy commercial successes at any price, there are three very similar titles in which nudity abounds, like the bulk of the production of identical characteristics: **Zorrita Martínez** (Foxy Martínez) by Vicente

Escrivá, **Las alegres chicas de El Molino** (The Carefree Girls at the El Molino) by José Antonio de la Loma, and **La zorrita en bikini** (The Foxy Girl in the Bikini) by Ignacio F. Iquino.

Among the youngest directors, Francesc Bellmunt's **La nova canço,** about the universe of this Catalonian song movement, especially stands out. The same is true of the absurd **País, S. A.** (Country Ltd.), by the cartoonist Forges, which is brimming over with jokes and which hardly exists as a feature.

Francisco Regueiro, who once again has a go at the chimeras like those of his previous pictures, makes a black humor and absurd comedy called **Las bodas de Blanca** (Blanca's Weddings). Finally, Narciso Ibáñez Serrador, a successful TV director, makes a thriller called **¿Quién puede matar a un niño?** (Who Can Kill a Child?), a spectacular and gruesome feature which is somewhere between fantasy and terror.

In summary, 1975 is a mediocre year for film, too similar in fact to what is done in the years immediately preceeding it. A great crisis and decadence is seen in the veterans, while the younger directors have enormous difficulties in expressing themselves. Even though the success of some of the more overanxious and innovative films point in the way of possible solutions, what can be felt —as the general context would later show—is the agony and decomposition of an oppressed film world.

Alfredo Landa in El puente **(1976) by J. A. Bardem.**

1976-1977: The biennial take-off

After the dictator physically disappeared from the Spanish scene and in the midst of a society which searches, fights for and tries to win democratic liberties, Spanish cinema attempts to recuperate and occupy the ground that it had yielded and lost during the previous restrictive decades. Among a flood of foreign and Spanish premiers —including the local films **Canciones para después de una guerra** (Songs for After a War; 1971), **La respuesta** (The Reply; 1969) and **Viridiana** (1961)— that reached Spanish screens after finally defeating the censorship blockade, film-makers shoot films which for one reason or another would have been inconceivable, impossible or difficult to have produced only a few months before. Of particular significance is the work done in the field of **documentary** film-making —the reconstruction of archive material and carrying out modern-day interviews— in which points of view are taken that would have been flatly denied by the censors of General Franco. At the same time, the more or less audacious development of the treatment given to sex and eroticism with widely varying results only confirms these points of view. The period also marks the return or recovery of directors who either did not shoot films —Berlanga— or who did so by making pictures about questions or circumstances which they did not consider personal in nature —Bardem

and Fernán Gómez.
Let ut begin, then by speaking of those film-makers who make come-backs. Antonio Bardem, for example, shoots a screenplay by Daniel Sueiro called **El puente** (The Long Weekend; 1976). The picture does not dismiss commercial possibilities —heading the cast is Alfredo Landa who makes a big change from his normal and repetitive sex-obsessed roles in male chauvinist and repressive comedies of the previous decade, but it tries to make a serious and involved commentary on numerous aspects of Spanish life, which until that time had been masked, and in a tone that is something between a testimony and an accusation. After various years of silence, Luis García Berlanga returns with a virulent satire of what can be described as the Francoist fauna. **La escopeta nacional** (The National Shotgun; 1977) is about a high-society hunting-party in which ministers and important mandatories of the Francoist Spain of only a few years before, reveal their climbing, hypocritical and rascally natures. It is a kind of choral comedy, very much in line with the best known films by Berlanga and with a sensational cast. Fernando Fernán Gómez directs **Mi hija Hildegart** (My Daughter Hildegart; 1977), a story about feminism —a complete novelty for Spanish cinema as is the case with explicit homosexualism. The film is set during the times of the II Republic and has a harsh and powerful way of studying the problem at hand,

Mónica Randal and José Sazatornil in La escopeta nacional **(1976) by Luis García Berlanga.**

Camada negra **(1977) by Manuel Gutiérrez Aragón.**

impossible to pin down during the long night of Francoism.
A very similar phenomenon happens with young film-makers who had their careers more or less blocked until this time. This is the case with Basilio Martín Patino, whom we will talk about later on; Manuel Gutiérrez Aragón, who after four years of silence makes **Camada negra** (Black Brood; 1977) an unusual film which broached the question of the violent and fanatical extreme rightist groups which had increased their extortionist activities in recent times; José Luis García Sánchez, who with his **Colorín colorado** (They All Lived Happily Ever After; 1978) reworked the characters of the film **El love feroz** (The Fierce «Love»/Wolf; 1973), creating a comedy in which the leading characters allude to discussions between supporters of rightist and leftist positions in Spanish life, never done before in Spanish cinema; Eloy de la Iglesia, who took a spectacular turn in his **strong melodramas,** delving into sex and society and destroying many taboos in **La otra alcoba** (The Other Alcove; 1975) and especially in **Los placeres ocultos** (Hidden Pleasures; 1976), a fundamental statement on homosexuality; Jaime Chávarri, who reappears with his **El desencanto** (Disenchantment; 1976), an Elías Querejeta production which we will later discuss in detail, and who later makes a suggestive film about homosexuality with passages from García Lorca and

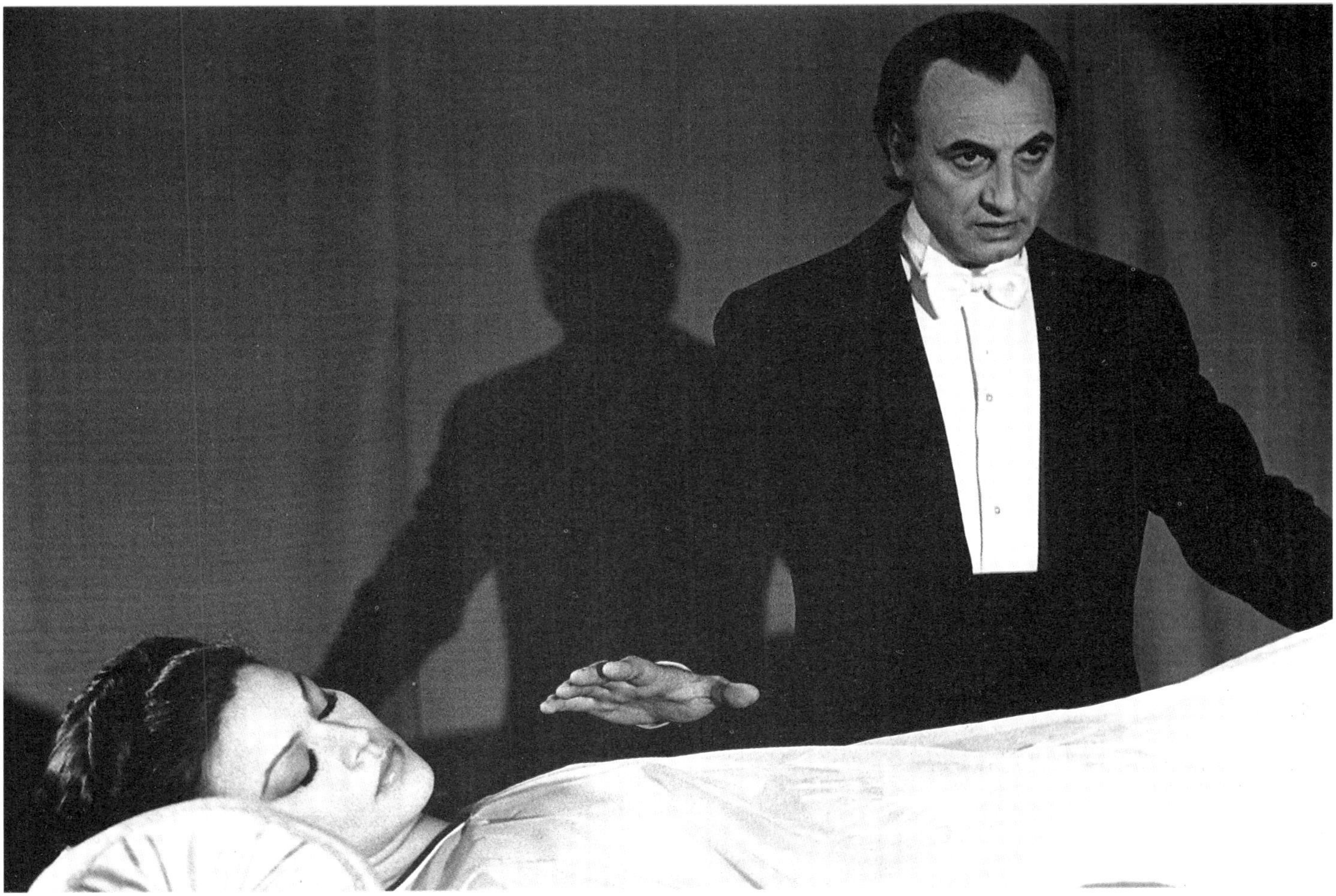

Mirta Miller and Héctor Alterio in *A un Dios desconocido* **(1977) by Jaime Chávarri.**

Michi, Juan Luis and Leopoldo Panero in El desencanto (1976) by Jaime Chávarri.

containing a kind of contrived silence titled **A un Dios desconocido** (To an Unknown God; 1977); and finally Miguel Picazo, a somewhat forgotten director, who gives with his ambitious **El hombre que supo amar** (The Man Who Knew Love; 1976) the biography of a well-known religious figure who is set in a serious and perhaps ambiguous light, very much opposed to the canons which had ruled over the pseudo-religious cinema sponsored under Francoism.

As can be seen, it is a two-year period in which almost all the directors try to make **their** film. Everyone shoots a film: veterans, young directors and first timers. It is a two-year period in which whatever the genre, documentary or fiction, comedy or drama, directors would deal with problems and would give opinions in a way that had never been done before in Spanish cinema. For better or for worse, the names of this two-year period would establish the principles, the bases and the keys for the future of Spanish cinema, a cinema that could compete on a national and international level.

The film that best mirrored or used the general state of affairs of that time in obtaining the biggest success is undoubtedly **Asignatura pendiente** (Pending Exam; 1977), the first feature-length film by José Luis Garci, a former critic and a well-known screenwriter of the **third way.** It is a love story, but done as a comedy with sorrowful overtones. The film is set

Fiorella Faltollano and José Sacristán in
Asignatura pendiente **(1977) by José Luis Garci.**

precisely at the time of the arrival of democracy and the end of Spain's period of repression. The title refers to the relations and feelings denied to students under a state-controlled education system, a system that blocked the way of people with ideas of their own. The leading characters of the film belong to a generation that was born at the beginning of the forties. The public easily identified with them and **Asignatura pendiente** played to packed houses.
We mentioned that we would speak about Patino and Chávarri and the documentaries they made. The large volume of documentary or non-fictional films made during this period is highly significant. As we pointed out, this was basically true because Francoism had only permitted the **documentary** as a kind of propagandistic news report or newsreel. These films were logically presented from the manipulated point of view of the winning side in the civil war.
Patino is finally able to premier his **Canciones para después de una guerra** (Songs for After a War) in 1976. That same year he makes another montage documentary put together from archive material called **Caudillo** (Leader). The film centers on the figure of General Franco. However, it is a risky venture and the documentary is described as too ambiguous. Neither did the film poke fun at Franco, nor did it really make a man out of the myth. Chávarri's **El desencanto** is unanimously acclaimed by the critics. Similar to cinema-vérité, the documentary interviews the wife and children of Francoist poet Leopoldo Panero and allows them to have their say. It shows the truth of a situation which the former regime had disguised behind the univocal outward appearance of the family unity; it is the symbolic image of the crumbling Francoist institutions.
Something similar takes place in **Raza, el espíritu de Franco** (Race: The Spirit of Franco; 1977), directed by Gonzalo Herralde. It uses fragments from **Raza** (Race; 1941), by José Luis Sáenz de Heredia, which was based on a screenplay by Francisco Franco himself, using the pseudonym of Jaime de Andrade. The film interviews the sister of General Franco and the lead in the forties film, Alfredo Mayo. It minutely examines the obvious: that Franco wanted to tell his own story in the way which most interested him, using the slant of a patriotic myth. He descended from a family of military heroes, the Churrucas, he was always on the side of the **true** Spain and if one of his family members were tempted by the **red** Spain, there would be no doubt that he would repent before his death becoming a martyr to the **crusade.** Herralde's film, practically a unique case in the history of Spanish cinema, is enormously enlightening and entertaining.
Two other documentaries which employ archive material and modern-day

Caudillo **(1976) by Basilio Martín Patino.**

interviews in dealing with the civil war are **Por qué perdimos la guera** (Why We Lost the War; 1977) by Galindo and Santillán, and **La vieja memoria** (The Old Memory; 1977) by Jaime Camino. The first is a highly controversial film which gives an anarchistic view of the war and which clashes head on with fascism, but at the same time constantly attacking the leftist government of 1936. The second film, on the other hand, centers its attention on the fact that the leaders of the country forty years before were very old. Most of the interview time is dedicated to two women, the communist Dolores Ibarruri, and the anarcho-syndicalist Federica Montseny. The people interviewed are the ones who give their opinions and contradict each other. The film simply illustrates their statements and lets them talk.

The zeal found in the 1976-1977 period for everyone to make **their** film is especially true of the first time directors. A large number of films of this type are produced, the most noteworthy of which are **Con mucho cariño** (With a Lot of Love) by Gerardo García, **Caperucita y roja** (Little Hood and Red) by Aitor Goiricelaya and Luis Revenga, **Marian** by Luis Cortés, **Dios bendiga cada rincón de esta casa** (God Bless Every Corner of This House) by Chumy Chúmez, **El anacoreta** (The Anchorite) by Juan Estelrich, **La tercera puerta** (The Third Door) by Alvaro Forqué, **Pantaleón y las visitadoras** (Pantaleón and the Visitors) by José María Gutiérrez, **Las palabras de Max** (Max's Words) by Emilio Martínez-Lázaro, **Vámonos, Bárbara** (Let's Go, Barbara) by Cecilia Bartolomé, **La petición** (The Demand) by Pilar Miró, **Tatuaje** (Tattoo) by Bigas Luna, **Tigres de papel** (Paper Tigers) by Fernando Colomo, **In memoriam** by Enrique Brasó, **Con uñas y dientes** (Tooth and Nail) by Paulino Viota, etc.

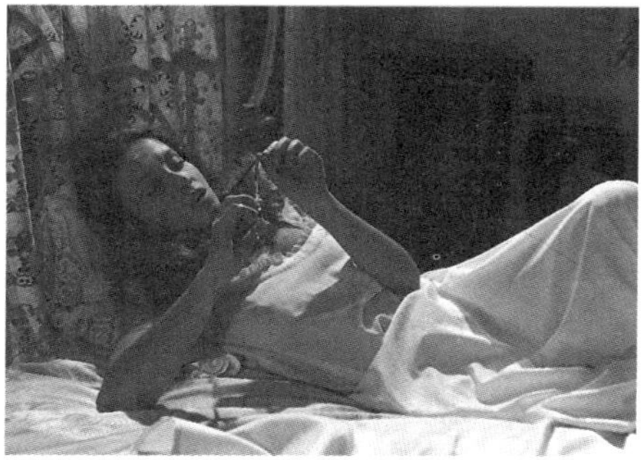

Ana Belén in La peticion **(1976) by Pilar Miró.**

Even though these films are quite different from one another, they generally have the common denominator of renovating comedy or drama and of explaining with a freedom that previously would have been impossible, unusual or taboo topics. They are shaky, irregular and even unsuccessful productions. The majority do only so-so at the box office, but a few are able to create their own schools. The directors of these productions come from all sorts of fields: television, criticism, advertising, graphic cartoon or from the industry itself, where they worked as screenwriters or assistant directors. The overall result was not very satisfactory, but it is undoubtedly much better and far different from what was done in other periods.

In a socio-political context, this two-year period is marked by a struggle to conquer new liberties, and as a result, to achieve the rights of the different peoples, regions or historical nationalities of Spain. While home rule is awaited, some films clearly express regional-nationalist sympathies, a faith

in cinema which springs from a non-central source. The best example of this is **La ciudad quemada** (The Burnt City; 1976), by Antoni Ribas. The picture is shown in many provincial capitals in its Catalonian-language version —unthinkable a few years before— and conceived as a huge historical fresco, almost a super-production, which narrates the events of the **Tragic Week** of Barcelona at the beginning of the century. **La ciudad quemada** has a big cast, employs impressive technical means, uses scale models, etc. All these ingredients make for a very particular finished product, only possible in a region like Catalonia which is the most aware of its national identity.
Carlos Saura, perhaps the only director who regularly makes films in his career, shoots another Elías Querejeta production in 1977 called **Elisa, vida mía** (Elisa, My Love). The film is very much in line with Saura's style. Once again, he centers his attention on family relations, and more concretely on the universe of a woman who is torn between her role as a wife and daughter and her strong attraction towards the father figure. Luis Buñuel, who finally sees the Spanish premier of **Viridiana** (1961) —a film which had been formerly banned in Spain and the distribution of which is only authorized as a Mexican film, shoots in his native country a basically French production, although with Spanish actors and

La vieja memoria (**1977**) **by Jaime Camino.**

actresses, called **Ese oscuro objeto del deseo** (That Obscure Object of Desire), his last film. Summers continues to look for easy commercial successes and directs **Mi primer pecado** (My First Sin; 1976), a male version of his popular **¡Ya soy mujer!** (Now I'm a Woman!; 1975). Vicente Aranda directs **Cambio de sexo** (Sex Change; 1977), situated somewhere between a testimonial and a commercial film and honestly dealing with a taboo subject. Francisco Betriu's **La viuda andaluza** (The Andalusian Widow; 1976) offers and absurd and nonsensical view of a classic work in erotic-picaresque literature, but set in a modern-day world of lumpen and prostitution. And finally, Pere Portabella, who will go from being a director to a senator, makes **Informe general** (General Report; 1977), a magnificent documentary that will not be distributed through normal channels, but is shown on non-commercial circuits.
There is one last consideration before we end our study of this two-year period. Even though censorship definitely disappears, established at the end of 1977 is the «S» anagram for films that contain an excessively erotic content and that, according to the authorities, could be «detrimental to the sensitivities of the viewer». A large number of films take advantage of this period without any kind of restrictive rating as well as the country's political liberalization process in order to play

on eroticism so as to become notable commercial successes. Another curious phenomenon is the immense success of **La guerra de papá** (Daddy's War; 1977), by Antonio Mercero, a film which is based on the world of children and the leading actor of which is a little boy. They are evidence that a great deal is still to be done and that Spanish cinema is still on the threshold of new horizons.

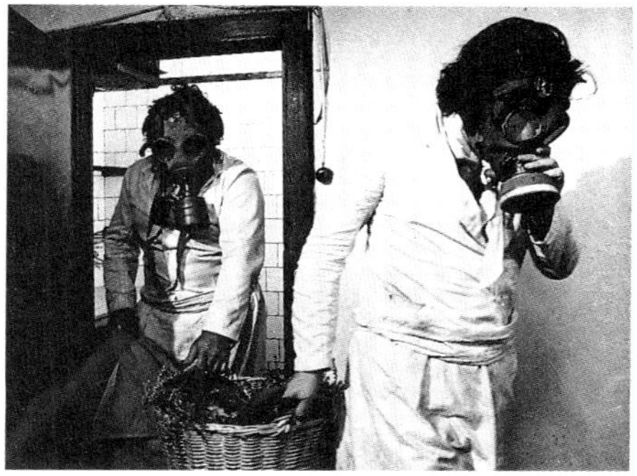

Las truchas (1977) by José Luis García Sánchez.

1978-1981: The transition

In spite of the predictions and in spite of the immense optimism resulting from the experiences of the two previous years, starting in 1978, precisely when legislation is entered on the books that could be used to change the entire industry, Spanish cinema enters into a period of crisis, lethargy and commonplace production. These years are spoken of as those of disenchantment and crisis. If we exaggerate in summarizing this period, we could say that there was a clash between the big hopes which have been placed in the democratization process —as opposed to the long night of Francosim— and the slowness which characterized the process as well as the crisis that had been inherited by the authorities, a crisis aggravated by the international situation and the fact that unemployment was having a dire effect on the Spanish economy. If to a certain extent, 1976 and 1977 had been the years in which a foundation was laid for the future of the industry from production to exhibition, the transitional years of 1978 to 1981 only contributed to the revision, the reinforcement and the decay of these foundations. Even though censorship did not raise its ugly head, legal problems with a few films reminded us of worse times. At the same time, we were faced with a less arbitrary but much more severe form of censorship: that of an economic nature. The fiasco of many films at the box office, the general crisis of the sector and the political deceptions of large sections of the Spanish population —especially among the young— which had a decisive effect on public attendance in certain areas of culture, all abruptly stopped the plans, dreams and hopes of those of us who, knowing the possibilities of our directors, confided in a boom for Spanish cinema.

In order to begin studying this period, it is necessary to point to the resurgence, especially starting in 1978, of a series of consumer films similar to those which were the lords and masters of the market just one decade previously. These productions are inexpensive light comedies of hardly any artistic merit which are generally produced at the service of enormously popular comedians and which make fun of some of the best known aspects of Spain's newly arrived

Fernando Rey, Geraldine Chaplin and Ana Torrent in *Elisa, vida mía* (1977) by Carlos Saura.

democracy. The growing importance of these films favoring vulgarity, rather coarse jokes and unimaginative situations, undoubtedly had their repercussions on the general production panorama. The same is true of the numerous soft-core films which invaded the market under the cover of the «S» rating and which served to draw the attention of producers who were eager for products that could be quickly amortized and that could even bring in a healthy profit. We are not trying here to establish a sterile manecheism on the quality of these films, but rather to briefly explain why a low budgeted and quickly made product designed for a fast turnover could never create a school, contribute to continuity or lay the foundations for a true film industry. The vulgarity of these pictures ends up boring the general public and it soon becomes too much of a bother to go to the local movie theater. It helps to explain the disappearance of the neighborhood or small-town cinemas, whose offerings were incapable of competing with the forms of entertainment acquired by the local people.

Even so, a long list of important films were made during this period, each one trying to carry on the fight alone They are generally much more relevant than the production of previous decades. Some directors remain true to the expectations which had been placed in them during the previous

José Luis López Vázquez, Luis Escobar, Amparo Soler Leal, Mary Santpere and José Ruiz Lifante in Patrimonio nacional **(1980) by Luis García Berlanga.**

two-year period, while others made their films according to their own or market interests, in spite of the fluctuations in consumer tastes. Precisely at the half-way mark of this stage are the first production accords with TVE (Spanish Television). These agreements establish a coproduction fund and producers and directors are asked to produce films based on well-known works from Spanish literature. With these accords, authorities attempt to give their support to worth-while films whose budgets would normally make them prohibitively expensive to produce. At any rate, a list of the most noteworthy films made during this period will make it easier to consider the pros and cons of the arguments we have been explaining.
Luis Berlanga shoots **Patrimonio nacional** (National Patrimony; 1980) a kind of continuation —especially with respect to the actors— of the much applauded **La escopeta nacional.** In spite of the reservations that one might have about second parts, this restrained satire offers the viewer some excellent moments and serves to acknowledge in Berlanga a kind of continuity which had never existed in his film-making before. Bardem makes one of the first films that reconstructs recent political events. **Siete días de enero** (Seven Days in January; 1978) narrates the murder of the labor lawyers in their offices on Madrid's

Atocha Street by a group of extreme rightists just one year after the event. It wins a prize in the Moscow Film Festival, but its commercial run at the box office can be termed as weak. The public reception is partly due to the boldness of the film's subject matter and partly to a general disinterest in films which exploit all-too-political topics. Josep María Forn makes **Companys, procés a Catalunya** (Companys, Catalonia on Trial; 1978), a film which historically reconstructs certain moments in the life of a former president of the regional Catalonian government during the forties who was arrested by the Nazis and who was executed by General Franco's forces. It mirrors the nationalistic feelings of the Catalan people and shows vast hatred towards the fascist centralism of the dictatorship, but it could have been more successful if it had been produced a few years before. Literary adaptations lead to praiseworthy films such as **La oscura historia de la prima Montse** (The Dark Tale of Cousin Montse; 1977) by Jordi Cadena, based on a work by Juan Marsé, **Soldados** (Soldiers; 1978) directed by Alfonso Ungría and based on a work by Max Aub, or **La muchacha de las bragas de oro** (The Girl with the Golden Panties; 1980) by Vicente Aranda and also based on a novel by Juan Marsé. A large part of their attraction comes from the original literary works, but

Fernando Rey and Angela Molina in Ese oscuro objeto del deseo **(1977) by Luis Buñuel.**

they are carefully directed and brilliant films. Noteworthy **regionalist** films include **El virgo de Visanteta** (The Virgin of Visanteta) and **Visanteta esta-te queta** (Hold Still Visanteta), both by Vicente Escrivá and **La portentosa vida del padre Vicente** (The Miraculous Life of Father Vicente), by Carles Mira, all of which date from 1978. These productions are particularly designed for the public of the Valencian region. The first two pictures are vulgar light comedies that include nude scenes, and risqué jokes and that are very local in flavor. The third film tries to ridicule one of the most venerated saints of the zone, the Dominican friar Vicente Ferrer, but the film is immediately attacked by the most reactionary and powerful forces of Valencia. The Catholic Church makes a protest and a bomb is set off in the movie theater where the film is being shown in a small town of Alcoy.
Even though far less are produced, a few documentary-inspired films are of undeniable interest. **Noche de curas** (Night of Priests; 1978), directed by Carlos Morales, records the dialogue of various priests, who, one way or another, have broken their clerical ties. The film is a testimonial of the open crisis in the very heart of the Spanish Catholic Church, where, with only a few exceptions, an attempt at maintaining the confessional spirit of national-Catholicism has been undertaken. **Ocaña, retrato intermitente** (Ocaña, an Intermittent Portrait; 1978),

by Ventura Pons is about the homosexual painter and transvestite, Ocaña, a well-known figure on the Barcelona Ramblas or boulevards. It is seriously done and has a pert manner that makes the film hardly acceptable fare for traditional Iberian machismo. A similar technique can be found in **El asesino de Pedralbes** (The Pedralbes' Muderer; 1978), by Gonzalo Herralde. The man interviewed or the protagonist of the story is a convict. José Luis García Sánchez and Andrés Linares present **Dolores** (1980), an emotive portrait of the president of the Spanish Communist Party. However, its distribution is limited. The Andalusian film. **Rocío,** by Fernando Ruiz, is on the one hand an example of how to make a documentary, and on the other, it is an obvious attempt at local or regional film-making. A lawsuit is brought against the documentary for alleged defamation and a judge orders the film withdrawn from Spain's cinemas. The director of **Rocío** is later sentenced and cuts are imposed on the film. It is the story of the «romería» of pilgrimage to the shrine of Our Lady of the Dew, giving glimpses of the local hysteria surrounding the event and its economic and ideological manipulation by reactionary sectors. Another important documentary linked to the idea of Basque cinema is **El proceso de Burgos** (The Burgos Trial; 1979), by Imanol Urribe. It compiles the

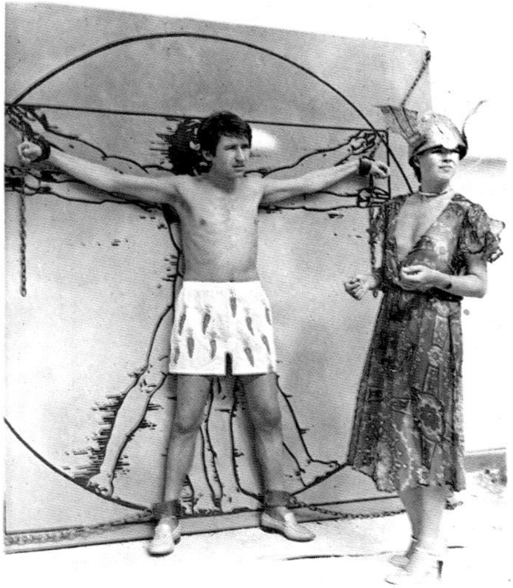

José Sacristán and Marilina Ross in Reina Zanahoria **(1978) by Gonzalo Suárez.**

testimonies of the ETA members who were tried in a court martial by General Franco's government. An **independent** effort is made by Angel García del Val who shoots the documentary **Cada ver es** (It's All Appearances; 1981), regarding the day-to-day life of an employee of the Department of Anatomy of Valencia's School of Medicine. It is given an «S» rating due to the continual presence of corpses and is the object of economic restrictions by the General Directorate of Cinematography when it is released in 16 mm. Something similar occurs to **Después de...** (After...; 1981), by Cecilia Bartolomé, which is a series of interviews regarding the situation in Spain following the death of General Franco. The film would have serious economic difficulties.
The results of the documentaries made during this period are rather poor. Even though they are all very interesting, most of them have a difficult time at the box office. It is a type of cinema that deserves a certain amount of aid and greater public support, since it deals with topics taken straight from Spain's socio-political situation, but quite to the contrary, it is necessarily condemned to marginal or specialized distribution and exhibition in circuits which do not even exist in Spain. In other countries, this vacuum is filled by universities or cultural centers.
Another testimonial film, but this time

Daniel Dicenta and José Manuel Cervino
in El crimen de Cuenca **(1979) by Pilar Miró.**

of a fictional nature, is **El crimen de Cuenca** (The Cuenca Crime; 1979) by Pilar Miró. It is about a police case at the beginning of the century in which torture carried out by members of the Civil Guard will make innocent men confess to crimes they did not commit. The film is withheld from release after a suit is brought by high-ranking members of the Civil Guard and is premiered several years afterwards. When it is released, the indirect publicity it received as a result of the legal proceedings —the whole affair is considered as an attack against Spain's newly won freedom of expression, the film becomes one of the most successful money-makers in the history of Spanish cinema.
During these years, Bigas Luna shows himself to be an original director. In **Bilbao** (1978) and **Caniche** (Poodle; 1979), sex and eroticism play an important role. The first film alludes to the obsessions of a morbid person who is in love with a prostitute, while the second is about the turbulent relations between a brother and sister whose lives revolve around dogs. The style of Bigas Luna is that of notable conciseness, and with close-ups of objects and details which contribute to the making of an oppressive universe.
José Luis Garci continues along the same lines which originally brought him success. **Solos en la madrugada** (Alone in the Early Hours; 1978) and **Las verdes praderas** (Green Pastures; 1979)

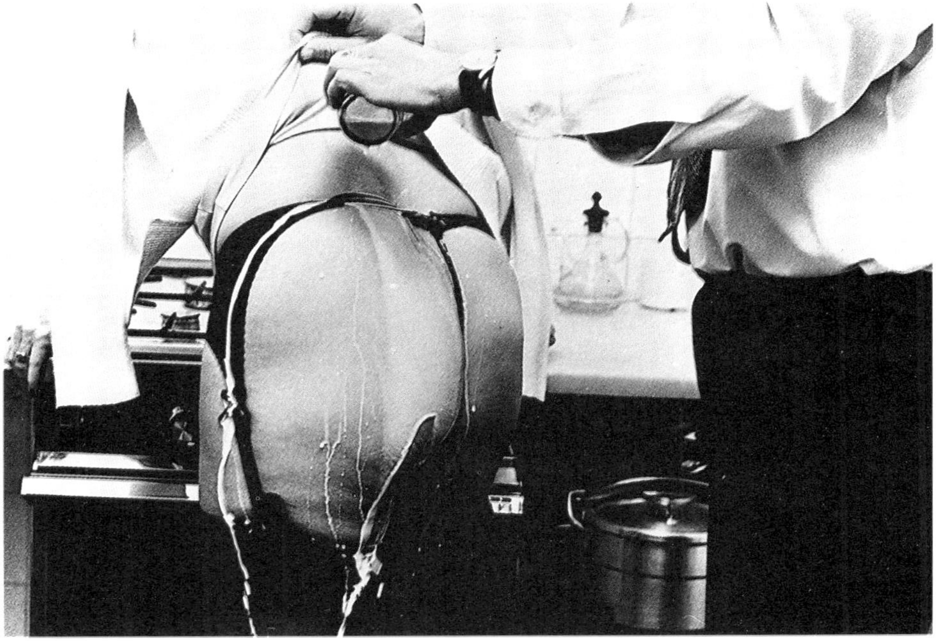

Bilbao (1978) by Bigas Luna.

José Sacristán and Emma Cohen in *Solos en la madrugada* **(1978) by José Luis Garci.**

as well as **Viva la clase media** (Long Live the Middle Class; 1980), by José María González Sinde —in which Garci is only screenwriter and actor—represent a type of nostalgic and commercial comedy which hopes to achieve a type of dignity that is different from the normal films designed for the Spanish consumer. Jaime de Armiñán follows a similar path during this period and makes **Nunca es tarde** (It's Never Too Late; 1977), **Al servicio de la mujer española** (At the Service of Spanish Womanhood; 1978) and **El nido** (The Nest; 1980), employing a style that could be described as sentimental and brilliant.

Comedies represent a large part of production. Sometimes they are satirical, other times they are comedies of manners, but for the most part these pictures are unpretentiously sentimental. However, the industry tries to attract cinema-goers, especially the youth who flee from movie theaters where brainy or intellectual fare is billed. The problem is that there is a difference in age and concerns between directors and that potential film-going public, and except in very concrete cases, these two groups are unable to get together. **La orgía** (The Orgy; 1978) and **Salut i força al canut** (Health, Lust and Fun; 1979) are two delightful examples by Francesc Bellmunt which move in that direction. The same director will be very

Angela Molina and Víctor Valverde in *El corazón del bosque* (1978) by Manuel Gutiérrez Aragón.

successful with his **La quinta del porro** (The Stoned Conscripts; 1980). Francisco Betriu is much shrewder and more critical with his **Los fieles sirvientes** (The Faithful Servants; 1979). The film is an amusing satire on the relations between servants and their masters within the framework of Catalonia's industrial middle-class society. It also has a firm grasp on the absurd side of their relationship. Fernando Colomo continues to specialize in comedies. Both **¿Qué hace una chica como tú en un sitio como éste?** (What's a Girl Like You Doing in a Place Like This?; 1978) and **La mano negra** (The Black Hand; 1980) contain a special sense of humor and deal with the day-to-day universe of people who are frustrated, absentminded and failures in life. Colomo's two films also have a certain detective element to them. Another film-maker who directs a theatrical and luxurious comedy is Fernando Fernán Gómez, even though his **Cinco tenedores** (Five Stars; 1979) is nothing more than a job he undertook at the spur of the moment. Finally, José Luis García Sánchez obtained first prize in the Berlin Film Festival with **Las truchas** (The Trout; 1977) a lavishly choral and biting comedy which reconstructs a delirious banquet organized by a fishermen's association. The people present mirror all the vices and obsessions of society in general, a little like Luis Buñuel's **El ángel exterminador** (Exterminating Angel;

1963). Another director who made a comedy, but who started off on the right foot, is Fernando Trueba with his **Opera prima** (A Cousin in Opera/First Work; 1980). The scope and success of the film would have their effects on the industry. It is about several young people who dream of traveling to Machu Picchu.

Ambitious films, small colossi of the Spanish film industry, are represented by **La Sabina** (The Sabina; 1979), by José Luis Borau, a coproduction with Sweden and whose director of photography is Sven Nikvist. The film tries to show a clash between two cultures together with a myth and an ancestral legend. Another ambitious project is **La verdad sobre el caso Savolta** (The Truth About the Savolta Case; 1978), by Antonio Drove. It is a kind of detective film of the masses based on a true event involving the trafficking of arms. The picture has an international cast and follows the example set by diverse French and Italian films.

Meanwhile, three directors continue to work with an enviable continuity. Manuel Gutiérrez Aragón, whose career is full of prizes and recognition given at both national and international film festivals, consecutively shoots **Sonámbulos** (Sleep Walkers; 1977), a parable about the confusing world of extreme leftist clandestine activity including a sensational sequence which gives an almost dream-like account of

Carol Kane and Angela Molina in La Sabina **(1979) by José Luis Borau.**

(Previous page)
Ana Belén in Sonambulos **(1977) by Manuel Gutiérrez Aragón.**

Cecilia Roth in *Arrebato* (1979) by Iván Zulueta.

(Following page)
Jorge Rigaud, Eduardo McGregor, Gerard Tichy, León Klimovsky and Cristina Marcos in *Maravillas* (1980) by Manuel Gutiérrez Aragón.

an assault by the Francoist police on the National Library; **El corazón del bosque** (The Heart of the Forest; 1978), a lovely story which narrates the useless death of the last **maquis** or guerilla opposed to the Franco regime; and **Maravillas** (1980), an unreal and dream-like story about the lives of adolescents on the very fringe of society and delinquents who clash with a world of haggard adults. Carlos Saura, whose work obtains considerable success in France, also makes film after film. **Los ojos vendados** (Blindfolded; 1978) touches on the question of torture and political persecution with Saura's usual aesthetic qualities. **Deprisa, deprisa** (Hurry, Hurry; 1980) is a true-to-life chronicle of a group of young bank robbers. **Mamá cumple cien años** (Mother Turns a Hundred; 1979) is a sardonic film which uses the same characters as in **Ana y los lobos** (Ana and the Wolves; 1972). The cast is the same and Rafaela Aparicio gives a sensational performance. Finally, Saura makes **Bodas de sangre** (Blood Wedding; 1981), a cross between a documentary and **cinema-vérité** and based on a dance version of García Lorca's play by the Antonio Gades dance company. Director Eloy de la Iglesia concentrates on a much more commercial product and makes **El sacerdote** (The Priest; 1977), **El diputado** (The Parliamentary Deputee; 1978), **Miedo a salir de noche** (Fearing To Go Out at Night; 1979) and **Navajeros**

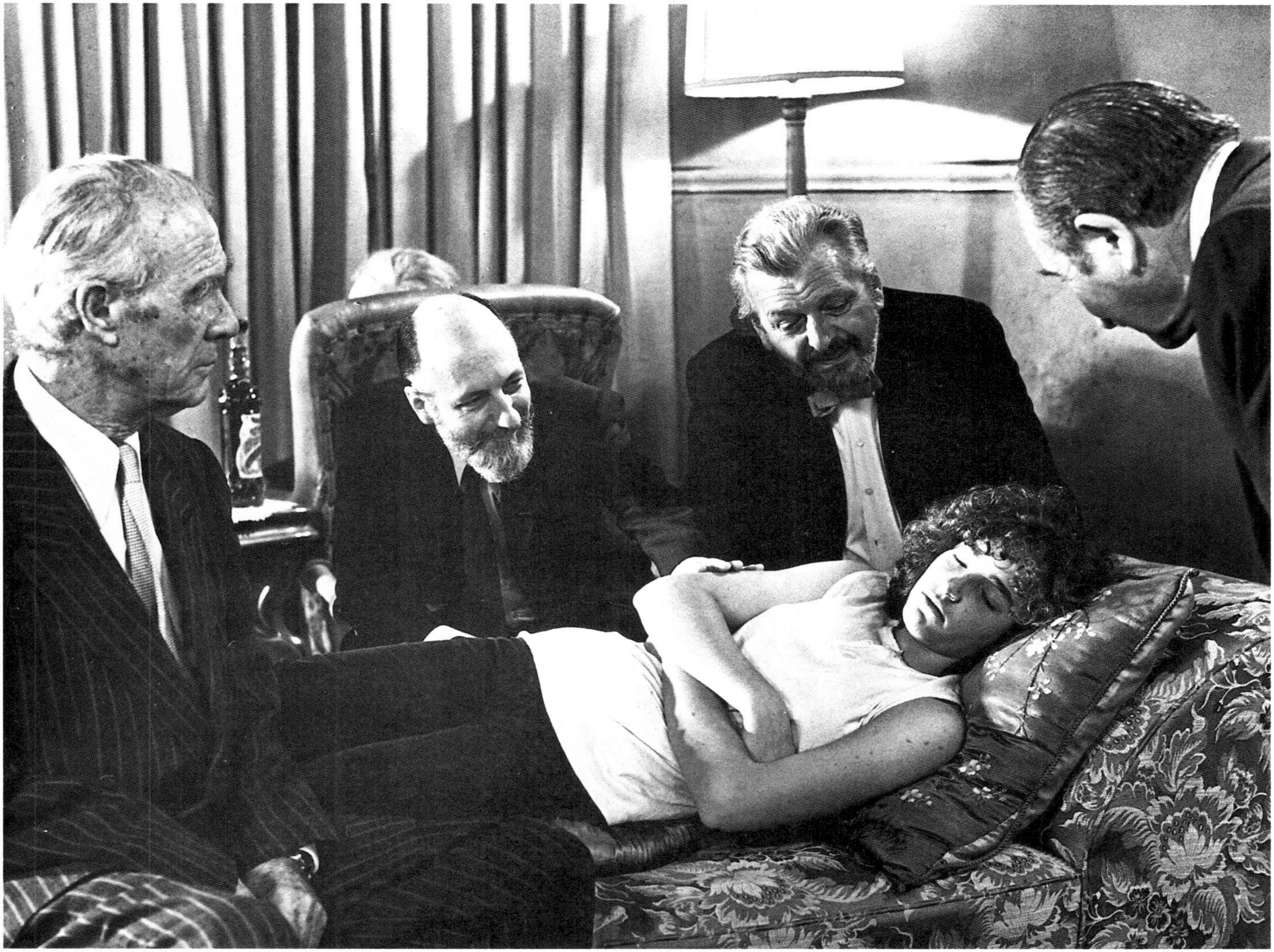

Ricardo Franco in Los restos del naufragio **(1978) by Ricardo Franco.**

(Knife Fighters; 1980). All these films show a constant concern for subjects with impact that are normally found in the sensationalist press and in the crime reports section of papers.
Up-and-coming directors such as Jaime Chávarri and Ricardo Franco have difficulty in trying to give their personal view of the world. Chávarri makes **Dedicatoria** (Dedication; 1980), a poetic film in which a journalist searches for the true identity of a strange writer at the same time as he is trapped into complex relations with his daughter. Franco directs a film that walks a fine line between the fantastic and the poetic called **Los restos del naufragio** (The Remains of the Shipwreck; 1978), which is a reflection on the impossibility of adventure and on the proximity of madness.
To sum up, the answers to many questions posed in this period would remain pending. A few tendencies would be established and quite a few careers would be consolidated, not only in the area of direction, but in production as well, including an important number of new and promising technicians and actors. It is a time full of doubts, timid attempts and frustrated perspectives. Something that should be kept in mind during this period are the provisional measures establishing a form of cooperation between TVE (Spanish Television) and the film industry. The resulting productions between television and the

film industry represent a kind of fund which are limited to the adaptation of literary works. In spite of these conditioning factors and limitations, the small advances made in this area would produce important works which are on the very frontier of a transitional stage full of doubts and another stage, much closer to us in time, which we trust will represent a settling in process, a stage in which the Spanish film industry will take a much closer look at itself.

1982-1983: Making up for lost time

Perhaps we could be accused of excessive optimism or inordinate favoritism. It should be made clear that if we give emphasis to the results of the last few months and if we place our explicit trust in Spain's socialist government, it is not so much because we identify with or respect their governmental program —in all likelihood we would not share the views of this program, but rather because we are strongly convinced that after forty years of dictatorship and after a long period of initiation to the democratic process, the definitive consolidation of democracy as well as the use and practise of freedoms should lead our cinema to serious reflection on its own possibilities and performance.
In general, we believe that during the brief period that has elapsed our cinema is taking stock of its own situation and is headed towards a rebirth. The industry is moving amidst what it inherited from the previous period and towards what film-makers in general and the guiding spirits would like Spanish cinema to achieve. All sectors are seeking new norms that will regulate the areas of production, distribution and exhibition. As we write this, a controversy is raging over a law that imposes the right of the Spanish film industry to use a language which foreign production, and very concretely the American film industry, has used for its exclusive benefit. These new norms will represent an important victory over the Francoist and fascist measures which forty years before had a harmful effect on our film industry and on the education and culture of our society. A worthy basis for collaboration between television and the film industry has appeared, while the government has begun to provide aid to the production sector —for example, an advance on money that a film will eventually take in at the box office. These measures will logically contribute to a sensible development of our cinema. Naturally, doubts still exist as to whether the norms will benefit everyone, if it is really possible to arrive at a situation in which the Spanish film industry is favored at all levels, if the aid the government provides will result in a sterile form of protectionism and an unproductive form of state control. The evident crisis in the film sector, the growing importance of video, the decompensation of certain locales and distribution and exhibition circuits, the mediocre work being done in the area by Spain's regional governments and a long list of other irregularities which have burdened the industry for decades, make us believe that we are faced with a road full of obstacles, a road that can only be smoothed over with an extensive and strict series of measures and controls.
Of considerable relevance are the numerous prizes and the large amount of recognition which the most important films of this period receive, although similar awards and recognition had their effect at other moments of the history of Spanish cinema. When the debatable **Volver a empezar** (Starting Over; 1982), by José Luis Garci, obtained the first Hollywood Oscar for Spanish cinema all the bells were set ringing, pealing out the international competitiveness of our cinema. A similar situation is created out of the brilliant career of Carlos Saura, from our point of view less personal today than in the past, but nevertheless the object of immense critical and public acclaim outside our frontiers as a result of **Carmen** (1983), a film based on the works of Merimée and Bizet and on the splendid dance company of Antonio Gades.

The applause received by the serious coproductions that the industry makes with TVE also serve as an example for what can be done. Francisco Betriu does a film adaption of a magnificent novel by Mercé Rodoreda called **La plaza del Diamante** (Diamond Square; 1982), which is first exhibited on commercial circuits in its feature format and later as a series on television. The work is an impassioned portrait of a woman who is a victim of the Spanish Civil War. Mario Camús wins a prize in the Berlin Film Festival with **La colmena** (The Beehive; 1982), produced with a similar exhibition criterion and based on a novel by Camilo José Cela, set in postwar Spain. Antonio José Betancor adapts **Crónica del alba,** by Ramón J. Sender, and makes two separate films from the novel, films that would also be made into a television series: **Valentina** (1982) and **1919, Crónica del alba** (1919, Dawn Chronicle; 1983). These ambitious and more or less costly productions that deal with the past make their presence felt on the Spanish film scene. **Bearn** (1983), by Jaime Chávarri, is the adaptation of a highly esteemed work by the writer Llorenç Villalonga. The film is set in Majorca and is produced by Alfredo Matas, one of the most noteworthy producers of recent years. Matas and Chávarri team up again to shoot **Las bicicletas son para el verano** (Bicycles Are for Summer; 1984), based on a theater piece by Fernando Fernán Gómez that is set in a Civil War Madrid.

Patricia Adriani in Sus años dorados **(1980) by Emilio Martínez-Lázaro.**

Marilina Ross in Soldados **(1978) by Alfonso Ungría.**

(Previous page)
Laura del Sol and Cristina Hoyos in Carmen **(1983) by Carlos Saura.**

Another example of what we can term as gigantism is **La conquista de Albania** (The Conquest of Navarre; 1983), by Alfonso Ungría. It is a superproduction that is partially backed by the Basque regional government and tells of events which took place in the fourteenth century. The same thing occurs with **¡Victoria!** (Victory; 1983) by Antoni Ribas. It is a six-hour long super-production that focuses on recent Catalonian history.
Apart from these big productions which aspire to be big successes with the public, there are smaller pictures which also try to occupy an important place on the market. This is the case with **Asesinato en el comité central** (Murder in the Central Committee; 1982), in which director Vicente Aranda prepares a screenplay from an entertaining detective story created by writer Manuel Vázquez Montalbán which springs from an imaginary crisis in the Spanish Communist Party. Other examples of this are the latest films by Eloy de la Iglesia, especially **El Pico** (The Shoot Up; 1983), a picture about drugs and the clash between different generations in the Basque region in Northern Spain, including direct references to the Civil Guard and the local nationalist movement. The same is true of the first film by actor José Sacristán called **Soldados de plomo** (Tin Soldiers; 1983), a well-made picture with excellent actors. The film is a

Francisco Rabal, Francisco Algora, Mario Pardo and José Sacristán in La colmena **(1982) by Mario Camus.**

mixture of a comedy, a detective story and a melodrama. Another noteworthy film is **El arreglo** (The Rendering; 1983), by another first-timer, José Antonio Zorrilla, a story about police corruption which tries to make its way in the detective genre, although it is only half successful.

One of the most outstanding cases of continuity and coherence is offered to us by the team made up by producer Luis Megino and director Manuel Gutiérrez Aragón who make the relevant and timely **Demonios en el jardín** (Demons in the Garden; 1982), starring the leading actresses Angela Molina and Ana Belén. The picture is about family bickerings regarding a young boy and is set in the postwar period of the fifties when the black market and the official newsreels, or the NO-DO, were of significance to Spaniards.

In the area of documentaries, **Vestida de azul** (Dressed in Blue; 1983), should be mentioned, a film which marks the return to cinema of Antonio Giménez-Rico. The picture includes interviews and testimonies of different Spanish transvestites and transsexuals who explain their sexual, labor and human experiences with praiseworthy sincerity. Pedro Olea also reappears with his **Akelarre** (Witches' Sabbath; 1984), a story about the Spanish Inquisition and witchcraft whose action takes place in a town in sixteenth century Navarre. Another director who

Angela Molina, Ana Belén, Alvaro Sánchez and Encarna Paso in Demonios en el jardín **(1982) by Manuel Gutiérrez Aragón.**

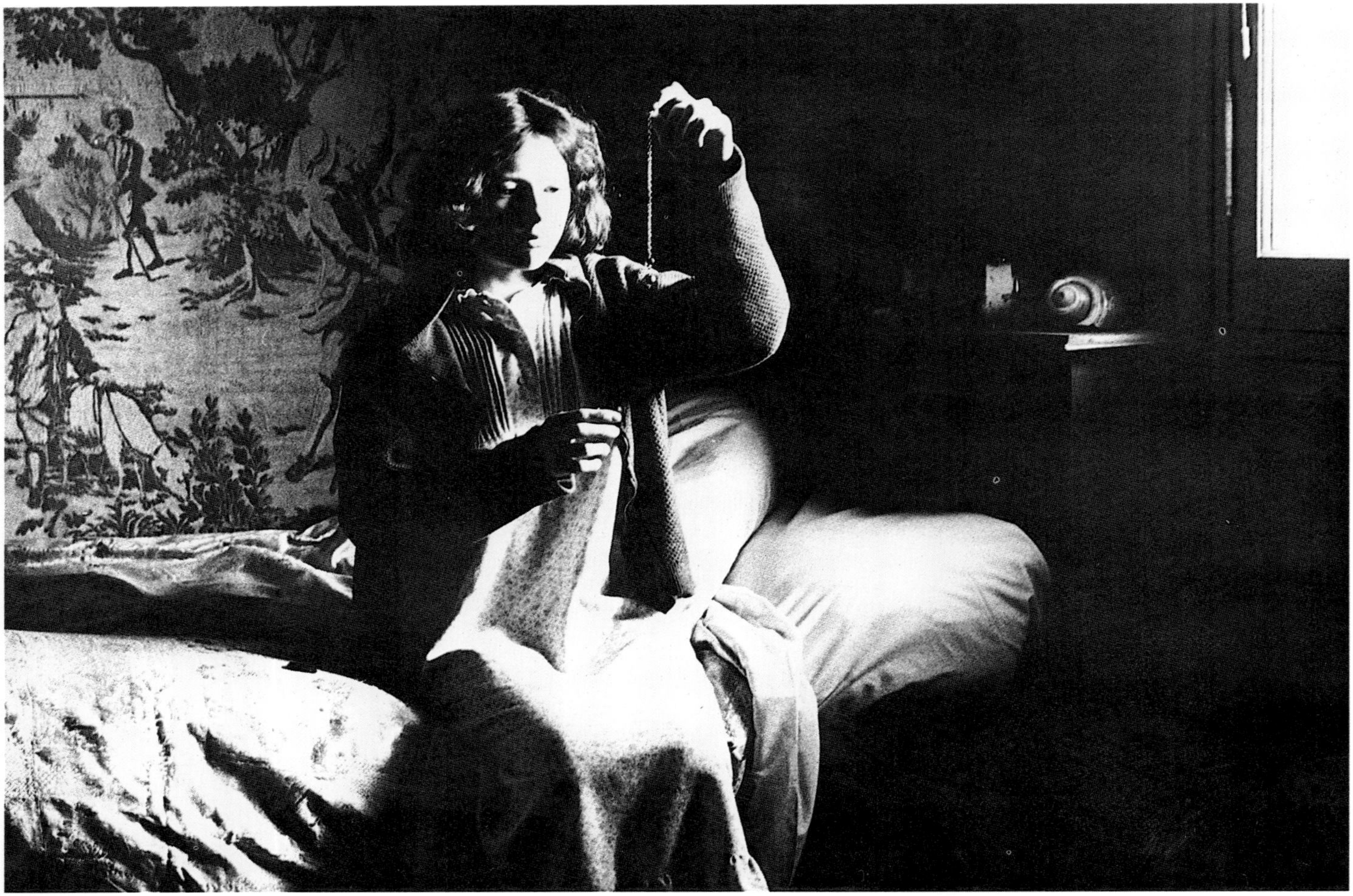

Iciar Bollain in El sur **(1983) by Víctor Erice.**

makes a come-back is Gonzalo Suárez with **Epílogo** (Epilogue; 1984). But the director who makes the most awaited come-back and the film-maker who awakens the greatest expectation is Víctor Erice. Ten years after directing **El espíritu de la colmena** (The Spirit of the Beehive; 1973), Erice shoots **El Sur** (The South; 1983) for Querejeta.
The film is similar to his first feature in that it delves into the life of an adolescent in a Spain of the fifties. Starring Omero Antonutti, it tells of the relationship between a father and his daughter, posing several questions which are not necessarily answered in the picture.
The comedy genre is the field which is most cultivated both by those who at the beginning of their careers are looking for a good reception and a quick return on the investment and by those veterans who have made humor a constant element in their films. Luis F. Berlanga culminates a kind of saga or trilogy —for the moment— with his **Nacional III** (National III; 1982). The film is the continuing adventures of the Leguineche family, a group of aristocrats who started out in **La escopeta nacional** (National Shotgun). Carles Mira tries to create with his **Que nos quiten lo bailao** (No One Can Take Away Our Good Times Together; 1983), a satire in relations between Moors and Christians. The film has elements of a musical or a variety show. Madrid director Pedro Almodóvar continues to make such comedies as **Laberinto de pasiones** (Labyrinth of Passions; 1982) which involves an alleged double of the Shah's son, and **Entre tinieblas** (In the Dark; 1983), a burlesque story with nuns —and with a delightful combination of good actresses— which was presented in the Mostra of Venice.
The appearance of «X» rated cinemas for the exhibition of material commonly called pornographic, and a decree regarding the classification of films, open the door for the production of soft-core films. The so-called «S» rated films which had swept through the market are now doomed to an agonizing death. Those directors who specialize in light comedies continue to be successful with easily produced and distributed films, but for the majority of film-makers in Spain, the solutions to the industry's problems point to a quality cinema, one of technical solvency and undeniable dignity. It is a type of film which is winning ground both on the domestic market and abroad, representing an alternative to a cinematography whose tradition and history deserve much better modern-day results.

AVANT-GARDE

Cecilia Roth and Pedro Díaz del Corral during the shooting of the film short Historias paralelas **(1983) by Tote Trenas.**

AVANT-GARDE

Manuel Palacio

I. Introduction

A point should be made before writing about the history of avant-garde cinema in Spain. There has never been an avant-garde film movement that has worked in an organized and lasting way. There have been, however, isolated individuals who have made works of notable interest. The directors of these films have normally had to produce their own works, they have never been able to count on a stable distribution and exhibition structure, they have generally been forgotten or have been pushed to one side by specialized film magazines, and they have never been comprehended when it comes time for public institutions or the administration to carry out research work in the area of cinema. Added to this is the fact that the very structure of the Spanish film industry makes it impossible for formal experimentation to be carried out in its midst as well as the fact that limitations have been imposed by our own socio-political situation throughout a large part of the century. The result of all this is that our avant-garde cinema has never gone beyond the embryonic stage.

In order to remedy this lack of tradition, the authors of the only two existing essays on the question (Francisco Aranda, 1953, and Eugeni Bonet/Manuel Palacio, 1982) describe as avant-garde films those works with certain restless and **advanced** qualities,

films which would have difficulties being included in what in an international context would currently be considered as avant-garde or experimental works.
The examples of novel documentary film-makers (Carlo Velo, for one) are found in the Spanish equivalent of the new cinema phenomenon —principally called independent cinema in the sixties/seventies and to a lesser extent, the **Barcelona School**— or in a concept which is even further away from avant-garde cinematography, the burlesque-satirical films of the thirties or the international mimicries that **amateur** film-makers reproduced during those same years. These are examples that one should cite when historically dealing with Spanish avant-garde cinema. At this point, one should not dismiss the possibility of clearing up the confusion which repeatedly exists when a film is defined as avant-garde simply because it is an alternative type of production to the industry norm. This confusion frequently pops up in Spain, a country where avant-garde cinematography is synonymous with boredom or something **strange** or where this work has no other function than filmic research which does not have the industry as a frame of reference. This is true whether it is opposed to the industry itself —based on the Narrative-Representative-Industrial parameters, or the NRI of Claudine Eizykman or on the Modes of Institutional Representation of Noël Burch— or whether it permits a circular process between its resulting innovations and their later industrial use. Not making then, a distinction between a linguistic form of research using the parameters of the industry— even though in many cases with radical differences in production, distribution or exhibition, and as such, potentially directed towards a non-deferential public, and linguistic form of research which is the very essence of the work, more than opposing, it simply avoids any reference to the industry. With these first considerations in mind, we can now go on to refer to the works themselves.

II. From the historic avant-garde to the postwar

The Spain of the first decades of the century offers enormous differences in its economic, social and cultural evolution with that of the rest of Europe. It is not until the second half of the twenties that the first works appear that can be listed as avant-garde or advanced in their outlook.
The rickety historical avant-garde of Spanish cinema does not exist except as a series of isolated films which have no unity of purpose among them. Then too, their late appearance would result in Spanish film-makers copying what is being done elsewhere in the world, following the tracks of what is easily detectable as futurism, expressionism and impressionism. It is not strange, then, that Buñuel had to leave Spain in order to undertake the filmic subversion of his first two works.
Prior to this one should first cite the work of the architect Nemesio Sobrevila. He is the author of two films, **El sexto sentido** (Sixth Sense; 1926) and **Lo más español** or **Al Hollywood madrileño** (The Most Spanish/To Madrid's Hollywood; 1927-1928), which in their own right make him the first confounded author of Spanish cinema. Neither of the two films are ever released and the later attempts by this Basque to direct are not very successful either. Currently, only **El sexto sentido** is conserved. It is a melodrama whose avant-garde innovations are secondary to the main plot. They are limited to the film short that the eccentric Professor Kamus shows to León, who is always falling in love, in order to teach him the extrasensorial advantages of the film camera. It amounts to nothing when compared to modern concepts of avant-garde cinematography, but in any case, it is the first example that we have of such concepts as urban symphony, **cineojo** (an eye for cinema) or **voyeurism.** His second film is lost. According to references, Sobrevila

worked very hard on the film, even building the sets himself. The work was conceived as episodes that were parodies of the different styles and genres which were in vogue at that time.
Another film which has disappeared is **Historia de un duro** (The Story of a Five Peseta Coin; 1927), by Santino Micón. Arriving in the world of film as a critic, his cinematographic career includes several commercial titles. **Historia de un duro** can be described then, as an exception in his film credits. The film is not very original when seen in a European context —briefly, it is about the travels of a five peseta coin, while the spectator only has the opportunity of seeing shots of the extremities of the different characters in the film— but there is no doubt that it is an unusual work in the Spanish film panorama.
When speaking about the development of Spanish avant-garde cinema, the magazine **La gaceta literaria** (The Literary Gazette; 1927-1932) should be cited. It is the main point of reference and the spokesman of avant-garde films in Spain. Founded by Ernesto Giménez Caballero and published twice monthly, **La gaceta literaria** was very much in line with other avant-garde European magazines and gave great importance to this new medium —standing out, for example, is issue number 43, totally dedicated to film. Its pages dedicated to cinema, first edited by Buñuel and later by Juan Piqueras, have become obligatory reading when studying avant-garde cinematography in Spain. **La gaceta literaria** did not support a parallel production structure for avant-garde film, since it was more than evident that this sector had no ties with the industry. Principally, in articles of theoretical reflection it talked about the very essence of film or about more concrete questions or issues, written by Piqueras or Luis Buñuel himself. This did not mean, however, that the magazine did not give detailed accounts of films made by Buñuel or Giménez Caballero.
As a kind of film extension of itself, on October 1, 1928, **La gaceta literaria** created the **España** Film Society. According to the words of Giménez Caballero, the original idea «like those clubs which existed in Paris, is to bring to the literary and artistic people of Spain the innovation of film». The film society, in spite of a few changes, remained faithful during the three years of its existence to the original program scheme: showing avant-garde, documentary and repertory films. Practically all the European avant-garde films —including the Soviet— were seen in its cinemas, a circumstance which would not have been possible if it had not been for the simple-minded programing of other cinemas. In a certain sense, the **España** Film Society became the main meeting place for most of the film-makers who worked in the avant-garde area. Even so, seeing the potential of what could be done in the field was to a certain extent frustrating for Spanish film-makers since they did not have the financial and technical possibilities to do the same.
In order to end this survey of Spanish avant-garde film of the period, it is necessary to consider the work of Ernesto Giménez Caballero. He took part in international congresses of independent film in **Sarraz** (1929) and **Brussels** (1930) and was very close to everything that was done in the avant-garde field during these years. Starting in 1930, he becomes increasingly enamored of fascism. His support for this ideology continues during Francoism and he becomes one of its main apologists.
Giménez Caballero's films did not lack the financial and technical means of the other avant-garde works produced at the time. They are not avant-garde films strictly speaking, but rather **advanced** films within the Spanish context. **Esencia de verbena** (The Essence of the Fair; 1930) was premiered in the film society or club on November 29, 1939, and was later shown in the Brussels Congress and in the Ursuline Studio in Paris. It is a «documentary poem of Madrid in twelve sequences» as can be read in the credits. **Noticiario del cine-club** (Film Society Newsreel; 1930) is a silent film

short in which a large part of the intelligentsia of the period can be seen. Standing out among them is Ramón Gómez de la Serna, the true catalyst of the Spanish avant-garde movement as can be seen from the fact that Luis Buñuel insisted on shooting his first film with Gómez de la Serna as the screenwriter.

Ernesto Giménez Caballero would have been the perfect person to have begun a tradition of Spanish avant-garde film. His work was not born out of individual heroism, but rather out of a favorable context in which he participated both in union with the motives of the artistic-literary avant-garde by means of the **La gaceta literaria** magazine and with his presence in international events —the result being Spain's exemplary participation in the Brussels and Sarraz congresses. However, it was not possible to begin a tradition since Spanish avant-garde cinema could not make up for the time lost. When it was on the point of seriously starting production in this area, Europe was on the verge of being swallowed up by the socio-political movements of the thirties. Giménez Caballero himself had also begun to walk down the path of fascism, a road that would definitively lead him away from avant-garde ideals. Formal experimentation within the film industry is the great novelty of Spanish cinema of the II Republic. For the first time in

Una de fieras (1934) by Eduardo García Maroto.

its history, Spanish cinematography was provided with a minimal professional organization that allowed for linguistic research work in the field. This is what is behind the work of Carlos Velo and Fernando Mantilla, probably the most notable production carried out during the Republican period. Both men produced for Cifesa an appreciable number of film shorts between 1934 and 1936. Their production can be included within the interest shown for the social documentary, a movement which flourished in Europe following the end of the historical avant-garde. The most notable example of this type of film produced before that time is **Las Hurdes (Tierra sin pan)** (Las Hurdes, Land without Bread; 1932), by Luis Buñuel. From our point of view, the most interesting work make by the Velo-Mantilla team is perhaps **Infinitos** (Infinites; 1935), a film which is now lost to us. Based on an idea by Maurice Maeterlinck and with music by Rodolfo Halffter, images and sounds are juxtaposed in the work. In 1936, Velo and Mantilla were contracted to direct five feature-length films, a project which the civil war stopped. Some films were made inside the industry during these years—oftentimes self-produced— that were quite different from more normal productions. It is very difficult to consider them as avant-garde works, but they can be mentioned due to

Una de miedo (1934) by Eduardo García Maroto.

their relationship to the literary avant-garde of that time which used the parody, the caricature or the art of buffoonery as forms of expression. These works include **Yo quiero que me lleven a Hollywood** (I Want Them To Take Me to Hollywood Too; 1931), **Falsos noticieros** (False News; 1934) and **Do re mi fa sol la si** (1934), by Edgar Neville; **Cinco minutos de españolada** (Five Minutes of an Exaggerated Spain; 1936), by Rafael Gil and Menéndez Pidal; the **One about...** series (1934-1935) by Eduardo García Maroto; **Celuloides rancios** (Rancid Celluloides; 1933), and **Celuloides cómicos** (Comic Celluloides; 1936-1938), by Enrique Jardiel Poncela, etc.
Finally, in the Republican Spain before the civil war, an incipient **amateur** cinema could be found, primarily centered in Catalonia. With their own publication —published by the film section of the **Centre Excursionista de Catalunya,** the Catalonian **amateur** film-makers such as Doménec Giménec, Francésc Gibert, Eusebi Ferré or Delmir de Caralt felt the influences of the avant-garde movement and they tried to copy these ideas between 1932 and 1936.
During the civil war, almost all the production is centered on the documentary, but even in this area the series **Tres minutos** (Three Minutes; 1937) can be mentioned. Produced by **Socorro Rojo** (Red Aid), the films in the series employ different simultaneous

superimpositions and fades. Also noteworthy are the untitled **trailers** which are produced by the film services of the Sub-secretariat of Propaganda and directed by Manuel Villegas López, Fernando Mantilla and Francisco Camacho, who used fragmented images, visual metaphors, collages, etc.
The harsh repression of the forties and fifties is not conducive to experimentation. In the years immediately following the civil war, a few burlesque films are made along the same lines as those done during the II Republic: **Un bigote para dos** (A Moustache for Two; 1940), by Tono and Mihura, and **Mauricio, una víctima del vicio** (Mauricio, a Victim of Vice; 1940), by Enrique Jardiel Poncela. The documentary is the only area where a certain amount of experimentation is carried out —although this does not necessarily mean avant-garde experimentation. Of special interest is **Visión fantástica** (Fantastic Vision; 1957), a NO-DO production that was directed by Eugène Deslaw. The work is a meticulous solarization of different shots of the men and lands of Spain.
A general evaluation of Spanish avant-garde cinema of these years can be made with the word «scanty». The period is plagued with attempts and projects which never came off and avant-garde cinema had minimum repercussions on the industry, an indecisive industry when it came time to take part in avant-garde **adventures,** an industry which totally lacked pure or abstract film. The political conditions of this first period of avant-garde film are especially revealing, since the country went through a dictatorship, a civil war, and another dictatorship which imposed a harsh repression during the forties and fifties.

III. José Val del Omar, a bridge between generations

Paraphrasing Amos Vogel in his commentary in **Aguaespejo granadino** o **La gran seguiriya** (1955), it could be said that José Val del Omar «is one of the great unknown film-makers within world cinema». A self-taught man, he worked in many different areas. However, it is precisely in research and creative work where Val del Omar has displayed his genius. An individualistic and solitary researcher, he could never submit himself to the strict discipline which the audiovisual industry imposes on specialists who carry out research. His cinematographic work includes the results of a large part of his experimentations. These include diaphonic sound, what can be described as an «apanoramic» overflowing on the screen, and tactilvision. Perhaps the complications of screening films with these characteristics forced Val del Omar to withdraw his films from circulation at the beginning of the sixties.
Val del Omar's credits originally included two films, **Aguaespejo granadino** o **La gran seguiriya** (Granadan Mirror-water or The Great «Seguiriyan» Dance) and **Fuego en Castilla** (Fire in Castile), both dating from 1959. Until shortly before his death, Val del Omar had worked on the completion of two other parts, which, coupled with the first two works, would form a standard-length feature. As a result, the **Tríptico elemental de España** (Elemental Triptych of Spain) would have a structure which would cross through Spain with a diagonal line. The work would start in Galicia in northwestern Spain —a land of earth and mud— with **A carinho galaico** (Galician Endearment), would continue through central Castile —a land of fire— with **Fuego en Castilla** and would end up in southern and southeastern Spain with the Andalusian explosion —water and light— of **La gran seguiriya.** The triptych would also have a prologue, a kind of **film-vortice** called **Ojalá** (Let's Hope So) in which for the first time Val del Omar works with color, lasers and a multi-projection system.
At any rate, even though the film work of Val del Omar may not be extensive, it is very necessary when trying to understand the panorama or the history of Spanish cinema. And from a strictly avant-garde point of view, Val del Omar represents a bridge between the ideals of the historical avant-garde

Alvaro and Elena del Amo in *Paisaje con árbol* **(1974) by Alvaro del Amo.**

and the modern concepts of experimental cinema.

IV. From the sixties until the death of General Franco

The sixties represent the period in which probably the greatest socio-economic mutations take place in all the history of the Franco regime. At the end of the sixties when the possibilities of the so-called **New Spanish Cinema** have been exhausted, the **Independent Spanish Cinema** appears. In a contradictory way, it represents the first half-way coordinated avant-garde activity in Spain. The **Independent Spanish Cinema** movement lumps together a heterogeneous group of individuals who only have in common their struggle against the dominant structure of the film industry. The most important role was played by the so-called narrative reform cinema, an avant-garde group closer to the productive process of film. However, at that time in Spain persons who came from other artistic fields or disciplines began to make a non-narrative film. In the seventies, this non-narrative tendency would become even more pronounced. Among the first to make this type of film is Adolfo Arrieta. He makes two experimental-personal works before emigrating to France: **El crimen de la**

pirindola (The Spinning Top Crime; 1964) and **Imitación al ángel** (Imitation Angel-style; 1965-1966). Both were done in a craftsman-like fashion and they were never publically exhibited—impossible due to the strict political and economic censorship norms of the period, but they had their effect on small groups of initiates.
Alvaro del Amo's work is strongly influenced by the literary avant-garde of the time. His films would be the Spanish example —the shaky film industry allowing— of what Peter Wollen would call the second avant-garde. In any case, it should not be forgotten that the Spanish film panorama simply could not spark possible discussions on two concepts of the avant-garde movement. Alvaro del Amo has made several film shorts including **Zumo** (Juice; 1972), **Paisaje con árbol** (Landscape with Tree; 1974), **Una historia** (A Story; 1978) as well as one feature titled **Dos** (Two; 1980) which had a commercial release.
The difficulties that Alvaro del Amo had in making a cinema of narrative reform within the industry are the same that Antoni Padrós had in carrying through his projects. After making several shorts, Padrós made two features called **Lock-out** (1973) and **Shirley Temple Story** (1975-1976). This latter film received the **Prix L'Age d'Or.** In Padrós' works there exist constant symbolic references to Franco's Spain or to a culture of masses, with a very notable use of sound negative. None of his features are given a commercial release.
Other directors that should be mentioned are Augusto Martínez Torres, who makes **El espíritu del animal** (Animal's Spirit; 1971) and **Ciencias naturales** (Natural Sciences; 1974); Jesús Garay, who shoots **Nemo** (1978) and **Manderley** (1980); and Antonio Artero, who directs **Yo creo que...** (I Think That...; 1976). As an intermediate step towards non-narrative works, the feature **Esquizo** (Schizo; 1970) should be cited. A film made by the well-known architect Ricardo Bofill, **Esquizo** was never released or even legalized by the authorities. The film is a penetrating look at the world of madness, but adorned at times with the tiresome aesthetic of the **Barcelona School.**
Pere Portabella holds a privileged place in the history of Spanish —fringe— cinema. From the end of the fifties, he takes part in different projects that go against the grain of Spanish officialism—for example he is one of the producers of **Viridiana** (1961). As a director, he has made several film shorts and features which range from art documentaries to militant films—**Informe general** (General Report; 1975-1977). From a filmic avant-garde point of view, and independently of films reminiscent of literary avant-gardism such as **No contéis con los dedos** (Don't Count with Your Fingers; 1967) and **Nocturno 29** (Nocturnal 29; 1968), his most interesting film is **Cuadecuc** (1970), also known as **Vampir,** made in collaboration with the poet, Joan Brossa. It is very much in line with the exposing of the productive structure of cinema, a phenomenon which is in vogue at that time. It is not surprising, then, that Portabella's films follow on the heels of **El conde Drácula** (Count Dracula; 1970), by Jesús Franco. Portabella employs the high contrast expressivity of the sound negative and the force of Carles Santos' sound track to make a very notable film.
As a result of the **First International Film School Talks** held in Sitges in 1967, a series of directors with radically leftist viewpoints sprang up who tried to carry out a theoretical rennovation in the criticism of the Francoist opposition. Later, some of these directors along with others made several films adopting minimalist goals, a novelty in Spain, but not very original abroad. These directors include Antonio Artero with his **Del tres al once** (From Three to Eleven; 1968) and **Blanco sobre blanco** (White on White; 1969); Pere Costa, who shoots **Esta es la película** (This Is the Film; 1968); Manolo Calvo, who directs **El 17 de Elvira** (Elvira's 17; 1968); and Paulino Viota with **Duración** (Duration; 1970). An even more radical experiment is **La celosía** (The Lattice Window; 1972), by

Isidoro Valcárcel. The film is a transcription to the screen of pages from Robbe-Grillet's novel, but it does not have a sound track.
The work of Javier Aguirre can also be included in the minimalist parameters and in structural cinema. He is undoubtedly the most persistent experimental director in the history of our cinematography, a fact which does not prevent his work from being unoriginal when compared to what is filmed abroad. His principal corpus is constituted by the so-called **Anti-Cine,** a program of eight films made between 1967 and 1971, films in which this director insists on dealing with formal problems and perception. Aguirre, a Basque director who is known in the Spanish film industry as a maker of grade B commercial films, wrote a book of theoretical reflection on what he calls Anti-Cine. The films comprising the body of Anti-Cine vary in quality. The best are **Impulsos ópticos en progresión geométrica** (Optical Impulses in Geometric Progression), **Fluctuaciones entrópicas** (Entropic Fluctuations) or **Uts cero** (UTS Zero). A film that is not included in the Anti-Cine, but which should be mentioned is the notable **Tautólogos Plus-X** (Tautologists Plus-X; 1974).
Another tradition in Spanish avant-garde cinema has been the work done in experimental film by people who have originally come from the plastic arts. It is curious that Basque painters have done the most to maintain the tradition. These painters include Néstor Basterretxea, Ramón de Vargas, Ruiz Balerdi —the director of a magnificent picture that was made by painting on film called **Homenaje a Tarzán** (Tribute to Tarzan; 1971), Baquedano and Benet Rossel, who, along with J. Xifrá, make an interesting film short titled **Calidoscopio** (Kaleidoscope; 1971), which was distributed on a commercial basis. However, the monumental **Ere erera baleibu icik subua aruaren...** (1968-1970), by José Antonio Sistiaga, is the most impressive film made in this sector. Its dimensions are spectacular: 75 minutes long done in 35 mm. without a sound track and projected in scope. As someone once pointed out, all this makes the film one of the most beautiful non-figurative pictures ever made in the world.
Some musicians have also made films in Spain. Especially important is the work of Carles Santos. The pictures made by this Valencian are closely linked to his compositions of avant-garde music. His credits range from a first period (1965-1972) which is essentially conceptual in nature, to a second (beginning in 1977) in which his films directly overlap with his performances or with the repetitive structure of his music. His best works include **Acció Santos** (1972), **682-3133 Buffalo Minessota** (1967) and **La do re mi** (1979).
Other avant-garde films from this period that should be cited are those of Ramón Massats-Luis de Pablo, especially **Insular** (1971) or those which include the conceptual views of Jordi Cerdá or José Luis Seguí.

V. The latest years

A series of new directors appear between 1976 and 1979 after the death of Franco and the disappearance of censorship. They are responsible for the partial rennovation of the experimental film panorama. Their works are shown around the world and the interest they awaken abroad was the direct cause for the organization of the only anthological exhibition of Spanish avant-garde film, an exhibition held in April, 1982, in Paris' Georges Pompidou Center. It is also true that the structural conditions for film experimentation have not substantially improved during the last few years. It can also be said that since these avant-garde films are shot in non-commercial formats —a similar tendency can be seen in the evolution of experimental film all over the world. The specialized press has given little attention to this area of film, perhaps because film critics in Spain are more interested in the immediate political benefits of militant cinema or the cinema of the Spanish autonomies or regional nationalities. If we add to this

the fact that many film societies or clubs have disappeared or have been remodeled, the result is that the directors who have appeared during these years have had great difficulties showing their works publically.
Madrid, Valencia and Barcelona have been the main centers of avant-garde production during these years. Iván Zulueta, the director whose work has had the greatest impact on Spain's younger generations, works in Madrid. He has made two commercial films: **Un, dos, tres... al escondite inglés** (One, Two, Three... Playing at English Hide-and-seek; 1969) and **Arrebato** (Rage; 1979). Zulueta has also made no less than twenty films of all different formats and lengths. For different reasons, it is difficult to see these films in public. His work includes concepts of a personal lyrical cinema, of day-to-day experiences and of automatism in one's writings. His films are like home movies in which refilming and the collage principle are used to elaborate concepts of space and time. The most constant feature of his film-making is the culture of our times, a mixture of music, the Hollywood mythology, pop, drugs, etc. The most outstanding of his works are **Babia** (Head in the Clouds; 1975), **A Mal Ga Ma** (A-Mal-Ga-Mate; 1976) and **Leo es pardo** (Leo's Brown; 1976).
Along with Zulueta, Pedro Almodóvar is the main representative of a possible new wave in Spain's commercial cinema, an industry which does not take kindly to change and which is set in its ways. He has made three commercial pictures which have been fairly successful with the Spanish public. Between 1974 and 1978 he makes several madcap films in which he lays on the sound himself, giving a running commentary and creating the dialogues of the various characters or even singing. His works constitute true happenings. The best are **El sueño** (The Dream; 1975), a parody of different aspects of such genres as the Melodrama, and **Folle, folle, folleme Tim** (Screw, Screw, Screw Me Tim), a feature-length film shot in Super-8. Also doing work in Madrid is the photographer Eduardo Momeñe and Waldo Bartolomé.
In Valencia, Luis Rivera makes **Travelling** (1972), the usual film about how the commercial industry is on the verge of collapse, and **Una jornada más** (Just Another Day; 1976-1978), a reflection on the daily life of a working man. Other avant-garde Valencian directors are J. Gandía Casimiro, who makes **Sega Cega** (1968-1972); Ximo Vidal, who shoots **De la finestra estant** (1974); María Montes and her **Espacios imaginarios** (Imaginary Spaces; 1976), José Luis Seguí, who films his **Investigaciones de las formas estéticas por medio de la práctica fílmica** (Research into Aesthetic Forms by Means of Filmic Practice; 1980), etcetera.
Until very recently, Barcelona has been the principal center for avant-garde film in Spain. Eugeni Bonet combines his work as a theoretician of experimental film and video with that of director. Outstanding in this field are **Photomatons** (1976), an interesting film about the depersonalization and massification of modern city life, and **133** (1978-1979), co-directed with Eugenia Balcells. Balcells, who currently uses video as a form of expression, has made among other films: **Boy Meets Girl** (1978) and **Fuga** (Escape; 1979). Juan Bufill employs an aesthetic with few subjetive reminiscenses, and his most interesting works include **Caramelo** (Toffee; 1977) and **Green** (1978). Manuel Huerga is the director of **Brutal Ardour** (1978-1979), a film employing a pre-Rafaelite aesthetic in which the process of refilming is the most important feature. Jordi Artigas, working in experimental animation, has presented Spanish avant-garde cinema with **Metamorfosi** (1979).
Finally, Sierra Fornell, Carles Comas and Madrid's Tau group are more interested in punk/new wave/no wave. Their work can be characterized as being extensive and heterogeneous and their most important films include **Frankie** (1981), by Sierra Fornells, **Quieto todo el mundo** (Hands Up Everyone; 1981) and **Dan** (1982), by Carles Comas, and **Conferencia de San Odu** (San Odu Conference; 1982), by the Tau group.

ANIMATION

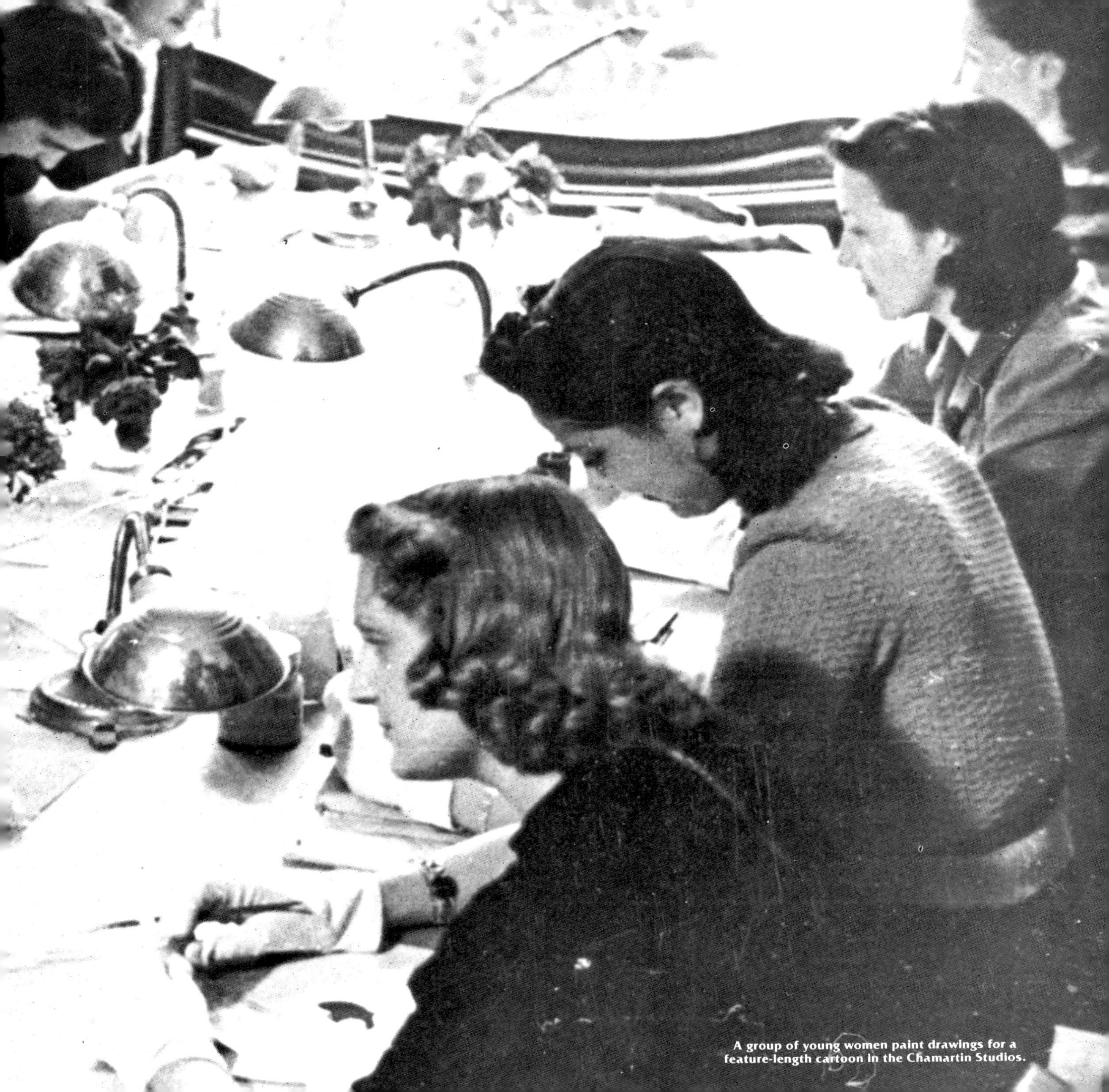

A group of young women paint drawings for a feature-length cartoon in the Chamartin Studios.

ANIMATION

Emilio de la Rosa

Animation began in Spain with Segundo de Chomón. He makes **El hotel eléctrico** (The Electric Hotel; 1905) in Barcelona, in which he mixes objects in real life scenes, cranking them through frame by frame. It is probably one of the first experiments in animation in the world. In 1906, Segundo de Chomón leaves Spain to work in France and Italy with the Pathé company, but his experiments in animation and animated drawings run parallel to Emile Cohl, who becomes the true pioneer in the field.
The industry would have to wait until 1917 when Fernando Marco makes **El toro fenómeno** (The Fantastic Bull), the first Spanish cartoon ever made. It is a parody on bullfights. The cartoon is currently lost to us, but it is not an extraordinary fact if we consider that hardly any cartoons made before the Spanish civil war are conserved today. The well-known cartoonist, Joaquín Xaudaró, who worked in the **Blanco y Negro** magazine and who had begun to work in animation around 1920 with animated caricatures of the Spanish edition of the **Public-cine** newsreel with **Un discípulo de caco** (The Crook's Disciple; 1930), in 1932 founded along with the cartoonists K. Hito and Antonio Got, the **Sociedad Española de Dibujos Animados** (SEDA). The company represented the first attempt at the creation of an industrial production structure to make cartoons. However, the venture fell apart after the death

El hotel eléctrico (1905) by **Segundo de Chomón.**

of Xaudaró in 1933. SEDA only made seven shorts, a few of which are unfinished. The best of these works include **Francisca, la mujer fatal** (Francisca, The Vamp; 1933) and **El rata primero** (Top Rat; 1933) by K. Hito, **Un drama en la costa** (A Drama on the Coast; 1933) by Joaquín Xaudaró, and **Serenata** (Serenade; 1932) by José López Rubio.
Two men who also produce a series of shorts in Madrid are José Martínez Romano (director) and the cartoonist Menda (graphic designer and screenwriter). Their most noteworthy work is **Buffalo Full, terror del Far West** (1935). Much more important from an historical point of view, however, is the appearance in Spain of the first films with animated puppets. Feliciano Pérez and Arturo Beringola make **El intrépido Raúl** (Intrepid Raul; 1930), Pablo Antonio Béjar and Miguel Ramos film **Arte, amor y estacazos** (Art, Love and Coming to Blows; 1935) and Adolfo Aznar creates **Pipo y Pipa en busca de Cocolín** (Pipo and Pipa Looking for the Bogeyman; 1936), based on drawings by Salvador Bartolozzi for **Estampa.** The forties represent a golden age for animation in Spain. As is the case with comic strips, Barcelona becomes the center of production for cartoons. During this period, more than one hundred shorts and four features are made, probably the only time during the history of animation in Spain that there is a certain amount of continuity

Don Cleque de los monos (**1943**) **by F. Tur.**

Civilón boxeador (**1944**) **by José Escobar.**

in production, but in spite of this fact, the cartoon industry does not consolidate as such.
First, the Baguñá brothers found the Hispano Grafic company and right after the end of the civil war, they present **La isla mágica** (The Magic Island; 1940), by Salvador Mestres. It is the first episode of an enormously popular series whose main hero, Juanito Milhombres, is based on a comic strip character known in pre-civil war Catalonia. Among the best episodes in the series are **Aventuras de Pulgarcito** (The Adventures of Tom Thumb; 1941) and **Juanito va de caza** (Juanito Goes Hunting; 1942).
In 1940, Alejandro F. de la Reguera founds a second cartoon production company in Barcelona called Dibsono Films, which employs such animators as Enrique Dibán, Francisco Tur, Ferrán, Tosquellas, etc. Dibsono makes the first animated cartoon after the end of the civil war called **SOS, Dr. Marabú** (1940), by E. Dibán, and begins what will later be a popular series, **Don Cleque** (1941-1945), by F. Tur.
Both of these production companies merge in 1941 to constitute Dibujos Animados Chamartín, the Barcelona affiliate of the Madrid production and distribution company.
Chamartín Barcelona, which employs practically all of the animators of that time, will create a large part of the Spanish cartoons made during those years. As a result of the pressures

Garbancito de La Mancha (1945) by Arturo Moreno.

brought to bear on the main officies to bring its capital back to Madrid, the studios close their doors in 1945. During its years in operation, Chamartín Barcelona groups its production into three different series. Francisco Tur takes over the production of the **Don Cleque** series. The best episodes are **Don Cleque marinero** (Don Cleque, Sailor; 1942) and **Don Cleque en el Oeste** (Don Cleque in the West; 1944). The team led by Enrique Dibán —the pseudonym of Enrique Ferrán—produces the series **Garabatos** (Scribbles; 1943-1945). The fourteen episodes have humorous reviews with caricatures of well-known figures of that time: **Garabatos y Greta Garbo** (1944), **Garabatos y Manolete** (1945), **Alady, Imperio Argentina,** etc. Finally, the third team, under the direction of José Escobar, makes the series **Toro Civilón** (The Civil Bull; 1942-1944) and **Gato Zapirón** (The Shoo Cat; 1944-1947). At the same time as the creation of Chamartín Barcelona, Arturo Moreno founds along with Armando Tosquella and Rosa Galcerán a semi-independent production company called Diarmo Films in 1942. They begin with the short, **El capitán Tormentoso** (Captain Stormy; 1942). Moreno looks for a distribution company for his film and finds Balet and Blay. Even though they are not particularly interested in the distribution of cartoons, they need Spanish productions to obtain import permits for foreign features. As a

result, they begin production on a feature-length color cartoon. Arturo Moreno and his team make **Garbancito de la Mancha** (1945), the first feature-length cartoon produced in Europe. Their notable effort is awarded with a clamorous critical and public success. The same team makes a second feature called **Alegres vacaciones** (Happy Holidays; 1946-1948) with the same characters: Garbancito, the giant Caramanca, the pair Chirili and Quiriqui, etc. The story line is about a trip that these heroes make through Spain, but this second feature is much less convincing that the first. Arturo Moreno leaves Spain in 1948 to work in Venezuela and Balet and Blay contract the Austrian Franz Winterstein to make a third feature called **Los sueños de Tai-Py** (Dreams of Tai-Py), which is a sonorous failure and which leads to the disappearance of the production company.
Series of very little interest are also made in Barcelona during this period such as **Quinito** (1943-1947), by Pérez Arroyo, the episodes of which are produced and distributed by Cifesa.
There is hardly any production in Madrid, and what there is can be considered of slight interest. Fernando Morales makes **Un día de feria** (A Day at the Fair; 1941), **La manzana encantada** (The Enchanted Apple; 1942), etc.
The team of animators which had formerly belonged to the Chamartín Barcelona studios —Francisco Tur, Juan Ferrándiz, E. Ferrán, etc.— joined in a new industrial venture called Estela Films —Jordi Tusell's company. They make a feature-length cartoon based on the story of Cinderella. A number of figures from the intelligentsia of Catalonia take part in the production including Josep Benet as the executive producer and Cirici Pellicer as the artistic director. The director of animation is José Escobar whom we have already cited as being in charge of the **Civilón** series, but who had previously worked in smaller film formats. Along with Joaquín Muntañola, Escobar had made the series **Faquir González** (Fakir González; 1941-1942). Escobar is especially known for the creation of important figures in the world of Spanish comic strips such as Carpanta and Zupi and Zape. He is so interested in animated cartoons that he is the only Spanish professional in the field to have written a course about animation (1961).
Estela's film is called **Erase una vez...** (Once Upon a Time...; 1950) due to pressures brought to bear by Walt Disney on the Spanish administration to keep **Cinderella** out of the title. It is probably the most interesting animated feature to have been made in Spain to date. In spite of the fact that it receives a prize in the Mostra of Venice, it is the only feature-length cartoon made by Estela Films.
Another project that should be mentioned is the one undertaken by the Baguñá brothers after the disappearance of the Estudios Chamartín Barcelona. They found the Editorial Científico-Cinematográfica in order to make educational films for primary and secondary school students. Their productions include **La circulación de la sangre** (The Circulation of Blood; 1945), **La fisiología de la audición** (The Physiology of Hearing; 1947), etc.
Among the films made with animated puppets, we should mention **Taruguete contra Ojo Pipa por el botijo de la buena vida** (1944) and **Aventuras de Esparadrapo** (The Adventures of «Esparadrapo»/Sticking Plaster; 1949), by Angel de Echenique, and **La ciudad de los muñecos** (Puppet City; 1945), by José María Elorrieta.
The fifties put a damper on the expansion of animation in Spain. As a matter of fact, production practically disappears due to the lack of profitability in the sector and draftsmen turn their talents to the comic strip.
The only notable productions are made by ICA Films: **Nausica** (1958), by José Serra Estruch, and **Pancho y Pincho en los infiernos** (Pancho and Pincho at the Back of Beyond; 1961), by Angel García.
Animated cartoons would make a recovery in the sixties. It is not so much due to the film industry, but to the advertising which would first be seen in movie theaters —Movierecord monopolizes this media from 1958 to

El mago de los sueños (**1966**) **by Francisco Marcián.**

about 1965— and later on TVE (Spanish Television). Spanish advertising animation —cartoons, objects, etc.— has won many prizes in international festivals. The Buch-Sanjuán studios— later Publi-Visión— in Barcelona would make TV commercials for brand names such as Pikolín, Moussel, Ben-Hur. Cera Alex, etc. The animators who work for this firm include Manuel Martínez Buch, Julio Taltavull, Jordi Amorós, Víctor Luna, Angel García, etc. The Estudios Moro company in Madrid is the main force behind advertising film. It also doubles as a true school of animation, since the majority of the industrial animators currently working in Spain work in Estudios Moro at one time including Francisco Macián, Robert Balser, José Ramón Sánchez, Pablo Núñez, etc. Among the most praiseworthy spots produced by Moro are those directed by Julio Alvarez, since they are made using objects —Tío Pepe, Camel, etc. José Luis Moro himself, perhaps the best Spanish animator, has directed commercial films. The most noteworthy is **Kati** (1983), a feature that was shown in episodes on Mexican television.

The main character is a caterpillar that meets different animals during its adventures.

Estudios Moro contracts Robert Balser to make advertisements —**Manos llenas de triunfo** (A Handful of Victory; 1964) and **Guapo** (Handsome; 1965), but they also produce together **El sombrero** (The

Hat; 1964), an innovative short within the field of animation. American Robert Balser decides to reside in Spain, and after separating from Estudios Moro, he creates his company called Pegbar Productions in Barcelona which currently works in the field of advertising and in the production of American television series. Balser has also produced **La doncella guerrera** (The Warrior Maiden; 1974), by Julio Taltavull, and **Crimen perfecto** (Perfect Crime; 1976), by Fernando Krann.
Another animator who works in Estudios Moro is Francisco Macián who even uses characters —the Telerín family in the **Vamos a la cama** (Let's Go to Bed) TV show— developed by José Luis Moro for his feature film, **El mago de los sueños** (The Dream Magician; 1963-1966), the picture with perhaps the most perfect technique and story line in the history of Spanish animated cartoons. The film is based on a story by Andersen and is produced by Macián's own studios. Later, he works on a new animation technique drawing on cibernetics called M-Tecnofantasy. He uses it in a sequence of the film **Dame un poco de amooor...** (Give Me a Little Bit of Looove...; 1968), by José María Forqué, and in **Memoria** (Memory; 1975), by Francisco Macián himself, a real-life picture which hardly makes a mark on the market. While preparing an old project called **Candelita,** a thirteen-episode cartoon series by José Ramón Sánchez, he prematurely dies in 1976. His production company is forced to close and Spanish animation loses one of its great hopes.
Cruz Delgado is the only animation director who constantly works in commercial film, making cartoons from **El gato con botas** (Puss 'N Boots; 1964) to **Los viajes de Gulliver** (Gulliver's Travels; 1983). He has a characteristic cartoon style, quite different from the Disney model. Delgado's work includes shorts such as **Andanzas de canguro Boxy** (The Adventures of Boxy the Kangaroo; 1966), series for TVE (Spanish Television) such as **Aventuras de Molécula** (Adventures of Molecula; 1968) or **Don Quijote de la Mancha** (Don Quixote of La Mancha; 1979-1981) —consisting of thirty-nine episodes lasting twenty-six minutes each, or features such as **Mágica aventura** (Magic Adventure; 1973).
José Ramón Sánchez, graphic designer of the electoral campaigns of the Spanish Socialist Workers Party, has also worked in animation. He directs an Estudios Moro production called **El gripoterio** (1972) and TVE productions titled **Paco Pum** (1973) or **Pablito,** a work about Picasso. His latest production is **El desván de la fantasía** (The Dream Loft; 1979), co-directed with Cruz Delgado and based on an original story by José Luis García Sánchez. TVE broadcast the film in ten episodes.
Continuing with the Madrid studios, Pablo Núñez and his company Pablo Núñez Story Film should be cited. He specializes in film titles and tricks and has worked in more than five hundred films during the last ten years. Among his film shorts, the most noteworthy is **Día tras día** (Day After Day; 1977), a work in which he mixes real life characters with cartoons. There is also the company of Rafael Vara, whose main work has been the series of twenty-two film shorts on the comic strip characters, **Mortadelo and Filemón,** which were later made into three feature-length films. Finally, the Estudios Castilla should be mentioned.
In the field of animated puppets, only Salvador Gijón works in a continual fashion. From the forties until 1970, he makes numerous works including **No la hagas y no la temas** (Don't Do It and Don't Fear It; 1943), **Rapto en palacio** (A Palace Kidnapping; 1945) and **Fiesta en Saturno** (Holiday on Saturn; 1969). His latest works are **Sombras de Granada** (Shadows of Granada; 1970) and **Juegos de naipes** (Card Games; 1970).
Apart from the Pegbar studios in Barcelona, we also find the work done by the Estudio Equip. Animator Jordi Amorós —known as Ja— is the visible head of these studios, even though the work done is a cooperative effort. Equip is the best example of a type of production which is between a purely craftsman-like method and an industrial outlook. In 1976, they make **Historias de amor y masacre** (Stories of Love and

Candelita (1976) by Francisco Macián.

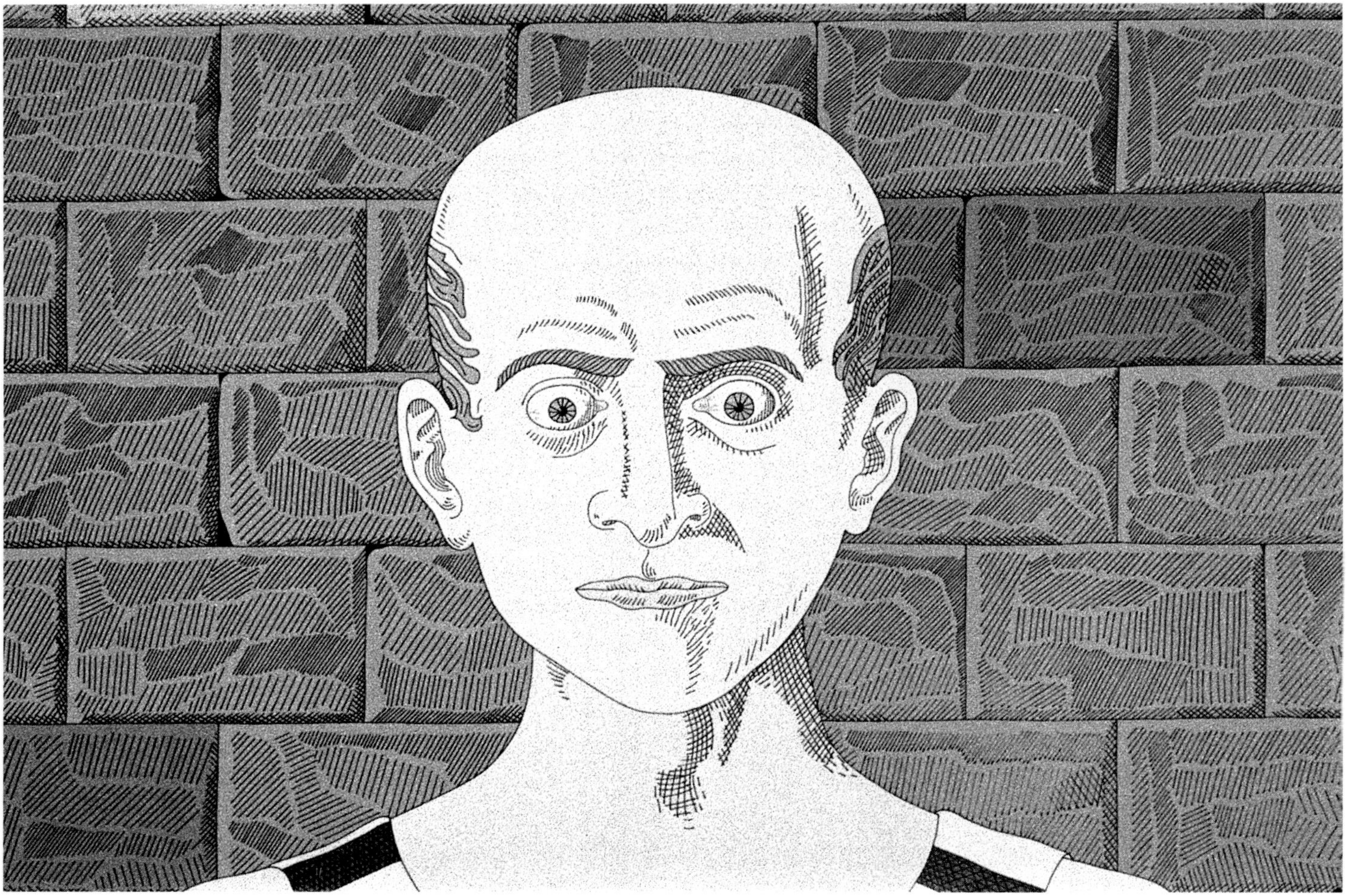

La edad del silencio **(1978) by Gabriel Blanco.**

Massacre), the first Spanish feature-length cartoon for adults. It is based on the characters which appear in the satirical magazine, **El Papus.** Jordi Amorós' film is both corrosive and very original. Among the people who work on this feature comprised of different episodes are such famous cartoonists as Gila, Chumy-Chúmez, Perich, etc. Iva's episode, **Hace un porrao de años o más** (It Was a Hell of a Long Time Ago or Even More), obtains a prize in the Zagreb Festival. Apart from their work in advertising, they have also made **Gu-Gú** (1981), using a character created by cartoonist Vázquez called Angelito, and **Prima donna** (1983).
Independent production has proliferated in the last few years, in other words, that type of production which does not have any relation with established studios or with advertising, the bread and butter of animators in Spain. Independent animation has made a certain degree of formal research and experimentation possible and is practically the only example of animated cartoon not specifically meant for children. Standing out in this area is Gabriel Blanco, the director of two film shorts, **La edad de la piedra** (Stone Age; 1964) and **La edad del silencio** (The Age of Silence; 1978, with drawings and cartoon ideas by Chumy-Chúmez and Ops, respectively. Both shorts are full of sharp social commentary. Rafael Ruiz Balerdi and José Antonio Sistiaga come from the world of plastic arts and have made films in which they directly paint on the celluloide. **Homenaje a Tarzán** (Tribute to Tarzan; 1971) is by Balerdi, while **Ere erera baleibu icik subua aruaren...** (1970) is created by Sistiaga, an abstract feature without a sound track.
Other animators and their works that should be mentioned are: Jaime Pascual, **Decó** (Decco; 1977) and **El bosque blanco** (The White Forest; 1981); Ana Mampaso, **Insomnio de una noche de verano** (Insomnia on a Summer's Night; 1981), one of the few examples of works close to the international concept of an Animation Workshop —made by children; Cisco Bermejo, **La caza del monstruo** (Hunting the Monster; 1981) and **Para qué una pistola** (The Wherefore of a Pistol; 1982); Raúl García Sanz, **Mujer esperando en un hotel** (Woman Waiting in a Hotel; 1982); or the productions of Brique Films —Iskra— such as **Darling** (1980), by Beni Russel; **Un final feliz** (A Happy Ending; 1982), by Ernesto Alvarez, and **La sorpresa** (The Surprise; 1982), by Alicia Carriazo.
Important work in independent animation is done in Catalonia as well. The most important animators are: Jordi Artigas, who is preparing a history of Catalonian animation, **Matamorfosi** (1979); Anna Miquel, **Gnochi el inconformista** (1977); the Joan Baca and Toni Garriga team, **Blanc negre** (1974); Miquel Esparbé, **Incubo rosa** (1973); Montse Ginesta, Toni Batllorí and Joma with their carefully done **Ploma daurada** (1981); Merche Hoyos, Xavier Roca and Fernando Marín, **Vols venir?** (1981); or **Cartas de un papa** (Letters from a Pope; 1980), by the Argentinians residing in Barcelona, Rodolfo Pastor and Petra Steinmeyer.
Several attempts at independent animation have also been made in the Basque Country such as **Por un pueblo verde** (For an Evergreen People; 1977), by Iñaki Núñez, and those films produced by the San Sebastián production company Jaizkibel and directed by Juan Bautista Berasategui: **Ekialdeko Izarra** (1978), **Fernando Amezketarra** (1981) and **Kukubilltxo** (1983).

CHRONOLOGY

1896

298 Anarchist terrorist attack against the Corpus Christi procession in Barcelona. The individuals responsible are tried in Montjuich. The Philippines insurrection breaks out.

Architecture.—Puig i Cadafalch: **Casa Martí** (Els quatre gats). Domenech i Estepá: **Church of Santa Eulalia de Vilapiscina.**
Painting.—Beruete: **Vista de Toledo, Paisaje de Madrid** and **Espinos en flor.** Nonell: **Cretíns de Boí.** Canals: **Café concierto.** Casas: **Plein-Air, Moulin Rouge, Moulin de la Galette** and **Montmartre.** Rusiñol: **Paisajes de Granada.**
Literature.—Ganivet: **Idearium español.**

Cinematographic presentation in Madrid and Barcelona by Lumière's representative, A. Promio. Jimeno shoots: **Salida de misa mayor del Pilar de Zaragoza** (Leaving High Mass at the Pilar of Zaragoza Cathedral), which is enormously successful when exhibited at the Maravillas Salon. At the end of the year a totally Spanish program is screened at the Actualidades Salon: **Corrida de toros del 18 de octubre** (October 18 Bullfight), **Parada en Palacio** (Palace Parade), **Sevillanas** («Sevillana» Dances), **Loreto Prado, Asalto a sable por los discípulos de Carbonell** (Sabre Charge by Carbonell's Disciples), **Salida de misa de las Calatravas** (Leaving Mass at the Calatravas) and **Puerta del Sol.**

Execution in Montjuich of the anarchists responsible for the terrorist attack. In taking revenge, anarchists assassinate Cánovas del Castillo, president of the Spanish cabinet and the man responsible for the Bourbon restoration following the coup headed by Generals Pavía and Martínez Campos, bringing the I Republic to an end.

Architecture.—Domenech: **Institut Pere Mata.**
Sculpture.—Llimona: **Primera comunión.** Reynés: **Monument to El Greco** in the city of Sitges.
Painting.—Inauguration of **Els quatre gats,** on whose walls Picasso paints **Veinticinco artistas.** Casas paints two plafonds: **Tándem** and **El automóvil.** Regoyos: **La España negra.** Gimeno: **Paisajes.** Casas: **Bal de tarda.** Rusiñol: **El Novici.**
Music.—Morera: **La Fada.** Millet: **Capella de Sant Felip Neri.**
Literature.—Galdós: **Misericordia.** Unamuno: **Paz en la guerra.** Gimerá: **Terra baixa.**
Various Wagnerian concerts are given in the Liceo. The Fourth Modernist Festivity in Sitges.

Gelabert shoots **Riña de café** (Café Brawl), the first fictional film made in Spain. Bravo sets up a screening stall in front of the Painting Museum and the widow of Beliós establishes another in the Puerta de la Paz, Barcelona.

1898

300 The explosion sinking the **Maine** in the port of Havana sparks off the war between the United States and Spain. The war ends with the **Paris Treaty** in which the last of the Spanish empire— Puerto Rico, Cuba and the Philippines— is lost. The Spanish army turns its eyes towards Africa. General Polavieja offers decentralizing solutions in a manifesto.
Spain's defeat in the Spanish-American war produces a national sentiment of anguish which results in an urgent need for change. It is necessary to make Spain more European in nature. Two different tendencies are born out of this sentiment: **revolutionary internationalism** and **nationalist exaltation.** The first of these tendencies has two different alternatives: anarchism or socialism. The second becomes an optimistic, decentralizing, constructive, middle-class and historicist solution in the different regions ringing Spain —Catalonia, Valencia, Murcia, the Basque Country, Galicia and Andalusia, while in Castile, it produces pessimism, ascesis, a break with the past, aristocratism and abstractionism.

Architecture.—Soria: **Ciudad Lineal.** Puig i Cadafalch: **Casa Amatller.** Domenech: **Casa Thomas.** Rubió: **Lavadero del Sanatorio del Tibidabo.** Gaudí: **Casa Calvet.**
Sculpture.—Mogroviejo: **Risveglio.**
Painting.—Romero de Torres: **El anarquista y su familia.** Zuloaga sets himself up in Segovia: **Las brujas de San Millán.** Casas: **La procesión del Corpus de Santa María del Mar.** Picasso: **El beso.** Anglada: **Moulin Rouge.** Mir: **La catedral de los pobres.** Rusiñol: **Jardins.** Casas draws the repatriates from Cuba.
Music.—Pedrell: **El último Abencerraje.** Bacarisse: **Balada romántica.** Granados: **María del Carmen.**
Literature.—Blasco Ibáñez: **La barraca.** Maragall: **Els tres Cants.** Verdaguer: **Santa Eulalia.** Maeztu: **Hacia otra España.** Costa: **Reconstitución y europeización.** The **Catalonia** magazine is founded. Adriá Gual offers the first session of **Teatre Intim.**

Bravo converts his screening stall into what can be termed the first stable movie theater called **El Palacio de la Electricidad.** Gelabert shoots his first two successes: **La Dorotea** and **Visita a Barcelona de doña María Cristina y don Alfonso XIII** (María Cristina and Alfonso XIII Visiting Barcelona).

In Morocco, the tribes of the Rif attack the railway which links Melilla with the Spanish iron mines. The result is the disaster in the Barranco del Lobo. The Minister of War calls up the reserves in Catalonia and there is a general strike. The lack of organization among the workers converts the strike into true subversion. The repressive measures and the outrages of violence will make these four days known as the **Tragic Week** of Barcelona. Accused of being the instigator of the events, Ferrer i Guardia, founder of the **Escuela Moderna** (Modern School), is shot. The government headed by Maura falls. The **Esquerra Catalana** wins the regional elections. The **Workers Solidarity** movement convokes the **First Syndical Congress,** from which the CRT is created. This is the embryo of the **National Workers Confederation** (CNT), the anarcho-syndicalist trade union that is founded the following year.

Architecture.—Moragas: **Bar «La Luna».** Gaudí: **Escuelas del Templo de la Sagrada Familia.** Planas: **Casa Pujadas.** Domenech: **Hospital de San Pablo.** Bassegoda: **Casa Berenguer.** Repullés: **Ayuntamiento de Valladolid.** Gaudí: **La Pedrera (Casa Milá).** Puig i Cadafalch: **Casa de les punxes.**
Painting.—Gris: **Tablero de ajedrez.** Picasso: **Horta de San Juan.** Casas: **Doscientos retratos al carbón.** Nonell: **Juana, La Xata, Roser, Florinda, La masía.** Sorolla: **El borracho** and **Alegría del agua.** Zuloaga: **Gregorio el botero.** Iturrino: **Caballos.** Echevarría: **La mestiza desnuda.** Blanchard: **La gitana y la campesina.** Torres: **Musa gitana.** Chicharro: **Las tres esposas.**
Music.—Granados: **Goyescas.** Albéniz: **Iberia.** Falla: **Trois melodies.** Turina: **Quinteto.** Del Campo: **Caprichos románticos.**
Literature.—Maragall: **Elogi de la poesía.** Baroja: **Zalacaín el aventurero.** Gómez de la Serna: **El drama del palacio deshabitado.**

Tramullas shoots scenes of the war in Africa. Baños does the same for Hispano Films and obtains his first big success: **La guerra del Rif** (The Rif War). Gelabert: **Guzmán el Bueno** and **Amor que mata** (Love That Kills). Hispano Films builds Spain's first film studios.

302 The First World War breaks out. The **Mancomunidad Catalana** (Catalonian Commonwealth) is constituted and Prat de la Riba is named president. Ortega y Gasset gives his speech **Vieja y Nueva política** (Old and New Politics) in Madrid's Comedia Theater where he proclaims the end of the Restoration process and urges the liberalization of Spanish life. In reply to the increasing workers trade unionism, the **Congress of Employers Federations** is created.

Architecture.—Gaudí reforms the **Catedral de Mallorca.** Masó: **Casa Masramón.** Jujol: **Casa Ximenis.** Berenguer: **Santuario de San José de la Montaña.**
Sculpture.—Hugué: **Torero.** Clará: **Diosa.** Galgallo: **Bailarina** and **La máscara de Jove.**
Painting.—Sorolla: **El baño del caballo** and **La condesa de Noailles.** Mir: **Costa Brava.** Romero de Torres: **Retablo del amor.** Miró: **El péndulo y la linterna.** Gris: **El chaquete.** Picasso: **Violín.**
Music.—Falla premiers **La vida breve** in Madrid. Pahissa: **Gala Placidia.** Mompou: **Impresions intimes.** Turina: **La procesión del Rocío** and **Margot.** Usandizaga: **Las golondrinas.**
Literature.—Catalá: **Solitut.** Jiménez: **Platero y yo.** Trigo: **Jarrapellejos.** Baroja: Trilogy **El mar.** Noriega: **Da Ruada.** Aguirre: **Ga roa.** Gómez de la Serna: **El Lunático.** Unamuno: **Niebla** and **El sentimiento trágico de la vida.** Ortega: **Meditaciones del Quijote.** Bergson, Einstein, Curie, Claudel, Valery, Max Jacob, Marinetti, Ravel, Milhaud and Poulenç visit the **Residencia de Estudiantes.** Codina: **Los siete niños de Ecija** and **El tonto de la huerta.** Togores: **La festa del blat.** Serena: **La última danza.**

Films.—Baños: **La Malquerida.** Marro: **Barcelona y sus misterios.** A. Gual: **El alcalde de Zalamea, La Gitanilla** and **Los cabellos blancos.** There are twelve production companies and four magazines dedicated to the world of film: **Arte y cinematografía, Mundo cinematográfico, El Cine** and **La vida gráfica.**

The troops of Abd-el-Krim inflict on the Spanish army one of its most serious defeats ever: the so-called **Annual Disaster** (Morocco). The activities of gunmen grow in importance. In 1920, the former parliamentary deputee Layret and the president of the Council of Ministers, Eduardo Dato, are shot. There is a struggle for power between the **Sindicato Libre** and the **Sindicato Unico** trade unions. Evil Boal, the secretary of the **CNT** is murdered. The **Fugitive Law** is voted upon. The Spanish **Communist Party (PCE)** is constituted.

Architecture.—Goday: **La Escola del Mar.** Jujol: **Vistabella Church.** Martinell: **Bodega de El Pinell de Brai.** Domenech: **Tomb of Jaime I** in Tarragona. Gaudí: **Templo de la Sagrada Familia.**
Sculpture.—Hugué: **El aragonés.** Inurria: **Forma.** Gargallo: **Maternidad.**
Painting.—Sert: **Murals in the Vic Cathedral.** Solana: **Tertulia de Pombo.** Cossío: **Pescadores.** Picasso: **Los tres músicos.** Chicharro: **Las intenciones de Buda.** Vázquez Díaz: **Retrato de Juan Ramón Jiménez** and **Alegría del campo vasco.** Blanchard: **La convaleciente.** Nogués: **Tarde de domingo.** Arteta: **Campesinos vascos.**
Music.—Guridi: **Amaya.** Bautista: **Interior.** Turina: **Sinfonía sevillana.** Pittaluga: **La romería de los cornudos.**
Literature.—Unamuno: **La tía Tula.** Pérez de Ayala: **Belarmino y Apolonio.** Arniches: **La señorita de Trévelez.** Felipe: **Versos y oraciones del caminante.**
Emilia Pardo Bazán dies three months after obtaining the chair of Comparative Literature at the University of Madrid.

Films.—Pérez Lugín: **La casa de la Troya** (The House of Troy). Baños: **Don Juan Tenorio.** Buchs: **La inaccesible** (The Inaccessible Girl) and **La verbena de la Paloma** (The Paloma Fair).
The arbitrary nature of the previous Film Censorship Law established in 1913, unleashes a protest campaign in 1913. In Barcelona there are three studios: Julio Sanz, Studios Films and Trilla, S. A., while in Madrid there are three others: Atlántida, Madrid Films and Films Española. Barcelona has ten laboratories and Madrid has four. There are also a total of seventy-five distribution companies in Madrid and Barcelona.

304 Abd-el-Krim surrenders in Morocco and General Sanjurjo draws up the document ending the war. The Spanish monarchs visit Morocco to bear witness to a peace that has come after a bloody war, a war that has impoverished Spain. The **Iberian Anarchist Federation** (FAI) is founded, a secretive group which is determined to «keep watch over the revolutionary essence of the Spanish libertarian movement».

Architecture.—Jujol: **Palacio del vestido** in Barcelona's Industrial Exposition. Zuazo: **Edificio de correos** in Bilbao. Labayen: **Restaurante del Monte Ulía.** Fernández Shaw: **Estación de servicio para automovilistas.** García Mercadal: **Rincón de Goya** in Zaragoza. Bergamín: **Casa del marqués de Villora.** Work is begun on Madrid's **Ciudad Universitaria** (University City).

Sculpture.—A. Sánchez: **Escultura de horizonte. Volumen que vuela en el silencio de la noche. Tres formas femeninas para arroyos de juncos.**

Painting.—Dalí: **La sangre es más dulce que la miel, Cabeza de mujer** and **Autorretrato desdoblándose en tres.** Blanchard: **El camelot du roi.** Salaverría: **La procesión del Cristo de Lezo.** Picasso: **El estudio.**

Music.—Falla: **Soneto a Córdoba.** Esplá: **Don Quijote velando las armas.** Turina: **Quinteto de viento.** Palau: **Gongorina.**

Literature.—Various young writers take part in the ceremonies marking the anniversary of the third centenary of the death of Góngora. They will later be known as the **generation of 27.** All linked to the **Residencia de Estudiantes,** they support the surrealistic movement and openly contradict the **generation of 98** literary movement. This divergence can be explained in a paragraph of a letter that Buñuel and García Lorca send to Juan Ramón Jiménez regarding his work **Platero y yo:** «We believe it our duty to tell you —yes, quite disinterestedly— that your work profoundly disgusts us because it is immoral, hysterical and arbitrary.» Larrea: **Oscuro dominio.** Valle-Inclán: **La hija del capitán.** Guillén: **Cántico.** Ortega: **La rebelión de las masas** and **Mirabeau o el político.** Margarita Xirgu premiers the play **Mariana Pineda,** by García Lorca. Giménez Caballero founds **La gaceta literaria.**

The Omnium Cine studios and the Cyma laboratories are inaugurated. The Fonofilm sound system is presented in the Callao movie theater in Madrid. The Fonofilm system allows audiences to hear speeches given by De Forest, Doctor Madariaga and the songs by Conchita Piquer. Sound pictures are practically a reality. The first weekly film magazine, **La pantalla,** appears. Buñuel edits the film section of **La gaceta literaria.**

Films.—Amichatis: **Baixant de la font del gat.** Buchs: **El dos de mayo** (The Second of May), **Los misterios de la imperial Toledo** (The Mysteries of Imperial Toledo) and **Los aparecidos** (The Ghosts). Perojo: **Malvaloca** (Hollyhock). Delgado: **Las de Méndez** (Those of Méndez). Rey: **La hermana San Sulpicio** (Sister San Sulpicio). Sobrevila: **Al Hollywood madrileño** (To Madrid's Hollywood). Orduña: **Una aventura de cine** (An Adventure in Film-making).

1929

306 The king dismisses General Primo de Rivera and appoints General Berenguer as president of the Council of Ministers, political decisions that end the **dictatorship** which had been sanctioned by the crown and which had administered Spain since 1923. General Primo de Rivera goes into exile in Paris where he dies shortly afterwards. The **Unión Patriótica** (Patriotic Union), the only party allowed under the dictatorship, is dissolved. The uprising led by Sánchez Guerra in order to establish a republic fails. It is an offshoot of the aborted «sanjuanada» in 1927. Guerra's attempt is backed by the generals Weyler, Aguilera and Batet, the intellectuals Blasco Ibáñez, Machado and Marañón, and by the politicians Melquiades Alvarez and the Count of Romanones. Sánchez Guerra and his son are arrested.

The **International Exposition** is held in Barcelona, while Seville organizes the Ibero-American Exposition.

Architecture.—Sert and Illescas found the GATPAC group and present the **Ciudad Reposo** project for Barcelona. Bergamín: **Fundación del Amo.** Folguera: **Casal de Sant Jordi.** Mestres: **Club Náutico** in Barcelona. Gutiérrez Soto: **Cine Barceló** in Madrid.

Sculpture.—Gargallo: **Greta Garbo** and **Bailarina.** González teaches iron sculpture technique to Picasso.

Painting.—Domínguez: **La máquina de coser electrosexual.** Dalí: **Espectros de dos automóviles.** Miró: **Interior holandés.** Solana: **La vuelta de la pesca.** Chicharro: **Dolor.** Zubiaurre: **Romería vasca.** Arteta: **Paisaje del caballo.** Nogués: **Cataluña pujante** and **El aventurero y el capitán.** Picasso: **Crucifixión.**

Music.—The **Grupo de los Ocho** is created. It is made up by Gerhard, Grau, Gilbert, Camins, Toldrá, Blancafort, Samper and Lamotte de Grignon. Bacarisse: **Corrida de feria.**

Literature.—Salinas: **Seguro azar.** Riba: **Tres suites.** Cabanillas: **Vento mareiro.** Gómez de la Serna: **Los medios seres.** Sagarra: **Judit.** Benavente: **Vidas cruzadas.** Machado: **La Lola se va a los puertos.** Menéndez Pidal: **La España del Cid.**

The **Unión Cinematográfica Española** demands that the state pass legislation protecting the film industry. The **International Institute of Educational Film** is created. Vítores undertakes sound experiments with Ramper and a group of Aragonese minstrels. Elías shoots the first Spanish fictional talkie, **El misterio de la Puerta del Sol** (The Puerta del Sol Mystery). Argilés: **L'auca del senyor Esteve.** Rey: **La aldea maldita** (The Cursed Village) and **Los claveles de la Virgen** (Carnations for the Virgin Mary). Guàl: **La hija del mar** (Daughter of the Sea). Claramunt: **La puntaine.** Buchs: **El Empecinado** (Martín Díaz, «The Obstinate»). Delgado: **Cuarenta y ocho pesetas de taxi** (A Taxi Costing Forty-eight Pesetas). Perojo: **Corazones sin rumbo** (Hearts without a Course). Camacho: **Zalacaín el aventurero** (Zalacaín the Adventurer). The España Film Society, founded in 1928 by Giménez Caballero, draws members of the **generation of 27** and leads to the creation of similar institutions.

Forty-eight films are produced. Buñuel and Dalí make **Un chien andalou** in Paris.

The municipal elections are won by the Republicans —whose **Revolutionary Committee** is constituted in San Sebastián in 1930 with Alcalá Zamora at its head. The II Republic is proclaimed. The king and his family go into exile in London. Cardinal Segura publishes a document ardently praising the monarch and a demonstration in support of the king is held in Madrid. The CNT and PCE —Spanish anarchists and communists, respectively— call a general strike which degenerates into disturbances and the burning of convents and churches over a two-day period. José Antonio Aguirre, the mayor of Guecho, convokes the representatives of the Basque town halls in Guernica in order to draw up an **Autonomy Statute.** In a referendum, 99 % of Catalonia's voters approve the **Nuria Statute** and the **Parlament Catalá** is elected. Companys is named president of the region's parliament and Maciá heads the **Generalitat,** or Catalonian regional government. The left wins the elections for the **Cortes Constituyentes** (constituent parliament) and the **Spanish Constitution** is drawn up and approved. Alcalá Zamora is named president of the II Republic and Azaña, who was acting president until that time, heads the Council of Ministers.

Architecture.—The group founded in Barcelona by Sert and Illescas is enlarged to include architects from all of Spain and is renamed GATEPAC. Their first project is the **Urbanización de la Diagonal.** G. Mercadal: **Ensanche de Ceuta.** Feduchi and Eced: **Edificio Carrión.** Bergamín and Blanco: **Parque-Residencia.** Delgado: **Teatro Fígaro** in Madrid. Gutiérrez Soto: **Aeropuerto de Barajas.** Illescas: **Casa Vilaró.** Zuazo: **Casa de las Flores.**
Sculpture.—González: **Mujer peinándose.**
A. Sánchez: **Toros ibéricos.**
Painting.—Anglada: **Jaleo flamenco.** Dalí: **Angelus de Millet** and **Retrato de Gala.** Solana: **Las chicas de la Claudia.** Arteta: **El trabajo en la industria.** Picasso: **Bañista sentada,** which receives the Carnegie Prize.
Music.—Esplá: **Himno de la República.** Sorozábal: **Katiuska.** Turina: **Rapsodia sinfónica.** Pahissa: **Monodia.**
Literature.—Cernuda: **Los placeres prohibidos.** García Lorca: **Poeta en Nueva York.** Aub: **Teatro Completo.**

The first **Hispano-American Film Congress** is held. Sound pictures take Spanish studios completely by surprise. Directors, screenwriters, actors and actresses emigrate to Paris or Hollywood to make talkies.
Film-makers who travel to Paris include Rey, De la Torre and Ardavín, while those who go to Hollywood include Martínez Sierra, Perojo, López Rubio, Neville and Jardiel Poncela. After the **La gaceta literaria** magazine disappears, Juan Piqueras founds **Nuestro cinema** in which the **generation of 27** collaborates as well as such figures as Epstein, L'Herbier, Florey, Moussignac, Beucler, MacOrlan, Cassou and Deslaw.
Films.—Perojo: **Niebla** (Mist). Marquina and Ardavín: **Rosa de Francia** (Rose of France). Martínez Sierra: **Primavera en otoño** (Spring in Autumn). Roldán: **Fermín Galán,** according to the screenplay of Alberti on the 1930 Jaca uprising.

308 The Catalonian town of Figols declares **libertarian communism.** Durruti and Ascaso, leaders of FAI-CNT, are deported to Bata (Guinea). The Jesuit order is dissolved and its goods are confiscated. Spanish parliament ratifies the **Estatut d'Autonomía de Catalunya** (Catalonia Autonomy Statute). General Sanjurjo heads a military uprising in Madrid and Seville. After it fails, he is deported to Villa Cisneros. The basis for the Galician Autonomy Statute is approved in Santiago de Compostela. The army Chaplain's Corps is done away with. The **Divorce Law** is passed. **Acción Católica** (Catholic Action) and its political arm, **Acción Popular** (People's Action) are created.

Architecture.—Zuazo: **La Castellana.** Sert: **Casa Bloc** and **Casa Galobart.** Aguirre: **Facultad de Letras.** Arniches: **Instituto-Escuela.** Gutiérrez Soto: Madrid's **Cine Capitol.** Labayen and Aizpurúa: Bilbao's **Club Náutico.** GATEPAC: **Plan urbanístico Maclá.**
Sculpture.—Gargallo: **El profeta.** Alberto Sánchez: **Mujer castellana.**
Painting.—Arteta: **Náufragos.** Zubiaurre: **Los remeros vencedores de Ondárroa.** Picasso: **Muchacha ante el espejo.**
Music.—Sorozábal: **Adiós a la bohemia,** with a libretto by Baroja. Pahissa: **Suite intertonal.** Gerhard: **Sis cançons populars de Catalunya.**
Literature.—Altolaguirre: **La lenta libertad.** Salinas: **La voz a ti debida.** García Lorca founds and directs the **La barraca** theater company in order to perform Golden Age classics throughout Spain's towns and villages—Benjamín Palencia paints the sets. Alejandro Casona creates the **Teatro del Pueblo** for the same purpose.

The CEA studios are created, while the Orfea studios and the Cinematiraje Riera and Arroyo laboratories are remodeled. The **Actualidades Sonoras Españolas** newsreel goes into production. The first totally spoken picture is made in Spain: **Pax,** by Elías.
Films.—Buchs: **Carceleras** («Carcelera» Songs). Roldán: **El sabor de la gloria** (Taste of Glory). De la Riva: **El nocturno de Chopin** (Chopin Nocturne). Buñuel: **Las Hurdes (Tierra sin pan)** (Las Hurdes, Land without Bread), banned by the government.

The Spanish parliament suspends the Catalonian Autonomy Statute after the **Estát Catalá** (Catalan nation) had been declared and Companys had surrendered in 1934 to General Batet. Alejandro Lerroux, the president of the Council of Ministers, hands in his resignation as a result of these events and the so-called Asturian revolution in 1934. The **black market** scandal breaks out in which various center-right ministers are implicated.

Architecture.—Torroja and Arcas: **Mercado de Algeciras.** Torroja and Zuazo: **Frontón Recoletos.** Sert: **Dispensario Antituberculoso.** Arcas: **Hospital Clínico.** Lacasa: **Residencia de Estudiantes.** Bergamín and Soler: **Colonia El Viso.** Labayen: **Proyecto para el ensanche de Amara** in San Sebastián. **Sculpture.**—Barral: **Monumento a Pablo Iglesias.** González: **Daphne.** Macho: **Dolores Ibárruri.** Sánchez: **Signo de mujer rural en el camino lloviendo.** **Painting.**—Zubiaurre exhibits in the **Primavera** Salon. Vázquez Díaz: **La dama de gris.** Prieto: **El caballo de bronce.** Palencia: **El Escorial.** Caballero: Illustrations for **Llanto por la muerte de Ignacio Sánchez Mejías** by García Lorca. **Music.**—Esplá: **Suite.** Formation of the **grupo de los cinco** —Garcés, Olmos, Sánchez, Asencio and Valdés— in Valencia in order to research the folk music of «Levante» or the eastern part of Spain. **Literature.**—Baroja ends the twenty-two novels of the series: **Memorias de un hombre de acción** and **Aviraneta o la vida de un conspirador.** Sender wins the National Literature Prize for **Mr. Witt en el Cantón.** Machado: First part of **Juan de Mairena.** Juan Ramón Jiménez: **Hojas.** De Torre: **El suicidio y el surrealismo.** Cernuda: **Invocaciones a las gracias del mundo.** Hernández: **El rayo que no cesa.** García Lorca: **Doña Rosita la soltera o el perfume de las flores.**

The Estudios Chamartín and Roptence studios are created as well as the Fotofilm laboratories. There are 10 studios, 17 laboratories, 13 dubbing studios, 20 production companies, 75 distributors and 3,337 movie theaters. **Films.**—Buchs: **El niño de las monjas** (The Nuns' Boy). Perojo: **Rumbo a El Cairo** (Off to Cairo) and **La verbena de la Paloma** (The Paloma Fair). Rey: **Nobleza baturra** (Nobility of Brute Action). Ardavín: **Vidas rotas** (Broken Lives). Delgado: **Currito de la Cruz.** Artola: **Rosario la Cortijera** (Rosario, the Farmer's Girl). Jardiel: **Angelina o el honor de un brigadier** (Angelina, or the Honor of a Brigadier). Maroto: **La hija del penal** (Prison Daughter). Pí: **El gato montés** (Wildcat). Buñuel produces for Filmófono **¡Centinela alerta!** (Sentry Alert!) by Gremillón, **La hija de Juan Simón** (The Daughter of Juan Simón) by Sáenz de Heredia, and **Don Quintín el amargao** (The Embittered Don Quintín) by Marquina.

310 The left joins forces and forms the **Frente Popular** (Popular Front) which wins an ample majority in the elections. The Catalonian Autonomy Statute is reestablished. Azaña is appointed president of the II Republic. General Mola creates a secret organization called the **Unión Militar** (Military Union). Lieutenant Castillo is murdered by an extreme rightist. The Assault Guard kills Calvo Sotelo, a parliamentary deputee on the extreme right. The garrison in Melilla begins the military rebellion. General Sanjurjo dies in Portugal. A state of war is declared. Cardenal Plá y Daniel declares a **Holy Crusade** against the II Republic. The **Partit dels Socialistes Catalans** (Catalonian Socialist Party), or PSUC, is founded. The Spanish parliament approves the **Estatuto de Autonomía de Euskadi** (Basque Autonomy Statute). The Galician people approve the Galician Autonomy Statute in a referendum, and autonomy is granted to that northwestern Spanish region by the parliament in 1938. On April 1, 1939, General Franco signs the orders ending the war after the fall of Madrid—1,200,000 dead, 270,000 arrested, 500,000 in exile and 19,776 million pesetas/gold in public debt is the sad and heart-rending result of the Spanish Civil War. The **Constitution** is abolished, **home rule** is also ended and it is forbidden to speak any other language than Castilian Spanish— to the detriment of such regional languages as Basque, Catalonian and Galician. Political parties are banned and the **Partido Unico** (Single Party) is created by means of the Unification Decree which constitutes the **Movimiento Nacional de FET y JONS** (National Movement of the Traditionalist Spanish Falange and of the National Syndicalist Juntas). General Franco begins a dictatorship which will last forty-one years.

Architecture.—Sert: **Pabellón Español** in the International Paris Exposition. Churruca: **Bloques expresionistas de Diagonal, 419.**
Sculpture.—González: **Montserrat.** Sánchez: **El pueblo español tiene un camino que le lleve a una estrella.**
Painting.—Picasso: **Guernica.** Sert: **Murales interiores de la Sociedad de Naciones** in Brussels. Dalí: **Canibalismo de otoño, El sueño** and **Enigma infinito.** Miró: **La revolución,** a fibrocement plaque placed in the FAD decorators' stand by GATEPAC. Palencia: **La trilla** and **Rosas.** Castelao: **Atila en Galicia** and **Galicia mártir.**
Music.—Gerhard: **Ariel.** Falla: **Homenajes.** R. Halffter: **Don Lino de Almería.** Sorozábal: **La tabernera del puerto.** Rodrigo: **Concierto de Aranjuez.**
Literature.—León Felipe: **Insignia** and **Oferta.** Salinas: **Razón de amor.** Hernández: **Viento de pueblo.** Guillén: second edition of **Cántico.** Aleixandre: **Sombra del Paraíso.** Alberti: **Entre el clavel y la espada.** Carranque: **Cinematógrafo.** Cabanillas: **O Mariscal.** Arconada: **Río Tajo.** Zambrano: **Filosofía y poesía.** Sender: **Contrataque.** Barea: **La llama.** Aub: **Laberinto mágico.** García Serrano: **Eugenio o la proclamación de la primavera.** Foxá: **Madrid, de Corte a Checa.** Pemán: **La bestia y el ángel.** Jiménez: **En el otro costado.**
Piscator is interested in editing **Terra baixa** in Barcelona, but the CNT is opposed. Alberti and León form the **Teatro de Arte y Propaganda.** Bergamín,

Aub and Altolaguirre create **El búho.** Valle-Inclán dies and García Lorca gives a reading of **La casa de Bernarda Alba** in Madrid. Three days afterwards, García Lorca is shot in Granada by rebel forces. The Republicans shoot Ramiro de Maeztu.

Apart from the España Film Society, also operating are Proa Filmófono, Cinestudio Universitario, Cinestudio Imagen, Cine-club Geci and Cine Amateur. Juan Piquera is shot by the rebels.

Films.—Buchs: **El rayo** (Lightning). Perojo: **Nuestra Natacha** (Our Natacha). Ardavín: **La reina mora** (The Moorish Queen). Delgado: **El genio alegre** (The Happy Genius). Elías: **María de la O** and **Bohemios** (Bohemians). Roldán: **Luis Candelas** and **Así venceremos** (That's How We'll Win). Iquino: **Diego Corrientes.** Marquina: **El bailarín y el trabajador** (The Dancer and the Worker). Sáenz de Heredia: **¿Quién me quiere a mí?** (Who Loves Me?). Puche: **Barrios bajos** (Lower-class Districts). Saus: **Aurora de esperanza** (Dawn of Hope). Rey: **Carmen, la de Triana** (Carmen, the Girl from Triana), **La canción de Aixa** (Aixa's Song) and **La Dolores.** Delgrás: **La tonta del bote** (The Girl Who's a Prize Fool).

Buñuel directs the film service of the II Republic. Ivens: **Tierra de España** (The Spanish Land) and Malraux: **L'Espoir (Sierra de Teruel).**

 The Society of Jesus is reinstated and all its wealth is returned. Spain reestablishes diplomatic relations with the Vatican. The crucifix returns to government offices and official centers.

The divorce law is abolished and the clergy is included in the General State Budget. As a result of the **Decree for the Political Guilty,** Julián Besteiro is condemned to thirty years imprisonment —he dies in prison, and Zugazagoitia, Companys and Masó Riera are shot, among thousands of others. The **Fuero de los españoles** (Code of Laws for Spaniards) substitutes the **Constitution.** The Code respects liberties, **if they do not offend the basic principles of the State.** The parliament and the senate are substituted by the **Cortes,** made up of «procurators» who are designated under the principles of **organic democracy.** The monarchist generals are discharged and a Restoration is requested by the outstanding men of the nation. By means of a referendum, Franco passes the **Ley de Sucesión** (Law of Succession), which makes Spain a kingdom without a king. Military men are forced to join the FET y JONS, whose executive body is the **National Council for the Movement** and whose national chief is General Franco. Also dependent on the **Movement** are: **the Magistrates Service, the Spanish University Union, the Syndical Organization, the Feminine Section, the National Social Security Institute and the Youth Front.**

Teachers, university students, workers, businessmen, the social security, primary and secondary education students are all controlled by the **FET y JONS.** Women are forced to do **Social Service** in the **Feminine Section.** The **Work Code** subordinates economics to politics. Industrial planning is handled by the **National Institute of Autarky** —later, the **National Institute of Industry,** controlled by the army. It is necessary to swear to the **Basic Principles of the Movement** to become liberal arts professionals, university professors, magistrates, etc. After France was initially defeated in the Second World War, Spain adopts a **neutral** and **non-belligerant** position and Franco occupies Tangiers. He meets with Hitler and Mussolini. A **workers' exchange program** is signed with Germany and the **Blue Division** is sent to fight on the Russian front. In 1944, foreign policy tilts towards the allies. The United Nations recommends to its member countries that they withdraw their ambassadors from Madrid. The so-called **seige** is broken in 1953 when Spain signs the **Economic and Military Pact** with the United States and the **Concordat** with the Vatican. Spain joins the UNESCO in 1952.

Architecture.—Moya: **Iglesia de la Ciudad Universitaria** and the **Universidad Laboral** in Gijón. Gutiérrez Soto: **Ministerio del Aire.** Fisac: **Instituto de Investigaciones Científicas, Instituto de Optica, Iglesia del Espíritu Santo** and the **Iglesia de los Dominicos.** Moragas: **Cine Fémina.** Muguruza and Méndez: **El Valle de los Caídos.** Del Amo: **Vegaviana** and **Belvís del Jarama.**

Sculpture.—Oteyza founds the **Grupo Espacio** and the **Grupo Escuela Altamira** is created. Chillida: **Forma** and **Peine del Viento.** Chirino: **Composición en hierro.** Oteyza: **Atarrabi.** Subirachs: **Europa, Dialeg** and sculpture pieces for the Sanctuary of **Nuestra Señora del Camino** in León. Ferrant: **Trabajos en hierro.** Ferreira: **Formas Bulbosas.** Serra: **Hoquedades.**

Painting.—Picasso: **Muchacha en azul, Cráneo de buey** and **Retrato de Mrs. H. P.** Miró: **El pájaro de mirada de fuego** and **Busto de figura quimérica y gato.** Dalí: **Galarina, La cesta del pan** and **El Cristo de San Juan de la Cruz.** Zabaleta: **Quesada** and **Mujeres en el campo.** Muntané: **El palco de la celestina.** Tapies, Cuixart, Tharrats and Ponç found the **Dau al Set.** Tapies: **La caja de bramante, La profundidad de las diademas Mudruc** and **Peluquería de señoras y elegidos.** Vela Zanetti: **Interior Murals** for the United Nations. Vázquez Días obtains the first prize in the **Hispano-American Biennial.** Palencia creates a rural painting school in Vallecas —a miserable suburb of Madrid.

Music.—Rodrigo: **Música para un códice salmantino** and **Concierto heroico.** Arámbarri: **Castilla.** Guridi: **Diez melodías vascas, Peña mariana** and **Sinfonía pirenaica.** Del Campo: **Poema de los caídos.** Montsalvatge: **Gato con botas** and **Canciones negras.** Albert: **Sinfonía levantina.** Suriñach: **El mozo que casó con mujer brava.** Ferrer: **Romance de la fragua.** Halffter: **Antifonía pascual.**

Literature.—Alonso: **Hijos de la Ira.** Panero: **Estancia vacía.** Rosales: **Retablo sacro del nacimiento del Señor.** De Otero: **Cántico espiritual.** Ridruejo: **Poesía en armas.** Vivanco: **Tiempo de dolor.** Gaos: **Arcángel de mi noche.** García Nieto: **Víspera de ti.** Crémer: **Nuevos cantos de vida y esperanza.** Mora: **España, pasión de vida.** Celaya: **Tranquilament hablando.** Hidalgo: **Los muertos.** Hierro: **Alegría.** Cela: **La familia de Pascual Duarte** and **La colmena.** Laforet: **Nada.** F. Flórez: **Lola, espejo oscuro.** Agustí: **Mariona Rebull** and **El viudo Rius.** Gironella: **Los cipreses creen en Dios.** Delibes: **La sombra del ciprés es alargada** and **Mi idolatatrado hijo Sisí.** Matute: **Los Abel.** Aldecoa: **El fulgor y la sangre.** Fernández Santos: **Los bravos.** Ferlosio: **Industrias y andanzas de Alfanuhí.** J. Goytisolo: **Juego de manos.** Laín: **España como problema.** Buero: **Historia de una escalera** and **En la ardiente oscuridad.** Sastre and De Quinto found the Teatro de Agitación Social (TAS). Sastre: **Escuadra hacia la muerte.** Mihura: **Tres sombreros de copa.** Pemán: **Cisneros.** C. Sotelo: **La muralla.** Neville: **El baile.** L. Rubio: **Celos del arie.** R. Iriarte: **Juego de niños.** Jardiel: **Eloísa está debajo de un almendro.** Paso: **Los pobrecitos.** Diego: **Alondra de verdad.** Espriu: **Antígona** and **Primera historia d'Esther.**

The film industry, like all the communications media, directly depends on the Vice-secretariat of People's Education of the **FET y JONS,** which later becomes the Ministry of Information. It is then when the General Directorate of Cinematography or Film Department is created. Censorship, which was instituted in 1938, is dependent on the Propaganda Service and is extended throughout Spain. It includes the previous censorship of screenplays. The **Sindicato de Espectáculo** (Show Business Union) establishes three categories for official protection in the film industry and prizes are created. Films are banned from being shown in any other language other than Castilian Spanish. It is made obligatory to show seven days of national film for every six weeks of foreign. The **Noticiario Documental** (NO-DO) newsreel is created. The NO-DO newsreels must be shown in all cinemas and no other newsreels or documentaries may be screened. The Delegation of Propaganda establishes the category of Films of National Interest. The National Board of Provincial Cinematography, on which the different unions depend, is the body in charge of watching over film interests. The Circle of Film Critics and Writers (CEC) is founded. The holding of the Hispano-American Fair, the First International Commercial Film Fair in Barcelona and the First International San Sebastian Film Week, which becomes an international festival. The **Cinema Research and Experiences Institute,** or IIEC, and Spain's **National Film Library** are created. The **National Federation of Film Clubs** is founded, while the **Objetivo** and **Primer Plano** film magazines appear. Mihura makes the first color film in Spain using the **Cinefotocolor** system developed by Aragonés and Pujol. The film is called **En un rincón de España** (In a Corner of Spain). Moreno directs the first feature-length color film in Spain: **Garbancito de la Mancha.**

Films.—Neville: **El crimen de la calle de Bordadores** (Crime on Bordadores Street), **Nada** (Nothing), **El último caballo** (The Last Horse), **La torre de los siete jorobados** (The Tower of the Seven Hunchbacks) and **La vida en un hilo** (Life Hanging on a Thread). López Rubio: **La malquerida** (The Unpopular Girl) and **Alhucemas.** Arévalo: **¡Harka!** Rey: **La Dolores, La aldea maldita** (The Cursed Village) (a new version), **La nao capitana** (The Lady Captain's Boat) and **La cigarra** (The Cicada). Gil: **Huella de luz** (A Sign of Light), **Reina Santa** (Holy Queen), **Don Quijote de la Mancha** (Don Quixote of La Mancha), **La guerra de Dios** (God's War) (Golden Shell Prize in the San Sebastian Film Festival and the OCIC Prize in Venice) and **El beso de Judas** (The Judas Kiss). Román: **Intriga** (Intrigue), **La casa de la lluvia** (The House of Rain), **Lola Montes** and **Los últimos de Filipinas** (The Last from the Philippines). Ardavín: **Forja de almas** (Forge of Souls). Perojo: **Goyescas.** Sáenz de Heredia: **Raza** (Race), **Mariona Rebull** and **Las aguas bajan negras** (The Water Flows Black). Mur-Oti: **Un hombre va por el camino** (A Man Goes Down the Road) and **Cielo negro** (Black Sky). Orduña: **Pequeñeces** (Little Things), **La Lola se va a los puertos** (Lola Goes to the Ports) and **Locura de amor** (Love Crazy). Serrano de Osma: **Embrujo** (Bewitched) and **La sirena negra** (The Black Siren). Vajda: **Barrio** (Neighborhood) and **Carne de horca** (Meat for Hanging) (prizes in San Sebastián and Venice). Nieves Conde: **Balarrasa** (Hothead) and **Surcos** (Furrows). Del Amo: **Día tras día** (Day After Day) and **Sierra maldita** (The Cursed Sierra) (Golden Shell in San Sebastian). Lucia: **Cerca de la ciudad** (Near the City). Bardem and Berlanga: **Esa pareja feliz** (That Happy Couple). Berlanga: **Bienvenido, Mr. Marshall** (Welcome, Mr. Marshall) (prize in Cannes). Bardem: **Cómicos** (Comedians) and **Felices Pascuas** (Happy Holidays).

An agrarian fascism begins to make way for a technocrat despotism. The government worries about being **presentable** before the eyes of the West. Ortega y Gasset dies and his funeral becomes an impressive **demonstration.** Laín sends the government a report about the **spiritual situation of the university youth.** The **National Students Congress** is held. There are clashes between liberal university students and Falangists and the university is closed. In the elections for the **union delegates** and **workers councils,** communists begin to appear. In 1956, there are **150,000 striking workers.** It is a harsh blow for the government to give Morocco its independence. General Franco promulgates the **Law of the Movement's Principles** —a mixture of neo-Falangist and traditional monarchist thought. The **Opus Dei** enters the government and the **Stabilization Plan** is prepared. Spain becomes a full member of the OECD and the International Monetary Fund. Salaries are practically frozen. Salaries and work conditions are directly negotiated by means of the **Collective Bargaining Law** and are no longer regulated by the Ministry of Labor. Clandestine trade unions are organized: USO —resulting from Catholic groups—and Workers Commissions. As a result of the 1956 university events, the **Popular Liberation Front** (FLP) appears, many of whose members come from the ASU, created by the socialist Amat. The «P», or **protest** campaign scrawled on walls, spreads in Catalonia; Pujol and Pizón are sentenced in a **Court Martial.** Dissidents of the PNV (Basque Nationalist Party) youth movement found the ETA terrorist organization. The **Unión Española** (clandestine monarchist party) is created. Three hundred thirty-nine Basque priests sign a document in which they demand liberties and protest against repression. The number of strikes grows. General Franco meets with Juan de Borbón and decides that Prince Juan Carlos, the son of the latter, should complete his education in Spain.

Architecture.—Giráldez: **Facultad de Derecho** in Barcelona. Carvajal: **Escuela de Comercio.** Bohigas-Martorell: **Fábrica PIHER.** V. Molezún: **Pabellón de España** in Brussel's Expo 58. Barbero and De la Joya: **SEAT.** Carvajal and Paredes: **Panteón de los Españoles** in Rome. Azpiroz: **Centro de Investigación Agropecuaria.**

Sculpture.—Serrano founds the **El Paso** group (Serrano, Saura, Millarés, Feito, Canogar). Serrano: **Bóvedas para el hombre** and **Monumento a Machado.** The **Grupo 57** is created in Córdoba. Ferrant: **Estático cambiante.** Chillida: **Abesti Gogora.** Chillida obtains first prize in the Venice Biennial, while Oteyza obtains that of the Säo Paulo Biennial. Berrocal: **Vía Apia.**

Painting.—Palazuelo: **Mandala.** Miró and Artigas: **Muro del Sol** in the UNESCO Palace. Canogar: **Serie negra.** Mignoni: **El mataor** and **A los pies de Cristo.** The **Hondo** group is created (Genovés, Jardiel, Mignoni, Vento, San Segundo). Genovés: **Crónica de la realidad.** Dalí: **La Cena** and **Corpus Hypercubicus.** Picasso: **Las meninas.**

Music.—Creation of the **Nueva Música** group (Moreno Buendía, Barce, Ember, Franco, García Abril, De Pablo, Blancafort and C. Halffter). Raxach: **Syntagma.** Del Campo: **Fantasía para piano y orquesta.** Remacha: **Vísperas.** Montsalvatge: **Desintegración morfológica de la Chacona de Bach.** Gómez: **Cuarteto plateresco.** Barce: **Alfa.** De Pablo: **Radial.** Homs: **El caminant i el**

mur. Blancafort: **Sonata.** C. Halffter: **Partita. Introducción, fuga y final.** Castillo: **Concierto festival.** Hidalgo: **Ukanga** and **Caurga.**

Literature.—Buero: **Un soñador para un pueblo** and **Hoy es fiesta.** Hierro: **Cuanto sé de mí.** Torrente: **Los gozos y las sombras.** Prado: **Oratorio del Guadarrama.** Vivanco: **El descampado.** Aleixandre: **En un vasto dominio** and **Los encuentros.** De Otero: **Que trata de España** and **Esto no es un libro.** Rodríguez: **Conjuros.** González: **Sin esperanza.** Valente: **Poemas a Lázaro.** Caballero Bonald: **Pliegos de cordel.** Figueras: **Vencida por el Angel.** Gil de Biedma: **Compañeros de viaje.** Labordeta: **Epilírica.** Cela: **Viaje a la Alcarria** and **Judíos, moros y cristianos.** Delibes: **La hora roja.** Aldecoa: **Gran Sol, Con el viento solano** and **El corazón y otros frutos amargos.** Fernández Santos: **En la hoguera** and **Cabeza rapada.** Sánchez Ferlosio: **El Jarama.** J. Goytisolo: **El mañana efímero,** the trilogy. Hortelano: **Nuevas amistades.** Marsé: **Encerrados con un solo juguete.** Gaite: **Entre visillos.** Mihura: **Maribel y la extraña familia.** Sastre: **Muerte en el barrio.** Sastre and De Quinto found the **GTR** (Grupo de Teatro Realista). Muñiz: **El tintero.** Mañas: **La feria de Cuernicabra.** Arrabal: **El triciclo** and **Cementerio de automóviles.**

The **Salamanca Film Conversations** are held in which the Spanish film industry is declared **politically ineffectual, socially false, intellectually the worst, aestheticallay nonexistent and industrially weak.** Valladolid's Religious and Human Values Film Festival and Barcelona's Color Film Week and Congress are created. The following magazines appear: **Cinema Universitario** —which carries on the spirit of the **Salamanca Conversations, Film Ideal** and **Nuestro Cine**— which assumes the same postures of **Cahiers du Cinema** and **Positif.**

Films.—Vajda: **Marcelino, pan y vino** (Marcelino, Bread and Wine) (prize in the Berlin Film Festival). Bardem: **Muerte de un ciclista** (Death of a Cyclist) (FIPRESCI in Cannes). Gil: **Un traje blanco** (A White Suit) (mention in Venice). Bardem: **Calle Mayor** (Main Street) (mention in Venice). Berlanga: **Calabuch** (OCIC in Venice). Nieves Conde: **Todos somos necesarios** (We're All Necessary) (prize in San Sebastián). Forqué: **Amanecer en Puerta Oscura** (Dawn in Puerta Oscura) (Silver Bear in Berlin). Bardem: **La venganza** (Revenge) (FIPRESCI in Cannes). Ardavín: **El lazarillo de Tormes** (The Blind Man's Guide of Tormes) (Golden Bear in Berlin). Klimowsky: **Salto a la gloria** (Leaping to Glory) (prize in San Sebastián). Berlanga: **Los jueves, milagro** (Miracles on Thursdays) (prize in Valladolid). Ardavín: **Cerca de las estrellas** (Close to the Stars) (prizes in Mar de Plata and Valladolid). Berlanga: **Plácido.** Bardem: **A las cinco de la tarde** (At Five in the Afternoon). Ferreri: **El pisito** (The Small Flat). Rovira Beleta: **Los atracadores** (The Robbers). Buñuel: **Viridiana** (Golden Palm in Cannes).

The **Primer Plan de Desarre** (First Emigration Plan) goes into effect. A million people emigrate. Tourism, money sent home by immigrants and capital investments from abroad contribute to a big trade balance in Spain's favor. Spain is transformed into an industrial and urban society, leaving behind an agricultural past. The number of tractors in the country quadruples. Modernization goes hand in hand with a rural exodus, the tourist revolution and television advertising, stimulating consumerism and well-being. The **Law for the Basis of Social Security** unifies the former system of dispersed benefits. The **Organic Law of the Nation** goes into effect —a Francoist pseudo-constitution which consecrates the so-called **organic democracy.** Juan Carlos de Borbón is designated succesor to the **title of king.** The **Organic Law of the Nation** separates the posts of chief of state and of government as well as the trade unions from the Movement. Freedom of religion is recognized and the **Council of the Kingdom** is given wider powers. The new **Press Law** does away with previous censorship. Ifni and Guinea are decolonized. The **Movement and the Associations Statutes** pave the way for the appearance of **Acción Política, Reforma Social** (politically more open), and **Fuerza Nueva** —an extreme-rightist organization. Admiral Carrero Blanco is appointed head of government in order to give greater continuity to Francoism in case of the possible death of General Franco. **The MATESA financial scandal blows up.** The **Fourth Congress of the European Movement** is held in Munich with representatives of Spain's moderate interior opposition forces and the **Spanish Socialist Workers Party** attending. The people who attend the congress and who do not choose to go into exile are sent to Fuerteventura in the Canary Islands. The communist leader Grimau is executed. The abbot of Montserrat makes a series of statements to **Le Monde,** and among other things says: **subversion comes from the government and the people must have the right to elect the government.** A court martial is held against members of the PSUC. Professors Tierno, Aranguren and García Calvo are separated from their chairs at the university. In 1967, the numbers of strikes is 402. The 564 workers of the **Laminados de Bandas de Echeverri** firm strike for 163 days. **Workers Commissions** organizes the biggest workers demonstration in the postwar years and 170 people are arrested. The Spanish **Bishops' Conference** signs a document asking for **trade union freedom.** ETA member Echevarrieta dies in a shoot-out and Sarasketa is sentenced to death and later pardoned by General Franco in the face of international pressure. ETA kills the chief of San Sebastián political police force. A **state of emergency** is declared. The **Democratic Junta** is formed in Paris. The **Spanish Socialist Workers Party** and the Christian Democrats create the **Plataforma.** More than 300 Basque Nationalists are arrested in 1970. The bishops of Bilbao and San Sebastián denounce the enforcement of the **Banditry and Terrorism Law.** The **Burgos trial** is held against sixteen members of the ETA terrorist organization. Demonstrations against the trial are held all over Spain, Catalonian intellectuals lock themselves up in the Montserrat Monastery and the army calls for a forceful solution. The prosecution asks for nine death sentences and 519 years imprisonment for the ETA members being tried. General Franco grants a pardon in the face of the international outcry. The **Assemblea de Catalunya** is secretly constituted. The **1,001 trial** is held against ten members of **Workers Commissions.** The same day ETA assassinates Admiral Carrero Blanco. Five members of ETA and FRAP are executed. **On November 20, 1975 General Franco dies.** Juan Carlos de Borbón becomes chief of state.

Architecture.—Bohigas and Martorell: **Escola THA.** De la Sota: **Gimnasio del Colegio Maravillas.** Sáenz de Oiza: **Torres Blancas.** Coderch: **Edificio Girasol.**
Sculpture.—Chillida: **Temblor de hierro.** Alfaro: **Plano curvo.** Millares: **Artefacto para la paz.** Marinelo: **Maqueta para un monumento en plaza pública.** Basterrechea: **Monumento a Iztueta.** Serrano: **San Valero.** Berrocal: **Richelieu.** Sempere: **El órgano.** Oteyza: **Conjunción triple vacía.** López Hernández: **El pintor y su esposa.**
Painting.—Canogar: **La policía en acción.** Saura: **Retratos de Felipe II.** Genovés: **Stop.** López García: **Atocha.** Mateos: **Las sombras.** Valle: **Tipos de mar.** Ibarrola: **Pintura.** Cortijo: **Niños corriendo.** Equipo Crónica: **El vendedor de lavadoras.** Ortega: **La trata.** Vázquez Díaz: **Murales de La Rábida.** Barjola: **Protesta.** Sempere: **Círculo amarillo.** Redondela: **Feria.** Alcorlo: **Homenaje a Mozart.** Picasso: **El pintor y su modelo.** Dalí: **El sueño de Cristóbal Colón.** Zabaleta: **Campesino fumando.** Calvo: **Pintura normativa.** Colmeiro: **Mujeres con fruta.**
Music.—De Pablo: **Cesuras.** C. Halffter: **Espejos.** Coria: **Vértices.** Padrós: **Klavierquintett.** Soler: **Edipo y Yocasta.** Ibarrondo: **Baña zargaitik.** Marco: **Escorial.** Bernaola: **Superficies.** Arteaga: **La mona de imitación.** García Abril: **Homenaje a Miguel Hernández.** Barce: **Coral hablado.** Escudero: **Zígor.** Esplá: **Sinfonía haitiana.** Montsalvatge: **Una voz en off.** Benguerel and Mestres-Quadreny: **Canon en homenaje a Galileo.**
Literature.—Aleixandre: **Diálogos de conocimiento.** Gil-Albert: **Valentín.** Martín Santos: **Soliloquios.** Rodríguez: **Alianza y condena.** Prado Nogueira: **Miserere en la tumba de R. N.** Gil de Biedma: **Colección particular.** Hierro: **Libro de las alucinaciones.** Bousoño: **Oda en la ceniza.** Grande: **Blanco Spirituals.** Gimferrer: **Arde el mar.** Ullán: **Maniluvios.** Valente: **Sobre el lugar del canto.** Marsé: **Ultimas tardes con Teresa.** J. Goytisolo: **Reivindicación del conde don Julián.** Torrente: **La saga-fuga de J. B.** Benet: **Volverás a Región.** Cunqueiro: **Las crónicas del sochantre.** Sueiro: **Corte de corteza.** Delibes: **Las ratas.** Umbral: **Las ninfas.** Buero: **El concierto de San Ovidio.** Mihura: **Ninette y un señor de Murcia.** Sastre: **Oficio de tinieblas.** Olmo: **La camisa.** Rodríguez Méndez: **Bodas que fueron famosas del Pingajo y la Fandanga.** M. Recuerda: **Las salvajes en Puente San Gil.** Mañas: **La historia de los tarantos.** Diosdado: **Olvida los tambores.** Gala: **Anillos para una dama.** Espríu: **Ronda de mort a Sinera.** Arrabal: **Guernica.**

The new Film Department reorganizes the **Classification and Censorship Board** and the **National Film Institute,** and it gives greater importance to the **Cinema Research and Experiences Institute** whose name is changed to the **Official Film School,** or EOC. Protection to Spanish cinema is increased to include those films of **Special Quality.**
Films.—Rovira Beleta: **Los tarantos** (a mention in the Mar del Plata Film Festival). Summers: **Del rosa al amarillo** (From Rose to Yellow) (Silver Shell at the San Sebastian Film Festival). Berlanga: **El verdugo** (The Executioner) (FIPRESCI in Venice). Camus: **Young Sánchez** (mention in Mar del Plata). Picazo: **La tía Tula** (Aunt Tula) (prize in San Sebastian) Diamante: **Tiempo de amor** (Times for Love) (prize in Valladolid). Summers: **La niña de luto** (The Girl in Mourning) (prize in Cannes) and **Juguetes Rotos** (Broken Toys) (prize in Valladolid). Patino: **Nueve cartas a Berta** (Nine Letters to Berta) (Silver Shell Award in San Sebastian). Saura: **La caza** (The Hunt) (Silver Bear in Berlin). Fons: **La busca** (The Search) (prizes in Venice and Valladolid). Forn: **La piel quemada** (Burnt Skin) (prize in Valladolid). Guerín, Egea and Erice: **Los desafíos** (The Challenges) (Silver Shell at San Sebastian). Borau: **Furtivos** (Poachers) (Golden Shell at San Sebastian). Olea: **El bosque del lobo** (The Wolves's Forest) (prize in Valladolid). Gil: **La duda** (The Doubt) (prize in San

Sebastian). Saura: **Peppermint frappé** (prize in Berlin). Grau: **Noche de verano** (Summer Night) (prize in Mar del Plata), **Una historia de amor** (A Love Story) (prize in San Sebastian) and **El espontáneo** (The Spontaneous Bullfighter). Armiñán: **Mi querida señorita** (My Dear Young Miss) and **El amor del capitán Brando** The Love of Captain Brando). Guerín: **La casa de las palomas** (The Dove House). Esteva: **Dante no es únicamente severo** (Dante Is Not Only Strict) and **Lejos de los árboles** (Far from the Trees). Olea: **No es bueno que el hombre esté solo** (A Man Shouldn't Be Alone), **La casa sin frontera** (The House without Frontiers) and **Tormento** (Torment). Regueiro: **El buen amor** (Good Love) and **Si volvemos a vernos** (Smashing-up). Erice: **El espíritu de la colmena** (The Spirit of the Beehive). Saura: **Llanto por un bandido** (Lament for a Bandit), **Ana y los lobos** (Ana and the Wolves) and **La madriguera** (The Den). Gutiérrez: **Habla, mudita** (Speak, Mute Girl). Patino: **Canciones para después de una guerra** (Songs for After a War). Bodegas: **Españolas en París.** (Spanish Women in Paris). Boráu: **Hay que matar a B** (B Must Die). Suárez: **La regenta** (The Regent). Eceiza: **De cuerpo presente** (Laid Out). Aranda: **Fata Morgana.**

 Demonstrations and strikes in favour of an amnesty for political prisoners. **Junta Democrática** and **Plataforma** join to form **Coordinación Democrática.** Repression in Vitoria. The **Cortes** approves a new **Law of Political Association,** and later the **Reform Project.** All political parties are legalized —the communist is the last, and becomes legal in the midst of Holy Week— as well as the trade unions. A joint commission made up of members of the opposition and the government draw up the **electoral law.** Ninety percent of the electorate votes in the **elections,** the winner of which is the Democratic Center Union (UCD) with 34.7 percent of the vote. The opening of the **Cortes:** a commission is entrusted with the job of drawing up the **Constitution.** The provisional **Generalitat** is reestablished and President Tarradellas returns to Catalonia. Spain is admited into the **Council of Europe.** The **pre-autonomous regime of Euskadi** (Basque Country) is established. The **Cortes** or Spanish parliament approves the **Constitution.** The **Constitutional Referendum** is held and 87.87 percent of the electorate vote affirmatively. Parliament is dissolved and legislative elections are convoked. The **autonomous systems of government** are approved for the regions of Valencia, Aragon, the Canary Islands, Extremadura, Andalusia, the Balearic Islands and Castile-Leon. It is the true end of the dictatorship.

Architecture.—Bofill: **Ciudad en el Espacio.** Moreno Bescós: **BANKINTER.**
Sculpture.—Soto: **Anillo con tres.** Negret: **Matamorfosis.** Mompó: **Alaró.** Chillida: **La sirena varada.**
Painting.—Cillero: **Díptico.** López: **En la azotea.** Feito: **1977.**
Music.—C. Halffter obtains the RAI Prize. Marco wins the International Composers' Tribunal Prize, while Prieto earns that of the **Cajas de Ahorro** (Savings' Banks).
Literature.—Plá: **Cuaderno gris.** Soto: **El libro de Tobías.** García Nieto: **Sonetos y revelaciones de Madrid.** Rodríguez: **Resurrección.** Umbral: **Memorias de un niño de derechas.** Chacel: **Barrio de Maravillas.** L. Goytisolo: **Recuento.** J. Goytisolo: **Señas de identidad.** Buero: **La doble historia del Dr. Valmy.** Nieva: **La carroza de plomo candente.** Martínez Mediero: **Las hermanas de Búfalo Bill.** Salom: **La piel del limón.** Gala: **Los buenos días perdidos.**

Censorship is abolished.
Films.—Chávarri: **El desencanto** (Disenchantment). Franco: **Pascual Duarte** (prize in the Cannes Film Festival). Camino: **Las largas vacaciones del 36** (The Long Vacation of 36) (FIPRESCI in Berlin). Bodegas: **Libertad provisional** (Provisional Freedom) (prize in San Sebastian). Saura: **Cría cuervos...** (Raising Ravens...). Ribas: **La ciutat cremada** (The Burnt City). Estelrich: **El anacoreta** (The Anchorite). Giménez-Rico: **Retrato de familia** (Family Portrait). Saura: **Elisa, vida mía** (Elisa, My Love) (prize in Cannes). Gutiérrez: **Camada negra** (Black Brood) (Silver Bear in Berlin). Bardem: **El puente** (The Long Week-end) (first prize in Moscow). Chávarri: **A un Dios desconocido** (To an Unknown God) (prize in San Sebastian). Garci: **Asignatura pendiente** (Pending Exam). Colomo: **Tigres de papel** (Paper Tigers). Mercero: **La guerra de papá** (Daddy's War). Fernán Gómez: **Mi hija Hildegard** (My Daughter Hildegard). Isasi: **El perro** (The Dog). García Sánchez: **Las truchas** (The Trout) (Golden Bear in Berlin). Martínez-Lázaro: **Las palabras de Max** (Max's Words) (Golden Bear in Berlin). Gutiérrez: **Sonámbulos** (Sleepwalkers) (prize in San Sebastian). Olea: **Un hombre llamado «Flor de Otoño»** (A Man Called «Autumn Flower») (prize in San Sebastian). Herralde: **El asesino de Pedralbes** (The Pedralbes' Murderer) (prize in San Sebastian). Camino: **La vieja memoria** (The Old Memory)

(FIPRESCI in San Sebastian). Camus: **Los días del pasado** (Days Gone By) (prize in Karlovy-Vary). Franco: **Los restos del naufragio** (The Remains of the Shipwreck). Saura: **Los ojos vendados** (Blindfolded). Berlanga: **La escopeta nacional** (The National Shotgun). Buñuel: **Ese oscuro objeto del deseo** (That Obscure Object of Desire). Bigas: **Bilbao.**

322 The **Democratic Center Union** wins the **general elections,** while the leftist coalition wins the municipal elections. For the first time since the Second Republic, a civilian becomes Minister of Defense. The autonomous government systems of Murcia, Asturias and Castile-La Mancha are approved. A referendum is held on the Basque, Catalonian and Andalusian autonomy statutes. The nationalists (PNV) win the elections to the Basque parliament, while the same is true in the Catalonian legislative body (CIU and ERC). Suárez resigns as premier and Calvo Sotelo is appointed to replace him. Lieutenant Colonel Tejero takes the Congress of Deputees by storm. He gives himself up after King Juan Carlos I addresses the nation on TVE. Two generals and more than ten officers are arrested. **An enormous demonstration is held in favor of the democratic system in Spain.** The government, the trade unions and the employers' associations subscribe the **National Agreement on Employment** (ANE). **The Divorce Law.** The adulterated cooking oil affair explodes —more than a hundred dead. **Popular Alliance** wins in the elections to the **Galician parliament.** The houses of parliament are dissolved and **general elections** are held: The Spanish Socialist Workers Party wins a majority while both the Democratic Center Union and the Spanish Communist Party suffer severe setbacks. Santiago Carrillo resigns as communist secretary general. The first socialist government comes to office.

Architecture.—Bofill: **Proyecto para el mercado de Les Halles.**
Sculpture.—Cardells: **Parada.** Mateos: **Nuevos hormigones.** Valdés: **La reina Mariana IX.** Luque: **Composición.** Mignoni: **Collage doble 523.**
Painting.—Delgado: **Campesino fumando.** Equipo Crónica: **Crónica de transición** and **Los viajes.** Gordillo: **Doble morado.** Villar: **Desnudo en arrecife** and **Bañista en la orilla.** Collective exhibition: **La última cena.** Canogar: **Con el polvo de la lid sangrienta.** Cardona: **En cas de drame...** Lozano: **Barcas** and **Paisaje de Levante.** Guinovart: **Aguafuertes retocados.** Portales: **Esferoides.**
Music.—García Abril: **Concierto Aguediano para guitarra.** De Pablo: **Kiu.**
Literature.—Guillén: **Antología del mar.** Serrano Plaja: **Los álamos oscuros.** Roig: **La hora violeta** and **La ópera cotidiana.** Gaite: **El cuento de nunca acabar** and **Retahílas.** Torrente: **La isla de los jacintos cortados.** Gil-Albert: **Los arcángeles.** Trapiello: **Las tradiciones.** Umbral: **Mortal y Rosa** and **La bestia rosa.** Marsé: **Un día volveré.** Hortelano: **Gramática parda.** Núñez: **Ocaso en Poley.** Guelbenzu: **El río de la luna.** Montalbán: **Asesinato en el Comité Central** and **Los pájaros de Bangkok.** Conde: **Breixo.** Azúa: **Ultima lección.** Suárez: **La reina roja.** Matute: **Los hijos muertos.** J. Goytisolo: **La resaca.** Fernández Santos: **Cabrera.** Sampedro: **Octubre, octubre.** Bergamín: **Al fin y al cabo.** Andújar: **Secretos augurios.** Semprúm: **Aquel domingo.** Caballero Bonald: **Toda**

la noche oyeron pasar los pájaros. De Otero: **Expresión y reunión.** Rosales: **Poesía reunida.** Alonso: **Gozos de la vista.** Valente: **Estancias.** Zubiri: **Inteligencia** and **Logos.** Sánchez Dragó: **Gárgoris and Habidis.**

Films.—Bardem: **Siete días en enero** (Seven Days in January) (prize in Moscow). Saura: **Mamá cumple cien años** (Mama Turns a Hundred) (prize in San Sebastian). Miró: **Gary Cooper que estás en los cielos** (Gary Cooper Who Art in Heaven) and **El crimen de Cuenca** (The Cuenca Crime). De la Iglesia: **El diputado** (The Parliamentary Deputee) and **El pico** (The Shoot-up). Burau: **La Sabina** (The Sabina). Gutiérrez: **El corazón del bosque** (The Heart of the Forest), **Maravillas** and **Demonios en el jardín** (Demons in the Garden). Armiñán: **El nido** (The Nest) (prize in Montreal) and **En septiembre** (In September). Forn: **Companys.** Drove: **La verdad sobre el caso Savolta** (The Truth about the Savolta Case). Zulueta: **Arrebato** (Rage). Trueba: **Opera prima** (A Cousin in Opera/First Work) (prize in Venice). García Sánchez: **Dolores.** Salgot: **Mater amatísima** (Mother Beloved). Molina: **Función de noche** (Night Performance). Berlanga: **Patrimonio nacional** (National Patrimony). Betriú: **La plaça del Diamant** (Diamond Square). Almodóvar: **Laberinto de pasiones** (Labyrinth of Passions). Chávarri: **Dedicatoria** (Dedication) and **Bearn.** Méndez-Leite: **El hombre de moda** (A Man in Fashion). Uribe: **La fuga de Segovia** (The Segovia Escape). Camus: **La colmena** (The Beehive). Betancor: **Valentina** and **1919.** Saura: **Bodas de sangre** (Blood Wedding) and **Carmen.** Erice: **El sur** (The South). Garci: **Volver a empezar** (Starting Over). Aguirre: **Vida perra** (Dog's Life). Martínez-Lázaro: **Sus años dorados** (Golden Years). Zorrilla: **El arreglo** (The Rendering).

DIRECTORS

JAVIER AGUIRRE
1935, San Sebastián

Begins his film activities in 1950. He organizes a film club, writes criticism and makes **amateur** films. In 1956 he moves to Madrid in order to study in the **Cinema Research and Experiences Institute,** but he does not obtain a degree. Starting in 1960, he directs film shorts and wins prizes in the festivals of San Sebastian, Venice, Bordighera, Bilbao, Strassburg, Valladolid, etc. Among other magazines, he writes for **Radiocinema, Primer Plano** and **Film Ideal.** Assistant director and screenwriter. He makes industrial shorts and advertising spots. Ever since 1967, he makes experimental film shorts, the style of which he describes as **Anti-Cine.** In 1972, he publishes **Anti-Cine, Apuntes para una teoría** (Anti-Cine, Notes on a Theory), in which he explains his ideas.

CREDITS (incomplete)

1964: **España insólita**
(Unusual Spain).
1967: **Los chicos con las chicas**
(The Boys with the Girls).
1970: **Pierna creciente, falda menguante**
(Growing Leg, Diminishing Skirt).
1973: **El gran amor del conde Drácula**
(Count Dracula's Great Love).
Volver a nacer
(Being Born Again).
1975: **Ligeramente viudas**
(Slightly Widowed).
1976: **La iniciación al amor (Dafnis y Cloe)**
(Initiation to Love —Daphne and Chloë).
1977: **Acto de posesión**
(Act of Possession).
1980: **La guerra de los niños**
(The Children's War).
1981: **Vida perra**
(Dog's Life).
1982: **Ni te cases ni te embarques**
(Neither Marry nor Sail the Sea).

PEDRO ALMODOVAR
1949, Calzada de Calatrava (Ciudad Real)

He moves into the film industry from the fringe areas of cinema. He makes several medium-length films in super-8 and a feature called **Folle, folle, folleme Tim** (Screw, Screw, Screw Me Tim; 1978). Afterwards, he makes the short called **Salomé** in 16 mm. He splits his time in film with his activities as an office worker in the telephone company. He works as an actor in the theater group, **Los Goliardos.** He has written stories and articles and has published a short novel: **Fuego en las entrañas** (Fire Deep Inside; 1982).

CREDITS

1980: **Pepi, Luci, Bom, y otras chicas del montón**
(Pepi, Luci, Bom and a Whole Lot of Other Girls).
1982: **Laberinto de pasiones**
(Labyrinth of Passions).
1983: **Entre tinieblas**
(In the Dark).
1984: **¿Qué he hecho yo para merecer esto?**
(What Have I Done to Deserve This?).
1986: **Matador**

ANTONIO DEL AMO

1911, Valdelagua (Madrid)

He writes criticisms and essays in the **Popular Films** and **Nuestro Cinema** magazines in the thirties. During the Spanish Civil War, he heads the film section of the **Lister Brigade** in which he makes several documentaries. After the war, he works as an assistant director with Rafael Gil, Antonio Román and I. F. Iquino. At the same time, he writes screenplays and makes documentaries. He is a professor at the **Cinema Research and Experiences Institute** until 1959 and editing professor at the **Official Film School** from 1965 to 1968. The author of several books, including the noteworthy **Estética del montaje** (Aesthetics of Editing). He discovers the young singing star Joselito and directs almost all his films.

CREDITS (incomplete)

1947: **Cuatro mujeres**
(Four Women).
1948: **El huésped de las tinieblas**
(The Guest of Darkness).
1949: **Noventa minutos**
(Ninety Minutes).
1950: **Historia de dos aldeas**
(Story of Two Villages).
1951: **Día tras día**
(Day After Day).
1952: **Puebla de las mujeres**
(Women's Town).
1954: **Sierra maldita**
(The Cursed Sierra).
1955: **El sol sale todos los dias**
(The Sun Comes Up Every Day).
1956: **El pequeño ruiseñor**
(The Small Nightingale).
1958: **Escucha mi canción**
(Listen To My Song).
1961: **Bello recuerdo**
(Lovely Memory).
1964: **Las gemelas**
(The Twins).
El hijo de Jesse James
(The Son of Jesse James).
1966: **Un perro en órbita**
(A Dog in Orbit).
1975: **Madres solteras**
(Unmarried Mothers).

VICENTE ARANDA

1926, Barcelona

After spending his youth in his native city, he goes to live in Venezuela from 1952 to 1959. There he works in NCR, installing accounting systems. On returning to Spain, he tries to enter the **Cinema Research and Experiences Institute** in Madrid and the IDHEC in Paris. Finally moving to Barcelona, he sets up his own production company. He is one of the founders of the **Barcelona School.**

CREDITS

1964: **Brillante porvenir** (with R. Gubern)
(Brilliant Future).
1966: **Fata Morgana.**
1969: **Las crueles**
(The Cruel Women).
1972: **La novia ensangrentada**
(The Bloody Bride).
1974: **Clara es el precio**
(Clara Is the Price).
1977: **Cambio de sexo**
(Sex Change).
1980: **La muchacha de las bragas de oro**
(The Girl with the Golden Panties).
1982: **Asesinato en el comité central**
(Munder in the Central Committee).
1984: **Fanny Pelopaja**
(Fanny Straw Top).
1986: **Tiempo de silencio**
(Time of Silence).

B

JAIME DE ARMIÑAN
1927, Madrid

He comes from a family of writers and politicians. He contributes articles to the magazines **Fotos** and **Dígame.** He writes plays and wins the national prizes, **Calderón de la Barca** and **Lope de Vega.** Until he begins to direct, he mainly works as a screenwriter both in television and in film. Among his scripts for TVE are those for the series **Galería de maridos** (Gallery of Husbands), **Galería de esposas** (Gallery of Wives), **Las 12 caras de Eva** (Eve's Twelve Faces), **Fábulas** (Fables) and **Confidencias** (Secrets). His screenplays include: **El secreto de Mónica** (Monica's Secret; 1961) by Forqué, **La becerrada** (The Fight with Yearling Bulls; 1962), by Forqué, **Sólo para dos** (Just for Two; 1968) by Lucía, and **El Bengador Gusticiero y su pastelera madre** (The Vengeful Avenger and His Cookie-baking Mother; 1976), by Forges.

CREDITS

1969: **Carola de día, Carola de noche** (Carola by Day, Carola by Night).
1970: **La Lola dicen que no vive sola** (They Say Lola Doesn't Live Alone).
1971: **Mi querida señorita** (My Dear Young Miss).
1973: **Un casto varón español** (The Chaste Spanish Male).
1974: **El amor del capitán Brando** (The Love of Captain Brando).
1975: **¡Jo, papá!** (Gee, Papa!).
1977: **Nunca es tarde** (It's Never Too Late).
1978: **Al servicio de la mujer española** (At the Service of Spanish Womanhood).
1980: **El nido** (The Nest).
1981: **En septiembre** (In September).
1984: **Stico**
1985: **La hora bruja** (The Witching Hour).

RICARDO DE BAÑOS
1882, Barcelona, 1939, Barcelona

His first work as an apprentice in the film industry dates from 1902 in Gaumont in Paris. In 1904, he makes his first film reports in Barcelona. In 1905, he shoots scenes of **zarzuelas** (Spanish light operas) with records according to Gaumont's **chronophone** system. Along with his brother Ramón, close collaborator and camera operator by profession, he associates himself with Hispano Film in 1907 and sets up a laboratory to develop negatives and print copies. In 1916, both brothers create the Royal Films production company and they direct fictional films until 1922 such as **Los arlequines de seda y oro** (Harlequins of Silk and Gold). For a time, he works as a director of photography and sets up business deals in the film industry. He returns to direct **El relicario** (The Reliquary).

CREDITS (imcomplete)

1907: **Don Juan Tenorio.**
1909: **La guerra de Rif** (The Rif War).
Locura de amor (Love Crazy).
Baixant de la Font del Gat.
1910: **Don Juan de Serrallonga.**
1911: **Don Pedro el Cruel.**
1914: **La malquerida** (The Unpopular Girl).

1916: **El idiota de Sevilla**
(The Fool from Seville).
Sangre y arena
(Blood and Sand).
1918: **Fuerza y nobleza**
(Strength and Nobility).
1919: **Los arlequines de seda y oro**
(The Harlequins of Silk and Gold).
1920: **El judío polaco**
(The Jewish Pole).
1921: **Don Juan Tenorio.**
1933: **El relicario**
(The Reliquary).

JUAN ANTONIO BARDEM

1922, Madrid

Son of actor Rafael Bardem and actress Matilde Muñoz Sampedro. He studies in Madrid, Barcelona, San Sebastián and Seville as a result of his parent's continual tours and the civil war. He becomes an agronomist in 1948, but his first love is film. In 1946, he works in the film department of the Ministry of Agriculture. In 1947, he joins the first class of the **Cinema Research and Experiences Institute,** but he does not obtain a degree since he fails the practice project at the end of the course of studies. He writes film criticism in the magazines **Indice** and **La hora** and he is a founding member of **Objetivo.** His close work with Berlanga leads them to direct **Esa pareja feliz** (That Happy Couple) together and to write the screenplay for **Bienvenido, Mr. Marshall** (Welcome, Mr. Marshall). He presents the report, **The current situation of the Spanish film industry** in the **Salamanca Conversations.** His films have been prize-winners in numerous festivals. President of the Uninci production company. President of ASDREC. Between 1965 and 1975 he is obliged to make a purely commercial product, completely different from the rest of his work.

CREDITS

1951: **Esa pareja feliz** (with Berlanga)
(That Happy Couple).
1953: **Cómicos**
(Comedians).
1954: **Felices Pascuas**
(Happy Holidays).
1955: **Muerte de un ciclista**
(Death of a Cyclist).
1956: **Calle Mayor**
(Main Street).
1957: **La venganza**
(Revenge).
1959: **Sonatas.**
1960: **A las cinco de la tarde**
(At Five in the Afternoon).
1962: **Los inocentes**
(The Innocents).
1963: **Nunca pasa nada**
(Nothing Ever Happens).
1965: **Los pianos mecánicos**
(Player Pianos).
1968: **El último día de la guerra**
(The Last Day of the War).
1970: **Varietés.**
1971: **La isla misteriosa**
(The Mysterious Island).
1972: **La corrupción de Chris Miller**
(The Corruption of Chris Miller).
1975: **El poder del deseo**
(The Power of Desire).
1976: **El puente**
(The Long Weekend).
1978: **Siete días de enero**
(Seven Days in January).
1982: **La advertencia** (in Bulgaria)
(The Warning).

FRANCESC BELLMUNT

1947, Sabadell (Barcelona)

Having obtained a degree in the Humanities from the University of Barcelona, he writes poetry and is a drummer in the **Los Duendes** musical band. He writes film criticism in a local newspaper and makes a film in 8 mm., winning a prize from the **Circle of Film Writers.** During 1970 and 1971, he directs the film shorts **Catherine, Semejante a Pedro** (Like Pedro) and **La mano de Belgrado** (Belgrade's Hand). He draws for the magazines **Por favor** and **Muchas gracias.** He shoots industrial shorts and directs newsreels for the **Institut de Cinema Catalá: Copel, presos en lucha** (Copel, A Prisoners' Fight) and **El conflicto de las gasolineras** (The Service Station Conflict).

CREDITS

1972: **Pastel de sangre** (an episode) (A Blood Cake).
1974: **Robin Hood nunca muere** (Robin Hood Never Dies).
1975: **Canet Rock**
1978: **L'orgia** (The Orgy).
1979: **Salut i força al canut** (Health, Lust and Fun).
1980: **La quinta del porro** (The Stoned Conscripts).
1984: **Pa d'angel** (Angel Bread).
1985: **Un par de huevos** (A Pair of Balls).
1986: **La radio folla** (Radio Screwball).

ANTONIO JOSE BETANCOR

1942, Santa Cruz de Tenerife

He studies law and obtains a degree in the **Official Film School** with the film project, **El último trabajo** (The Last Job; 1971). He receives a scholarship from the March Foundation and studies film in the University of Southern California in the United States. He works as an assistant director for Mario Camus. He makes various episodes of **Paisajes con figuras** for TVE.

CREDITS

1978: **Sentados al borde de la mañana con los pies colgando** (Seated at the Edge of Morning with Your Legs Hanging Over).
1982: **Valentina.**
1983: **1919. Crónica del alba** (1919. Dawn Chronicle).

FRANCISCO BETRIU

1940, Orgaño (Lérida)

His artistic experiences begin during his military service in Africa. He organizes a theater company made up of soldiers and stages several works that are so successful that a tour is made of numerous barracks. He joins the **Official Film School,** but he does not complete the study program. He starts to produce and direct film shorts in the Inscram production company. He directs the shorts **Gente de mesón** (The Tavern Crowd; 1969) and **Bolero de amor** (The Love Bolero; 1970). Editor-in-chief of the magazine **Nuevos Fotogramas.** He belongs to the Editorial Staff of Barcelona's **Noticiari,** part of the **Institut de Cinema Catalá.**

CREDITS

1972: **Corazón solitario** (Lonely Heart).
1974: **Furia española** (Spanish Fury).
1976: **La viuda andaluza** (The Andalusian Widow).
1980: **Los fieles sirvientes** (The Faithful Servants).
1982: **La plaza del diamante** (Diamond Square).
1985: **Réquiem por un campesino español** (Requiem for a Spanish Peasant).

JOSE JUAN BIGAS LUNA

1946, Barcelona

He founds the graphic design studio **Gris** and works in that field until 1970. He works as a professor and collaborator in the schools of communication and design **Eina** and **Elisava** between 1973 and 1974. A member of the INFAD committee and designer in the ADI-FAD group. His works are on show in the Dalí Museum in Figueras and form part of various private collections. He also works with the director, J. L. Fábregas Poveda in the creation of departments for **Psychotherapy Recuperation in Art.** Between 1972 and 1976, he makes thirteen film shorts. He is the co-founder and member of the **Barcelona Grup,** a Spanish film export organization.

CREDITS

1976: **Tatuaje**
(Tattoo).
1978: **Bilbao.**
1979: **Caniche**
(Poodle).
1981: **Renacer** (in USA)
(Reborn).
1985: **Lola**

ROBERTO BODEGAS

1933, Madrid

He studies for the merchant marine in Barcelona and later takes a course in the Humanities in Madrid. He is an employee in the telephone company until he gets his first jobs in the film industry: unpaid trainee, second assistant director, assistant director, second unit director and screenwriter in such films as **O salto** (1969), by Christian de Chalonge. He works in these activities in different countries with such directors as Sergio Leone, Denys de la Patteliere, Jean Dreville, Serge Bourgignon, Christian-Jacque, Fred Zinnemann, Christian de Chalonge, etc.

CREDITS

1970: **Españolas en París**
(Spanish Women in Paris).
1973: **Vida conyugal sana**
(A Healthy Married Life).
1974: **Los nuevos españoles**
(The New Spaniards).
1975: **La adúltera**
(The Adulteress).
1976: **Libertad provisional**
(Provisional Freedom).
1982: **Corazón de papel**
(Paper Heart).

JOSE LUIS BORAU

1929, Zaragoza

After having received a law degree from the University of Zaragoza, he writes film criticism in the **El Heraldo de Aragón** newspaper. Driven by his interest in film and his desire to live in Madrid, he passes a competitive examination for a post in the Ministry of Housing. In 1957, he joins the **Cinema Research and Experiences Institute** and graduates with the film project **En el río** (On the River; 1960). He leaves his job in the ministry to work in advertising. He makes various shorts until he directs his first feature. In 1967, he founds his own production company called **El Imán,** giving opportunities to such directors as Iván Zulueta, Jaime de Armiñán and Manuel Gutiérrez Aragón. Professor of screenwriting techniques at the **Official Film School** and of direction in the Cinema Chair of the University of Valladolid. He currently resides in Hollywood.

CREDITS

1964: **Brandy.**
1965: **Crimen de doble filo**
(Double-edged Crime).
1974: **Hay que matar a B**
(B Must Die).
1975: **Furtivos**
(Poachers).
1979: **La Sabina**
(The Sabina).

1984: **Río abajo** (in USA)
(On the Line).

JOSE BUCHS

1893, Santander. 1973, Madrid

Member of the Academy of Music and Declamation. He works as an actor, assistant director and production chief in **Los intereses creados** (Vested Interests; 1918), by Jacinto Benavente—a work based on Benavente's theater piece. He directs four films in 1920 and works as an actor in several. He founds his own production company and between 1926 and 1931, he makes eight films, some of which with big budgets such as **El dos de mayo** (The Second of May) and **Prim.** He directs the first totally Spanish sound film called **Carceleras** («Carcelera» Songs; 1932).

CREDITS (incomplete)

1920: **Expiación**
(Atonement).
La inaccesible
(The Inaccessible Girl).
La verbena de la Paloma
(The Paloma Fair).
1922: **Alma rifeña**
(The Soul of Rif).
La reina mora
(The Moorish Queen).
Carceleras
(«Carcelera» Songs).
1923: **Doloretes**
Rosario, la cortijera
(Rosario, the Farmer's Girl).
Curro Vargas.
1924: **Diego Corrientes.**
1925: **La hija del corregidor**
(The Magistrate's Daughter).
El abuelo
(The Grandfather).
1926: **Pilar Guerra.**
Una extraña aventura de Luis Candelas
(A Strange Adventure Involving Luis Candelas).
1927: **El conde de Maravillas**
(Count Maravillas).
El dos de mayo
(The Second of May).
1928: **Pepe-Hillo.**
1929: **El rey que rabió**
(The King Who Raved).
1930: **Prim**
1932: **Carceleras**
(«Carcelera» Songs).
1935: **El niño de las monjas**
(The Nun's Boy).
1936: **El rayo**
(Lightning).
1939: **El rey que rabió**
(The King Who Raved).
1942: **Un caballero famoso**
(A Famous Gentleman).
1943: **El ilustre Perea**
(The Illustrious Perea).
1947: **Aventuras de don Juan de Mairena**
(The Adventures of Don Juan de Mairena).

1953: **Brindis al cielo**
(A Dedication to the Heavens).
1957: **Cara de goma**
(Rubber Face).

LUIS BUÑUEL

1900, Calanda (Teruel). 1983, México.

He first studies with the Jesuits in Zaragoza. Later, he moves to Madrid in 1917 where he stays in the famous **Residencia de Estudiantes** (Student Residency). He begins a course of studies to become an agronomist, but he soon starts to study the Humanities. He becomes Spain's amateur boxing champion in 1921. A member of the Platerías cafe «tertulias» or get-togethers along with García Lorca, Rafael Alberti, Dámaso Alonso, Ramón Gómez de la Serna, Jorge Guillén, Eugenio d'Ors, etc. In 1925, he moves to Paris and one year later starts his film career as an aid to J. Epstein. He forms part of the surrealist group along with Dalí and Man Ray. His first film, **Un chien andalou** (An Andalusian Dog; 1928) is directed along with Dalí and is financed thanks to the money his mother sends him from Spain. He works in dubbing jobs for Paramount in Paris and Warner in Madrid. He is a production supervisor for Filmófono, working in pictures directed by new directors (1935-1937). During the civil war he puts together various propaganda documentaries for the Republican government. From 1938 to 1946, he works in the United States, first in New York's Modern Art Museum and later in dubbing for Warner between 1944 and 1946. He leaves for Mexico where he lives and works. In 1961, he returns to Spain to shoot **Viridiana** which wins the Golden Palm in the Cannes Film Festival and which is banned in Spain for sixteen years. It is only recognized as a Spanish film in 1982.

SPANISH CREDITS

1932: **Las Hurdes** (Tierra sin pan)
Las Hurdes (Land without Bread).
1961: **Viridiana.**
1970: **Tristana.**
1977: **Ese oscuro objeto del deseo**
(That Obscure Object of Desire).

JAIME CAMINO

1936, Barcelona

A degree in law and professor of piano and harmony. He writes for the magazines **Indice** and **Nuestro cine** and contributes to the screenplays for all his films. He is a finalist for the Nadal Prize for novels. Before he directs his first feature, he makes shorts in various film formats. He owns the Tibidabo production company. He participates in the founding of the **Institut de Cinema Català.** He is the author of the book, **Intimas conversaciones con la Pasionaria** (1977).

CREDITS

1965: **Los felices sesenta** (The Happy Sixties).
1966: **Mañana será otro día** (Tomorrow's Another Day).
1968: **España otra vez** (Spain Again).
1969: **Un invierno en Mallorca (Jurtzenka)** (A Winter in Mallorca, Jurtzenka).
1972: **Mi profesora particular** (My Private Teacher).
1975: **Las largas vacaciones del 36** (The Long Vacation of 36).
1977: **La vieja memoria** (The Old Memory).
1979: **La campanada** (The Ringing of the Bells/Scandal).
1984: **El balcón abierto.** (The Open Balcony).

MARIO CAMUS

1935, Santander

He studies law. Joining the **Cinema Research and Experiences Institute** he received his diploma after completing his project called **El borracho** (The Drunk; 1963). Later he becomes a professor. He works with Saura on the scripts for **Los Golfos** (The Scoundrels; 1959) and **Llanto por un bandido** (Lament for a Bandit; 1963). He works for TVE in some of the episodes for the series **Conozca usted España** (Get To Know Spain), **Cuentos y leyendas** (Stories and Legends), **Si las piedras hablaran** (If Stones Could Speak) and **Curro Jiménez.** Other TVE productions he has made include **Los camioneros** (The Truck Drivers), **La leyenda del alcalde de Zalamea** (The Legend of the Mayor of Zalamea), **Fortunata y Jacinta** and **Los desastres de la guerra** (Disasters of War).

CREDITS

1963: **Los farsantes** (The Actors). **Young Sánchez.**
1964: **Muere una mujer** (A Woman Dies).
1965: **La visita que no toçó el timbre** (The Visitor Who Did Not Ring the Doorbell). **Con el viento solano** (With the East Wind).
1966: **Cuando tú no estás** (When You Aren't There). **Volver a vivir** (Living Again).
1967: **Al ponerse el sol** (When the Sun Sets).
1968: **Digan lo que digan** (No Matter What They Say).
1969: **Esa mujer** (That Woman).
1970: **La cólera del viento** (The Wind's Wrath).
1975: **Los pájaros de Baden-Baden** (The Birds of Baden-Baden) **La joven casada** (The Young Married Woman).
1977: **Los días del pasado** (Days Gone By).
1982: **La colmena** (The Beehive).
1984: **Los santos inocentes** (The Holy Innocents).
1985: **La vieja música** (That Old Music).

JAIME CHAVARRI

1943, Madrid

Degree in law and a student of the **Official Film School** for two courses. The director of various features in super-8, including **Run, Blancanieves, run** (Run, Snow White, Run; 1967) and **Ginebra en los infiernos** (Confusion in Hell; 1970). His career also includes work as a critic, art director, screenwriter, assistant director, and director of shorts and advertising spots. He works in TVE, where he has directed some of the episodes of such series as **Los libros** (Books), **Pintores del Prado** (Painters of the Prado), **Ficciones** (Fictional Tales) and **Cuentos y Leyendas** (Stories and Legends), as well the production **Luis y Virginia** (1982).

CREDITS

1971: **Pastel de sangre** (episode: The Dance)
(The Bood Cake).
1973: **Los viajes escolares**
(School Trips).
1976: **El desencanto**
(Disenchantment).
1977: **A un Dios desconocido**
(To an Unknown God).
1979: **Cuentos eróticos** (episode: The Small Planet)
(Erotic Tales).
Cuentos para una escapada (episode: The Deaf Woman)
(Stories of an Escapade).
1980: **Dedicatoria**
(Dedication).
1983: **Bearn o la sala de las muñecas**
(Bearn or the Doll Room).
1984: **Las bicicletas son para el verano**
(Bicycles Are for Summer).
1986: **El río de oro**
(The Golden River).

SEGUNDO DE CHOMON

1871, Teruel. 1927, París

Creator, technician, camera operator and director. He discovers a system to animate objects, and he also invents animated drawings and puppets as well as transparent and moveable backgrounds. He discovers the traveling shot and uses it for the first time in **La vie et la passion de Jesus-Christo** (1907) by Zecca, and **Cabiria** (1914) by Pastrone. Contracted by Pathé, he makes close to 150 films of about 100 to 150 meters in length with trick shots. From Paris, he goes to Turin where he works until 1923.

CREDITS

1902: **Choque de trenes**
(Train Crash).
Montserrat.
1905: **Eclipse de sol**
(Eclipse of the Sun).
El hotel eléctrico
(The Electric Hotel).
1906: **Las sombras animadas**
(**Les ombres chinoises,** made in France).
(The Animated Shadows)
1907: **La casa de los duendes**
(**La maison hantée,** made in France).
(Ghost House).
1909: **Cuisine magnetique** (made in France).

JULIO COLL

1919, Campodrón (Gerona)

Professor of mercantile law and operations, and theater critic for the magazine **Destino.** He has published various novels, stories and essays. An expert on flamenco song as well as Gypsy and Andalusian dance. He is also a specialist in jazz, having written on the subject for several years in the magazine **Cine en siete días.** He has written numerous screenplays and several theater pieces. Sub-director of the **Official Film School** in 1969 and later head of studies, professor in theory and professor of direction and acting techniques. Producer of his own films since 1958, employing the name Juro Films. A director who has received a degree specializing in television productions, he has made the following programs for TVE: **La Rosa** (Rosa), **La familia Colón** (The Columbus Family), **José Iturbi** and **En víspera de la Olimpiada** (On the Eve of the Olympics), among others.

CREDITS

1955: **Nunca es demasiado tarde**
(It's Really Never Too Late).
1956: **La cárcel de cristal**
(The Glass Prison).
1957: **Distrito quinto**
(Fifth District).
1958: **Un vaso de whisky**
(A Glass of Whiskey).
1959: **El traje de oro**
(The Golden Suit).
1961: **Los cuervos**
(Ravens).
La cuarta ventana
(The Fourth Window).
1962: **Ensayo general para la muerte**
(A General Rehearsal in Death).
1963: **Los muertos no perdonan**
(The Dead Don't Forgive).
Fuego
(Fire).
1964: **Jandro.**
1966: **Las viudas** (an episode).
(The Widows).
Comando de asesinos
(Death Squad).
1968: **Persecución hasta Valencia**
(Persecution to Valencia).
1969: **El mejor del mundo**
(The Best in the World).
1971: **La Araucana**
(The Araucanian).

FERNANDO COLOMO

1946, Madrid

Receives a degree from Madrid's Higher School of Architecture and another from the **Official Film School** as an art director. He makes films in super-8 and in 16 mm. His film shorts made in 35 mm. called **En un París imaginario** (In an Imaginary Paris; 1975) and **Pomporrutas imperiales** (1976) receive various prizes. He has fostered and formed part of various production companies specialized in making shorts or features: Meridion Films, La Salamandra P. C. and Zeppo Films.

CREDITS

1977: **Tigres de papel**
(Paper Tigers).
1978: **¿Qué hace una chica como tú en un sitio como éste?**
(What's a Girl Like You Doing in a Place Like This?)
1979: **Cuentos eróticos** (episode: Koñensonatten)
(Erotic Tales).
1980: **La mano negra**
(The Black Hand).
1982: **Estoy en crisis**
(I'm Having a Crisis).
1983: **La línea del cielo**
(Skyline).
1985: **El caballero del dragón**
(The Knight of The Dragon).

D

CRUZ DELGADO
1929, Madrid

Graduate of Madrid's School of Fine Arts, he also studies graphic arts and cinematography. In 1956, he begins to work in Estudios Moro as an assistant animator. Illustrator of comic strip stories and professor of animation in the Film Department of the University of Valladolid. Founder and owner of Estudios Cruz Delgado, dedicated to animated film. From 1964 he makes a number of shorts such as **Molécula** (1965), **Andanzas del canguro Boxy** (Adventures of Boxy the Kangaroo; 1966) and **¿Conoces las señales?** (Do You Know the Signs?; 1970). For TVE, he has made 13 episodes of the series **Aventuras de Molécula** (Adventures of Molecula; 1968) and 39 episodes of the series **Don Quijote de la Mancha** (Don Quixote of La Mancha; 1981).

CREDITS

1973: **Mágica aventura** (Magic Adventure).
1979: **El desván de la fantasía** (with J. R. Sánchez) (The Dream Loft).
1983: **Los viajes de Gulliver** (Gulliver's Travels).

FERNANDO DELGADO
1891, Madrid. 1950

Son of the writer and journalist Sinesio Delgado and grandson of the actress Balbina Valverde. He studies law, but he gives it up due to his interest in theater acting. He makes his debut on the stage with a work by the brothers Alvarez Quintero in 1909. He contributes to the founding of the Madrid daily, **La noche.** Working in the company of Madrid's Teatro de la Comedia, he makes the acquaintance of Benito Perojo, who in 1916 gives him his first opportunity to work in film. In 1918, Jacinto Benavente contracts him as assistant director for the film version of **Los intereses creados** (Vested Interests). Between 1919 and 1924 he works as an actor and takes part in the creation of the Madrid Films studios and laboratories. He makes his debut as a director in 1924, but the appearance of sound pictures prevents him from making any more between 1929 and 1934. During the Spanish Civil War he makes documentaries for the insurrectionists, produced by Cifesa.

CREDITS

1924: **Los granujas** (The Rogues).
1925: **Ruta gloriosa** (The Glorious Road).
Cabrita que tira al monte (The Kid Takes to the Hills).
1927: **La terrible lección** (The Terrible Lesson).
Las de Méndez (Those of Méndez).
1928: **El tren o la pastora que supo amar** (The Train or the Shepherdess Who Knew Love).
¡Viva Madrid, que es mi pueblo! (Long Live Madrid, Which Is My Town!)
1929: **Cuarenta y ocho pesetas de taxi** (A Taxi Costing Forty-eight Pesetas).
El gordo de Navidad (The Big Christmas Lottery).
1934: **Doce hombres y una mujer** (Twelve Men and a Woman).
1935: **Currito de la Cruz.**
1939: **El genio alegre** (The Happy Genius).
1940: **La gitanilla** (The Little Gypsy Girl).
1941: **Fortunato.**
1943: **La patria chica** (The Home Town).
La maja del capote (The Pretty Girl of the Cape).
1946: **Lluvia de hijos** (It's Raining Sons and Daughters).
1947: **La calumniada** (The Woman Who Was Slandered).

JULIO DIAMANTE
1930, Cádiz

He works in Spanish National Radio and Radio Madrid in different culture programs. He contributes to the theater, film, poetry and music sections of the magazines **Indice, Estudio, Primer Acto, Nuestro Cine** and **L'Europa Letteraria.** Founder and director of the theater company of the **Cinema Research and Experiences Institute,** from which he receives a degree in direction for his research project **La lágrima del diablo** (The Devil's Tear; 1961). Later, he becomes a professor in the **Official Film School.** His professional career begins with the shooting of film shorts such as **Velázquez y lo velazqueño** (Velázquez and Everything Velázquez). He has directed the Benalmádena Film Festival for years.

CREDITS

1962: **Los que no fuimos a la guerra**
(Cuando estalló la paz)
(Those of Us Who Didn't Go to War —When Peace Broke Out).

1964: **Tiempo de amor**
(Time for Love).

1965: **El arte de vivir.**
(The Art of Living).

1969: **Tiempos de Chicago**
(Times in Chicago).

1970: **Helena y Fernanda**
(Helena and Fernanda).

1974: **Sex o no sex**
(Sex or No Sex).

1975: **La Carmen.**

ANTONIO DROVE
1942, Madrid

He studies electronic engineering. Writer for the **Griffith** magazine. He receives a degree from the **Official Film School** for the film project, **La caza de brujas** (Witch Hunt; 1968), which was banned from public screening. One year later he directs his first commercial medium-length film, **¿Qué se puede hacer con una chica?** (What Can You Do with a Girl?; 1969). For TVE he has made: **La noche de los tiempos** (The Night of Our Times; 1971), **Pura coincidencia** (Pure Coincidence; 1972), **Velázquez, la nobleza de la pintura** (Velázquez, the Nobility of Painting) and **La gran batalla de Andalucía** (The Great Battle of Andalusia). As a screenwriter, he has worked on the script of **Hay que matar a B** (B Must Die; 1974), by Borau.

CREDITS

1974: **Tocata y fuga de Lolita**
(Lolita's Toccata and Fugue/Elopement).
Mi mujer es muy decente dentro de lo que cabe
(My Wife Is Very Decent As Far As That's Possible).

1976: **Nosotros que fuimos tan felices**
(We Who Were So Happy).

1978: **La verdad sobre el caso Savolta**
(The Truth about the Savolta Case).

CARLOS DURAN

1935, Barcelona

Photographer who works in fashion and advertising. He receives a degree in direction from Paris' IDHEC in 1963. On his return to Barcelona, he works as an assistant director, technical director, set supervisor, production chief, etc., in the **Barcelona School.** His first short, **Raimon,** is banned for several years. Forming part of the **Institut de Cinema Catalá,** during the last few years he has made several documentaries based on Catalonian themes: **L'assemblen de Catalunya** (1981), **El barri del Besós** (1979) and **Escoles** (1980).

CREDITS

1967: **Cada vez que...** (Each Time...).
1970: **Liberxina 90.**

ANTON ECEIZA

1935, San Sebastián

He receives a degree in law and studies in the **Official Film School,** but never graduates. He writes in the magazines **Cinema Universitario, Film Ideal** and **Nuestro Cine.** He works as an assistant director and screenwriter with Bardem, Mur-Oti, Grau, Cottafavi, etc. He makes several documentaries in collaboration with producer Elías Querejeta. He works in advertising. In 1973, he leaves Spain due to political reasons. He lives in Paris and later in Mexico, where he directs two films. Currently, he lives in the Basque Country and makes film shorts in «euskera» or the Basque language.

CREDITS

1963: **El próximo otoño** (Next Autumn).
1965: **De cuerpo presente** (Laid Out).
1966: **Ultimo encuentro** (The Last Encounter).
1969: **Las secretas intenciones** (Secret Intentions).
1976: **Mina, viento de libertad** (made in Mexico) (Mina, Wind of Freedom).
1977: **El complot mongol** (made in Mexico) (The Mongolian Plot).

FRANCISCO ELIAS

1890. Huelva 1977, Barcelona

He begins to work in film in 1909 as a specialist in the translation and preparation of titles. He works in Gaumont's Parisian studios, Eclair and Manufactura del Film, his own company. He sets up a workshop, press and laboratory in New York, a company which operates until 1930. In 1925, he works in the literary department of the First National in Paris. He directs **El misterio de la Puerta del Sol** (The Puerta del Sol Mystery), the first Spanish sound film employing the Phonofilm system. In 1931, he helps found the Orphea studios in Barcelona. Until 1938, he writes screenplays and directs films in Spain. He returns from Mexico in 1948 to continue his work in direction and as a screenwriter.

CREDITS (incomplete)

1928: **El fabricante de suicidios** (The Maker of Suicides).
1929: **El misterio de la Puerta del Sol** (The Puerta del Sol Mystery).
1932: **Pax.**
1933: **Boliche.**
1935: **Rataplán.** (Rub-a-dub).
1936: **María de la O**
1937: **Bohemios** (Bohemians).
1954: **Marta.**

JOSE MARIA ELORRIETA

1921. Madrid 1974, Madrid

Doctor in law. Founder and president of various film writer societies. Director of the Technical School of Cinematography, assistant professor of the **Cinema Research and Experiences School** and censor of screenplays in the Department of Film and Theater in the ministry. Screenwriter and director of film shorts, and after 1946, he begins to make features. After 1962, he produces his own films, many of which as coproductions and including all types of genres such as melodramas, comedies, religious, westerns, horror, action and musicals. He makes these films either under his own name or using such pseudonyms as Elio Riett, Joe Lacy, Joseph de Lacey and J. Douglas.

CREDITS (incomplete)

1946: **La ciudad de los muñecos** (The City of the Dolls).
1949: **La tienda de antigüedades** (The Antique Shop).
1952: **Encuentro en la ciudad** (Encounter in the City).
1953: **El milagro del sacristán** (The Sacristan's Miracle).
1954: **Tres huchas para Oriente** (Three Moneyboxes for the East).
1955: **Torero por alegrías** (Bullfighter to the Beat of «Alegrías»).
1956: **El fenómeno** (The Terrific Guy).
1957: **El hincha** (The Fan).
1958: **Habanera.**
1959: **Pasa la tuna** (The Student Minstrels Go By).
1960: **La corista** (The Chorus Girl).
La bella Mimí (The Lovely Mimí).
1961: **Rosa de Lima** (Rosa From Lima).
Mi adorable esclava (My Adorable Slave).
Canción de cuna (Lullaby).
1962: **El diablo en vacaciones** (The Devil on Holiday).
Usted tiene ojos de mujer fatal (You Have the Eyes of a Vamp).
1964: **El hombre de la diligencia** (The Stagecoach Man).
1965: **El halcón de Castilla** (The Hawk of Castile).
1966: **Los siete de Pancho Villa** (Pancho Villa's Seven).
1969: **Las joyas del diablo** (The Devil's Jewels).
1971: **Los amantes del diablo** (The Devil's Lovers).
1972: **El espectro del terror** (The Spectre of Terror).
1973: **La llamada del vampiro** (The Call of the Vampire).

VICTOR ERICE

1940, San Sebastián

After receiving a degree in political science, he joins the **Cinema Research and Experiences School** and graduates with the film project, **Los días perdidos** (Lost Days; 1963). He writes in the magazines **Cuadernos de Arte y Pensamiento** and **Nuestro Cine.** He works on scripts together with Antón Eceiza and Miguel Picazo. Between the making of **El espíritu de la colmena** (The Spirit of the Beehive; 1973) —which receives the Golden Shell Award in the San Sebastian Film Festival— and **El sur** (The South; 1983)— which obtains First Prize in the Chicago Film Festival, he works in advertising.

CREDITS

1969: **Los desafíos** (an episode) (The Challenges).
1973: **El espíritu de la colmena** (The Spirit of the Beehive).
1983: **El Sur** (The South).

VICENTE ESCRIVA

1913, Valencia

Doctor in the Humanities, writer, screenwriter and producer. In 1940 he is appointed to the post of program chief for Latin America in National Radio. In 1941, he publishes an historical essay called **Tomás de Villanueva,** and in 1947, he comes out with **Jornadas de Juan de Ribera.** In 1947 he obtains the National Literature Prize for **Jornadas de Miguel de Cervantes.** Author of various novels and of a few plays. During the fifties he is the most valued producer and screenwriter in Spain. He regularly works with Rafael Gil at this time and is responsible for making a long list of political-religious films. Apart from producing and writing, he begins to direct starting in 1959.

CREDITS

1959: **El hombre de la isla**
(The Island Man).
1962: **Dulcinea.**
1968: **El golfo**
(The Scoundrel).
1969: **El ángel**
(The Angel).
Johnny Ratón
(Johnny Mouse/Ratón).
1970: **Sin un adiós**
(Not Even a Good-bye).
1971: **Aunque la hormona se vista de seda**
(Even Though Hormones Dress in Silk).
1972: **La curiosa**
(The Curious Girl).
1973: **Lo verde empieza en los Pirineos**
(Eroticism Begins at the Pyrenees).
1974: **Polvo eres**
(Dust You Are).
Una abuelita de antes de la guerra
(A Grandmother Like the Ones Before the War).
1975: **Zorrita Martínez**
(Foxy Martínez).
1976: **La lozana andaluza**
(The Robust Girl from Andalusia).
1977: **Niñas... ¡al salón!**
(Girls... To the Parlor!).
1978: **El virgo de Visanteta**
(The Virgin of Visanteta).
Visanteta esta-te queta
(Hold Still, Visanteta).
1979: **Gata caliente**
(Hot Kitty).
1980: **Esperando a papá**
(Waiting for Daddy).

JACINTO ESTEVA GREWE

1936, Barcelona 1985, Barcelona.

He studies the Humanities in Barcelona and Architecture in Geneva, specializing in Urban Planning in the Institute of the Sorbonne in 1961. Along with Paolo Brunatto he directs the short, **Notas sobre la emigración** (Notes on Emigration), which receives a prize in the Moscow Film Festival. He returns to Spain in 1962 and makes documentaries at the same time as he works as an architect. In 1965 he founds the Filmscontacto production company. He is one of the members of the **Barcelona School.**

CREDITS

1967: **Dante no es únicamente severo**
(with J. Jordá)
(Dante Is Not Only Strict).
1968: **Después del diluvio**
(After the Flood).
1970: **Lejos de los árboles**
(Far from the Trees).
1971: **Metamorfosis**
(Metamorphosis).
1973: **El hijo de María**
(Maria's Son).

F

342 CESAR FERNANDEZ ARDAVIN

1923, Madrid

He begins to work in the world of film in 1947 as an assistant director for his uncle, Eusebio Fernández Ardavín. Later, he works as a screenwriter. He has his own production company, Aro Films, with which he has made more than 300 films shorts to date—principally tourist or art documentaries. Important among the prizes he has received is the Golden Bear from the Berlin Film Festival for **El lazarillo de Tormes** (The Blind Man's Guide from Tormes).

CREDITS

1952: **La llamada de Africa** (The Call of Africa).
1954: **Crimen imposible** (Impossible Crime).
1956: **La puerta abierta** (The Open Door).
1957: **Y... eligió al infierno** (And... Hell Was Chosen).
1959: **El lazarillo de Tormes** (The Blind Man's Guide from Tormes).
1960: **Festival** (Festival).
1961: **Cerca de las estrellas** (Close to the Stars).
1963: **La frontera de Dios** (God's Frontier).
1965: **Quijote, ayer y hoy** (Quixote, Yesterday and Today).
1969: **La Celestina.**
1970: **Hembra (Prohibido)** (Female [Forbidden]).
1974: **No matarás** (Thou Shall Not Kill).
1977: **Doña Perfecta** (Mrs. Perfect).

EUSEBIO FERNANDEZ ARDAVIN

1898, Madrid 1965, Albacete

He belongs to a family of artists, painters and poets. He studies industrial engineering, but he gives it up for film. In 1917, he shoots his first two shorts. Between 1929 and 1932, he works in Paramounts Joinville Studios as a dialogue supervisor for films shot in Spanish. He takes part in the founding of the Estudios CEA which were inaugurated in 1933.

CREDITS (incomplete)

1925: **El reloj del anticuario** (The Antique Dealer's Watch). **Del Rastro a la Castellana** (From the Rastro to the Castellana).
1926: **La bejarana** (The Girl from Béjar). **El bandido de la sierra** (The Mountain Bandit).
1927: **Rosa de Madrid** (Rosa from Madrid).
1934: **El agua en el suelo** (Water on the Ground).
1935: **Los claveles** (The Carnations).
1936: **La reina mora** (The Moorish Queen).
1939: **La marquesona** (The Big Marchioness).
1940: **La florista de la reina** (The Queen's Florist).

1941: **Unos pasos de mujer**
(The Steps Taken by a Woman).
1943: **Forja de almas**
(The Forge of Souls).
El abanderado
(The Standard-Bearer).
1946: **El doncel de la reina**
(The Queen's Page).
La rueda de la vida
(The Wheel of Life).
1947: **La dama del armiño**
(The Lady in Ermine).
1949: **Neutralidad**
(Neutrality).
1953: **La bella de Cádiz** (with R. Bernard)
(The Lovely Lady from Cádiz).
1954: **La reina mora** (with R. Alfonso)
(The Moorish Queen).
1958: **Llegaron dos hombres**
(with A. Mattson)
(Two Men Came).

FERNANDO FERNAN GOMEZ

1921, Buenos Aires

Brought to Spain when he was very young. When the Spanish civil war broke out, he ended his studies of the Humanities. At the end of the civil war, he works both in theater and film. As an actor, he has made more than 120 films. In theater, he has performed the works of a wide range of playwrights: Jardiel Poncela, Ibsen, Brecht, Valle-Inclán, etc. He has formed his own theater company on various occasions. He has also dubbed films and has worked in radio and television. In 1950, he begins to direct both film and theater. He wins the Lope de Vega Literary Prize for his theater work, **Las bicicletas son para el verano** (Bicycles Are for Summer). He also publishes novels and books of verse. In 1973 he writes, performs in and directs the 13-episode series called **El pícaro** (The Rascal) for TVE as well as the program **Juan Soldado.** He wins the best actor award in the Berlin Film Festival for his role in **El anacoreta** (El Anchorite), by Juan Estelrich. He received the Fine Arts Gold Medal in 1981.

CREDITS

As an actor (incomplete)

1944: **El camino de Babel,** by J. Mihura.
El destino se disculpa, by J. L. Sáenz de Heredia.
1945: **Domingo de carnaval,** by E. Neville.
1946: **Los habitantes de la casa deshabitada,** by G. Delgrás.
1947: **Botón de ancla,** by R. Torrado.
1948: **Vida en sombras,** by L. Llobet.
La mies es mucha, by J. L. Sáenz de Heredia.
1950: **El capitán Veneno,** by L. Marquina.
El último caballo, by E. Neville.
Balarrasa, by J. A. Nieves Conde.
1951: **Esa pareja feliz,** by J. A. Bardem and L. G. Berlanga.
1953: **Aeropuerto,** by L. Lucia.
1954: **La otra vida del capitán Contreras,** by R. Gil.
1955: **La ironía del dinero,** by E. Neville.
El malvado Carabel, by F. Fernán Gómez.
1956: **Viaje de novios,** by L. Klimovsky.
1957: **El inquilino,** by J. A. Nieves Conde.
1958: **La vida por delante,** by F. Fernán Gómez.
1959: **La vida alrededor,** by F. Fernán Gómez.
1961: **La venganza de don Mendo,** by F. Fernán Gómez.
1963: **El mundo sigue,** by F. Fernán Gómez.
1965: **Ninette y un señor de Murcia,** by F. Fernán Gómez.
1968: **La vil seducción,** by J. M. Forqué.
1972: **Ana y los lobos,** by C. Saura.
1973: **El espíritu de la colmena,** by V. Erice.
1974: **El amor del capitán Brando,** by J. de Armiñán.

1975: **Pim, pam, pum... ¡fuego!,** by P. Olea.
1976: **El anacoreta,** by J. Estelrich.
Gulliver, by A. Ungría.
1977: **Arriba Hazaña,** by J. M. Gutiérrez.
1978: **Los restos del naufragio,** by R. Franco.
1980: **Maravillas,** by M. Gutiérrez Aragón.
1984: **Feroz,** by M. Gutiérrez Aragón.
Los zancos, by C. Saura.
La noche más hermosa, by M. Gutiérrez Aragón.

As a director

1952: **Manicomio** (with L. M. Delgado) (Insane Asylum).
1953: **El mensaje** (The Message).
1955: **El malvado Carabel** (The Wicked Carabel).
1958: **La vida por delante** (Your Life Ahead of You).
1959: **La vida alrededor** (Life Around You).
1960: **Sólo para hombres** (Just for Men).
1961: **La venganza de don Mendo** (Don Mendo's Revenge).
1963: **El mundo sigue** (Life Goes On).
1964: **El extraño viaje** (The Strange Trip).
Los palomos (The Pigeons/Idiots).
1965: **Ninette y un señor de Murcia** (Ninette and a Gentleman from Murcia).
1966: **Mayores sin reparos** (Adults without a Consideration).
1969: **Cómo casarse en 7 días** (How To Get Married in Seven Days).
1970: **Crimen imperfecto** (Imperfect Crime).
1974: **Yo la vi primero** (I Saw Her First).
1975: **La querida** (The Mistress).
1976: **Bruja, más que bruja** (Witch, Nothing but a Witch).
1977: **Mi hija Hildegart** (My Daughter Hildegart).
1979: **Cinco tenedores** (Five Stars).
1986: **Mambrú se fue a la guerra** (Mambrú Went to War).

MARCO FERRERI

1928, Milán

He begins to work in film advertising. He founds an important filmed cinema magazine called **Documento Mensile.** He works in production. He arrives in Spain in 1955 as the representative of Totalscope camera lens. He gets to know the writer and humorist, Rafael Azcona. He begins his career as a director with three Spanish films, two of them, **El pisito** (The Little Flat) and **El cochecito** (The Little Car), based on novels by Azcona and with the screenplay written by both men. In 1961, he returns to Italy to continue his directing career and becomes one of the most important names in European cinema.

SPANISH CREDITS

1958: **El pisito** (with I. M. Ferry) (The Little Flat).
1959: **Los chicos** (The Boys).
1960: **El cochecito** (The Little Car).

IGNACIO FERRES IQUINO

1910, Valls (Tarragona)

Son of a composer and an actress, he studies music and painting. At twelve years of age, he draws, sculptures in clay, paints in oils and plays the violin. He exhibits his caricatures at the age of fifteen and later works in Barcelona as a cartoonist and draftsman for newspapers and magazines. In Paris he works as a costume designer and a decorator-director. In 1934 he creates the Emisora Films production company in order to work in the different facets of film: scenographer, camera operator, musician, screenwriter, director and producer. Owner of the IFI, S. A., company, including studios and distribution concerns. He has directed a great number of films since 1931.

CREDITS (incomplete)

1935: **El crimen del expreso de Andalucía**
(The Crime on the Andalusian Express).
1936: **Diego Corrientes.**
1940: **¿Quién me compra un lío?**
(Who Wants To Buy a Mess?).
1941: **Alma de Dios**
(Soul of God).
El difunto es un vivo
(The Dead Man Is Alive).
1942: **Los ladrones somos gente honrada**
(We Crooks Are Really Honest).
El pobre rico
(The Poor Rich Man).
La culpa del otro
(The Other's Blame).
Boda accidentada
(A Troubled Marriage).
1943: **Un enredo de familia**
(A Family Muddle).
El hombre de los muñecos
(The Puppet Man).
1944: **Una sombra en la ventana**
(A Shadow on the Window).
1945: **El obstáculo**
(The Obstacle).
1946: **Aquel viejo molino**
(That Old Mill).
1947: **Noche sin cielo**
(A Skyless Night).
1948: **El tambor de Bruch**
(Bruch's Drum).
1950: **Brigada criminal**
(Criminal Brigade).
Historia de una escalera
(Story of a Stairwell).
1951: **El sistema de Pelegrín**
(Pelegrin's System).
1952: **El Judas**
(Judas).
1953: **Fuego en la sangre**
(Fire in the Blood).
1956: **El golfo que vio una estrella**
(An Urchin Who Saw a Star).
1957: **Los ángeles del volante**
(Angels at the Wheel).
1963: **Trigo limpio**
(Clean Wheat).
1973: **Aborto criminal**
(Criminal Abortion).
Chicas de alquiler
(Girls for Rent).

ANGELINO FONS

1935, Madrid

He studies the Humanities in Murcia where he runs a university film society. After moving to Madrid, he studies in the **Cinema Research and Experiences Institute** and he receives his degree with the film project, **A este lado del muro** (On This Side of the Wall; 1963). He writes for the magazines **Acento, Cuadernos de Arte y Pensamiento** and **Nuestro Cine.** He makes a few shorts and works as a screenwriter on such films as **La caza** (The Hunt; 1965), **Peppermint frappé** (1967) and **Stress es tres, tres** (Stress Is Three; 1968), by Saura. He works sporadically in TVE where he has done **Granada y García Lorca** (Granada and García Lorca;1967).

CREDITS

1966: **La busca**
(The Search).
1968: **Cantando a la vida**
(Singing to Life).
1969: **Fortunata y Jacinta.**
1971: **La primera entrega**
(The First Delivery).
1972: **Marianela.**
1973: **Separación matrimonial**
(Matrimonial Separation).
Mi hijo no es lo que parece
(My Son Isn't What He Seems To Be).
1974: **La casa**
(The House).
1975: **De profesión, polígamo**
(Polygamist by Profession).
1976: **Emilia... parada y fonda**
(Emilia... Roadside Motel).
1977: **Esposa y amante**
(Wife and Mistress).
1982: **Mar brava**
(Wild Sea).
1983: **El Cid Cabreador**
(The Valiant/Infuriating Cid).

JOSEP MARIA FORN

1928, Barcelona

Since 1948, he has worked as an unpaid trainee, assistant, director and producer. He is the owner of Teide Films since 1958, a production company which finances his own films and promotes Catalonian films: **La ciutat cremada** (The Burnt City; 1976) by Ribas, **Ocaña, retrat intermitent** (Ocaña, and **Vicario de Olot** (The Vicar from Olot; 1981) by Pons. He edits the **Panorama Literario** magazine. He has been one of the founders of the **Institut de Cinema Catalá.** He directs the first **Noticiari** documentary-newsreel in Barcelona.

CREDITS

1955: **Yo maté**
(I Killed).
1957: **La rana verde**
(The Green Frog).
1959: **Muerte al amanecer**
(Death at Dawn).
1960: **La vida privada de Fulana de Tal**
(The Private Life of Mrs. So-and-so).
1961: **Pena de muerte**
(Death Sentence).
1962: **Los culpables**
(The Culprits).
La ruta de los narcóticos
(The Narcotics Route).
1963: **José María.**

1964: **La barca sin pescador**
(The Boat without a Fisherman).
1967: **La piel quemada.**
(Burnt Skin).
1969: **La respuesta.**
(The Reply).
1979: **Companys, procés a Catalunya.**
(Companys, Catalonia on Trial).

JOSE MARIA FORQUE

1923, Zaragoza.

He studies in the Higher School of Architecture of Barcelona. He is a quantity surveyor and works as a draftsman to pay for his studies. Interested in theater, he collaborates with the TEU in Zaragoza and soon becomes the director of the company. Drawn to film, he makes more than twelve film shorts before directing his first feature. He wins the Silver Bear Award at the Berlin Film Festival with **Amanecer en Puerta Oscura** (Dawn in Puerta Oscura). In 1967, he founds his own production company, Orfeo Films. Among other productions he makes for TVE the series **El español y los 7 pecados capitales** (The Spaniards and the Seven Deadly Sins), **Ramón y Cajal** and **El jardín de Venus** (The Garden of Venus).

CREDITS (incomplete).

1951: **Niebla y sol**
(Mist and Sun).
1953: **El diablo toca la flauta**
(The Devil Plays the Flute).
1954: **Un día perdido**
(A Day Lost).
1955: **La legión del silencio**
(with J. A. Nieves Conde)
(The Legion of Silence).
1956: **Embajadores en el infierno**
(Ambassadors in Hell).
1957: **Amanecer en Puerta Oscura**
(Dawn in Puerta Oscura).
1958: **La noche y el alba**
(Night and Dawn).
Un hecho violento
(An Awkward Fact).
1960: **Maribel y la extraña familia**
(Maribel and the Strange Family).
091, policía al habla
(091-Police, May We Help You?)
1961: **Usted puede ser un asesino**
(You Can be a Murderer).
El secreto de Mónica
(Monica's Secret).
1962: **Atraco a las tres**
(Robbery at Three).
Accidente 703
(Accident 703).
La becerrada
(The Fight with Yearling Bulls).
1963: **El juego de la verdad**
(The Game of Truth).
1965: **Yo he visto la muerte**
(I Saw Death).
1967: **Un millón en la basura**
(A Million in the Trash).
1968: **La vil seducción**
(The Vile Seduction).
1969: **Estudio amueblado 2-P**
(Furnished Study 2-P).
El triangulito
(The Little Triangle).
1970: **El monumento**
(The Monument).
El ojo del huracán
(The Eye of the Hurricane).

1972: **Tarots.**
1974: **No es nada, mamá, sólo un juego** (It's Just a Game, Mom).
1976: **El segundo poder** (The Second Power).
1980: **El canto de la cigarra** (The Cricket's Cry).

JESUS FRANCO
1930, Madrid

He studies Humanities and Law in the University of Madrid and music in Madrid's Royal Conservatory. He takes courses for two years in the **Cinema Research and Experiences Institute** in Madrid in the area of direction, a course of studies in Paris' IDHEC, as well as several courses in the Sorbonne. He works as an assistant director for Bardem, Berlanga, Romero Marchent and Klimovsky. He writes screenplays along with Alfonso Paso, J. L. Dibildos and Luis de Diego and composes the musical scores for films. He directs a few documentaries: **Arbol de España** (The Spanish Tree; 1957) and **Baroja** (1958). Since 1959, he has directed more than a hundred films in just about every genre including horror films, espionage, musicals, science fiction and comedy. Starting in 1970 he basically specializes in sex films, ranging from erotic to hard-core and uses the pseudonyms of Clifford Brown, James P. Johnson, Frank Hollmann, Charlie Christian and Jess Frank. He has shot films in Spain, France, Portugal, Germany, Switzerland, the United States, Italy, the Eastern European countries, etc. He has also worked as an actor, both in his own films and those of other directors. He plays the piano and trumpet. He has written novels under the pseudonym David Khune.

CREDITS (incomplete)

1959: **Tenemos 18 años** (We're Eighteen Years Old).
1960: **Labios rojos** (Red Lips).
La reina del Tabarín (The Tabarin Queen).
1961: **Gritos en la noche** (Cries in the Night).
1962: **Vampiresas 1930** (Lady Vampires 1930).
La muerte silba un blues (Death Whistles the Blues).
1963: **La mano de un hombre muerto** (A Dead Man's Hand).
1964: **El secreto del Dr. Orloff** (Dr. Orloff's Secret).
Miss Muerte (Miss Death).
1966: **Cartas boca arriba** (Cards Face Up).
1967: **Residencia para espías** (Spy Residence).
Bésame, monstruo (Kiss Me, Monster).
1968: **Fu-Manchú y el beso de la muerte** (Fu-Manchu and the Kiss of Death).
99 mujeres (USA) (Ninety-nine Women).
1969: **Justine** (France).
El proceso de las brujas (Witches' Trial).
1970: **El conde Drácula** (Count Dracula).

1971: **Vuelo al infierno**
(Flight to Hell).
1972: **Un capitán de 15 años**
(Captain Courageous).
1974: **La noche de los asesinos**
(Night of the Assassins).
Al otro lado del espejo
(The Other Side of the Mirror).
1977: **Cartas de amor a una monja portuguesa**
(Love Letters to a Portuguese Nun).

RICARDO FRANCO
1949, Madrid

He started working in film when he was very young. After finishing his studies he works as an assistant director on various films made by his uncle, Jesús Franco. He produces his first short, **Gospel** (1969), and his first feature in 16 mm., **El desastre de Annual** (The Annual Disaster). Elías Querejeta produces his short, **El increíble aumento del coste de la vida** (The Incredible Cost of Living Increase; 1974) and his feature, **Pascual Duarte.**

CREDITS

1970: **El desastre de Annual**
(The Annual Disaster).
1976: **Pascual Duarte.**
1978: **Los restos del naufragio**
(The Remains of the Shipwreck).
1984: **San Judas de la Frontera** (México).

JOSE LUIS GARCI
1944, Madrid

Film critic for the magazines **Signo, Aún** and **Cinestudio** and editor-in-chief for **Reseña** and **Revista SP.** In 1968 he is awarded the prize for the best literary work from the **Circle of Film Writers.** He has published various books: **Ray Bradbury, humanista del futuro, Cine de ciencia-ficción, La cabina** and **La Gioconda está triste.** Starting in 1970 he starts to write for film and TVE. He works on treatments and screenplays for producer José Luis Dibildos. The TVE program called **La cabina** (The Telephone Booth; 1972) by Antonio Mercero, and based on his own screenplay, wins an Emmy. In 1975, he directs three film shorts: **¡Al futbol!** (Let's See Football!), **Mi Marilyn** (My Marilyn) and **Tiempo de gente acobardada** (Time for Discouraged People). In 1983, he wins the Oscar for the best foreign film for **Volver a empezar** (Starting Over).

CREDITS

1977: **Asignatura pendiente**
(Pending Exam).
1978: **Solos en la madrugada**
(Alone in the Early Hours).
1979: **Las verdes praderas**
(Green Pastures).
1980: **El crack**
(The Crack).

1982: **Volver a empezar** (Starting Over).
1983: **El crack II** (Crack II).
1984: **Sesión continua.** (Double Feature).

LUIS GARCIA BERLANGA
1921, Valencia

His first artistic leanings are towards poetry, painting and film criticism. In 1947 he becomes part of the first class of the **Cinema Research and Experiences Institute.** He works closely with Bardem, who helps direct his first film and who contributes to the screenplay of **Bienvenido, Mr. Marshall** (Welcome, Mr. Marshall). Since 1961, he has written his screenplays in collaboration with Rafael Azcona. A professor in the **Official Film School** until he resigns in opposition to the selection procedure of students. Editor of the erotic literary collection, **La sonrisa vertical.** President of the National Film Library. He has received numerous prizes and tributes in festivals both in Spain and abroad.

CREDITS

1951: **Esa pareja feliz** (with Bardem) (That Happy Couple).
1952: **Bienvenido, Mr. Marshall.** (Welcome, Mr. Marshall).
1953: **Novio a la vista** (Boyfriend in Sight).
1956: **Calabuch.**
1957: **Los jueves, milagro** (Miracles on Thursdays).
1961: **Plácido.**
1962: **Las cuatro verdades** (episode: Death and the Woodcutter) (The Four Truths).
1964: **El verdugo** (The Executioner).
1967: **La boutique** (Argentina).
1969: **¡Vivan los novios!** (Long Live the Bride and Groom).
1973: **Tamaño natural** (France) (Life Size).
1977: **La escopeta nacional** (The National Shotgun).
1980: **Patrimonio nacional** (National Patrimony).
1982: **Nacional III** (National III).
1984: **La vaquilla.** (The Heifer).

EDUARDO GARCIA MAROTO

1904, Jaén

From 1923, his entire life has been dedicated to all kinds of technical and artistic endeavors in film. He works for the Madrid Films laboratories and appears in various films as an actor. He is also a reporter and an editor in the CEA studios. He makes his debut as a director with film shorts that were written along with Miguel Mihura: **Una de fieras** (One about Wild Beasts; 1934), **Una de miedo** (One about Fear; 1934) and **Y ahora, una de ladrones** (And Now, One about Crooks; 1935). His first feature is produced by Cifesa. Following the medium-length film, **Aventuras de don Quijote** (The Adventures of Don Quixote; 1961), he never directs again. He is a theater director and contributor to magazines specializing in theater and film criticism, but he stands out as a humorist in such magazines as **Cine revista, Hermano Lobo,** etc. Since 1975 he is production supervisor and in charge of second units for some of the American films shot in Spain. He works in such films as **The Pride and the Passion** (1957) by Stanley Kramer, **Solomon and Sheba** (1959) by King Vidor, **Spartacus** (1960) by Stanley Kubrick, **The Pleasure Seekers** (1964) by Jean Negulesco; **Von Ryan's Express** (1966) by Mark Robson, and **Patton** (1969) by Franklin J. Shaffner.

CREDITS

1935: **La hija del penal**
(Prison Daughter).
1939: **Los cuatro Robinsones**
(The Four Robinsons).
1942: **Canelita en rama.**
(Cinnamon on a Stick).
¿Por qué vivir tristes?
(Why Live Sadly?)
1943: **Oro vil**
(Vile Gold).
Mi fantástica esposa
(My Fantastic Wife).
1946: **La mantilla de Beatriz** (Portugal)
(Beatriz' Mantilla).
1948: **No hay muchachos malos**
(Portugal)
(No Boys Are Bad).
La otra sombra
(The Other Shadow).
1950: **Truhanes de honor**
(Honorable Misfits).
1954: **Tres eran tres**
(Three Were Three).

GONZALO GARCIA PELAYO

1947, Madrid

He studies direction in the Official Film School for two one-year courses. He works in Popular Radio and National Radio as head of musical programs and as a disk jockey. He has produced records for the musical groups **Triana, Smash, Alameda** and **Medinazzara** and for the soloists Gerena, Pau Riba, María Jiménez and Amancio Prada. In TVE he directs the series Beat-club and collaborates with Moncho Alpuente in Mundo Pop. His films are an attempt to make Andalusian cinema.

CREDITS

1975: **Manuela.**
1978: **Vivir en Sevilla**
(Living in Seville).
1979: **Frente al mar**
(Facing the Sea).
1980: **Corridas de alegría**
(Bullfights of Happiness/«Alegría» Songs).
1982: **Rocío y José**
(Rocío and José).

JOSE LUIS GARCIA SANCHEZ

1941, Salamanca

A degree in law from the University of Madrid and in sociology from the CSIC. He graduates from the **Official Film School** and alternates his theoretical studies with work as an assistant director with Basilio M. Patino and Carlos Saura. He directs a few film shorts before his first feature. Not only does he work in film, but he writes children's books. More than seventy of his works have been published. As a screenwriter, he has worked on the scripts of **Habla, mudita** (Speak, Mute Girl; 1973) and **Camada negra** (Black Brood; 1977) by Gutiérrez Aragón, **Corazón solitario** (Lonely Heart; 1972) and **Furia española** (Spanish Fury; 1974) by Betriu, and **Queridísimos verdugos** (Dearest Hangmen; 1973) by Patino. He also writes scripts for TVE. In 1978, he wins the Golden Bear Prize in the Berlin Film Festival with **Las truchas** (The Trout). He works a great deal in video.

CREDITS

1972: **El love feroz** (The Fierce «Love»/Wolf).
1976: **Colorín colorado** (They All Lived Happily Ever After).
1979: **Cuentos para una escapada** (episode: A Multi-colored Gift) (Stories of an Escapade).
1980: **Dolores.**
1985: **La corte de faraon** (The Pharaoh's Court).

FRUCTUOSO GELABERT

1874, Barcelona. 1955, Barcelona

Photographer and mechanic by profession, he is one of the founders of the Spanish film industry. Impressed by the new invention presented in Spain in 1896 by the Lumière brothers, he builds a similar movie camera and projector and makes **Riña de café** (Café Brawl). After that, he works as a producer, screenwriter, director, cameraman, builder of film devices, installer of equipment and founder of studios and laboratories. He makes more than a hundred films.

CREDITS (incomplete)

1897: **Riña de café** (Café Brawl).
Salida de los trabajadores de «La España Industrial» (Getting Off Work in the «Industrial Spain»).
1899: **Choque de dos transatlánticos** (Collision of Two Transatlantics).
1905: **Los guapos de la vaquería del parque** (The Handsome Guys at the Park's Dairy Shop).
1907: **Tierra baja** (Lowland).
1908: **María Rosa.**
Los calzoncillos de Toni (Toni's Shorts).
La Dolores.
1909: **Amor que mata** (Love That Kills).
Gúzman el Bueno.
1912: **Ana Cadova.**
1915: **El cuervo del campamento** (The Encampment's Raven).
El nocturno de Chopin (Chopin's Nocturne).
1918: **La España trágica** (Tragic Spain).
1928: **La puntaire (La encajera)** (The Laceworker).

RAFAEL GIL
1913, Madrid

In 1930 he begins to write about film in such magazines as **Popular Film, Films selectos, Nuestro cinema** and **Cinema Sparta** as well as in such newspapers as **La voz, Claridad** and **ABC.** In 1933, he is a founding member of the **Group of Independent Film Writers.** He publishes **Luz de cinema** (1936).
In 1935, he makes three film shorts in 16 mm. During the Spanish Civil War, he makes documentaries for the Republic. After the civil war he joins the Fox Movietone Newsreel team as a screenwriter and a director. He is a professor of the **Cinema Research and Experiences Institute.** He has not stopped working since 1941. During the fifties, he wins several prizes in international festivals with films written and produced by Vicente Escrivá. He is the owner of the Coral PC production company.

CREDITS (incomplete)

1941: **El hombre que se quiso matar** (The Man Who Wanted to Kill Himself).
1942: **Viaje sin destino** (A Trip without Destination).
1943: **Huella de luz** (A Sign of Light).
Eloisa está debajo de un almendro (Eloisa Is Underneath the Almond Tree).
1944: **El clavo** (The Nail).
El fantasma y doña Juanita (The Ghost and Doña Juanita).
1946: **La pródiga** (The Prodigy).
Reina Santa (Holy Queen).
1947: **La fe** (Faith).
Don Quijote de la Mancha (Don Quixote of La Mancha).
1948: **La calle sin sol** (The Sunless Street).
1949: **Una mujer cualquiera** (Just Any Woman).
1950: **Teatro Apolo** (Apollo Theater).
1951: **El gran galeoto** (The Great Pimp).
La señora de Fátima (The Lady of Fatima).
1952: **Sor Intrépida.**
1953: **La guerra de Dios** (God's War).
El beso de Judas (The Judas Kiss).
1954: **Murió hace 15 años** (Dead Fifteen Years Ago).
La otra vida del capitán (The Captain's Other Life).
Contreras.
1955: **El canto del gallo** (The Rooster's Crow).
1956: **Un traje blanco** (A White Suit).
1957: **Viva lo imposible** (Long Live the Impossible).
1959: **El Litri y su sombra** (Litri and His Shadow).
1960: **Siega verde** (Green Harvest).
1963: **Chantaje a un torero** (Blackmailing a Bullfighter).
1964: **Samba.**
1965: **Currito de la Cruz.**
1968: **Sangre en el ruedo** (Blood in the Ring).
1971: **Nada menos que todo un hombre** (Nothing Less Than Every Bit a Man).
1972: **La duda** (The Doubt).
La guerrilla (The Guerilla Fighter).
1974: **Los novios de la muerte** (The Lovers of Death).
1975: **Los buenos días perdidos** (The Good Days Lost).
1979: **... Y al tercer año resucitó** (He Came to Life After the Third Year).
1982: **De camisa vieja a chaqueta nueva** (From an Old Shirt to a New Jacket).

ANTONIO GIMENEZ-RICO

1938, Burgos

A law degree from the University of Valladolid. Later, he studies music and journalism. For several years he runs a film club. He is a critic for the **Cinestudio** magazine and does radio and university theater. He works as an assistant director for Vittorio Cattafavi, Eugenio Martín, Pascual Cervera, Javier Setó, Ernst Hofbauer, etc. He makes four film shorts before he directs his first feature. Since 1970 he has worked in TVE, where he makes the series **Plinio** (Pliny), a few episodes for **Los libros** (Books), **Cuentos y leyendas** (Tales and Legends), **Crónicas de un pueblo** (Chronicles of a People) and undertakes several literary adaptations. He has lately made five episodes of the series **La máscara negra** (The Black Mask) and fifteen of **Rasgos** (Features).

CREDITS

1966: **Mañana de domingo**
(Sunday Morning).
1968: **El hueso**
(The Bone).
1969: **El cronicón**
(The Short Chronicle).
¿Es usted mi padre?
(Are You My Father?).
1976: **Retrato de familia**
(Family Portrait).
Al fin solos, pero...
(Alone at Last, but...).
1977: **Del amor y de la muerte**
(On Love and Death).
1983: **Vestida de azul.**
(Dressed in Blue).

JORGE GRAU

1930, Barcelona

He studies in the **Instituto del Teatro** in Barcelona. Actor, scenographer, radio scriptwriter and theater director. He has written books on theater, stories, articles and the book **El actor y el cine** (1962). As a painter he has had several one-man shows —1952, 1956 and 1982— and has taken part in a collective exhibition dedicated to Miro—1973. He discovers the world of film when in 1955 he directs a group of actors in an amateur movie. He works as an assistant director before he goes to study in the **Centro Sperimentale di Cinematografia** in Rome. He makes several documentaries. He has been a professor of the **Official Film School** from 1969 to 1975 and professor in the School of **Informational Sciences** from 1973 to 1976.

CREDITS

1962: **Noche de verano**
(Summer Night).
1964: **El espontáneo**
(The Spontaneous Bullfighter).
1965: **Acteón**
(Actaeon).
1966: **Una historia de amor**
(A Love Story).
1969: **Historia de una chica sola**
(Story of a Lonely Girl).
1970: **Chicas de club (Cántico)**
(Girls in the Club —Canticle).

1972: **Ceremonia sangrienta**
(Bloody Ceremony).
1973: **Pena de muerte**
(Death Sentence).
1974: **No profanar el sueño de los muertos**
(Don't Desecrate the Resting Place of the Dead).
1975: **La trastienda**
(The Back Room).
El secreto inconfesable de un chico bien
(The Unconfessed Secret of a Boy from a Good Family).
1976: **La siesta.**
1978: **Cartas de amor de una monja**
(Love Letters from a Nun).
1981: **La leyenda del tambor**
(The Legend of the Drum).
1983: **Coto de caza**
(Hunting Ground).
1984: **Muñecas de trapo.**
(Rag Dolls).
1986: **El extranjero de la cruz del sur**
(The Foreigner of Southern Cross).

CLAUDIO GUERIN

1939, Alcalá de Guadaira (Seville).
1973, Noya (La Coruña)

He studies Finance and the Humanities. He works in advertising and makes radio programs as a scriptwriter and director. He is a film critic in the magazines **Cuadernos Universitarios de Cine** and **Nuestro Cine.** He receives a degree in direction from the **Official Film School** with the project **Luciano** (1965). Standing out among his documentaries are **Galicia** (1966), **La Mancha** (1967) and **La Meseta** (1969). He attends special courses specializing in theater and television. He directs for the second channel of TVE tourist programs, dramas, musicals and a few live shows. He dies in an accident during the shooting of **La campana del infierno** (Hell's Chime).

CREDITS

1969: **Los desafíos** (an episode)
(Challenges).
1971: **La casa de las palomas**
(The Dove House).
1973: **La campana del infierno**
(Hell's Chime).

MANUEL GUTIERREZ ARAGON

1942, Torrelavega (Santander)

Receives a degree in the Humanities from the University of Madrid and graduates from the **Official Film School** in direction and with the project **Hansel y Gretel** (1970). He has made various shorts and has worked on the screenplays of such films as **Furtivos** (Poachers; 1975) by Borau, **Las largas vacaciones del 36** (The Long Vacation of 36; 1976) by Camino and **Las truchas** (The Trout; 1977) by García Sánchez. His first two films received respectively the Critics Prize (1974) and the Director Prize (1977) at the Berlin Film Festival. In 1979, he directs in Madrid the theater version of Peter Weiss' **The Trial,** by Kafka.

CREDITS

1973: **Habla, mudita**
(Speak, Mute Girl).
1977: **Camada negra**
(Black Brood).
Sonámbulos
(Sleep Walkers).
1978: **El corazón del bosque**
(The Heart of the Forest).
1979: **Cuentos para una escapada**
(episode: Test for Children).
(Stories of an Escapade).
1980: **Maravillas.**
1982: **Demonios en el jardín**
(Demons in the Garden).

1984: **Feroz**
(Fierce).
La noche más hermosa.
(The Most Beautiful Night).

H

GONZALO HERRALDE
1949, Barcelona

Interested in psychology, he studies medicine for a while, but he gives it up for theater and enters the **Academia de Arte Dramático de Adriá Gual.** After a brief period studying in the **Institut de Formation Cinematographique** in Paris, he shoots his first short called **El cartel** (The Poster; 1970). In 1974, he creates his own production company. Until he makes his first feature, he spends his time making shorts and studying the Semiotics and History of Art in the University of Barcelona.

CREDITS

1975: **La muerte del escorpión**
(Death of a Scorpion).
1977: **Raza, el espíritu de Franco**
(Race, the Spirit of Franco).
1978: **El asesino de Pedralbes**
(The Pedralbes' Murderer).
1980: **Vértigo en Manhattan** (USA)
(Jet Lag).
1984: **Ultimas tardes con Teresa**
(The Last Afternoons with Teresa).

I

ELOY DE LA IGLESIA
1944, Zarauz (Guipúzcoa)

He makes his first shorts on 8 mm. film at the age of fifteen. He is unable to enter the **Official Film School** since he is still under age. He directs the **Teatro Popular Infantil.** He moves to Barcelona where he works in TVE in a series of films on children's books. His first feature called **Fantasía... 3** (Fantasy... 3; 1966) is born out of three of these stories.

CREDITS

1966: **Fantasía... 3)**
(Fantasy... 3).
1967: **Algo amargo en la boca**
(Something Bitter-tasting).
1969: **Cuadrilátero**
(Quadrilateral).
1971: **El techo de cristal**
(The Glass Ceiling).
1972: **La semana del asesino**
(The Week of the Murderer).
Nadie oyó gritar
(No One Heard the Scream).
1973: **Una gota de sangre para morir amando**
(A Drop of Blood To Live Dying).
Juego de amor prohibido
(The Game of Forbidden Love).
1975: **La otra alcoba**
(The Other Alcove).
1976: **Los placeres ocultos**
(Hidden Pleasures).

1977: **La criatura**
(The Creature).
El sacerdote
(The Priest).
1978: **El diputado**
(The Deputee).
1979: **Miedo a salir de noche**
(Fearing To Go Out at Night).
1980: **Navajeros**
(Knife Fighters).
1981: **La mujer del ministro**
(The Minister's Wife).
1982: **Colegas**
(Pals).
1983: **El pico**
(The Shoot Up).
1984: **El pico II**
(The Shoot Up II).
1985: **Otra vuelta de tuerca**
(The Turn of the Screw).

ANTONIO ISASI

1927, Madrid

He is educated in Barcelona and works as an errand boy in Emisora Films. Between 1947 and 1954 he edits numerous films. Later he works as a screenwriter and directs shorts. In 1963 he creates his own production company and studios. From 1963, his films are big productions made along American lines. In 1976, he is elected member of the High Council for Cinematography, but he resigns since he does not agree with the organization's basic guidelines.

CREDITS

1954: **Relato policiaco**
(A Police Story).
1955: **La huida**
(The Flight).
1956: **Pasión bajo el sol**
(Passion Under the Sun).
1957: **Rapsodia de sangre**
(Rhapsody in Blood).
1959: **Diego Corrientes.**
1960: **La mentira tiene cabellos rojos.**
(The Lie Is a Red-head).
Sentencia contra una mujer
(A Sentence against a Woman).
1961: **Tierra de todos**
(Every Man's Land).
1962: **Vamos a contar mentiras**
(Let's Tell Lies).
1963: **La máscara de Scaramouche**
(Scaramouche).
1965: **Estambul 65**
(Istanbul 65).
1968: **Las Vegas 500 millones**
(500 Million in Las Vegas).
1972: **Un verano para matar**
(Summertime Killer).
1975: **Rafael en Raphael.**
1976: **El perro**
(The Dog).

PEDRO LAZAGA

1918, Valls (Tarragona)
1979, Madrid

Interested in film since he was a boy, he writes for the bulletin of the Circle of Film Writers. In 1946, he sells an adaptation of **Abel Sánchez,** by Unamuno, which is later directed by Serrano de Osma. This serves as his introduction to film and he works as an assistant director, screenwriter and production chief. During his thirty years as a director, he has made more than 90 films.

CREDITS (incomplete)

1948: **Encrucijada** (Crossroads).
1950: **Hombre acosado** (The Pursued Man).
1954: **La patrulla** (The Patrol).
1955: **Cuerda de presos** (Chain Gang).
La vida es maravillosa (Life Is Marvelous).
1956: **El frente infinito** (The Infinite Front).
Torrepartida.
1957: **El aprendiz de malo** (Apprentice at Being Bad).
La frontera del miedo (Fear's Frontier).
Muchachas de azul (Blue Girls).
1958: **Ana dice sí.** (Ana Says Yes).
1959: **Los tramposos** (The Swindlers).
La fiel infantería (The Faithful Infantry).
1961: **Trampa para Catalina** (A Trap for Catalina).
1962: **Aprendiendo a morir** (Learning To Die).
1964: **El tímido** (The Bashful Fellow).
1965: **Posición avanzada.** (Advanced Position).
1966: **La ciudad no es para mí** (The City Isn't the Place for Me).
1967: **Los guardiamarinas** (Midshipmen).
1968: **No desearás la mujer de tu prójimo** (Thou Shall Not Lust After Thy Neighbor's Wife).
1969: **El otro árbol de Guernica** (Guernica's Other Tree).
1970: **Vente a Alemania, Pepe.** (Come to Germany, Pepe).
1972: **No firmes más letras, cielo** (Don't Sign Any More Bills of Exchange, Darling).
1973: **El chulo** (The Dandy).
1975: **Yo soy Fulana de Tal** (I'm a So-and-so).
1977: **Vota a Gundisalvo** (Vote for Gundisalvo).

JOSE ANTONIO DE LA LOMA

1924, Barcelona

He studies the Humanities, specializing in history. He directs for three seasons the TEU theater company. He publishes three novels: **Sin la sonrisa de Dios, Estación de servicio** and **El undécimo mandamiento.** He writes his first screenplay in 1951 for Ignacio F. Iquino. In 1954, he receives the Annual Screenplay Prize for his adaptation of his own novel, **Sin la sonrisa de Dios** (Without God's Smile), which is directed by Salvador in 1956. He has written an infinite number of screenplays, many of which he has directed himself. For many years now he has specialized in directing co-productions.

CREDITS (incomplete)

1956: **Manos sucias.** (Dirty Hands).
1963: **Vivir un largo invierno** (Living a Long Winter).
1964: **Totó de Arabia** (Toto from Arabia).
1967: **Misión en Ginebra** (Mission in Geneva).
1968: **El magnífico Tony Carrera** (The Magnificent Tony Carrera)
1969: **Golpe de mano** (Raid).

1971: **El más fabuloso golpe del Far-West**
(The Most Fabulous Master Stroke in the Far West).
1972: **Razzia**
(Foray).
1974: **Metralleta Stein**
(Machine Gun Stein).
1975: **Las alegres chicas de El Molino**
(The Carefree Girls at the El Molino).
1977: **Perros callejeros**
(Street Dogs).
1978: **Nunca en horas de clase**
(Never during Class).
1980: **Los últimos golpes de «El Torete»**
(The Last Stickup Jobs of «El Torete»).
1982: **Jugando con la muerte**
(Playing with Death).

JOSE LOPEZ RUBIO

1903, Motril (Granada).

In 1930, he goes to Hollywood to write screenplays for film versions in Spanish. When he returns to Spain, he begins a short, but interesting career as a director. He directs three film shorts: **Rosa de Africa** (Rosa from Africa), **La petenera** («Petenera» Andalusian Song) and **A la lima y al limón** (To the Lime and to the Lemon). Afterwards, he begins to write theater pieces and he soon makes a name for himself due to the quality of his comedies such as **Celos del aire** (1951) and **Un trono para Cristi** (1956). He also writes numerous screenplays. Member of the Spanish Royal Academy.

CREDITS

1940: **La malquerida**
(The Unpopular Girl).
1941: **Pepe Conde.**
1942: **Sucedió en Damasco**
(It Happened in Damascus).
1944: **Eugenia de Montijo.**
1946: **El crimen de Pepe Conde**
(Pepe Conde's Crime).
1947: **Alhucemas.**

GERMAN LORENTE

1932, Vinaroz (Castellón)

After receiving a law degree, he starts to send contributions when he is very young to the magazines **Imágenes, Cinemundo, Otro Cine,** etc., and publishes a few novels. He starts his film career as a screenwriter for the Este Films production company and eventually becomes the executive producer of the company.

CREDITS (incomplete)

1963: **Antes de anochecer**
(Before Dusk).
1964: **Donde tú estés**
(Where You Are).
1965: **Playa de Formentor.**
(The Beach at Formentor)
Vivir al sol
(Living Under the Sun).
1966: **Su nombre es Daphne**
(Her Name Is Daphne).
1967: **Un día después de agosto**
(A Day After August).
Cover Girl.
1968: **Sharon vestida de rojo**
(Sharon Dressed in Red).
1969: **Las nenas del mini-mini**
(The Mini-mini Girls).
1970: **Coqueluche**
(Whooping Cough).
1971: **Una chica casi decente**
(An Almost Decent Girl).
1973: **La chica de Vía Condotti**
(The Girl on Via Condotti).

1974: **Atraco en la Costa Azul.**
(Robbery on the Costa Azul)
1976: **Strip-tease.**
La violación
(The Rape).
1980: **Tres mujeres de hoy**
(Three Women of Today).
1981: **Adolescencia**
(Adolescence).

LUIS LUCIA

1914, Valencia 1984, Madrid

Son of an important Christian Democratic politician. He receives a law degree after having studied in the Universities of Valencia and Madrid. At the end of the Spanish Civil War, he begins to work in Cifesa as a legal advisor, manager, and later, as a production chief with such directors as Marquina, Orduña, Gil, etc. Interested in drawing, he collaborates with the magazines **Gutiérrez** and **Buen Humor.** He takes part in the writing of the screenplays of almost all the forty films he has directed. He discovers the child stars Marisol, Rocio Dúrcal and Ana Belén.

CREDITS (incomplete)

1943: **El 13-13.**
1945: **Un hombre de negocios**
(A Businessman).
1947: **Dos cuentos para dos**
(Two Stories for Two).
La princesa de los Ursinos
(The Princess of the Ursines).
1948: **Currito de la Cruz.**
1949: **La duquesa de Benamejí**
(The Duchess of Benamejí).
1950: **El sueño de Andalucía** (with R. Vernay)
(The Andalusian Dream).
1951: **Lola la piconera**
(Lola, The Coalgirl).
Cerca de la ciudad
(Close to the City).
1952: **La hermana San Sulpicio**
(Sister San Sulpicio).
Gloria Mairena.
1953: **Aeropuerto**
(Airport).
Jeromín.
1954: **Un caballero andaluz**
(An Andalusian Gentleman).
Morena Clara
(Clara the Brunette).
1955: **Esa voz es una mina**
(That Voice Is Worth a Fortune).
1956: **La vida en un bloc**
(Life on a Notebook).
1958: **La muralla**
(The Wall).
1959: **Molokai.**
Un ángel tuvo la culpa
(An Angel Was To Blame).
1960: **El príncipe encadenado**
(The Chained Prince).
Un rayo de luz
(A Ray of Light).
1961: **Ha llegado un ángel**
(An Angel Has Arrived).
1962: **Canción de juventud**
(Song of Youth).
Tómbola
(Tombola).
1965: **Zampo y yo**
(Zampo and I).
1968: **Sólo para dos**
(Just for Two).

1970: **La orilla**
(The Shore).
1973: **Entre dos amores**
(Between Two Loves).

M

ANA MARISCAL
1925, Madrid

Pseudonym of Ana María Arroyo. She studies Natural Sciences at the same time as she works in an amateur theater group. She makes her debut as a film actress in **La florista de la reina** (The Queen's Florist; 1940), by E. Fernández Ardavín. Almost at the same time, she makes her debut as the leading lady in the National Theater under the direction of Luis Escobar. She has starred in more than 40 films and has performed a great number of works on the stage. In 1952, she founds the Bosco Films production company and begins to finance her own films. Acting professor at the **Cinema Research and Experiences Institute** from 1956 to 1961. She publishes various novels and an autobiography. She has formed her own theater company on numerous occasions.

CREDITS

As an actress (incomplete)

1940: **El último húsar** by L. Marquina.
1941: **Raza** by J. L. Sáenz de Heredia.
1942: **Vidas cruzadas,** by L. Marquina.
1946: **Dulcinea,** by Luis Arroyo.
1947: **La princesa de los Ursinos,** by L. Lucía.
1948: **Vida encadenada,** by A. Román.
1949: **Pacto de silencio,** by A. Román.
Un hombre va por el camino, by M. Mur-Oti.
1950: **De mujer a mujer,** by L. Lucia.
1952: **Segundo López,** by A. Mariscal.
1953: **Jeromín,** by L. Lucia.
1958: **La violetera,** by L. C. Amadori.
1959: **El magistrado,** by L. Zampa.
1962: **La reina del Chantecler,** by R. Gil.
1964: **El camino,** by A. Mariscal.
La otra mujer, by F. Villiers.

As a director

1952: **Segundo López.**
1957: **Con la vida hicieron fuego**
(They Made Fire with Their Lives).
1959: **La quiniela**
(The Football Pools).
1960: **Feria en Sevilla** (with Carreras)
(The Seville Fair).
1961: **¡Hola, muchachos!**
(Hello, Boys!).
1962: **Occidente y sabotaje**
(The West and Sabotage).
1964: **El camino**
(The Road).
1965: **Los duendes de Andalucía**
(The Spirits of Andalusia).
1966: **Ojos verdes**
(Green Eyes).
Vestida de novia.
(Dressed as a Bride).

1968: **El paseíllo**
(The Opening Parade at the Bullfight).

LUIS MARQUINA

1904, Barcelona. 1980, Madrid

Son of the poet Eduardo Marquina. When he finishes studying Industrial Engineering he travels to the Tobis studios in Paris and the UFA studios in Berlin to specialize in sound engineering. On his return to Spain, he occupies the post of technical sub-director and sound engineer at the recently created CEA studios in Madrid. Buñuel, the production chief at Filmófono, gives him the opportunity to shoot his first film, **Don Quintín el amargao** (The Embittered Don Quintín). He has directed more than 25 films and has worked as a screenwriter, director general of production, sound technician and professor of production, technology and editing at the **Cinema Research and Experiences Institute.** He is the author of various comedies and scripts for the TVE series, **Al margen de la historia** (On the Fringe of History).

CREDITS (incomplete)

1935: **Don Quintín el amargao**
(The Embittered Don Quintín).
1936: **El bailarín y el trabajador**
(The Dancer and the Worker).
1940: **El último húsar** (Italy).
(The Last Hussar).
1941: **Torbellino**
(Whirlwind).
1942: **Malvaloca**
(Hollyhock).
1943: **Noche fantástica**
(Fantastic Night).
1944: **Santander, la ciudad en llamas**
(Santander, the City in Flames).
1949: **Filigrana**
(Filigree).
1950: **El capitán Veneno**
(Captain Venom).
1952: **Amaya.**
1953: **Así es Madrid**
(This Is Madrid).
1956: **Aventura para dos** (with Don Siegel)
(A Spanish Affair).
1961: **La viudita naviera**
(The Little Shipowning Widow).
1968: **Tuset Street.**
1971: **Cerco de terror**
(Surrounded by Fear).

EUGENIO MARTIN

1925, Granada

He studies law in the University of Granada and founds and runs a university film society. He publishes poetry and essays in university magazines. After receiving a degree in direction from the **Cinema Research and Experiences Institute,** he makes a few shorts. He works as an assistant director to Guy Hamilton, Michael Anderson, Nathan Juran, Nicholas Ray, etc. He directs all types of film genres and obtains a big success with the spaghetti western, **El precio de un hombre** (A Man's Price).

CREDITS (incomplete)

1958: **Despedida de soltero** (Stag Party).
1962: **Hipnosis** (Hypnosis).
1964: **Duelo en el Amazonas** (Duel in the Amazons).
1966: **El precio de un hombre** (A Man's Price).
1969: **Las leandras** (The Pesetas).
La vida sigue igual (Life Goes On).
1970: **La última señora Anderson** (The Last Mrs. Anderson).
1972: **Pánico en el transiberiano** (Panic on the Trans-Siberian Express).
1973: **Una vela para el diablo** (A Candle for the Devil).
La chica del Molino Rojo (The Girl from the Molino Rojo).
1975: **No quiero perder la honra** (I Don't Want To Lose My Honor).
1979: **Aquella casa de las afueras** (That House on the Outskirts).
1981: **Sobrenatural** (Supernatural).

BASILIO MARTIN PATINO

1930, Lombrales (Salamanca)

A degree in the Humanities from the University of Salamanca. He founds the university film society of that city as well as the magazine, **Cinema Universitario.** In 1955, he actively takes part in the **Salamanca Conversations.** He studies in the **Cinema Research and Experiences Institute** and receives his diploma with the film project, **Tarde de domingo** (Sunday Afternoon; 1960). He also works in advertising and makes two shorts: **El noveno** (The Ninth; 1960) and **Torerillos** (The Little Bullfighters; 1961). His work in TVE is limited to a medium-length film based on **Rinconete y Cortadillo,** by Cervantes, which was never shown. Since 1971, he has made montage films: **Canciones para después de una guerra, Queridísimos verdugos** and **Caudillo.** Recently, he only works in video.

CREDITS

1965: **Nueve cartas a Berta** (Nine Letters to Berta).
1969: **Del amor y otras soledades** (On Love and Other Solitudes).
1961: **Canciones para después de una guerra** (Songs for After a War).
1973: **Queridísimos verdugos** (Dearest Hangmen).
1975: **Caudillo.** (Leader).
1985: **Los paraísos perdidos** (Paradise Lost).

EMILIO MARTINEZ-LAZARO

1945, Madrid

He studies the physical sciences in the University of Madrid. His first contacts with the world of film are by means of film societies and the contributions he makes to the magazines **Griffith** and **Nuestro Cine.** He tries to enter the **Official Film School.** He shoots his first film short called **Circunstancias del milagro** (Circumstances of a Miracle; 1968) in 16 mm. His first jobs in film are as an assistant director, screenwriter —**Pascual Duarte,** (1976) by Franco— and as an adaptor and director in TVE. In 1979, he wins the Golden Bear Prize in the Berlin Film Festival with **Las palabras de Max** (Max's Words).

CREDITS

1971: **Pastel de sangre:** (episode: Victor Frankenstein)
(A Blood Cake).
1976: **Las palabras de Max**
(Max's Words).
1980: **Sus años dorados**
(Golden Years).
1985: **Lulú de noche**
(Lulu by Night).

PEDRO MASO

1927, Madrid

Ever since 1943 he has worked in all kinds of film-related activities: extra, actor, production assistant, production chief, screenwriter, etc. His most important work has been as a producer, having made more than 40 films, as a screenwriter, having written more than 30 scripts, and as a director, with 13 features to his credit. He has written, produced and directed the series **Anillos de oro** (Gold Rings; 1983) for TVE.

CREDITS

1971: **Las Ibéricas FC.**
(Las Ibéricas Football Club).
Las colocadas
(The Highly Placed Women).
1972: **Experiencia prematrimonial**
(Premarital Experience).
1973: **Una chica y un señor**
(A Girl and a Man).
1974: **Un hombre como los demás**
(A Man Like the Rest).
1975: **Las adolescentes**
(The Adolescents).
1976: **La menor**
(The Minor).
1977: **La coquito**
(Baby Face).
1979: **La miel**
(Honey).
La familia bien, gracias
(The Family's Fine, Thanks).
1980: **El divorcio que viene**
(Divorce Is on Its Way).
1981: **Puente aéreo**
(Air Shuttle).
127 millones libres de impuestos
(127 Million Tax Free).

ANTONIO MERCERO
1936, Lasarte (Guipúzcoa)

A law degree from the University of Valladolid. In 1959, he enters the **Cinema Research and Experiences Institute** and graduates with the film project **Trotín Troteras** (1962). After directing his first feature, he writes scripts and directs shorts for the NO-DO. Since 1964 he has worked in TVE, directing film reports, documentaries, special programs and a few series. His most important works include: **La cabina** (The Telephone Booth; 1972), which wins 10 national and international prizes including an Emmy; **Don Juan** (1974), a prize-winner in Montreux; **La Gioconda está triste** (Mona Lisa Is Sad; 1976) and the series **Ese señor de negro** (That Man Dressed in Black; 1975) and **Verano azul** (Blue Summer; 1982).

CREDITS

1963: **Se necesita chico**
(A Boy Wanted).
1974: **Manchas de sangre en un coche nuevo**
(Blood Stains in a New Car).
1976: **Las delicias de los verdes años**
(The Delights of Erotic Years).
1977: **La guerra de papá**
(Daddy's War).
1978: **Tobi.**
1982: **La próxima estación**
(The Next Station).
Buenos días, señor monstruo
(Good Morning, Mr. Monster).

JERONIMO MIHURA
1902, Cádiz

He joins the Technical Service of the Postal Department in 1922. Film critic in various magazines, including **La pantalla,** as well as the daily newspaper **La Nación** in Madrid. Starting in 1933 he works as an assistant director for Perojo, Ardavín, Sáenz de Heredia and Marquina. Dubbing director in the Estudios Fono España, with Hugo Donnarelli, and in the Estudios CEA. Director of 20 documentaries for Magister, a production company tied to the Catholic Church. Beween 1942 and 1959 he directs 16 features, many of the screenplays of which are written by his brother, playwright Miguel Mihura. In 1965, he begins to work in NO-DO, contributing scripts and directing.

CREDITS

1942: **Aventura**
(Adventure).
1943: **Castillo de naipes**
(House of Cards).
1944: **El camino de Babel**
(The Road to Babel).
1946: **Cuando llegue la noche**
(When Night Falls).
1947: **Confidencia**
(Confidence).
Vidas confusas
(Confused Lives).
1948: **Siempre vuelven de madrugada**
(They Always Return at Dawn).
En un rincón de España
(In a Corner of Spain).
Mi adorable Juan.
(My Adorable Juan)
1950: **Me quiero casar contigo**
(I Want To Marry You).
El señorito Octavio
(Young Master Octavio).
1954: **Muchachas de Bagdad** (with Edgar G. Ulmer)
(Girls from Bagdad).
1953: **Maldición gitana**
(Gypsy Curse).
1956: **Los maridos no cenan en casa**
(Husbands Don't Dine at Home).
1959: **La copla andaluza**
(The Andalusian Ballad).

CARLES MIRA

1947, Valencia

He studies political science in the University of Madrid and does theater at the same time. He enters the **Official Film School,** but he is not able to receive a degree since he participates in a strike. Assistant to José Luis Gómez in the staging of several theater works. Since 1973, he has directed several shorts which have received prizes in different festivals.

CREDITS

1978: **La portentosa vida del padre Vicente**
(The Miraculous Life of Father Vicente).
1979: **Cuentos para una escapada**
(episode: Memories of the Sea)
(Stories of an Escapade).
1980: **Con el culo al aire**
(Caught with Your Pants Down).
1981: **Jalea real**
(Royal Jelly).
1983: **Que nos quiten lo bailao**
(No One Can Take Away Our Good Times Together).
1985: **Karnabal**

PILAR MIRO

1940, Madrid

She studies law and journalism. In 1968, she graduates from the **Official Film School** with the specialty of screenwriting. She later teaches editing and screenwriting in the same educational institution. She works in TVE since 1960. Beginning as a program assistant, she becomes the first woman director in TVE at 23 years of age. Her first program is **Revista de mujer,** while her first dramatic show is **Lili,** a five-episode soap opera. She has adapted and directed works by such authors as Balzac, Dickens, O'Neill, Strindberg, Lope de Vega and Unamuno. She has worked with Summers on the screenplays of **La niña de luto** (The Girl in Mourning; 1964) and **El juego de la oca** (Snakes and Ladders; 1964) directed by Summers. She has also directed two theater works. Co-producer of her films **Gary Cooper que estás en los cielos** (Gary Cooper Who Art in Heaven) and **Hablamos esta noche** (Let's Talk Tonight). From 1983 to 1985, she is Director General of the Film Department of the Ministry of Culture.

CREDITS

1976: **La petición**
(The Demand).
1979: **El crimen de Cuenca**
(The Cuenca Crime).
1980: **Gary Cooper que estás en los cielos**
(Gary Cooper Who Art in Heaven).
1982: **Hablamos esta noche**
(Let's Talk Tonight).

JOSEFINA MOLINA REIG
1936, Córdoba

Studies political sciences and in 1962 founds the **Teatro de Ensayo Medea** in Córdoba. She stages works by Ibsen, Sartre and Shaffer. In 1967, she works in television as an assistant director to Claudio Guerin and Pilar Miró. One year later, she directs her first documentaries for TVE in the programs: **Aquí España** (Spain Here) and **Fiesta.** She is the first woman to obtain a degree in direction at the **Official Film School.** She has adapted and directed more than 50 dramatic programs for TVE. She is a film critic in Madrid's Radio Popular. In 1979, she makes her professional debut in theater by directing **Cinco horas con Mario** (Five Hours with Mario), by Miguel Delibes. She directs the series **Teresa de Jesús** (1984) for TVE.

CREDITS

1973: **Vera... un cuento cruel** (Vera... a Cruel Story).
1979: **Cuentos eróticos** (episode: The Linden-blossom Tea) (Erotic Tales).
1981: **Función de noche** (Night Performance).

RAFAEL MORENO ALBA
1942, Madrid

He studies law and subject matter related to the merchant marine, but his interests lead him to work in film where he makes his debut in 1961. He has been an unpaid trainee, a script (boy), assistant director and second unit director. He directed the medium-length film **Silencio** (Silence; 1967), which has been given several prizes, and six documentaries shot in Egypt. He directs for TVE 13 episodes of the series **Los gozos y las sombras** (Joys and Shadows; 1981).

CREDITS

1969: **Gallos de pelea** (Fighting Cocks).
1971: **Triángulo** (Triangle).
1972: **Las melancólicas** (The Melancholic Women).
1975: **Pepita Jiménez.**
1979: **Mis relaciones con Ana.** (My Relations with Ana).

MANUEL MUR-OTI
1908, Vigo (Pontevedra)

In 1921, he moves to Cuba and begins to study law, but he gives it up for writing. He lives in the Americas more than twenty years and travels throughout the world. He comes back to Spain after the end of the Spanish Civil War and begins to write his first treatments and screenplays. He is the author of novels and dramatic works. In 1953 he founds the Celta Films production company. He adapts literary works such as **Cañas y barro** and **La barraca** by Blasco Ibáñez for TVE.

CREDITS

1949: **Un hombre va por el camino** (A Man Goes Down the Road).
1951: **Cielo negro** (Black Sky).
1953: **Condenados** (Sentenced).
1955: **Orgullo** (Pride).
1956: **El batallón de las sombras** (The Shadow Batallion).
Fedra.
1957: **La guerra empieza en Cuba** (The War Begins in Cuba).
1958: **Una chica de Chicago** (A Girl from Chicago).
1959: **Duelo en la cañada** (Duel in the Gorge).

1960: **Pescando millones**
(Fishing Millions).
1961: **Milagro a los cobardes**
(Miracle for the Cowards).
1962: **A hierro muere**
(Die by Iron).
1964: **Loca juventud**
(Crazy Youth).
1966: **El escuadrón del pánico**
(The Panic Squadron).
1968: **Our Regiment** (USA).
1972: **La encadenada**
(The Chained Girl).
1973: **El diario de una asesina**
(The Diary of a Lady Killer).
1975: **Morir, dormir... tal vez soñar**
(To Die, To Sleep ... Perhaps To Dream).

N

EDGAR NEVILLE

1899, Madrid. 1967, Madrid

Count of Berlanga de Duero, he studies the Humanities and Law. In 1922, he enters the diplomatic corps. He holds various diplomatic posts in Europe, Asia and the Americas. In 1929 he heads the Spanish consulate in Los Angeles, later beginning his film career there by writing dialogues for Spanish versions of American films. On returning to Spain he makes three shorts before directing his first feature. During the Spanish Civil War he shoots a few documentaries for the insurrectionists. His literary activity is very extensive and he has written novels, poems, comedies, stories and essays.

CREDITS

1935: **El malvado Carabel**
(The Villainous Carabel).
1936: **La señorita de Trévelez**
(The Young Lady from Trevelez).
1939: **Santa Rogelia** (Italy)
Frente de Madrid (Italy).
(Madrid Front)
1941: **La muchacha de Moscú**
(The Girl from Moscow).
1942: **Correo de Indias**
(Mail from the Indies).
1943: **Café de París**
(Paris Café).
1944: **La torre de los siete jorobados**
(The Tower of the Seven Hunchbacks).
1945: **La vida en un hilo**
(Life Hanging from a Thread).
Domingo de carnaval
(Shrove Sunday).
1946: **El crimen de la calle de Bordadores**
(Crime on Bordadores Street).
El traje de luces
(The Bullfighting Suit).
1947: **Nada**
(Nothing).
1948: **El señor Esteve**
(Mister Esteve).
El marqués de Salamanca
(The Marquess of Salamanca).
1950: **El último caballo**
(The Last Horse).
1951: **Cuento de hadas**
(Fairy Tale).
1952: **El cerco del diablo** (an episode)
(Besieging the Devil).
Duende y misterio del flamenco
(The Spirit and Mystery of Flamenco).
1955: **La ironía del dinero**
(The Irony of Money).
1959: **El baile**
(The Dance).
1960: **Mi calle**
(My Street).

JOSE ANTONIO NIEVES CONDE
1915, Segovia

Film critic for the **Pueblo** newspaper and writer in the magazine **Primer Plano.** Between 1941 and 1946, he works as an assistant director for Gil. One year later, the producer of these films gives him the opportunity to direct his first feature film. Vice-president of the ASDREC. During a time, he works in TVE.

CREDITS

1946: **Senda ignorada** (Ignored Path).
1947: **Angustia** (Anguish).
1949: **Llegada la noche** (Nightfall).
1950: **El cerco del diablo** (an episode) (Besieging the Devil).
Balarrasa (Hothead).
1951: **Surcos** (Furrows).
1953: **Rebeldía** (Rebelliousness).
1955: **La legión del silencio** (with J. M. Forqué) (The Legion of Silence).
Los peces rojos (The Red Fish).
Todos somos necesarios (We're All Necessary).
1957: **El inquilino** (The Tenant).
1960: **Don Lucio y el hermano Pío** (Don Lucio and Brother Pío).
1963: **El diablo también llora** (The Devil Cries Too).
1965: **El sonido de la muerte** (The Sound of Death).
1966: **Cotolay.**
1971: **Marta.**
1972: **Historia de una traición** (The Story of Treachery).
1976: **Volvoreta.**

JOSE MARIA NUNES
1930, Faro (Portugal)

In 1942, he moves to Seville and later he goes to Barcelona. From 1950 to 1956, he works in more than 30 films as an unpaid trainee, script(boy), assistant, editor, actor, etc. He writes scripts and directs theater. He belongs to the **Barcelona School.** Due to problems of nationality, his daughter Virginia has received the film credit for his latest films.

CREDITS (incomplete)

1957: **Mañana** (Tomorrow).
1961: **No dispares contra mí** (Don't Shoot Me).
1962: **Silencio** (Silence).
La alternativa (The Alternative).
1966: **Noches de vino tinto** (Nights of Red Wine).
Superespectáculos del mundo (with R. Bianchi) (Super-shows of the World).
1967: **Biotaxia.**
1968: **Sexperiencias.**
1975: **Iconokaut.**
1983: **Gritos a ritmo fuerte** (Heavy Rhythm Cries).

PEDRO OLEA

1938, Bilbao

He studies economics and at the same time runs a university film club and makes a few films in 8 and 16 mm. He gives up his former studies when he travels to Madrid and enters the **Official Film School,** where he graduates with the film project **Anabel** (1964). He writes in the magazine, **Nuestro cine.** He directs different programs for TVE: **La Ronca, La ría de Bilbao, El Rastro de Ramón, Ultimo grito** and **Especial Víctor Manuel.** He later works in television, film and advertising. He is also the producer of his films, **El bosque del lobo** (The Wolves' Forest), **La casa sin fronteras** (The House without Frontiers) and **Akelarre** (Witch's Sabbath).

CREDITS

1967: **Días de viejo color**
(Days of Fading Color).

1969: **Juan y Junior en un mundo diferente**
(Juan and Junior in a Different World).

1970: **El bosque del lobo**
(The Wolf's Forest).

1972: **La casa sin fronteras**
(The House without Frontiers).

1973: **No es bueno que el hombre esté solo**
(A Man Shouldn't Be Alone).

1974: **Tormento**
(Torment).

1975: **Pim, pam, pum... ¡fuego!**
(Ready, Aim... Fire!).

1976: **La Corea.**

1977: **Un hombre llamado «Flor de Otoño»**
(A Man Called «Autumn Flower»).

1984: **Akelarre**
(Witch's Sabbath).

JUAN DE ORDUÑA

1907, Madrid. 1974, Madrid

Actor, director, producer and screenwriter. He begins very young as a theater actor. He receives a degree in law, while appearing in his first films. In 1923, he makes his debut with the Emilio Thuillier theater company and the year after works in his first film called **La casa de la Troya** (The House of Troy), by Pérez Lugín and Manuel Noriega. Noteworthy among the more than 20 films he acted in before 1941 are: **La revoltosa, Boy, Pilar Guerra, El misterio de la Puerta del Sol, Nobleza baturra, Luna gitana** and **La gitanilla.** After briefly directing film shorts, he basically works as a director of more than 40 films. Between 1968 and 1970, he shoots for TVE 13 **zarzuelas** (Spanish light operas) for the series **Teatro lírico español** (Spanish Lyrical Theater).

CREDITS (incomplete)

1941: **Porque te vi llorar**
(Why I Saw You Cry).

1942: **¡A mí la Legión!**
(I Like the Foreign Legion!).

1943: **Rosas de otoño**
(Autumn Roses).
Deliciosamente tontos
(Deliciously Foolish).

1944: **Ella, él y sus millones**
(Hers, His and the Millions).

1946: **Misión blanca**
(White Mission).
1947: **La Lola se va a los puertos**
(Lola Goes to the Ports).
1948: **Locura de amor**
(Love Crazy).
1949: **Pequeñeces**
(Little Things).
1950: **Agustina de Aragón.**
1951: **La Leona de Castilla**
(The Lioness of Castile).
Alba de América
(America's Dawn).
1953: **Cañas y barro**
(Reeds and Mud).
1954: **Zalacaín el aventurero**
(Zalacaín the Adventurer).
1957: **El último cuplé**
(The Last Song).
1961: **Teresa de Jesús**
1964: **Abajo espera la muerte**
(Death Waits Below).
1965: **Nobleza baturra**
(Nobility of Brute Action).
1973: **Me has hecho perder el juicio**
(You've Made Me Lose My Mind).

MARIANO OZORES

1926, Madrid

Son of actor Mariano Ozores and actress Luisa Puchol and brother of actors José Luis (1923-1968) and Antonio. He makes his debut as a screenwriter in 1957 and two years later, directs his own screenplays. He is one of Spain's most prolific directors, having made more than 75 films in 25 years.

CREDITS (incomplete)

1959: **Las dos y media y veneno**
(Two-thirty and Venom).
1961: **Salto mortal**
(Somersault).
1962: **Alegre juventud**
(Happy Youth).
1965: **Morir en España**
(Dying in Spain).
Historia de la fiesta
(The Story of a Festivity).
1966: **Operación secretaria**
(Operation Secretary).
1968: **Objetivo bikini**
(Objective: Bikini).
1970: **En un lugar de la Manga**
(In a Place in La Manga).
1971: **En la red de mi corazón**
(Somewhere in My Heart).
1973: **Señora doctor**
(Lady Doctor).
1974: **El reprimido**
(The Wallflower).
1975: **Mayordomo para todo**
(A Butler for Everything).
1976: **Alcalde por elección**
(Mayor by Choice).
1977: **El apolítico**
(Apolitical Man).
1979: **Los bingueros**
(The Bingo Players).
1980: **Yo hice a Roque III**
(I Did in Roque III).
1981: **Brujas mágicas**
(Magic Witches).
1982: **Todos al suelo**
(Hit the Floor).
¡Qué vienen los socialistas!
(The Socialists Are Coming!).

P

372 **BENITO PEROJO**
1894, Madrid 1974, Madrid

He studies in England. He works in innumerable pictures as an actor. He directs his first film in 1913 and the last in 1950. After that date he dedicates himself exclusively to production. Between 1918 and 1924 he works in France. In 1930, he is contracted by Paramount to direct Spanish versions of films in the Joinville studios. In 1931 he shoots **Mamá** in Hollywood. From 1936 to 1939 he shoots three films in Germany and in Italy. He also directs nine films in Argentina between 1942 and 1948.

CREDITS (incomplete)

1913: **Fulano de tal se enamora de Manon** (So-and-so Falls in Love with Manon).
1915: **Garrotazo y tentetieso** (Cudgel and Tumbler). **Peladilla, cochero de punto** (Peladilla, Cabby at the Ready).
1922: **La bien pagada** (A Well-paid Girl).
1924: **Más allá de la muerte** (Beyond Death).
1925: **Boy.**
1927: **Malvaloca** (Hollyhock). **El negro que tenía el alma blanca** (The Black Who Had a White Soul).
1933: **Susana tiene un secreto** (Susan Has a Secret). **Se ha fugado un preso** (A Convict Has Escaped).
1934: **El negro que tenía el alma blanca** (The Black Who Had a White Soul). **Crisis mundial** (World Crisis).
1935: **Rumbo a El Cairo** (Off to Cairo). **Es mi hombre** (He's My Man). **La verbena de la Paloma** (The Paloma Fair).
1936: **Nuestra Natacha** (Our Natacha).
1938: **El barbero de Sevilla** (Germany) (The Barber of Seville). **Suspiros de España** (Germany) (Sighs from Spain). **Mariquilla Terremoto** (Germany)
1939: **Los hijos de la noche** (Italy) (Children of the Night). **La última falla** (Italy) (The Last «Falla»).
1940: **Marianela.**
1942: **Goyescas** (Argentina).
1944: **La casta Susana** (Argentina) (The Chaste Susana).
1946: **La maja de los cantares** (Argentina) (The Singing Maja).
1947: **La copla de la Dolores** (Argentina) (Dolores' Song).
1950: **Sangre en Castilla** (Blood in Castile).

MIGUEL PICAZO

1927, Cazorla (Jaén)

He studies law in the University of Madrid. Interested in cinema, he enters the **Cinema Research and Experiences Institute** and graduates with the film project, **Habitación de alquiler** (Room for Rent; 1960). Shortly afterwards he becomes an assistant professor in the **Official Film School.** He receives a degree as psychologist in the specialites of Child Pyschology, Sexology and Psychotherapy in the International Institute (University of Boston Foundation). Following two failed attempts, one of which is **Jimena,** which was to be produced by Ferreri, he finally is able to direct **La tía Tula** (Aunt Tula). He adapts and directs more than 70 programs for TVE, including: **El hombre de la esquina rosada** (The Man on the Rose Corner) by Borges, **Cartas de mamá** (Letters from Mama) by Cortázar, **El gato negro** (The Black Cat) by E. A. Poe, **Soledad** (Solitude) by Unamuno, **Entre visillos** (Between the Curtains) by Martín Gaite, **El hombre de los santos** (The Man of the Saints) by Fernández Santos, **Rinconete y Cortadillo** (Corner and Tumbler) by Cervantes and **Sonata de Primavera** (Spring Sonata) by Valle-Inclán.

CREDITS

1964: **La tía Tula**
(Aunt Tula).

1967: **Oscuros sueños de agosto**
(Obscure August Dreams).

1976: **El hombre que supo amar**
(The Man Who Knew Love).
Los claros motivos del deseo
(The Clear Motives of Desire).

1985: **Extramuros**
(Beyond the Walls).

PERE PORTABELLA

1929, Figueras (Gerona).

He studies chemistry and takes part in the avant-garde artistic movements, collaborating with Antoni Tàpies, Antonio Saura, Eduardo Chillida, etc. In 1959 he creates Films 59, in which Saura, Fons, Ferreri, Cuadrado, etc. also have an interest and produces **Los golfos** (The Scoundrels; 1959) by Saura, **El cochecito** (The Little Car; 1960) by Ferreri and **Viridiana** (1961) by Buñuel, a film which was coproduced with Uninci. As a screenwriter, he works on **El momento de la verdad** (The moment of Truth; 1964), by Rosi. He has directed five shorts on the painter Joan Miró and various of a political nature: **Poetas catalanes** (Catalonian Poets; 1970), **Abogados laboralistas** (Labor Lawyers; 1973) and **El sopar** (1974). His film and political activities have always been inter-connected. A founding member of the **Assembly of Catalonia** (1971) and senator between 1977 and 1982.

CREDITS

1968: **Nocturno 29**
(Nocturnal 29).

1970: **Cuadecuc (Vampir).**

1972: **Umbracle/Umbráculo**
(Latticework Shed).

1977: **Informe general**
(General Report).

R

FRANCISCO REGUEIRO
1934, Valladolid

A professor of commerce, he studies law and journalism. He writes stories and screenplays. In 1962, he wins the Sésamo Prize with the story **La muchacha de los cabellos de lino.** He publishes jokes in **La Codorniz** and **El Norte de Castilla.** He receives a degree from the **Cinema Research and Experiences Institute** with the film project **Sor Angelina, virgen** (1961). Between 1956 and 1963, he participates in collective exhibitions of drawings and paintings. For TVE, he has made programs for the series **Pintores del Prado** (Painters of the Prado), among others.

CREDITS

1963: **El buen amor**
(Good Love).
1965: **Amador**
(Lover).
1967: **Si volvemos a vernos**
(Smashing Up).
1969: **Me enveneno de azules**
(I'm Poisoning Myself with the Blues).
1973: **Carta de amor de un asesino**
(Love Letter from an Assassin).
1974: **Duerme, duerme, mi amor**
(Sleep, Sleep, My Love).
1975: **Las bodas de Blanca**
(Blanca's Weddings).
1985: **Padre nuestro,**
(Our Father)

FLORIAN REY
1894, La Almunia (Zaragoza).
1962, Alicante.

Pseudonym of Antonio Martínez. Between 1910 and 1920, he works in the editorial offices of various newspapers in Zaragoza and Madrid. Actor in theater and film. He directs his first film in 1924. In 1927, he discovers the actress Imperio Argentina and marries her in 1934. He directs the actress in 15 films. Between 1930 and 1933, he works in Paramount's studios in Joinville, making European versions of American films. In 1938, he makes two films in the German studios of Hispano-Film Produktion in Berlin. In 1957, he leaves the world of films.

CREDITS (incomplete)

1924: **La revoltosa**
(The Mischievous Girl).
1925: **Los chicos de la escuela**
(The Schoolboys).
El lazarillo de Tormes
(The Blindman's Guide of Tormes).
Gigantes y cabezudos
(Giants and Bigheads).
1926: **El cura de aldea**
(The Village Priest).
1927: **La hermana San Sulpicio**
(Sister San Sulpicio).
1928: **Agustina de Aragón.**
1929: **La aldea maldita**
(The Cursed Village).
1934: **La hermana San Sulpicio**
(Sister San Sulpicio).
1935: **Nobleza baturra**
(Nobility of Brute Action).
1936: **Morena Clara**
(Clara the Brunette).
1938: **Carmen, la de Triana** (Germany)
(Carmen, the Girl from Triana).
1939: **La canción de Aixa** (Germany)
(Aixa's Song).
La Dolores.
1941: **¡Polizón a bordo!**
(Stowaway on Board!).
1942: **La aldea maldita**
(The Cursed Village).
1944: **Orosia.**
1945: **La luna vale un millón**
(The Moon Is Worth a Million).
1946: **Audiencia pública**
(Public Hearing).
1947: **La nao capitana**
(The Lady Captain's Boat).
1948: **Brindis a Manolete**
(Toast to Manolete).
1950: **Cuentos de la Alhambra**
(Tales of the Alhambra).
1953: **Tres citas con el destino**
(an episode)
(Three Appointments with Destiny).
1954: **La danza de los deseos**
(The Dance of Desires).
La cruz de Mayo
(The May Cross).
1957: **Polvorilla**
(Quick-tempered).

ANTONI RIBAS

1935, Barcelona.

He receives a degree in law and economics in 1958. He works as an unpaid trainee and script (boy). Between 1961 and 1965, he is assistant director to Isasi, Gil, Lucia, Amadori and Torrado. In 1964, he directs educational films for the Encyclopaedia Britannica. He is a finalist for the 1957 **Ciudad de Barcelona** Theater Prize. Member of the Institut de Cinema Catalá. He makes the documentary **Catalans universals** (Universal Catalonians; 1978) for TVE.

CREDITS

1966: **Las salvajes en Puente San Gil** (The Savages on San Gil Bridge).
1968: **Palabras de amor** (Words of Love).
1969: **Medias y calcetines** (Stockings and Socks).
1972: **La otra imagen** (The Other Image).
1976: **La ciutat cremada** (The Burnt City).
1983: **¡Victoria! La gran aventura d'un poble.** (Victory! The Great Adventure of a People).
¡Victoria! II. La disbauxa del 17 (Victory II).
1984: **¡Victoria! III, El seny i la rauxa** (Victory III).
1985: **El primer torero porno** (The First Porno Bullfighter).

ANTONIO ROMAN

1911, Orense

He moves to Madrid to study pharmacy and begins to write as a film critic in such magazines as **Popular Films, Films selectos** and **Cinegramas.** Among his shorts made from 1934 to 1941 are: **Canto de emigración** (Emigration Song), **Ritmo de un día** (Rhythm of a Day), **De la Alhambra al Albaicín** (From Alhambra to Albaicin) and **El hombre y el carro** (The Man and the Cart). He works on the screenplays for **Raza** (Race; 1941), by Sáenz de Heredia, and **Las últimas banderas** (The Last Flags). He works as a scriptwriter in TVE.

CREDITS (incomplete)

1941: **Escuadrilla** (Squadron).
1942: **Boda en el infierno** (Wedding in Hell).
Intriga (Intrigue).
1943: **La casa de la lluvia** (The House of Rain).
1944: **Lola Montes.**
1945: **Los últimos de Filipinas** (The Last from the Philippines).
1947: **Fuenteovejuna.**
1948: **La vida encadenada** (The Chained Life).
1949: **Pacto de silencio** (A Pact of Silence).
El amor brujo (Bewitched Love).
1952: **Ultimos días** (The Last Days).
1955: **Congreso en Sevilla** (Congress in Seville).
La fierecilla domada (The Taming of the Shrew).
1957: **Madrugada** (Dawn).
1958: **Los clarines del miedo** (The Bugles of Fear).
Bombas para la paz (Bombs for Peace).
1962: **El sol en el espejo** (Sun in the Mirror).
1963: **Pacto de silencio** (A Pact of Silence).
1964: **Un tiro por la espalda.** (A Shot in the Back).
1969: **El mesón del gitano** (The Gypsy's Inn).

FRANCISCO ROVIRA BELETA

1912, Barcelona

He studies architecture, the humanities and law. He produces cartoon shorts (the **El Faquir** series), animated and directed by Joaquín Muntañola. He directs film shorts for Cifesa. He works as an assistant director. Nominated for Oscars for the best foreign film with his pictures **Los tarantos** and **El amor brujo** (Bewitched Love). He has also directed a few episodes for the TVE series: **Cuentos y leyendas** (Tales and Legends) and **Curro Jiménez.**

CREDITS

1948: **Doce horas de vida** (Twelve Hours of Life).
1949: **39 cartas de amor** (Thirty-nine Love Letters).
1950: **Luna de sangre** (Blood Moon).
1953: **Hay un camino a la derecha** (There's a Road on the Right).
1954: **Once pares de botas** (Eleven Pairs of Boots).
1955: **Familia provisional** (Provisional Family).
1956: **Expreso de Andalucía** (Andalusian Express).
1957: **Historias de la feria** (Fair Stories).
1960: **Altas variedades** (Varieties).
1961: **Los atracadores** (The Robbers).
1962: **Los tarantos.**
1965: **La dama del alba** (The Lady of Dawn).
1967: **El amor brujo** (Bewitched Love).
1969: **La larga agonía de los peces fuera del agua** (The Long Agony of Landed Fish).
1972: **No encontré rosas para mi madre** (I Found No Roses for My Mother).
1976: **La espada negra** (The Black Sword).

ARTURO RUIZ CASTILLO

1910, Madrid

Son of the publisher José Ruiz Castillo. After receiving a degree in Natural Sciences from the University of Madrid, he enters the School of Architecture. He soon gives up these studies to work in theater. Along with García Lorca he works in the **La barraca** University Theater as a technician and designer. Artistic director of the **Biblioteca Nueva** publishing company. Along with Gonzalo Menéndez Pidal, he makes experimental and avant-garde shorts in 9.5 and 16 mm. in 1933. Between 1940 and 1945, he makes more than 50 shorts. In 1946, he founds the Horizonte Films production company for which he directs **Las inquietudes de Shanti-Andía** (The Worries of Shanti-Andía), based on the novel by Pío Baroja.

CREDITS (incomplete)

1946: **Las inquietudes de Shanti-Andía** (The Worries of Shanti-Andía).
1948: **La manigua de Dios** (The Godless Brushland).
1949: **El santuario no se rinde** (The Sanctuary Refuses To Surrender).
1950: **María Antonia la Caramba.**
1951: **Catalina de Inglaterra** (Catalina of England).
1952: **La laguna negra** (The Black Lagoon).

1953: **Dos caminos**
(Two Roads).
1955: **El guardián del paraíso**
(The Guardian of Paradise).
1956: **Pasión en el mar**
(Passion at Sea).
1959: **Los ases buscan la paz**
(The Aces Look for Peace).
1960: **Pachín.**
1962: **Llovidos del cielo**
(Raining from Heaven).

JOSE LUIS SAENZ DE HEREDIA
1911, Madrid

He studies architecture. At a very early age he begins to write comedies which are performed by amateur theater groups. In 1933, he subtitles foreign films in Spanish. He writes the screenplay for **Patricio miró a una estrella** (Patricio Looked at a Star) which he ends up directing after Fernando Delgado argues with the producer. He makes **La hija de Juan Simón** (The Daughter of Juan Simón) for Filmófono with Buñuel as executive producer. During the civil war he joins the insurrectionists, but rejects a proposal for work in General Franco's film services. He directs **Raza** (Race) based on a screenplay by General Franco. In 1949, he founds the Chapalo Films production company, under whose banner he makes the majority of his films. Between 1961 and 1963, he is director of the **Official Film School.**

CREDITS (Incomplete)

1934: **Patricio miró a una estrella**
(Patricio Looked at a Star).
1935: **La hija de Juan Simón**
(The Daughter of Juan Simón).
1941: **A mí no me mire usted**
(Don't Look at Me).
Raza
(Race).
1943: **El escándalo**
(The Scandal).
1944: **El destino se disculpa**
(Destiny Says It's Sorry).
1945: **Bambú.**
1946: **Mariona Rebull.**
1947: **Las aguas bajan negras**
(The Water Flows Black).
1948: **La mies es mucha**
(That's a Lot of Corn).
1950: **Don Juan.**
1952: **Los ojos dejan huellas**
(Eyes Leave Tracks).
1954: **Todo es posible en Granada**
(Everything's Possible in Granada).
1955: **Historias de la radio**
(Radio Stories).
1960: **Diez fusiles esperan**
(Ten Rifles Are Waiting).
1963: **La verbena de la Paloma**
(The Paloma Fair).
1964: **Franco, ese hombre**
(Franco, That Man).
1965: **Historias de la televisión**
(Television Stories).
1970: **Los gallos de la madrugada**
(The Roosters at Dawn).
1974: **Proceso a Jesús**
(Jesús on Trial).
1976: **El último héroe**
(The Last Hero).

CARLOS SAURA

1932, Huesca

His secondary education is in Madrid. He is interested in photography from the time he is fifteen and eventually becomes a professional, participating in various collective exhibitions. In 1953, he collaborates with the **First International Abstract Art Exhibition** in Santander. He studies in the **Cinema Research and Experiences Institute** and graduates with the film project **La tarde del domingo** (Sunday Afternoon; 1957). Shortly afterwards, he occupies the chair of direction in the Institute, but in 1964 he is dismissed from the post due to political reasons. Among the immense number of prizes received by his pictures are the Silver Bears for **La caza** (The Hunt) and **Peppermint frappé** and the Golden Bear for **Deprisa, deprisa** (Hurry, Hurry) at the Berlin Film Festival.

CREDITS

1959: **Los golfos**
(The Scoundrels).
1963: **Llanto por un bandido**
(Lament for a Bandit).
1965: **La caza**
(The Hunt).
1967: **Peppermint frappé.**
1968: **Stress es tres, tres**
(Stress in Three).
1969: **La madriguera**
(The Den).
1970: **El jardín de las delicias**
(The Garden of Delights).
1972: **Ana y los lobos**
(Ana and the Wolves).
1973: **La prima Angélica**
(Cousin Angelica).
1975: **Cría cuervos...**
(Raising Ravens...)
1977: **Elisa, vida mía**
(Elisa, My Love).
1978: **Los ojos vendados**
(Blindfolded).
1979: **Mamá cumple 100 años**
(Mama Turns a Hundred).
1980: **Deprisa, deprisa**
(Hurry, Hurry).
1981: **Bodas de sangre**
(Blood Wedding).
Dulces horas
(Sweet Hours).
1982: **Antonieta.**
1983: **Carmen.**
1984: **Los zancos.**
(The Stilts).
1986: **El amor brujo**
(Bewitched Love).

CARLOS SERRANO DE OSMA

1916, Madrid.
1984, Alicante

Film critic and essayist, he writes in the magazines **Nuestro Cinema, Popular Film, Gran Film, Filmar, Cinegramas, Radiocinema, Tajo** and in the newspaper **Ahora.** During the Spanish Civil War he joins the film service of Madrid's Communist Party. At the end of the civil war he directs a series of documentaries for official bodies. From 1947 to 1968, he is porfessor of direction at the **Cinema Research and Experiences Institute.** He also becomes the sub-director of the Institute for six years. He directs a few programs for TVE including the biographies of **Juan Ramón Jiménez** (1968) and **Cánovas** (1969). From 1971 to 1979 he runs his own art gallery. Director of archives at the National Film Library. In 1983, he receives a tribute for his work in film from the Valladolid Film Festival.

CREDITS

1946: **Abel Sánchez.**
1947: **Embrujo**
(Bewitched).
La sirena negra
(The Black Siren).
1948: **La sombra iluminada**
(The Illuminated Shadow).
1951: **Rostro de mar**
(Sign of the Sea).
Parsifal (with D. Mangran).

1960: **La rosa roja**
(The Red Rose).

GONZALO SUAREZ
1934, Oviedo

He studies the humanities at the University of Madrid, specializing in French philology. In 1953, he joins the TEU theater group and later other companies. He has performed the works of Seneca, Saroyan, Aristophanes, Berri, Anouilh, Shakespeare, etc. He resides successively in Madrid, Paris and Barcelona. He works in journalism under the pseudonym of Martín Girard. In 1963, he gives up journalism and embarks on a literary career: **De cuerpo presente** (1963), **Los once y uno** (1964), **Rocabruno bate a Ditirambo** (1965), **Operación doble dos** (1974), **Gorila en Hollywood** (1980) and **La reina rosa** (1981). He makes his first film short called **Ditirambo vela por nosotros** (Dithyramb Watches Over Us) in 1966 and since then he has alternately worked in film, literature and advertising.

CREDITS

1967: **Ditirambo**
(Dithyramb).
1969: **El extraño caso del doctor Fausto**
(The Strange Case of Dr. Faustus).
1970: **Aoom.**
1971: **Morbo**
(Disease).
1972: **Al diablo con amor**
(To the Devil with Love).
1973: **La loba y la paloma**
(The Wolf and the Dove).
1974: **La regenta**
(The Regent).
1976: **Beatriz.**
1977: **Parranda.**
(Binge).
1978: **Reina zanahoria.**
(Queen Carrot).
1979: **Cuentos para una escapada**
(episode: Miniman and Super-wolf).
(Stories of an Escapade).
1984: **Epílogo.**
(Epilogue).

MANUEL SUMMERS

1935, Seville

He begins to study law, but he gives it up in order to work in the area of drawing. He specializes in caricatures and cartoon strips. He works with the Madrid daily **Pueblo** and with TVE. He studies in the **Cinema Research and Experiences Institute** and receives a degree after submitting the film project **El viejecito** (The Little Old Man; 1960). He has also worked as an actor and as a screenwriter on different films.

CREDITS

1963: **Del rosa al amarillo**
(From Rose to Yellow).
1964: **La niña de luto**
(The Girl in Mourning).
1965: **El juego de la oca**
(Snakes and Ladders).
1966: **Juguetes rotos**
(Broken Toys).
1968: **No somos de piedra**
(We're Only Flesh and Blood).
1969: **¿Por qué te engaña tu marido?**
(Why Does Your Husband Cheat On You?).
1970: **Urtain, el rey de la selva o así.**
(Urtain, the King of the Jungle or Something Like That).
1971: **Adiós cigüeña, adiós**
(Good-bye, Stork).
1973: **El niño es nuestro**
(The Baby Is Ours).
1975: **¡Ya soy mujer!**
(Now I'm a Woman).
1976: **Mi primer pecado**
(My First Sin).
1978: **El sexo ataca**
(Sex Attacks).
1980: **Angeles gordos**
(Fatty Angels).
1981: **Tó er mundo é güeño**
(Everyone's Great).
1982: **Tó er mundo é... imejó!**
(Everyone's... Even Better!).
1984: **La biblia en pasta**
(A Holy Lot of Hoax).
1985: **Tó er mundo é... demasiao**
(Everyone's... Too Much).

T

RAMON TORRADO

1905, La Coruña

He has exhibited in many cities in Spain and Latin America as a painter. In the film industry he has worked as a scenographer, a technical advisor, production chief, storywriter, screenwriter and director. He has directed fifty films and has obtained numerous prizes from the National Show Business Union for his story lines and scripts.

CREDITS (incomplete)

1942: **Campeones**
(Champions).
1945: **Castañuela**
(Castanet).
1946: **Mar abierto**
(Open Sea).
1947: **Botón de ancla**
(Anchor Button).
1949: **Rumbo**
(Course).
1950: **Debla, la virgen gitana**
(Debla, The Gypsy Virgin).
1951: **La niña de la venta.**
(The Girl at the Inn).
La trinca del aire.
(The Air Lashing).
1952: **La estrella de Sierra Morena.**
(The Star of Sierra Morena).
1953: **La alegre caravana**
(The Happy Caravan).
1954: **Amor sobre ruedas**
(Love on Wheels).

Malvaloca
(Hollyhock).
1955: **Suspiros de Triana**
(Sighs from Triana).
1956: **Un fantasma llamado amor**
(A Ghost Called Love).
1956: **María de la O.**
1959: **La ruinas de Babilonia**
(The Ruins of Babylon).
1960: **Un paso al frente**
(A Step Forward).
1961: **Fray Escoba**
(Friar Escoba).
1962: **Cristo Negro**
(The Black Christ).
1965: **Mi canción es para ti**
(My Song Is for You).
1969: **Amor a todo gas**
(Pushing Down the Accelerator on Love).
1972: **Los caballeros del botón de ancla**
(The Gentlemen of the Anchor Buttons).
1976: **Guerreras verdes**
(The Erotic Lady Fighters).
1978: **Pasión inconfesable**
(Unconfessed Passion).

FERNANDO TRUEBA
1955, Madrid

He studies image/camera in the School of Informational Sciences. Film critic for the **El País** newspaper and the magazines **La guía del ocio** and **Casablanca,** of which he is a founding member. Since 1974, he has directed the shorts: **Urculo, En legítima defensa** (In Self-defense), **Homenaje a trois** (Homage a trois) and **Oscar y Carlos 82** (Oscar and Carlos, 82). He also helped write the screenplays for **La mano negra** (The Black Hand; 1980), by Colomo, and **A contratiempo** (Offbeat; 1981), by Ladoire.

CREDITS

1980: **Opera prima**
(A Cousin in Opera/First Work).
1982: **Mientras el cuerpo aguante**
(While the Body Lasts).
1984: **Sal gorda**
(Coarse Salt/Get Lost, Fatso).
1985: **Sé infiel y no mires con quién**
(Move Over, Miss).

U

ALFONSO UNGRIA
1946, Madrid

He studies economics. He collaborates with the TEU, staging works by Arrabal, Adamov and O'Neiil. His first picture is a medium-length film in 16 mm called **Querido Abraham** (Dear Abraham; 1968). In 1969, he directs more than a hundred three-minute shorts on particular subjects for the NO-DO newsreel. The medium-length film **La vida en los teleclubs** (Life in the Tele-Clubs; 1969) cost him his job since it was highly criticized by the executives who entrusted him with the film. Since 1971, he directs episodes for the TVE series **Los libros** (Books), **Cuentos y leyendas** (Tales and Legends) and **Cervantes.**

CREDITS

1970: **El hombre oculto**
(The Hidden Man).
1971: **Tirarse al monte**
(Take to the Hills).
1976: **Gulliver.**
1978: **Soldados**
(Soldiers).
1979: **Cuentos eróticos** (episode: Love is Marvellous)
(Erotic Tales).
1983: **La conquista de Albania**
(The Conquest of Albania).

V

IMANOL URIBE

1950, San Salvador (El Salvador)

He comes to Spain at a very early age and studies journalism and direction at the **Official Film School,** from where he graduates in 1974. He makes two documentaries: **Off** (1976) and **Ez** (No; 1977). All his work in film, in and shorts as well as features, is linked to the Basque Country.

CREDITS

1979: **El proceso de Burgos** (The Burgos Trial).
1981: **La fuga de Segovia** (The Segovia Escape).
1984: **La muerte de Mikel** (Mikel's Death).

LADISLAO VAJDA

1906, Budapest (Hungary).
1965, Barcelona

Son of the writer, playwright and theater director of the same name. He directs his first film in 1933 in Budapest. Afterwards, he shoots in England, Italy, France and Portugal. He decides to settle in Spain in 1942. In 1952 he is awarded the Cross of Isabella the Catholic Queen and in 1954 he obtains Spanish nationality. He dies of a heart attack while shooting **La dama de Beyrut** (The Lady from Beirut: 1965).

CREDITS (incomplete)

1943: **Se vende un palacio** (A Palace Is for Sale).
Doce lunas de miel (Twelve Honeymoons).
1945: **Cinco lobitos** (Five Little Wolves).
1950: **Séptima página** (Seventh Page).
1951: **Ronda española** (Spanish «Ronda»).
1952: **Doña Francisquita.**
1953: **Carne de horca** (Meat for Hanging).
1954: **Aventuras del barbero de Sevilla** (The Adventures of the Barber of Seville).
Marcelino, pan y vino (Marcelino, Bread and Wine).
1955: **Tarde de toros** (Afternoon of Bulls).
1956: **Mi tío Jacinto** (Uncle Jacinto).
1957: **Un ángel pasó por Brooklyn** (An Angel Passed Through Brooklyn).
1958: **El cebo** (Bait).
1960: **María, matrícula de Bilbao.** (Maria, License Plate from Bilbao).

Z

PAULINO VIOTA
1948, Santander

A degree in economics. Film critic in Radio Popular and in the **Diario Montañés** newspaper of Santander. At 18 he makes his first shorts on super-8 mm. He directs his first 16 mm. film called **Fin de un invierno** (Winter's End) in 1968. One year later he tries to enter the **Official Film School.** He also makes in 16 mm. a feature called **Contactos** (Contacts), considered an avant-garde work.

CREDITS

1970: **Contactos** (Contacts).
1978: **Con uñas y dientes** (Tooth and Nail).
1982: **Cuerpo a cuerpo** (Hand-to-hand).

IVAN ZULUETA
1943, San Sebastián

He studies decoration at Madrid's **Centro de Nuevas Profesiones,** and in 1964, he travels to New York to study painting and design at the **Art Students League.** Later, he enters the **Official Film School,** but he does not graduate from the institution. For a year and a half he makes **Ultimo grito** (Latest Fashion) for TVE, a weekly musical program lasting half an hour. He does all types of graphic design, from the jackets of records to posters for films. Borau produces his first feature, which he finishes in spite of labour problems. He also works as an assistant director.
A number of shorts, medium-length and feature-length films in super-8 mm, with a style all their own.

CREDITS

1969: **Un, dos, tres... al escondite inglés** (One, Two, Three... Playing at English Hide-and-seek).
1979: **Arrebato** (Rage).

ACTORS

386 **VICTORIA ABRIL**

1959. Madrid

Pseudonym for Victoria Mérida. Her ballet studies give her the opportunity to appear in small cameo roles starting in 1974. Two years later, she acts in her first important role in **Caperucita y Roja.** She combines her work in film with television and becomes one of Spain's most popular TV hosts and announcers in such programs as «Un, dos, tres» (One, Two, Three) and «625 líneas» (625 Lines). She also performed in the series «La Barraca».

CREDITS

1974: **Obsesion,** by F. L. Polop.
1975: **... Y le llamaban Robin Hood,** by T. Ricci.
1976: **Robin and Marian** (Robin y Marian), by R. Lester.
El hombre que supo amar, by M. Picazo.
Caperucita y Roja, by A. Goiricelaya and L. Revenga.
El puente, by J. A. Bardem.
1977: **Cambio de sexo,** by V. Aranda.
Esposa y amante, by A. Fons.
Doña Perfecta, by C. Fernández Ardavín.
1979: **La muchacha de las bragas de oro,** by V. Aranda.
Mater amatísima, by J. A. Salgot.
Le coeur à l'envers (France), by F. Abprederis (Otra mujer).
Mieux vaut etre riche et bien portant que fauche et mal foutu, by M. Pecas (Más vale pájaro en mano).
La casa del paraíso, by S. San Miguel.
1981: **Comin'at ya!,** by F. Bardi.
J'ai epouse une ombre, by R. Davis.
1981: **La batalla del porro,** by F. Bellmunt.
1982: **La colmena,** by M. Camús.
Asesinato en el Comité Central, by V. Aranda.
L'odyssee de Monsanto (Portugal), by P. Kast.
Entre paréntesis, by S. Fábregas.
Sem sombra de pecado (Portugal), by J. Fonseca e Costa.
Le batard, by B. van Effenterre.
L'addition, by D. Amar.
Le voyage, by M. Andriev.
1983: **La luna dans le caniveau,** by J. Beinex.
Las bicicletas son para el verano, by J. Chávarri.
1984: **Río abajo** (On the Line), by J. L. Borau.
La noche más hermosa, by M. Gutiérrez Aragón.
After Darkness, by D. Othenin-Girard and S. Guerroz.
Rouge Gorge, by P. Zucca.
1985: **Padre nuestro,** by F. Regueiro.
La hora bruja, by J. de Armiñán.
Tiempo de silencio, by V. Aranda.
1986: **Max Mon Thour,** by N. Oshina.

IMPERIO ARGENTINA

1906, Buenos Aires

The pseudonym of Magdalena Nile. She is born in Argentina during a theatrical tour of her parents. She makes her debut al twelve in the dance school company of the **Comedia de Buenos Aires Theater.** After making various tours through Latin America, she definitively comes to Spain in 1923. While she is acting in Madrid's Romea Theater in 1927, she is discovered by Florián Rey, who directs her in several pictures and who finally marries her. In 1931, she works in Paramount's Joinville Studios. During the Spanish Civil War, she makes various films in Italy and Germany. She becomes one of the most popular Spanish film actresses. Since 1951, she has basically presented musical and theater shows. She acts in New York's Carnegie hall in 1952. In 1957, she performs the theater piece, **Un sueño para Constanza,** by Luis Matilla. In recent years, she has been paid tributes in different film festivals and on TVE.

CREDITS (incomplete)

1927: **La hermana San Sulpicio,** by F. Rey.
1928: **Corazones sin rumbo** (Germany), by B. Perojo (Herzen Ohne Ziel).

1930: **El profesor de mi mujer** (Germany), by F. Rey (L'amour chante).
1931: **Cinópolis** (France), by J. M. Castellví (Elle veut faire du cinéma).
Su noche de bodas (France), by L. Mercanton and F. Rey (Marions-nous).
1934: **El novio de mamá,** by F. Rey.
La hermana San Sulpicio, by F. Rey.
1935: **Nobleza baturra,** by F. Rey.
1936: **Morena Clara,** by F. Rey.
1938: **Carmen, la de Triana** (Germany), by F. Rey.
1939: **La canción de Aixa** (Germany), by F. Rey.
1940: **Tosca** (Italy), by K. Koch.
1942: **Goyescas,** by B. Perojo.
1945: **Bambú,** by J. L. Sáenz de Heredia.
1946: **Los majos de Cádiz** (Argentina), by B. Perojo.
1947: **La copla de la Dolores** (Argentina), by B. Perojo.
1948: **La cigarra,** by F. Rey.
1960: **Ama Rosa,** by L. Klimovsky.
1965: **Con el viento solano,** by M. Camus.

IMANOL ARIAS

1956, Riaño (León)

He begins to work in independent theater companies in the Basque Country. Later, he is contracted by Madrid's National Drama Center. Cuban director, Humberto Solás, gives him his first big opportunity in film, offering him the leading role in **Cecilia.** He has performed in the following series for TVE: «Juanita la larga», «Anillos de oro» and «La bella Otero».

CREDITS

1975: **La Corea,** by P. Olea.
1981: **Cecilia** (Cuba), by H. Solás.
1982: **La colmena,** by M. Camús.
Laberinto de pasiones, by P. Almodóvar.
Demonios en el jardín, by M. Gutiérrez Aragón.
1983: **Bearn o la sala de las muñecas,** by J. Chávarri.
La muerte de Mikel, by I. Uribe.
1984: **Fuego eterno,** by J. A. Rebolledo.
Camila, by M. L. Bemberg.
1985: **Luces de bohemia,** by M. A. Díez.
Lulú de noche, by E. Martínez-Lázaro.
Tiempo de silencio, by V. Aranda.

AURORA BAUTISTA

1925, Villanueva de los Infantes (Valladolid)

She studies acting and makes her debut in the Lola Membrives' company. Later she works in Madrid's Español Theater and in the Cámara Theater. She performs in such works as Shakespeare's **Midsummer Night's Dream,** Anouilh's **Atigone,** Cocteau's **Two-headed Eagle,** García Lorca's **Yerma,** Aristophanes' **Lysistrata,** etc. Discovered by Juan de Orduña, she is put under contract by Cifesa and thanks to the success of **Locura de amor** (Love Crazy), she becomes one of the most popular actresses in Spain and in Latin America. She goes on tour with theater companies in Mexico and Argentina and enjoys immense success. After marrying, she leaves theater and film for a few years.

CREDITS (incomplete)

1948: **Locura de amor,** by J. de Orduña.
1950: **Pequeñeces,** by J. de Orduña.
Agustina de Aragón, by J. de Orduña.
1953: **Condenados,** by M. Mur-Oti.
1956: **La gata,** by M. Alexandre y R. Torrecilla.
1959: **Sonatas,** by J. A. Bardem.
1961: **Teresa de Jesús,** by J. de Orduña.
1964: **La tía Tula,** by M. Picazo.
1969: **Pepa Doncel,** by L. Lucía.

1973: **Una vela para el diablo,** by E. Martín.
1977: **El mirón,** by J. R. Larraz.
1985: **Extramuros,** by M. Picazo.

ANA BELEN
1951, Madrid

Pseudonym of Pilar Cuesta. She has worked in film, theater, television and song from an early age. She makes her debut at fourteen with **Zampo y yo** in Madrid's Teatro Estudio and directed by Miguel Narros. Under his direction she performs in Cervantes' **Numancia,** Moratín's **El sí de las niñas,** Shakespeare's **King Lear,** Zorrilla's **Don Juan Tenorio,** etc. Among her works for TVE are **Crimen y castigo** (Crime and Punishment), **Las mocedades del Cid** (The Pranks/Youth of El Cid) and **Fortunata y Jacinta** (Fortunata and Jacinta; 1979), by M. Camus.

CREDITS (incomplete)

1965: **Zampo y yo,** by L. Lucía.
1979: **Españolas en París,** by R. Bodegas.
1971: **Morbo,** by G. Suárez.
1973: **Separación matrimonial,** by A. Fons.
Vida conyugal sana, by R. Bodegas.
1974: **Tormento,** by P. Olea.
El amor del capitán Brando, by J. de Armiñán.
1975: **¡Jo, papá!** by J. de Armiñán.
Emilia, parada y fonda, by A. Fons.
1976: **La petición,** by P. Miró.
El buscón, by L. Berriatúa.
1977: **La oscura historia de la prima Montse,** by J. Cadena.
La criatura, by E. de la Iglesia.
Sonámbulos, by M. Gutiérrez Aragón.
1978: **Jaque a la dama,** by F. Rodríguez.
1982: **La colmena,** by M. Camus.
Demonios en el jardín, by M. Gutiérrez Aragón.
1985: **La corte de faraón,** by J. L. García Sánchez.
Sé infiel y no mires con quién, by F. Trueba.

C

SONIA BRUNO
1945, Barcelona

Pseudonym of Antonia Cyamburu. Begins to work at fourteen years of age in diverse programs for TVE. In 1961, she makes her first feature. From that year until 1969, she performs in 36 films. She then leaves the film industry to get married. She makes her debut with the Mary Carrillo theater company in **El mantel.**

CREDITS (incomplete)

1961: **Los atracadores,** by F. Rovira Beleta.
1962: **La ruta de los narcóticos,** by J. M. Forn.
1963: **Crimen,** by M. Lluch.
El próximo otoño, by A. Eceiza.
1964: **El juego de la oca,** by M. Summers.
1966: **Mañana será otro día,** by J. Camino.
1967: **La boutique,** by L. García Berlanga.
1968: **Oscuros sueños de agosto,** by M. Picazo.
No desearás la mujer de tu prójimo, by P. Lazaga.
La chica de los anuncios, by P. Lazaga.
Sharon, vestida de rojo, by G. Lorente.
1969: **Las amigas,** by P. Lazaga.
Las chicas del mini-mini, by G. Lorente.

PABLITO CALVO
1949, Madrid

Chosen from among hundreds of children to play the lead in **Marcelino, pan y vino** (Marcelino, Bread and Wine) at seven years of age. After his exclusive contract runs out with Chamartín, he makes a few more pictures and retires from the industry at the age of fourteen. He currently works as an industrial engineer.

CREDITIS

1955: **Marcelino, pan y vino,** by L. Vajda.
1956: **Mi tío Jacinto,** by L. Vajda.
1957: **Un ángel pasó por Brooklyn,** by L. Vajda.
1958: **Totó e Marcelino** (Italia), by A. Musu.
1960: **Juanito,** by F. Palacios.
1961: **Alerta en el cielo,** by L. C. Amadori.
1962: **Barcos de papel,** by R. Viñoly Barreto.
1963: **Dos años de vacaciones,** by E. Gómez Muriel.

ANTONIO CASAL
1910, Santiago de Compostela (La Coruña)
1973, Madrid

He makes his debut at eighteen years of age in the Maravillas Theater in Madrid. Later he becomes Spain's most well-known comedian in such musical comedies as **Monte Carmelo** and **La madre guapa.** Discovered by Florián Rey, he begins his film career with **Polizón a bordo** (Stowaway on Board). Between 1950 and 1957 he does variety shows with the comedian Angel de Andrés. In 1958, he joins the company of Madrid's Goya Theater. Noteworthy among his works for TVE is the series **Plinio** (Pliny; 1972), by Giménez-Rico.

CREDITS (incomplete)

1941: **Polizón a bordo,** by F. Rey.
Pepe Conde, by J. López Rubio.
1942: **Viaje sin destino,** by R. Gil.
1943: **Huella de luz,** by R. Gil.
1944: **El fantasma y doña Juanita,** by R. Gil.
1946: **Un hombre de negocios,** by L. Lucía.
1947: **Botón de ancla,** by R. Torrado.
1949: **La guitarra de Gardel,** by L. Klimovsky.
1950: **El sueño de Andalucía,** by L. Lucía y R. Vernay.
La trinca del aire, by R. Torrado.
1952: **Doña Francisquita,** by L. Vajda.

1955: **Familia provisional,** by F. Rovira Beleta.
1957: **Camarote de lujo,** by R. Gil.
1958: **Secretaria para todo,** by I. F. Iquino.
1964: **La nueva Cenicienta,** by G. Sherman.
1968: **El cronicón,** by A. Giménez-Rico.
1973: **Me has hecho perder el juicio,** by J. de Orduña.

ESTRELLITA CASTRO

1912, Seville
1983, Madrid

Well-known flamenco dancer and singer since she was ten due to her particular style. At age twelve she wins a contest that opens the doors of Madrid's Novedades Theater to her. She tours through Spain and Latin America. In 1935, she performs in her first film. During the Spanish Civil War, she performs in Germany and Italy under the direction of B. Perojo. Since the middle of the fifties, she basically works in theater shows and in TVE.

CREDITS

1935: **Rosario la Cortijera,** by L. Artola.
1938: **El barbero de Sevilla** (Germany), by B. Perojo.
Suspiros de España (Germany), by B. Perojo.
1939: **Mariquilla Terremoto** (Germany), by B. Perojo.
Los hijos de la noche (Germany), by B. Perojo.
1940: **La gitanilla,** by F. Delgado.
1941: **Torbellino,** by L. Marquina.
1942: **Los misterios de Tánger,** by C. Fernández Cuenca.
1943: **La patria chica,** by F. Delgado.
La maja del capote, by F. Delgado.
1953: **Gitana tenías que ser** (Mexico), by R. Baledón
1967: **La niña del patio,** by A. de Ossorio.
1972: **Casa Flora,** by R. Fernández.

ALBERTO CLOSAS

1921, Barcelona

The Spanish Civil War forces him to leave for Buenos Aires just after finishing his secondary education. He joins the Margarita Xirgú Dramatic Arts School and in whose company he becomes a leading actor. Later, he forms his own company and tours Latin America. In the forties he takes part in more than thirty films and diverse plays in Argentina. In 1954, he returns to Spain and soon becomes a popular theater and film actor.

CREDITS (incomplete)

1955: **Muerte de un ciclista,** by J. A. Bardem.
La fierecilla domada, by A. Román.
1956: **Todos somos necesarios,** by J. A. Nieves Conde.
1957: **Distrito quinto,** by J. Coll.
1958: **Una muchachita de Valladolid,** by L. C. Amadori.
1959: **El baile,** by E. Neville.
1960: **María, matrículo de Bilbao,** by, L. Vajda.
1961: **Usted puede ser un asesino,** by J. M. Forqué.
1962: **La gran familia,** by F. Palacios.
1964: **Casi un caballero,** by J. M. Forqué.
1965: **La familia y uno más,** by F. Palacios.
De cuerpo presente, by A. Eceiza.
1972: **Experiencia prematrimonial,** by P. Masó.
1979: **La familia, bien, gracias,** by P. Masó.
1980: **El divorcio que viene,** by P. Masó.

ANTOÑITA COLOME

1912, Seville

She makes her debut in the Eslava Theater in Madrid, and shortly afterwards, performs in variety shows in Barcelona's Tívoli. In the thirties she is contracted by Paramount's Joinville studios to make Spanish versions of films. She returns to Spain in 1932. During the fifties, she tours Latin America for six years. In 1951, she retires from film.

CREDITS (incomplete)

1932: **Luces de Buenos Aires,** by A. Millar.
El hombre que se reía del amor, by B. Perojo.
1934: **El negro que tenía el alma blanca,** by B. Perojo.
Crisis mundial, by B. Perojo.
1935: **Rataplán,** by F. Elías.
El malvado Carabel, by E. Neville.
1936: **Una mujer en peligro,** by J. Santugini.
La señorita de Trévelez, by E. Neville.
El bailarín y el trabajador, by L. Marquina.
1941: **Héroe a la fuerza,** by B. Perojo.
1942: **La rueda de la vida,** by E. Fernández Ardavín.
El puente de los suspiros, by J. de Orduña.
1943: **Forja de almas,** by E. Fernández Ardavín.

D

Mi fantástica esposa, by E. G. Maroto.
1945: **La gitana y el rey,** by M. Bengoa.
1946: **El crimen de Pepe Conde,** by J. López Rubio.
1950: **María Antonia la Caramba,** by A. Ruiz Castillo.
1951: **Tercio de quites,** by E. Gómez Muriel.

MARUJA DIAZ
1932, Seville

She begins her artistic career by singing and dancing in folk shows. She is given a few small roles, but her first big opportunity is **El sueño de Andalucía.** Shortly afterwards, she becomes one of the biggest box office draws in the musical genre. As a result, she founds her own production company, and later, a theater company with which she does her own musical comedies such as **Caridad de noche.**

CREDITS (incomplete)

1950: **El sueño de Andalucía,** by L. Lucía and R. Vernay.
1952: **Puebla de las mujeres,** by A. del Amo.
1953: **El pescador de coplas,** by A. del Amo.
1955: **Good-bye Sevilla,** by I. F. Iquino.
El ceniciento, by J. Lladó.
1956: **Polvorilla,** by F. Rey.
El genio alegre, by G. Delgrás.
1959: **Y después del cuplé,** by E. Arancibia.
1960: **La corista,** by J. M. Elorrieta.
1961: **Pelusa,** by J. Setó.
La Cumparsita, by E. Carreras.
1962: **Abuelita Charlestón,** by J. Setó.
Lulú, by J. Setó.
1963: **La casta Susana,** by L. C. Amodori.
1965: **La pérgola de las flores** (Argentina), by E. Viñoly Barreto.
1971: **Carmen Boom,** by N. Nostro.

ROSITA DIAZ GIMENO
1911, Madrid

She studies in the National Music Conservatory. Her debut comes in theater in the Martínez Sierra company. She tours through France and Latin America. In 1931, she is contracted by Paramount's Joinville studios to make Spanish versions of films. In 1934, she shoots **La Dolorosa,** by Jean Gremillon in Spain. In 1935, she stars in two films in Hollywood. A year later she returns to Spain to make her last Spanish film, **El genio alegre,** a picture that is finished after the civil war. However, she does not receive credit for having made it since she is a republican. For some years she lives and works in Mexico. Currently, she resides in New York where in 1983 Spanish cinema paid her a tribute.

CREDITS (incomplete)

1931 **Su noche de bodas** (France), by F. Rey.
Un caballero de frac (France), by C. San Martín.
1932: **El hombre que se reía del amor,** by B. Perojo.
1933: **Sierra de Ronda,** by F. Rey.
Susana tiene un secreto, by B. Perojo.
Se ha fugado un preso, by B. Perojo.
1934: **La Dolorosa,** by J. Gremillon.

1935: **Angelina o el honor de un brigadier** (USA), by Louis King.
Rosa de Francia (USA), by G. Wiles.
1936 - 1939: **El genio alegre,** by F. Delgado.
1945: **Pepita Jiménez** (Mexico), by E. Fernández.
Me enamoré de una sirena (Mexico), by N. Foster.
1946: **El último amor de Goya** (Mexico), by J. Salvador.

RAFAEL DURAN
1911, Madrid

He begins his artistic career by acting in important theater conpanies. For a time he dubs for Metro-Goldwyn-Mayer. After starring in **La tonta del bote,** he works for a long time as a leading man. He takes part in the production of some of his films.

CREDITS (incomplete)

1935: **Rosario la cortijera,** by L. Artola.
1939: **La tonta del bote,** by G. Delgrás.
1940: **Muñequita,** by R. Quadreny.
1941: **Pimentilla,** by J. López de Valcárcel.
Un marido a precio fijo, by G. Delgrás.
1942: **La condea María,** by G. Delgrás.
1943: **Eloísa está debajo de un almendro,** by R. Gil.
1944: **Ella, él y sus millones,** by J. de Orduña.
El clavo, by R. Gil.
1945: **El destino se disculpa,** by J. L. Sáenz de Heredia.
La vida en un hilo, by E. Neville.
1946: **La pródiga,** by R. Gil.
1947: **La fe,** by R. Gil.
1948: **Tuvo la culpa Adán,** by J. de Orduña.
1950: **Séptima página,** by L. Vajda.
1953: **Jeromín,** by L. Lucía.
1955: **El Piyayo,** by L. Lucía.
1958: **La rebelión de los gladiadores,** by V. Cottafavi.
Una chica de Chicago, by M. Mur-Oti.
1959: **La quiniela,** by A. Mariscal.
1961: **Teresa de Jesús,** by J. de Orduña.
1962: **El valle de las espadas,** by J. Setó.
Bochorno, by J. de Orduña.
1963: **El escándalo,** by J. Setó.
Isidro el labrador, by R. J. Salvia.
1964: **La vida nueva de Pedrito de Andía,** by R. Gil.

F

ROCIO DURCAL

1945, Madrid

Pseudonym of Angeles de las Heras. Discovered by producer Luis Sanz when she was participating in a contest of new singers in TVE and launched in the film **Canción de juventud.** As a singer she tours through Spain and Latin America, especially Mexico. Noteworthy among her theater work is **Un domingo en Nueva York,** directed in 1965 by Adolfo Marsillach. She currently works exclusively as a singer.

CREDITS (incomplete).

1961: **Cancion de juventud,** by L. Lucía.
1962: **Rocío de la Mancha,** by L. Lucía.
1963: **La chica del trébol,** by S. Greco.
1964: **Tengo diecisiete años,** by J. M. Forqué.
1965: **Más bonita que ninguna,** by L. C. Amadori.
1966: **Acompáñame,** by L. C. Amadori.
1967: **Buenos días, condesita,** by L. C. Amadori.
Amor en el aire, by L. C. Amadori.
1968: **Cristina Guzmán,** by L. C. Amadori.
1969: **Las leandras,** by E. Martín.
1971: **La novicia rebelde,** by L. Lucía.
1972: **Marianela,** by A. Fons.
1973: **Díselo con flores,** by P. Grimblat.
1977: **Me siento extraña,** by E. Martín Maqueda.

ARTURO FERNANDEZ

1929, Barcelona

He begins a theater career at twenty. Important among his first plays are **La bruja en zapatillas** and **La herencia,** which was performed with the Rafael Rivelles theater company. Later performed in such plays as Williams' **Sweet Bird of Youth, La tercera palabra** and **Pato a la naranja.** He makes small appearances in films starting in 1951 such as **La trinca del aire** (1951), by R. Torrado and **El beso de Judas** (1954), by R. Gil. In 1957 he begins to do leading film roles.

CREDITS (incomplete)

1955: **Nunca es demasiado tarde,** by J. Coll.
1957: **Rapsodia de sangre,** by A. Isasi.
Distrito quinto, by J. Coll.
1958: **Un vaso de whisky,** by J. Coll.
1960: **María, matrícula de Bilbao,** by L. Vajda.
1961: **Los cuervos,** by J. Coll.
El último verano, by J. Bosch.
La viudita naviera, by L. Marquina.
1962: **Bahía de Palma,** by J. Bosch.
1964: **Jandro,** by J. Coll.
1965: **Currito de la Cruz,** by R. Gil.
1968: **No desearás la mujer de tu prójimo,** by P. Lazaga.
Pecados conyugales, by J. M. Forqué.
1972: **Casa Flora,** by R. Fernández.
1974: **Tocata y fuga de Lolita,** by A. Drove.
1976: **Mauricio, mon amour,** by J. Bosch.
1978: **El hombre que yo quiero,** by J. J. Porto.
1981: **Esperando a papá,** by V. Escrivá.
1983: **Truhanes,** by M. Hermoso.

ANTONIO FERRANDIS

1923, Paterna (Valencia)

He makes his theater debut in 1950 with the Antonio Vico theater company. Later he joins the Rafael Rivelles company as well as those of the Español and María Guerrero theaters in Madrid. In 1972, he definitively leaves the world of theater. He continuously works in the television media and has become very popular in Spain as a result of the series **Verano azul** (Blue Summer; 1982). Among the prizes he has received is that for the best actor in the Karlovy-Vary Festival for **Y el prójimo.** He also did the leading role in **Volver a empezar** which received the Oscar for the best foreign film.

CREDITS (incomplete)

1961: **Plácido,** by L. garcía Berlanga.
1962: **Los derechos de la mujer,** by J. L. Saenz de Heredia.
1963: **El diablo también llora,** by J. A. Nieves Conde.
1964: **Historias de la televisión,** by J. L. Saenz de Heredia.
1965: **Con el viento solano,** by M. Camús.
Posición avanzada, by P. Lazaga.
1966: **Fata Morgana,** by V. Aranda.
1967: **¿Pero en qué país vivimos?,** by J. L. Saenz de Heredia.
1968: **No desearás la mujer de tu prójimo,** by P. Lazaga.
1969: **Tristana,** by L. Buñuel.
1970: **Varietés,** by J. A. Bardem.
1971: **Mi querida señorita,** by J. de Armiñán.
1972: **Las colocadas,** by P. Masó.
1973: **Vida conyugal sana,** by R. Bodegas.
... Y el prójimo, by A. del Pozo.
1974: **El amor del capitán Brando,** by J. de Armiñán.
Los nuevos españoles, by R. Bodegas.
1975: **Leonor,** by J. L. Buñuel.
¡Jo, papá!, by Jaime de Armiñán.
La casa grande, by F. Rodríguez.
1976: **Gusanos de seda,** by F. Rodríguez.
Retrato de familia, by A. Giménez Rico.
El hombre que supo amar, by M. Picazo.
1977: **Vota a Gundisalvo,** by P. Lazaga.
La escopeta nacional, by L. García Berlanga.
Parranda, by G. Suárez.
1978: **Tobi,** by A. Mercero.
1979: **Miedo a salir de noche,** by E. de la Iglesia.
1980: **Dos y dos son cinco,** by J. L. Comerón.
1981: **Profesor eróticus,** by L. M. Delgado.
1982: **Corazón de papel,** by R. Bodegas.
Volver a empezar, by J. L. Garci.
1983: **Vivir mañana,** by N. Quevedo.
1984: **Memorias del General Escobar,** by J. L. Madrid.
1985: **Réquiem por un campesino español,** by F. Betriu.

LOLA FLORES

1925, Jeréz de la Frontera (Cádiz)

From an early age she works as a dancer and Andalusian folk singer in the Manolo Caracol company. Later, she appears in musical reviews. Her first film appearance is in **Martingala** (1939), by F. Mignoni, dancing with Niño de Marchena. Her first leading role is in **Embrujo.** She becomes one of the myths of Spanish folk cinema and works in Mexico, Cuba and Argentina.

CREDITS (incomplete)

1947: **Embrujo,** by C. Serrano de Osma.
1951: **La niña de la venta,** by R. Torrado.
1952: **La estrella de Sierra Morena,** by R. Torrado.
1954: **La danza de los deseos,** by F. Rey.
La hermana Alegría, by L. Lucía.
Morena Clara, by L. Lucía.
1955: **La faraona** (México), by R. Cardona.
1957: **María de la O,** by R. Torrado.
Maricruz (México), by M. Zacarías.
Sueño de oro (México), by M. Zacarías.
1958: **Venta de Vargas,** by E. Cahén Salaberry.
1962: **El balcón de la luna,** by L. Saslavsky.
1967: **Una señora estupenda,** by E. Martín.
1972: **Casa Flora,** by R. Fernández.
1973: **El asesino no está solo,** by J. García Dueñas.
1983: **Truhanes,** by M. Hermoso.

MARUCHI FRESNO

1916, Madrid

She gives up her studies to star in **El agua en el suelo.** During the Spanish Civil War, she gives a series of poetry recitals in Argentina. In Spain she performs in **La leyenda rota,** the first of a long series of films that make her popular during the forties and fifties. She alternates her work in film with theater. Among other works, she performs in Shakespeare's **Romeo and Juliet, Midsummer Night's Dream,** as well as **Mary Stuart.**

CREDITS (incomplete)

1934: **El agua en el suelo,** by E. Fernández Ardavín.
1935: **Vidas rotas,** by E. Fernández Ardavín.
1940: **La leyenda rota,** by C. Fernández Cuenca.
La última falla, by B. Perojo.
1941: **Una conquista difícil,** by P. Puche.
1943: **Dora, la espía,** by R. Matarazzo.
1946: **Mar abierto,** by R. Torrado.
1947: **Reina Santa,** R. Gil.
1948: **El capitán de Loyola,** by J. Díaz Morales.
1950: **Historia de una escalera,** by I. F. Iquino.
Brigada criminal, by I. F. Iquino.
1951: **Catalina de Inglaterra,** by A. Ruiz Castillo.
1952: **La laguna negra,** by A. Ruiz Castillo.
1963: **El camino,** by A. Mariscal.
1968: **Algo amargo en la boca,** by E. de la Iglesia.

TERESA GIMPERA

1936, Igualada (Barcelona)

Discovered by photographer Leopoldo Pomés, she soon becomes a highly paid model. She makes her debut in film with some of the members of the **Barcelona School.** She works a number of times for TVE, directed by J. de Armiñán and N. Ibáñez Serrador. She wins the **Lady Europe** contest in 1969.

CREDITS (incomplete)

1965: **Fata Morgana,** by V. Aranda.
1966: **Una historia de amor,** by J. Grau.
1967: **Novios 68,** by P. Lazaga.
Lucky el intrépido, by J. Franco.
1968: **Tuset Street,** by L. Marquina.
Las secretarias, by P. Lazaga.
1969: **La cena,** by J. Grau.
Las crueles, by V. Aranda.
El extraño caso del Dr. Fausto, by G. Suárez.
1970: **Aoom,** by G. Suárez.
1971: **La novicia rebelde,** by L. Lucía.
1972: **Las petroleras,** by Christian-Jaque.
1973: **El espíritu de la colmena,** by V. Erice.
1976: **La ciutat cremada,** by A. Ribas.
1977: **La guerra de papá,** by A. Mercero.
1978: **Cartas de amor de una monja,** by J. Grau.
1983: **¡Victoria!** by A. Ribas.
1985: **Luces de bohemia,** by M. A. Díez.
Stico, by J. de Armiñán.
1986: **Mambrú se fue a la guerra,** by F. Fernán Gómez.

JOSE LUIS GOMEZ

1940, Huelva

He studied acting in the Westphalia Dramatic Arts Institute in Bochum and in Paris with Jacques Lecoq. Before he worked in his first film, he performs intensely as a theater actor and director in Nuremburg, Munich, Hamburg, Poland, Kiel, Brazil and Spain. Among his prizes, he has received the best actor's award in the Cannes Film Festival for **Pascual Duarte.**

CREDITS

1975: **Pascual Duarte,** by R. Franco.
1976: **Parranda,** by G. Suárez.
In Memoriam, by E. Brasó.
1977: **Nunca es tarde,** by J. de Armiñán.
Sonámbulos, by M. Gutiérrez Aragón.
Las rutas del sur, by J. Losey.
1979: **Los ojos vendados,** by C. Saura.
1980: **Dedicatoria,** by J. Chávarri.

AGUSTIN GONZALEZ

1930, Madrid

He begins his long career in the **Teatro Universitario** (T.E.U.) where in 1953 he obtains his first big success with Alfonso Sastre's play, **Esquadra hacia la muerte.** He has widely and simultaneosly worked in theater, television (in such dramatic series as **El jardín de Venus, Cervantes,** etc.) and film, where he has made more than 120 films at the present time. He received the best actor award in the Karlovy-Vari Film Festival for **Las bicicletas son para el verano.**

CREDITS (incomplete)

1961: **Plácido,** by L. García Berlanga.
1962: **Los que no fuimos a la guerra** (Cuando estalló la paz), by J. Diamante.
1963: **Rififí en la ciudad,** by J. Franco.
El mundo sigue, by F. Fernán Gómez.
1964: **Tiempo de amor,** by J. Diamante.
Llanto por un bandido, by C. Saura.
1965: **La muerte viaja demasiado,** by J. M. Forqué.
Estambul 65, by A. Isasi.
1969: **El mejor del mundo,** by J. Coll.
1971: **Me debes un muerto,** by J. L. Saenz de Heredia.
1976: **Gusanos de seda,** by F. Rodríguez.
Volvereta, by J. A. Nieves Conde.
1978: **El diputado,** by E. de la Iglesia.
Companys, proces a Catalunya, by J. M. Forn.
1979: **Cinco tenedores,** by F. Fernán Gómez.
1980: **Sus sueños dorados,** by E. Martínez. Lázaro.
El nido, by J. de Armiñán.
Gary Cooper que estás en los cielos, by P. Miró.
1981: **Patrimonio nacional,** by L. García Berlanga.
En septiembre, by J. de Armiñán.
1982: **La colmena,** by M. Camús.
Volver a empezar, by J. L. Garci.
Nacional III, by L. García Berlanga.
La próxima estación, by A. Mercero.
1983: **El crack dos,** by J. L. Garci.
Un genio en apuros, by J. L. Comerón.
Las bicicletas son para el verano, by J. Chávarri.
1984: **El caso Almería,** by P. Costa.
Los Santos Inocentes, by M. Camús.
El pico II, by E. de la Iglesia.

JOSITA HERNAN

1919, Mahón (Menorca)

She works in dubbing and makes her debut with the Juan Guerrero Zamora theater company. Since 1931 she does small roles, but she makes a name for herself with her portrayal in **La tonta del bote** (1940). She publishes various books of verse as well as novels. In the mid-fifties she leaves for Paris to study in the Theater Conservatory and in the National Conservatory of Dramatic Art which is directed by R. Ferdinand. Shortly afterwards, she decides to definitively stay in the French capital. She holds the chair of Spanish in the Paris conservatory and directs a theater group.

CREDITS (incomplete)

1940: **La tonta del bote,** by G. Delgrás.
Muñequita, by R. Quadreny.
1941: **El 13.000,** by R. Quadreny.
Pimentilla, by J. López de Valcárcel.
1943: **La chica del gato,** by R. Quadreny.
La niña está loca, by A. Ulloa.
Una chica de opereta, by R. Quadreny.
1944: **Ella, él y sus millones,** by J. de Orduña.
Mi enemigo y yo, by R. Quadreny.
Angela es así, by R. Quadreny.
1945: **Un hombre de negocios,** by L. Lucia.
1946: **Las inquietudes de Shanti-Andía,** by A. Ruiz Castillo.
1947: **Un viaje de novios,** by G. Delgrás.

I

J

398 **JOSE ISBERT**
1886, Madrid. 1966, Madrid

His long artistic career beings in 1902 as an unpaid trainee in Madrid's Apolo Theater. Between 1903 and 1908, he works as an actor in Madrid's Coliseo Imperial. Later he performs as a leading actor in the Infanta Isabel Theater and Lara Theater companies. In 1935, he forms his own theater company. He makes his debut in film in 1912, performing a small role in a short on the assassination of the politician Canalejas. He works in Paramount's Joinville studios making Spanish versions of films. After the Spanish Civil War he begins his true film career. He makes more than a hundred films. He is paid numerous tributes and he obtains a number of awards.

CREDITS (incomplete)

1929: **48 pesetas de taxi,** by F. Delgado.
1935: **Vidas rotas,** by E. Fernández Ardavín.
1936: **El bailarín y el trabajador,** by L. Marquina.
1941: **Alma de Dios,** by I. F. Iquino.
1942: **Aventura,** by J. Mihura.
1943: **Orosia,** by F. Rey.
1944: **La vida empieza a medianoche,** by J. de Orduña.
Ella, él y sus millones, by J. de Orduña.
1945: **Un hombre de negocios,** by L. Lucia.
1948: **El señor Esteve,** by E. Neville.
1950: **El capitán Veneno,** by L. Marquina.
1952: **Bienvenido, Mr. Marshall,** by L. G. Berlanga.
1955: **Historias de la radio,** by J. L. Sáenz de Heredia.
1956: **Calabuch,** by L. G. Berlanga.
1957: **Los jueves, milagro,** by L. G. Berlanga.
1958: **La vida por delante,** by F. Fernán Gómez.
1960: **El cochecito,** by M. Ferreri.
1961: **Los que no fuimos a la guerra,** by J. Diamante.
1963: **El verdugo,** by L. G. Berlanga.

JOSELITO
1946, Jaén

Pseudonym of José Jiménez. He is made famous at ten years of age by Antonio del Amo who directed him in **El pequeño ruiseñor.** Before his film debut, he sings on radio and gives a few recitals with Luis Mariano, who gets him contracts to perform in Paris on radio and television. He makes major tours throughout Latin America, Europe and the Arab world. In the Tenth Children's Film Mostra of Venice, **El ruiseñor de las cumbres** receives various prizes.

CREDITS

1956: **El pequeño ruiseñor,** by A. del Amo.
1957: **Saeta del ruiseñor,** by A. del Amo.
1958: **El ruiseñor de las cumbres,** by del Amo.
1959: **Escucha mi canción,** by A. del Amo.
Aventuras de Joselito en América, by del Amo.
1961: **Los dos golfillos,** by A. del Amo.
Bello recuerdo, by A. del Amo.
El caballo blanco, by R. Baledón.
1963: **El secreto de Tommy,** by A. del Amo.
Loca juventud, by M. Mur-Oti.
1964: **La nueva vida de Pedrito de Andía,** by R. Gil.
1965: **El falso heredero,** by M. Morayta.
1968: **Prisionero de la ciudad,** by A. de Jáen.

L

OSCAR LADOIRE

1955, Madrid

He studies in the School of Informational Sciences. He professionally works with Fernando Trueba. He acts in and helps write the scripts for Trueba's shorts **Oscar y Carlos** (Oscar and Carlos; 1974), **En legítima defensa** (In Self-defense; 1978), **El león enamorado** (The Amorous Lion; 1979) and **Oscar y Carlos 82** (Oscar and Carlos 82; 1982). He also stars in and helps write the screenplays for **Opera prima** (A Cousin in Opera/First Work; 1980) and **Sal gorda** (Coarse Salt/Get Lost, Fatso; 1984). He wins the best actor's prize in the Venice Mostra for **Opera prima.** He has directed the short, **La retención** (The Retention; 1977) and the feature, **A contratiempo** (Offbeat; 1981).

CREDITS

1980: **Opera prima,** by F. Trueba.
1981: **A contratiempo,** by O. Ladoire.
1984: **Sal gorda,** by F. Trueba.
Bajo en nicotina, by R. Artigot.
La noche más hermosa, by M. Gutiérrez Aragón.

ALFREDO LANDA

1933, Pamplona

He studies law in San Sebastián where he helps found the TEU. In 1958, he moves to Madrid where he begins to work in dubbing and theater. He makes his film debut in 1962 and since 1966, he has only worked in this area of the industry. He has made more than 80 films, 70 of which in the leading role. Until 1976, he specializes in comic roles, but this year marks the point when he begins to work in other genres.
The Best Actor's Award in the Cannes Film Festival for **Los santos inocentes.**

CREDITS (incomplete)

1962: **Atraco a las tres,** by J. M. Forqué.
1963: **El verdugo,** by L. G. Berlanga.
La niña de luto, by M. Summers.
1965: **Ninette y un señor de Murcia,** by F. Fernán Gómez.
De cuerpo presente, by A. Eceiza.
1967: **No somos de piedra,** by M. Summers.
1969: **El alma se serena,** by J. L. Sáenz de Heredia.
1970: **No desearás al vecino del quinto,** by R. Fernández.
1971: **Aunque la hormona se vista de seda,** by V. Escrivá.
1972: **París bien vale una moza,** by P. Lazaga.
1974: **Cuando el cuerpo suena,** by L. M. Delgado.
1975: **Los pecados de una chica casi decente,** by M. Ozores.
1976: **El puente,** by J. A. Bardem.
1978: **Las verdes praderas,** by J. L. Garci.
1979: **Paco el seguro,** by D. Haudepin.
1980: **El canto de la cigarra,** by J. M. Forqué.
El poderoso influjo de la luna, by A. del Real.
1981: **El crack,** by J. L. Garci.
1982: **La próxima estación,** by A. Mercero.
1983: **El crack II,** by J. L. Garci.
1984: **Los santos inocentes,** by A. Camus.
La Vaquilla, by L. G. Berlanga.
1985: **Los paraísos perdidos,** by B. M. Patino.

MIGUEL LIGERO

1897, Madrid. 1968, Madrid

He works in theater since he is twelve, both in Spain and in Latin America—principally in Argentina. He first works in film in one of the numbers of **Frivolinas** (1927). In 1930, he is contracted by Paramount to make talkies in Spanish in the Joinvile studios. In 1931, he goes to Hollywood under contract for Fox. Between 1930 and 1936 he assiduously works with Imperio Argentina and they become the most famous Spanish acting team the industry has ever produced.

CREDITS (incomplete)

1930: **Doña Mentiras** (France), by A. Millar.
Salga de la cocina (France), by L. Mercanton.
Hay que casar al príncipe (USA), by L. Seiler.
Eran trece (USA), by D. Howard.
1933: **Susana tiene un secreto,** by B. Perojo.
1934: **El novio de mamá,** by F. Rey.
La hermana San Sulpicio, by F. Rey.
Crisis mundial, by B. Perojo.
1935: **Rumbo a El Cairo,** by B. Perojo.
Nobleza Baturra, by B. Perojo.
La verbena de la Paloma, by B. Perojo.
1936: **Morena Clara,** by F. Rey.
1938: **El barbero de Sevilla** (Germany), by B. Perojo.
1939: **Los hijos de la noche** (Italy), by B. Perojo.
1940: **La última falla** (Italy), by B. Perojo.
1941: **Pepe Conde,** by J. López Rubio.
1945: **La luna vale un millón,** by F. Rey.
1954: **La cruz de mayo,** by F. Rey.
1956: **Polvorilla,** by F. Rey.
1963: **La verbena de la Paloma,** by J. L. Sáenz de Heredia.
1964: **Nobleza baturra,** by J. de Orduña.
1967: **Hamelín,** by L. M. Delgado

CHARO LOPEZ

1943, Salamanca

She studies humanities in Salamanca, where she also works in the TEU. She receives her degree in Madrid and studies acting in the **Official Film School.** She makes her debut as the lead in **Ditirambo.** Noteworthy among her theater performances are **El condenado por desconfiado** and **La marquesa Rolinda,** performed in Madrid's Español Theater and under the direction of Miguel Narros. She works constantly in TVE, working in soaps, dramatic programs and series. Among her best portrayals are those in the works **Aguila de blasón, Bodas de cobre** and **Orestes** and in the series **Entre visillos,** by Miguel Picazo, **Fortunata y Jacinta,** by Mario Camus and **Los gozos y las sombras,** by Moreno Alba.

CREDITS (incomplete)

1967: **Ditirambo,** by G. Suárez.
1968: **El hueso,** by A. Giménez-Rico.
1969: **La vida sigue igual,** by E. Martín.
Me enveneno de azules, by F. Regueiro.
1971: **Pastel de sangre** (episode by E. Martínez-Lázaro).
1973: **La guerrilla,** by R. Gil.
1974: **La regenta,** by G. Suárez.
Largo retorno, by P. Lazaga.
1975: **Manuela,** by G. García-Pelayo.

1977: **Los placeres ocultos,** by E. de la Iglesia.
Parranda, by G. Suárez.
Luto riguroso, by J. R. Larraz.
1982: **Interior rojo,** by E. Anglada.
La colmena, by M. Camus.
1984: **Epílogo,** by G. Suárez.
1985: **La vieja música,** by M. Camus.
Los paraísos perdidos, by B. M. Patino.

JOSE LUIS LOPEZ VAZQUEZ

1922, Madrid

His first jobs in the film industry are as a costume designer and later as an assistant director. He makes his debut as an actor in Madrid's María Guerrero Theater in the Conchita Montes and the Alberto Closas company. Since 1951, he has performed in more than 160 films, the majority in comic roles. Best actor in the Chicago Film Festival for **El bosque del lobo** and **Mi querida señorita.** Noteworthy among his works for TVE is **La cabina** (1972) for Antonio Mercero.

CREDITS (incomplete)

1951: **Esa pareja feliz,** by L. G. Berlanga and J. A. Bardem.
1953: **Novio a la vista,** by L. G. Berlanga.
1954: **Felices pascuas,** by J. A. Bardem.
Un día perdido, by J. M. Forqué.
1957: **Los jueves, milagro,** by L. G. Berlanga.
El inquilino, by J. A. Nieves Conde.
1958: **El pisito,** by M. Ferreri and I. M. Ferry.
1959: **Los tramposos,** by P. Lazaga.
1960: **091, policía al habla,** by J. M. Forqué.
El cochecito, by M. Ferreri.
1961: **Usted puede ser un asesino,** by J. M. Forqué.
Plácido, by L. G. Berlanga.
1962: **Atraco a las tres,** by J. M. Forqué.
1963: **El verdugo,** by L. G. Berlanga.
1965: **La visita que no tocó el timbre,** by M. Camus.
1967: **Peppermint frappé,** by C. Saura.
1969: **¡Vivan los novios!,** by L. G. Berlanga.
1970: **El jardín de las delicias,** by C. Saura.
El bosque del lobo, by P. Olea.
Españolas en París, by R. Bodegas.
1971: **Mi querida señorita,** by J. Armiñán.
1972: **No es bueno que el hombre esté solo,** by P. Olea.
1973: **Habla, mudita** by M. Gutiérrez Aragón.
La prima Angélica, by C. Saura.
1974: **Duerme, duerme, mi amor,** by F. Regueiro.
1975: **La ciutat cremada,** by A. Ribas.
1977: **La escopeta nacional,** by L. G. Berlanga.
1978: **La verdad sobre el caso Savolta,** by A. Drove.
1979: **La miel,** by P. Masó.
1980: **Patrimonio nacional,** by L. G. Berlanga.
1982: **La colmena,** by M. Camus.
Nacional III, by L. G. Berlanga.
1984: **Akelarre,** by P. Olea.
La vaquilla, by L. G. Berlanga.
1985: **La corte de faraón,** by J. L. García Sánchez.

M

MANUEL LUNA

1898, Seville. 1958, Madrid

From fourteen he works in theater as an amateur and makes his debut in film in 1915 as a professional. He acts in a few silent films, but his first great success is **Nobleza baturra.** He performs in about 70 films, the majority of which he plays the villain.

CREDITS (incomplete)

1935: **Nobleza baturra,** by F. Rey.
1936: **El cura de aldea,** by F. Camacho.
Morena Clara, by F. Rey.
1938: **Carmen la de Triana,** by F. Rey.
1939: **La canción de Aixa,** by F. Rey.
La Dolores, by F. Rey.
1941: **Torbellino,** by L. Marquina
1942: **¡A mí la Legión!,** by J. de Orduña.
1943: **El escándalo,** by J. L. Sáenz de Heredia.
1945: **Misión blanca,** by J. de Orduña.
1946: **El crimen de la calle de Bordadores,** by E. Neville.
Abel Sánchez, by C. Serrano de Osma.
1947: **La nao capitana,** by F. Rey.
Fuenteovejuna, by J. de Orduña.
1948: **Locura de amor,** by J. de Orduña.
1950: **Agustina de Aragón,** by J. de Orduña.
1951: **La Leona de Castilla,** by J. de Orduña.
Lola la piconera, by L. Lucia.
1954: **La hermana Alegría,** by L. Lucia.
1957: **María de la O,** by R. Torrado.

MARISOL

1948, Málaga

Pseudonym of Josefa Flores. Discovered by producer Manuel J. Goyanes during a performance on TVE. She is immensely successful in Spain and Latin America, becoming one of the most important child stars in the sixties. She has cut over a dozen records. In 1973, she makes her debut in theater with **Stay for Breakfast** by Cooney and Stone. During the seventies she tries to change her image but is unsuccessful. Currently she makes small appearances in films by Saura.

CREDITS

1960: **Un rayo de luz,** by L. Lucia.
1961: **Ha llegado un ángel,** by L. Lucia.
1962: **Tómbola,** by L. Lucia.
1963: **Marisol rumbo a Río,** by F. Palacios.
1964: **La nueva Cenicienta,** by G. Sherman.
La historia de Bienvenido, by A. Fenollar.
Búsqueme a esa chica, by F. Palacios.
1965: **Cabriola,** by Mel Ferrer.
1967: **Las cuatro bodas de Marisol,** by L. Lucia.
1968: **Solos los dos,** by L. Lucia.
1969: **Carola de día, Carola de noche,** by J. de Armiñán.
El taxi de los conflictos, by J. L. Sáenz de Heredia.
1972: **La corrupción de Chris Miller,** by J. A. Bardem.
1973: **La chica del Molino Rojo,** by E. Martín.
1975: **El poder del deseo,** by J. A. Bardem.
1976: **Los días del pasado,** by M. Camus.
1981: **Bodas de sangre,** by C. Saura.
1983: **Carmen,** by C. Saura.
1985: **Caso cerrado,** by J. Caño.

ADOLFO MARSILLACH

1928. Barcelona

Receives a law degree from the University of Barcelona. At age eighteen he begins to do work at the TEU theater in Barcelona and shortly afterwards, makes his debut as a professional. In 1947, he begins to work in film, along with theater and television. He has acted in and directed a great number of theater pieces including Peter Weiss' **Marat-Sade,** Molière's **Tartuffe** and **Socrates.** In 1956, he forms his own theater company for the first time. He has directed Madrid's Español Theater and in 1978, he is named director of the **National Drama Center.** He has appeared on TVE many times and his most important performances include **Silencio, vivimos, Silencio, se rueda, Habitación 508**, and **La señora García se confiesa.** He directs and acts in the film, **Flor de santidad** (Flower of Saintliness). Lately, he has acted in the TVE series **Ramón y Cajal** (1981) directed by J. M. Forqué.

CREDITS (incomplete)

1947: **Mariona Rebull,** by J. L. Sáenz. de Heredia.
1952: **Cerca de la ciudad,** by L. Lucía.
1953: **Jeromín,** by L. Lucia.
1956: **El frente infinito,** by P. Lazaga.
La cárcel de cristal, by J. Coll.
Torrepartida, by P. Lazaga.
1958: **Un hecho violento,** by J. M. Forqué.
1959: **Salto a la gloria,** by L. Klimovsky.
1960: **Maribel y la extraña familia,** by J. M. Forqué.
Mi calle, by E. Neville.
1961: **El secreto de Mónica,** by J. M. Forqué.
1963: **El tulipán negro,** by Christian-Jaque.
1966: **Las salvajes en Puente San Gil,** by A. Ribas.
Una historia de amor, by J. Grau.
1972: **Flor de santidad,** by A. Marsillach.
1974: **La regenta,** by G. Suárez.
1975: **La ciutat cremada,** by A. Ribas.
1978: **Al servicio de la mujer española,** by J. de Armiñán.
1980: **El poderoso influjo de la luna,** by A. del Real.
1984: **Sesión continua,** by J. L. Garci.
La vaquilla, by L. G. Berlanga.

FRANCISCO MARTINEZ SORIA

1904, Tarazona (Zaragoza). 1982, Madrid

He works in amateur theater groups until he becomes a professional in the thirties. In 1940, he successfully forms his own company. Since 1934, he has worked both in theater and film and he is one of the most popular actors in both areas.

CREDITS (incomplete)

1934: **El crimen del expreso de Andalucía,** by I. F. Iquino.
1935: **Error judicial,** by J. Faidella.
1938: **Paquete, el fotógrafo público número 1,** by I. F. Iquino.
1942: **Boda accidental,** by I. F. Iquino.
1943: **Deliciosamente tontos,** by J. de Orduña.
Viviendo al revés, by I. F. Iquino.
1951: **Almas en peligro,** by A. Santillán.
1953: **Fantasía española,** by J. Setó.
1955: **El difunto es un vivo,** by I. F. Iquino.
1957: **Su desconsolada esposa,** by M. Iglesias.
1965: **La ciudad no es para mí,** by P. Lazaga.
1966: **¿Qué hacemos con los hijos?,** by P. Lazaga.
1967: **El turismo es un gran invento,** by P. Lazaga.
1968: **Abuelo made in Spain,** by P. Lazaga.
Se armó el belén, by P. Lazaga.
1970: **Hay que educar a papá** by P. Lazaga.

1971: **El padre de la criatura,** by P. Lazaga.
1972: **El abuelo tiene un plan,** by P. Lazaga.
1975: **El alegre divorciado,** by P. Lazaga.
1977: **Vaya par de gemelos,** by P. Lazaga.
1980: **Es peligroso casarse a los sesenta,** by M. Ozores.
1981: **La tía de Carlos,** by L. M. Delgado.

ALFREDO MAYO

1911, Barcelona
1984, Palma de Mallorca

He makes his debut as an actor in the Ernesto Vilches company and acts in his first film, **El 113,** by R. J. Salvia, in 1935. During the Spanish Civil War he is an officer in the rebel air force. Since 1940, he has worked in a large number of films, at first as a leading man, but after 1965, he changes the type of roles he portrays. He has acted in more than 200 films. He also works in TVE.

CREDITS (incomplete)

1940: **La florista de la reina,** by E. Fernández Ardavín.
1941: **Harka,** by C. Arévalo.
Escuadrilla, by A. Román.
Raza, by J. L. Sáenz de Heredia.
1942: **¡A mí la Legión!** by J. de Orduña.
Malvaloca, by L. Marquina.
1943: **El abanderado** by E. Fernández Ardavín.
1946: **Audiencia pública,** by F. Rey.
1949: **El santuario no se rinde,** by A. Ruiz Castillo.
1951: **La Leona de Castilla,** by J. de Orduña.
1954: **Alta costura,** by L. Marquina.
1957: **El último cuplé,** by J. de Orduña.
1958: **Quince bajo la lona,** by A. Navarro.
1960: **La reina del Tabarín,** by J. Franco.
1964: **Sangre en Indochina,** by P. Schoendorffer.
1965: **La caza,** by C. Saura.
1967: **Peppermint frappé,** by C. Saura.
1970: **El bosque del lobo,** by P. Olea.
1972: **Marianela,** by A. Fons.
1973: **La letra escarlata,** by W. Wenders.
La campana del infierno, by C. Guerín.
Vera, un cuento cruel, by J. Molina.
1977: **Raza, el espíritu de Franco,** by G. Herralde.
1978: **Los restos del naufragio,** by R. Franco.
1980: **Patrimonio Nacional,** by L. G. Berlanga.
1982: **Cecilia,** by H. Solas.
Hablamos esta noche, by P. Miró.

JORGE MISTRAL

1920, Aldaya (Valencia).
1972, México D. F.

Pseudonym of Modesto Llosas. He begins to work as an actor in the Enrique Borrás, Ana Adamuz and Josita Hernán companies. He does his first leading role in a film in 1944 and soon becomes one of Spain's most coveted young stars. He is given an exclusive contract by Cifesa. In 1949 he marries, breaks the contract and moves to Mexico. From that time he works in Mexico, Cuba and in Spain. During his last years, he directs a film in Puerto Rico.

CREDITS (incomplete)

1944: **La llamada del mar,** by J. Gaspar.
1945: **Misión blanca,** by J. de Orduña.
1946: **Mar abierta,** by R. Torrado.
La nao capitana, by F. Rey.
1947: **La dama del armiño,** by E. Fernández Ardavín.
Botón de ancla, by R. Torrado.
1948: **Locura de amor,** by J. de Orduña.
Currito de la Cruz, by L. Lucia.
1949: **La duquesa de Benamejí,** by L. Lucia.
1950: **Pequeñeces,** by J. de Orduña.
1951: **El mar y tú** (México), by E. Fernández.
1952: **La hermana San Sulpicio,** by L. Lucia.
1953: **Reportaje** (México), by E. Fernández.
Abismos de pasión (México), by L. Buñuel.
1954: **Un caballero andaluz,** by L. Lucia.
1955: **La legión del silencio,** by J. A. Nieves Conde.
1957: **La sirena y el delfín** (Italy) (Boy on a Dolphin), by J. Negulesco.
La venganza, by J. A. Bardem.
1959: **Carmen la de Ronda,** by T. Demichelli.
1962: **Scherezade,** by P. Gaspard-Huit.
1963: **Los pistoleros de Casa Grande,** by R. Rowland.

ANGELA MOLINA

1956, Madrid

Daughter of singer and actor Antonio Molina, and elder sister of actress Paula and actor Miguel. She studies classical ballet, flamenco and Spanish dance and obtains a degree in ballet at sixteen. She studies dramatic art in Madrid's Higher School of Dramatic Arts. She is discovered thanks to magazine reports published in 1973. For a time she works in France with **Le Grand Magic Circus.** She normally makes films in Italy, France, West Germany and Spain.

CREDITS

1974: **No matarás,** by C. Fernández Ardavín.
No quiero perder la honra, by E. Martín.
Las protegidas, by F. Lara Polop.
1975: **La ciutat cremada,** by A. Ribas.
Las largas vacaciones del 36, by J. Camino.
1976: **El hombre que supo amar,** by M. Picazo.
Camada negra, by M. Gutiérrez Aragón.
Viva/Muera Don Juan, by T. Aznar.
1977: **Nunca es tarde,** by J. de Armiñán.
Ese oscuro objeto del deseo, by L. Buñuel.
A un Dios desconocido, by J. Chávarri.

La portentosa historia del padre Vicente, by C. Mira.

1978: **Los restos del naufragio,** by R. Franco.
El gran atasco, by L. Comencini.
El corazón del bosque, by M. Gutiérrez Aragón.
Operación Ogro, by G. Pontecorvo.

1979: **Buone notizie** (Italy), by E. Petri.
La sabina, by J. L. Boráu.

1980: **Marginado** (Kaltgestellt) (West Germany), by B. Sinkel.
Arrivano i bersagieri (Italy), by L. Magni.

1982: **Gli occhi, la bocca** (Italy), by M. Bellocchio.
Demonios en el jardín, by M. Gutiérrez Aragón.

1983: **Bearn o la sala de las muñecas,** by J. Chávarri.

1984: **Fuego eterno,** by J. A. Rebolledo.

1985: **Camorra,** by L. Wertmüller.
Lola, by J. J. Bigas Luna.
Coupe fourre, by G. Verga.
El río de oro, by J. Chávarri.

CONCHITA MONTENEGRO
1912, San Sebastián

She studies in the School of Dance in the Opera Theater in Paris. In 1927, she begins her film career in Spain. In 1929, she works in France and between 1930 and 1934 in the United States, under contract for Metro-Goldwyn-Mayer. Later, she returns to shoot in France and Italy. Her last films are made in Spain between 1942 and 1944. She gives up her film career when she gets married.

CREDITS (incomplete)

1927: **La muñeca rota,** by R. Blothner.
Rosa de Madrid, by E. Fernández Ardavín.

1929: **La femme et le pantin** (France), by J. de Baroncelli.

1930: **De frente... imarchen!** (USA), by E. Sedgwick.
Sevilla de mis amores (USA), by R. Novarro.

1931: **Besos al pasar** (USA), by G. Fitzmaurice (Strangers May Kiss).
Prohibido (USA), by W. S. Van Dyke (Never the Twain Shall Meet).

1932: **Audaz y galante** (USA), by A. L. Werker (The Gay Caballero).

1935: **Noches de París** (France), by R. Siodmak (La vie parisienne).
Luces de París (France), by R. Pottier (Lumières de Paris).

1939: **L'or du Cristobal** (France), by J. Becker and J. Stelli.

1940: **El último húsar** (Italy), by. L. Marquina.
Melodías eternas (Italy), by C. Gallone (Melodie eterne).

1941: **Rojo y negro,** by C. Arévalo.

1942: **Boda en el infierno,** by A. Román.
Aventura, by J. Mihura.

1943: **Idolos,** by F. Rey.

1944: **Lola Montes,** by A. Román.

CONCHITA MONTES

1914, Madrid

Pseudonym of Concepción Carro. Receives a degree in law and works as a translator and adaptator of comedies by foreign authors. From her first films in 1939, she combines her film activities with theater. Very close to director and author Edgar Neville for years, she works with him until his death.

CREDITS (incomplete)

1939: **Frente de Madrid** (Italy), by E. Neville.
1941: **La muchacha de Moscú** (Italy), by E. Neville.
1942: **Correo de Indias,** by E. Neville.
1943: **Misterio en la marina,** by C. de la Torre.
Café de París, by E. Neville.
1945: **La vida en un hilo,** by E. Neville.
Domingo de carnaval, by E. Neville.
1947: **Nada,** by E. Neville.
1948: **El marqués de Salamanca,** by E. Neville.
1949: **Mi adorado Juan,** by J. Mihura.
1950: **El último caballo,** by E. Neville.
1951: **Cuento de hadas,** by E. Neville.
1959: **El baile,** by E. Neville.
1960: **Mi calle,** by E. Neville.
1962: **55 días en Pekín,** by N. Ray (55 Days at Peking).
1969: **Solos los dos,** by L. Lucia.
1981: **Un pasota con corbata,** by J. Terrón.

SARA MONTIEL

1928, Campo de Criptana (Ciudad Real)

Pseudonym of Antonia Abad. Discovered by the producer Vicente Casanova, she makes her debut in a small role in **Te quiero para mí** (1944) by L. Vajda with the artistic name María Alexandra. In 1950, she leaves for Mexico to work in film, theater and television shows. She makes three films in the United States. Returning to Spain in 1957, she becomes one of the most popular singers and actresses of the sixties. During the last few years she has only put together theatrical musicals.

CREDITS (incomplete)

1945: **Bambú,** by J. L. Sáenz de Heredia.
1947: **Mariona Rebull,** by J. L. Sáenz de Heredia.
Don Quijote de la Mancha, by R. Gil.
1948: **Locura de amor,** by J. de Orduña.
La mies es mucha, by J. L. Sáenz de Heredia.
1950: **El capitán veneno,** by L. Marquina.
Pequeñeces, by J. de Orduña.
1953: **Reportaje** (México), by E. Fernández.
1954: **Veracruz** (USA), by R. Aldrich.
1955: **Dos pasiones y un amor** (Serenade) (USA), by A. Mann.
1957: **Yuma** (Run of the Arrow) (USA), by S. Fuller.
El último cuplé, by J. de Orduña.
1958: **La violetera,** by L. C. Amadori.
1960: **Mi último tango,** by L. C. Amadori.
1961: **Pecado de amor,** by L. C. Amadori
1962: **La reina del Chantecler,** by R. Gil.
1963: **Samba,** by R. Gil.
Noches de Casablanca, by H. Decoin.
1965: **La dama de Beirut,** by L. Vajda.
1968: **Tuset street,** by L. Marquina.
1969: **Esa mujer,** by M. Camus.
1971: **Varietés,** by J. A. Bardem.
1973: **Cinco almohadas para una noche,** by P. Lazaga.

N

408 PAUL NASCHY

1938, Madrid

Pseudonym of Jacinto Molina, who only uses the name as an actor. Student of architecture, champion Spanish weight-lifter and the author of a few stories and novels. He begins in film as a script (boy) and assistant director to Lazaga and Mur-Oti. As an actor he begins as an extra, later he does small roles in detective films and westerns, and starting in 1968, specializes in fantasy, horror and suspense films. He writes scripts, directs and portrays the key characters in the genre: the wolfman, Jack the Ripper, Mr. Hyde, the mummy, etc. The producer of some of his films, he has also directed, written and starred in his films since 1976. He receives a special mention for all of his work in the Sitges Film Festival in 1971. He wins the Georges Méliès acting prize in the French Convention of Fantastic Films in Paris for **El jorobado de la morgue** (The Hunchback of the Morgue). In 1974 he is named the most popular Spanish-speaking actor in New York.

CREDITS

As an actor (incomplete)

1968: **La marca del hombre lobo,** by E. L. Eguiluz.
1970: **El vértigo del crimen,** by P. Cervera.
La noche de Walpurgis, by L. Klimovsky.
1971: **Jack, el destripador de Londres,** by J. L. Madrid.
El doctor Jekyll y el hombre lobo, by L. Klimovsky.
1972: **La orgía de los muertos,** by J. L. Merino.
El gran amor del conde Drácula, by J. Aguirre.
El jorobado de la morgue, by J. Aguirre.
1973: **El retorno de Walpurgirs,** by C. Aured.
1974: **Exorcismo,** by J. Bosch.
1975: **La maldición de la bestia,** by M. Iglesias.
1976: **Inquisición,** by J. Molina.
1977: **El huerto del francés,** by J. Molina.
1978: **El caminante,** by J. Molina.
1980: **El retorno del hombre lobo,** by J. Molina.
1981: **La batalla del porro,** by J. Minguell.
1982: **Buenas noches, señor monstruo,** by A. Mercero.
1983: **La bestia y la espada mágica,** by J. Molina.

As a director

1976: **Inquisición** (Inquisition).
1977: **El huerto del francés** (The Frenchman's Garden).
1978: **Madrid al desnudo** (Madrid Uncovered).
El caminante (The Walker).
1979: **Los cántabros** (The Cantabrians).
1980: **El retorno del hombre lobo** (The Return of the Wolfman).
El carnaval de las bestias (Cannibal Feast).
1983: **La bestia y la espada mágica** (The Beast and the Magic Sword).
Latidos de pánico (Heart Beats of Panic).
1984: **Mi amigo el vagabundo** (My Friend the Vagabond).
El último kamikaze (The Last Kamikaze).
Operación Mantis (Operation Mantis).

JOSE LUIS OZORES
1923, Madrid. 1968, Madrid.

Son of actor Mariano Ozores and Luisa Puchol, brother of the film director Mariano and actor Antonio. He gives up his studies to join his parents' theater company. Later he joins the María Guerrero theater company in Madrid. Since 1950, he works extensively in comic film roles. He becomes extremely popular after his role in **Recluta con niño.** Incapacitated since 1963 due to a grave illness, during the last years of his life he paints and writes poetry. Even so, he does not totally give up acting, since he does perform in a few roles and presents a weekly spot for TVE for a time. He even plays the lead in a theater production called **El poder,** by Calvo Sotelo from a wheel chair.

CREDITS (incomplete)

1950: **El último caballo,** by E. Neville.
1951: **Esa pareja feliz,** by J. A. Bardem and L. G. Berlanga.
1953: **El diablo toca la flauta,** by J. M. Forqué.
1955: **Historias de la radio,** by J. L. Sáenz de Heredia.
Recluta con niño, by P. L. Ramírez.
1956: **Calabuch,** by L. G. Berlanga.
La gran mentira, by R. Gil.
Los ladrones somos gente honrada, by P. L. Ramírez.
1957: **Los ángeles del volante,** by I. F. Iquino.
El fotogénico, by P. Lazaga.
El tigre de Chamberí, by P. Lazaga.
El aprendiz de malo, by P. Lazaga.
1958: **El gafe,** by P. L. Ramírez.
1959: **Un ángel tuvo la culpa,** by L. Lucia.
Ahí va otro recluta, by R. Fernández.
1962: **Suspendido en sirvengüenza,** by M. Ozores.
1965: **Hoy como ayer,** by M. Ozores.

VICENTE PARRA
1931, Valencia

He makes his debut in film as an extra in the Luis Prendes theater company. Since 1949, he works both in theater and film. He becomes extremely popular at the end of the fifties when he portrays King Alfonso XII both on the screen and on the stage.

CREDITS (incomplete)

1950: **Debla, la virgen gitana,** by R. Torrado.
1953: **El pescador de coplas,** by A. del Amo.
1954: **La patrulla,** by P. Lazaga.
1956: **Fedra,** by M. Mur-Oti.
El expreso de Andalucía, by F. Rovira Beleta.
El batallón de las sombras, by M. Mur-Oti.
1957: **Rapsodia de sangre,** by A. Isasi.
1958: **¿Dónde vas, Alfonso XII?,** by L. C. Amadori.
1959: **Un mundo para mí,** by J. A. de la Loma.
¿Dónde vas, triste de tí?, by A. Balcázar.
1963: **La verbena de la Paloma,** by J. L. Sáenz de Heredia.
1964: **Nobleza baturra,** by J. de Orduña.
1966: **Buenos días, condesita,** by L. C. Amadori.
1971: **Varietés,** by J. A. Bardem.
1972: **Nadie oyó gritar,** by E. de la Iglesia.

1976: **Las largas vacaciones del 36,** by J. Camino.
La siesta, by J. Grau.
Nosotros que fuimos tan felices, by A. Drove.
1977: **La guerra de papá,** by A. Mercero.
El último guateque, by J. J. Porto.
1981: **La leyenda del tambor,** by J. Grau.

EMMA PENELLA
1931, Madrid

She makes her debut in Madrid's María Guerrero Theater and later in **La duquesa de Benamejí** on the screen. Her first important role in film is in **Barco sin rumbo.** In **La cuarta ventana,** she acts for the only time along with her sisters, Elisa Montés and Terele Pávez. After her marraige with the producer Emiliano Piedra, she only acts in his productions. She also works in TVE.

CREDITS (incomplete)

1949: **La duquesa de Benamejí,** by L. Lucia.
1951: **Barco sin rumbo,** by J. M. Elorrieta.
1952: **Los ojos dejan huellas,** by J. L. Sáenz de Heredia.
1953: **Carne de horca,** by L. Vajda.
Cómicos, by J. A. Bardem.
1956: **Fedra,** by M. Mur-Oti.
Un marido de ida y vuelta by L. Lucia.
1959: **De espaldas a la puerta,** by J. M. Forqué.
1961: **La cuarta ventana,** by J. Coll.
1963: **El verdugo,** by L. G. Berlanga.
1966: **Lola, espejo oscuro,** by F. Merino.
La busca, by A. Fons.
1969: **Fortunata y Jacinta,** by A. Fons.
1971: **La primera entrega,** by A. Fons.
1974: **La regenta,** by G. Suárez.
1985: **Padre nuestro,** by F. Regueiro.

EUSEBIO PONCELA
1947, Madrid

He studies in the **School of Dramatic Art.** He makes his debut with García Lorca's **Mariana Pineda.** Noteworthy among his theater works are Peter Weiss' **Marat-Sade,** Shakespeare's **Romeo and Juliet** and Arrabal's **El cementerio de automóviles.** Among other works, he has performed in the following dramatic programs for TVE: **The Robbers,** by Schiller; **Doña Luz,** by Valera; **Look Back in Rage,** by Osborne; **The Magic Mountain,** by Mann, and the series **Los gozos y las sombras,** by Torrente Ballester.

CREDITS (incomplete)

1971: **Pastel de sangre** (episode by E. Martínez-Lázaro).
La semana del asesino, by E. de la Iglesia.
Separación matrimonial, by A. Fons.
1974: **La larga noche de julio,** by L. J. Camerón.
1975: **La muerte del escorpión,** by G. Herralde.
1977: **In memoriam,** by E. Brasó.
1979: **Operación Ogro,** by G. Pontecorvo.
Arrebato, by I. Zulueta.
1982: **Entre paréntesis,** by S. Fabregas.
1983: **El arreglo,** by J. A. Zorrilla.

R

FRANCISCO RABAL

1926, Aguilas (Murcia).

He moves to Madrid in 1936 and begins to work as an electrician at the Chamartín Studios. Shortly afterwards, he begins to do small roles in the films that are shot there. He begins to work in the Luis Escobar theater company in the Infanta Isabel and María Guerrero Theaters and the José Tamayo company in the Lope de Vega Theater, all of which are in Madrid. In 1950, he makes his first films as a leading actor and since then he has worked in different countries with important directors. Among the programs he has made for TVE, the most important is the series **Cristóbal Colón** (1967), by Vittorio Cottafavi. He directs four shorts, the most noteworthy of which is **Rafael Alberti en Italia y en España.** The Best Actor's Award in the Cannes Film Festival for **Los santos inocentes.**

CREDITS (incomplete)

1950: **Luna de sangre,** by F. Rovira Beleta.
La honradez de la cerradura, by L. Escobar.
1953: **La guerra de Dios,** by R. Gil.
1954: **El beso de Judas,** by R. Gil.
Murió hace 15 años, by R. Gil.
Todo es posible en Granada, by J. L. Sáenz de Heredia.
1955: **Historias de la radio,** by J. L. Sáenz de Heredia.
1957: **Amanecer en Puerta Oscura,** by J. M. Forqué.
Prisionero del mar (Italy), by G. Pontecorvo (La lunda strada azzurra).
1958: **Nazarín** (México), by L. Buñuel.
1959: **Sonatas,** by J. A. Bardem.
1960: **A las 5 de la tarde,** by J. A. Bardem.
La mano en la trampa (Argentina), by L. Torre-Nilsson.
1961: **Viridiana,** by L. Buñuel.
El eclipse (Italy), by M. Antonioni (L'eclisse).
1962: **Noche de verano,** by J. Grau.
Setenta veces siete (Argentina), by L. Torre-Nilsson.
1963: **Llanto por un bandido,** by C. Saura.
1965: **La religiosa** (France), by J. Rivette (La religieuse).
Belle de Jour (France), by L. Buñuel.
1967: **Oscuros sueños de agosto,** by M. Picazo.
1970: **Cabezas cortadas,** by G. Rocha.
1974: **Tormento,** by P. Olea.
1975: **las bodas de Blanca,** by F. Regueiro.
1976: **Las largas vacaciones del 36,** by J. Camino.
1977: **Carga maldita** (USA), by W. Friedkin (Sorcerer).
1981: **Renacer** (USA), by Bigas Luna (Reborn).
1982: **La colmena,** by M. Camus.
1983: **Truhanes,** by M. Hermoso.
1984: **Sal gorda,** by F. Trueba.
Epílogo, by G. Suárez.
Los santos inocentes, by M. Camus.
Los zancos, by C. Saura.
1985: **Padre nuestro,** by F. Regueiro.
Los paraísos perdidos, by B. M. Patino.
Luces de bohemia, by M. A. Díez.
Camorra, by L. Wertmüller.
La hora bruja, by J. de Armiñán.
Tiempo de silencio, by V. Aranda.

412 FERNANDO REY

1917, La Coruña

Pseudonym of Fernando Casado. Son of a republican soldier. The Spanish Civil War interrupts his studies in architecture. He begins to work as a film extra in order to get by. He does a few small roles in Madrid's Español theater company and dubs films. His acting career begins with **Eugenia de Montijo** (1944), by J. López Rubio. He has worked in more than a hundred films and has made television shows in Spain, France, West Germany and Italy. Among the awards he has received is the best actor prize from the Cannes Film Festival for **Elisa, vida mía** and in the San Sebastián Film Festival for **La duda.**

CREDITS (incomplete)

1945: **Los últimos de Filipinas,** by A. Román.
1946: **La pródiga,** by R. Gil.
1947: **Don Quijote de la Mancha,** by R. Gil.
1948: **Locura de amor,** by J. de Orduña.
1950: **Agustina de Aragón,** by J. de Orduña.
1951: **Esa pareja feliz,** by J. A. Bardem and L. G. Berlanga.
1954: **Cómicos,** by J. A. Bardem.
Marcelino, pan y vino, by L. Vajda.
1957: **Un marido de ida y vuelta,** by L. Lucia.
Les bijoutiers au clair de lune (France), by R. Vadim.
1958: **La venganza,** by J. A. Bardem.
1959: **Sonatas,** by J. A. Bardem.
1961: **Viridiana,** by L. Buñuel.
1965: **Campanadas a medianoche,** by O. Welles (Falstaff).
1970: **Tristana,** by L. Buñuel.
1971: **Contra el imperio de la droga** (USA), by W. Friedkin (French Connection).
1972: **Blanco rojo y...,** by A. Lattuada (Bianco, rosso, e...)
La duda, by R. Gil.
El discreto encanto de la burguesía (France), by L. Buñuel (Le charme discret de la bourgeoisie).
1973: **Pena de muerte,** by J. Grau.
1975: **La gran burguesía** (Italy), by M. Bolognini (Fatte di gente bene).
Sietebellezas (Italy), by L. Wertmuller (Pasqualino settebellezze).
Excelentísimos cadáveres (Italy), by F. Rosi (Cadaveri eccellenti).
1976: **Nina** (USA), by V. Minnelli (A Matter of Time).
Il deserto dei tartari (Italy), by V. Zurlini.
1977: **Elisa, vida mía,** by C. Saura.
Ese oscuro objeto del deseo, by L. Buñuel.
1979: **Quinteto** (USA), by R. Altman (Quintet).
El crimen de Cuenca, by P. Miró.
1983: **Bearn o la sala de las muñecas,** by J. Chávarri.
1985: **Padre nuestro,** by F. Regueiro.
El caballero del dragón, by F. Colomo.

PAQUITA RICO
1929, Seville

At a very early age she works as a dancer performing Spanish ballet. She is discovered by F. Rey when he is looking for the lead for **Brindis a Manolete** (1948). A short time later, she becomes a very popular actress and performs in comedies, short comedies and dramas. She works both in film and on the stage.

CREDITS (incomplete)

1948: **¡Olé torero!,** by B. Perojo.
1949: **Rumbo,** by R. Torrado.
1950: **Luna de sangre,** by F. Rovira Beleta.
Debla, la virgen gitana, by R. Torrado.
1951: **María Morena,** by J. M. Forqué and P. Lazaga.
1953: **El duende de Jerez,** by D. Mangrané.
1955: **Suspiros de Triana,** by R. Torrado.
1957: **Las lavanderas de Portugal** (France), by P. Gaspard-Huit (Les lavandiéres du Portugal).
1958: **¿Dónde vas, Alfonso XII?,** by L. C. Amadori.
1961: **La viudita naviera,** by L. Marquina.
Historia de una noche, by L. Saslavsky.
1962: **El balcón de la luna,** by L. Saslavsky.
1963: **Los otoñales,** by M. Girolami.

AMPARO RIVELLES
1925, Madrid

Daughter of actor Rafael Rivelles and actress María Fernanda Ladrón de Guevara, she starts to perform roles at an early age in her mother's theater company. She makes her film debut at age sixteen in **Mari Juana** (1940), by A. Vidal. Later, she performs in a long list of films produced by Cifesa which makes her one of the most important actresses of the forties. Since 1957, she has worked and lived in Mexico, where, among other activities, she plays in a television soap opera lasting 400 programs and performs in a number of theater tours. She later returns to Spain, and among her important appearances is the theater piece, **The Human Voice,** by Cocteau, and the TVE series, **Los gozos y las sombras** (1981).

CREDITS (incomplete).

1941: **Los ladrones somos gente honrada,** by I. F. Iquino.
1942: **Malvaloca,** by L. Marquina.
1943: **Deliciosamente tontos,** by J. de Orduña.
Eloísa está debajo de un almendro, by R. Gil.
1944: **el clavo,** by R. Gil.
Eugenia de Montijo, by J. López Rubio.
1947: **La fe,** by R. Gil.
Fuenteovejuna, by A. Román.
1948: **La calle sin sol,** by R. Gil.
1949: **La duquesa de Benamejí,** by L. Lucia.
1950: **De mujer a mujer,** by L. Lucia.
1951: **La Leona de Castilla,** by J. de Orduña.
Alba de América, by J. de Orduña.
1955: **Mr. Arkadin,** by O. Welles.
1956: **El batallón de las sombras:** by M. Mur-Oti.
1959: **Un ángel tuvo la culpa,** by L. Lucia.
1974: **Presagio** (Mexico), by L. Alcoriza.
La madrastra (Mexico), by R. Gavaldón.
1977: **La coquito,** by P. Masó.
1983: **Soldados de plomo,** by J. Sacristán.

RAFAEL RIVELLES

1898, El Cabañal (Valencia). 1972

He gives up his studies at fifteen in order to work in theater. It does not take him long to form his own company and he tours through Spain and Latin America. He makes his film debut in a small role in **Prueba trágica** (1914), by J. de Togores. In 1930, he goes to Hollywood to work in Spanish-speaking films, contracted by Metro-Goldwyn-Mayer and Fox. Since 1940, he works both in theater and film, doing character roles.

CREDITS (incomplete)

1929: **El embrujo de Sevilla** (Germany), by B. Perojo.
1930: **La mujer X** (USA), by C. F. Borcosque.
El proceso de Mary Dugan (USA), by M. Desano.
1931: **¿Conoces a tu mujer?** (USA), by L. Seiler.
Mamá (USA), by B. Perojo.
Niebla (USA), by B. Perojo.
1932: **El hombre que se reía del amor,** by B. Perojo.
1936: **Nuestra Natacha,** by B. Perojo.
1938: **Carmen, la de Triana** (Germany), by F. Rey.
1939: **Frente de Madrid** (Italy), by E. Neville.
1942: **Goyescas,** by B. Perojo.
1943: **Lecciones de buen amor,** by R. Gil.
1947: **Don Quijote de la Mancha,** by R. Gil.
1954: **El beso de Judas,** by R. Gil.
Murió hace quince años, by R. Gil.
1955: **Marcelino, pan y vino,** by L. Vajda.
1960: **La rebelión de los esclavos,** by N. Malasomma.
1963: **Cyrano y D'Artagnan,** by A. Gance.

JOSE SACRISTAN

1937, Chinchón (Madrid)

He works in independent theater until he makes his debut as a professional in 1962. He works sporadically in film until he starts to perform in a number of secondary roles starting in 1965. His first leading role is in **Vida conyugal sana.** He regularly works in TVE. In theater he has starred in Molière's **The Miser, La balada de los tres inocentes,** by P. M. Herrero and Kafka's **The Trial,** directed by Gutiérrez Aragón. He directs, writes and performs in the feature **Soldados de plomo** (Tin Soldiers).

CREDITS (incomplete)

1965: **La familia y uno más,** by F. Palacios.
1968: **Sangre en el ruedo,** by R. Gil.
1969: **Cómo casarse en siete días,** by F. Fernán-Gómez.
1970: **Pierna creciente, falda menguante,** by J. Aguirre.
1971: **Españolas en París,** by R. Bodegas.
1973: **Vida conyugal sana,** by R. Bodegas.
1974: **Los nuevos españoles,** by R. Bodegas.
Mi mujer es muy decente dentro de lo que cabe, by A. Drove.
1975: **Pantaleón y las visitadoras,** by J. M. Gutiérrez and M. Vargas Llosa.

1976: **Las largas vacaciones del 36,** by J. Camino.
Beatriz, by G. Suárez.
Asignatura pendiente, by J. L. Garci.
1977: **Un hombre llamado «Flor de Otoño»,** by P. Olea.
Solos en la madrugada, by J. L. Garci.
Reina zanahoria, by G. Suárez.
1978: **El diputado,** by E. de la Iglesia.
1979: **Operación Ogro,** by G. Pontecorvo.
La muerte del tercer personaje, by H. Soto.
Miedo a salir de noche, by E. de la Iglesia.
1980: **Navajeros,** by E. de la Iglesia.
1981: **La cripta** by C. del Real.
1982: **La colmena,** by M. Camus.
Estoy en crisis, by F. Colomo.
1983: **Soldados de plomo,** by J. Sacristán.
1984: **La noche más hermosa,** by M. Gutiérrez Aragón.
1985: **A la pálida luz de la luna,** by J. M. González Sinde.
El extranjero de la Cruz del Sur, by J. Grau.

ASSUMPTA SERNA

1957, Barcelona.

Receives a degree from the Barcelona School of Dramatic Arts in 1976. She works in Catalonian independent theater companies and is noted for her work in **Antaviana** by the **Dagoll-Dagom** group. She makes her debut in the world of film with **L'Orgia.** For television, she has made episodes of **Estudio I, Encuentro con las Letras** and **Teatro breve.** She has performed in the film shorts **El despertar del árbol** (1981) and **Alimentación** (1981).

CREDITS

1978: **L'Orgia,** by F. Bellmunt.
1979: **Salut i força al canut,** by F. Bellmunt.
1979: **Polvos mágicos,** by J. R. Larraz.
Supermarket (México), by J. Sánchez.
El crimen de Cuenca, by P. Miró.
1980: **Siete cabalgan hacia la muerte,** by J. L. Merino.
Vecinos, by A. Bermejo.
1981: **La cripta,** by Cayetano del Real.
Dulces horas, by C. Saura.
La rebelión de los pájaros, by J. L. Comerón.
1982: **Círculo de pasiones,** by C. D'Anna.
1983: **Coto de caza,** by J. Grau.
Soldados de plomo, by J. Sacristán.
1984: **El jardín secreto,** by C. Suárez.
1985: **Extramuros,** by M. Picazo.
La vieja música, by M. Camus.
Lulú de noche, by E. Martínez-Lázaro.
1986: **Matador,** by P. Almodóvar.

CARMEN SEVILLA

1930, Seville

Pseudonym of Carmen García. When very young, she becomes the prima ballerina in the Montemar ballet company, and later, in the Estrellita Castro company. She belongs to the corps de ballet of Enrique Castro and Paco Reyes, and is the dance partner of Príncipe Gitano. She makes her film debut in **Serenata española** (1947), by J. de Orduña. Her first leading role is in **Jalisco canta en Sevilla.** She makes her name in the fifties with various films co-starring Luis Mariano.

CREDITS (incomplete)

1948: **Jalisco canta en Sevilla,** by F. de Fuentes.
1950: **Cuentos de la Alhambra,** by F. Rey.
El sueño de Andalucía, by L. Lucía and R. Vernay.
1952: **Violetas imperiales,** by R. Pottier y F. Bernal.
La hermana San Sulpicio, by L. Lucía.
1953: **Reportaje,** by E. Fernández.
1954: **Un caballero andaluz,** by L. Lucía.
La pícara molinera, by L. Klimovsky.
1955: **Congreso en Sevilla,** by A. Román.
La fierecilla domada, by A. Román.

1956: **Aventura para dos,** by D. Siegel and L. Marquina (A Spanish Affair).
1957: **La venganza,** by J. A. Bardem.
1961: **Rey de reyes,** by N. Ray (King of Kings).
El secreto de Mónica, by J. M. Forqué.
1962: **El balcón de la luna,** by L. Saslavsky.
1966: **Camino del Rocío,** by R. Gil.
1970: **El techo de cristal,** by E. de la Iglesia.
Marco Antonio y Cleopatra, by C. Heston (Anthony and Cleopatra).
1973: **La loba y la paloma,** by G. Suárez.
1974: **La cruz del diablo,** by J. Gilling.
1976: **Beatriz,** by G. Suárez.

AMPARO SOLER REAL

1923, Madrid.

The daughter of an actor and actress, she begins to work in theater at thirteen, performing small rolls in the María Guerrero theater company in Madrid, directed by Luis Escobar. Later, as a leading actress, she performs in works by both Spanish and foreign playwrights including Pirandello, Carlos Muñiz and Alfonso Sastre. She forms her own theater company and takes part in the **Realist Theater** group.
In 1975, she gives up the world of theater for television and film. She has been married to producer Alfredo Casado for the last 24 years.

CREDITS (incomplete)

1961: **Usted puede ser un asesino,** by J. M. Forqué.
1962: **La gran familia,** by F. Palacios.
Vamos a contar mentiras, by A. Isasi.
1963: **Vuelve San Valentín,** by F. Palacios.
1964: **Confidencias de un marido,** by F. Prósper.
1965: **La barca sin pescador,** by J. M. Forn.
1966: **Amador,** by. F. Regueiro.
1968: **Las que tienen que servir,** by J. M. Forqué.
1969: **Estudio amueblado 2 P,** by J. M. Forqué.
1970: **El bosque del lobo,** by P. Olea.
1972: **Casa Flora,** by R. Fernández.
1973: **Tamaño natural,** by L. García Berlanga.
1974: **Los nuevos españoles,** by R. Bodegas.
1975: **¡Jo, papá!,** by J. de Armiñán.
La adúltera, by R. Bodegas.
1976: **Retrato de familia,** by A. Giménez Rico.
Nosotros que fuimos tan felices, by A. Drove.
Vuelve, querida Nati, by J. M. Forqué.
1977: **¡Vámonos, Bárbara!,** by C. Bartolomé.
Mi hija Hildegart, by F. Fernán Gómez.
1979: **El crimen de Cuenca,** by P. Miró.
1980: **Los fieles sirvientes,** by F. Betriú.
Gary Cooper que estás en los cielos, by P. Miró.
1981: **Patrimonio nacional,** by L. García Berlanga.
Tac-tac, by L. Alcoriza.
1982: **Nacional III,** by L. García Berlanga.
Hablemos esta noche, by P. Miró.
1983: **Bearn o la sala de las muñecas,** by J. Chávarri.
Las bicicletas son para el varano, by J. Chávarri.
1984: **¿Qué he hecho yo para merecer esto?,** by P. Almodóvar.
1985: **La vaquilla,** by L. G. Berlanga.

T

JOSE SUAREZ

1919, Trubia (Asturias)
1981, Moreda (Asturias)

Discovered by G. Delgrás when he was working on the Asturian railway system, he makes his film debut in the leading role of **Altar mayor.** He acts in more than 30 films as a leading man. For several years he is the president of the Actors Film Union. He leaves the industry during the last years of his life and is the mayor of the Asturian town of Aller.

CREDITS (incomplete)

1943: **Altar mayor,** by G. Delgrás.
1947: **Un viaje de novios,** by G. Delgrás.
1950: **Brigada criminal,** by I. F. Iquino.
Historia de una escalera, by I. F. Iquino.
1951: **Alba de América,** by J. de Orduña.
1953: **Condenados,** by M. Mur-Oti.
1954: **Once pares de botas,** by F. Rovira Beleta.
1956: **Calle Mayor,** by J. A. Bardem.
1957: **El desafío** (Italy), by F. Rosi (La sfida).
1959: **El magistrado** (Italy), by L. Zampa.
1960: **Scano boa** (Italy), by R. Dall'Ara.
1964: **A tiro limpio,** by F. Pérez Dolz.
1965: **Siete hombres de oro** (Italy), by M. Vicario. (Sette uomini d'oro).
1966: **El primer cuartel,** by I. F. Iquino.
1968: **Mañana os besará la muerte,** by J. L. Gottlieb.
1969: **Il prezzo del potere** (Italy), by T. Valerii.
1975: **La trastienda,** by J. Grau.

ANA TORRENT

1966, Madrid

Discovered at seven by V. Erice when he is looking for the lead for **El espíritu de la colmena.** Best actress prize in the Montreal Film Festival for **El nido.** She has recently worked in a number of series for TVE.

CREDITS

1973: **El espíritu de la colmena,** by V. Erice.
1975: **Cría cuervos...,** by C. Saura.
1977: **Elisa, vida mía,** by C. Saura.
Misa en si menor de Juan Sebastián Bach (West Germany), by K. Kieschner.
1979: **Operación Ogro,** by G. Pontecorvo.
1980: **El nido,** by J. de Armiñán.
1982: **La hija rebelde,** by G. Ehmck.
1985: **Los paraísos perdidos,** by B. M. Patino.

V

CONCHA VELASCO

1939, Valladolid.

She studies classical dance from a very early age and dances flamenco with Manolo Caracol and Luisa Ortega. Afterwards, she works as a chorus girl in the shows staged by Celia Gámez. She does small roles in film until 1958, when she begins to play leading roles in comedies. Starting in 1972, she starts to do dramatic roles and to perform important roles in theater. Standing out among her work for TVE is the series **Teresa de Jesús** (1984), by Josefina Molina.

CREDITIS (incomplete)

1954: **El bandido generoso,** by J. M. Elorrieta.
1956: **Dos novias para un torero,** by A. Román.
1957: **Muchachas de vacaciones,** by J. M. Elorrieta.
1958: **Las chicas de la Cruz Roja,** by R. J. Salvia.
Una muchachita de Valladolid, by L. C. Amadori.
1959: **El día de los enamorados,** by F. Palacios.
Los tramposos, by P. Lazaga.
1960: **El indulto,** by J. L. Sáenz de Heredia.
Festival de Benidorm, by R. J. Salvia.
1961: **Trampa para Catalina,** by P. Lazaga.
1963: **La verbena de la Paloma,** by J. L. Sáenz de Heredia.
1964: **Historia de la televisión,** by J. L. Sáenz de Heredia.
1968: **Los que tocan el piano,** by J. Aguirre.
1969: **El alma se serena,** by J. L. Sáenz de Heredia.
1973: **El love feroz,** by J. L. García Sánchez.
1974: **Tormento,** by P. Olea.
Mi mujer es muy decente dentro de lo que cabe, by A. Drove.
1975: **Pim, pam, pum... ¡fuego!,** by P. Olea.
Las bodas de Blanca, by F. Regueiro.
1976: **Las largas vacaciones del 36,** by J. Camino.
Libertad provisional, by R. Bodegas.
1977: **Esposa y amante,** by A. Fons.
1982: **La colmena,** by M. Camus.
1985: **La hora bruja,** by J. de Armiñán.

ANTONIO VICO

1903, Santiago de Chile. 1977 Madrid.

He is the son of an actor and an actress and is born during a tour through South America. He makes his debut in the Concha Catalá theater company. Later he forms his own company with his wife, Carmen Carbonell. His first important role in film is in **Patricio miró a una estrella.** He performs in more than forty films, alternating with his work in theater.

CREDITS (incomplete)

1917: **El Doctor Rojo,** by R. Caralt.
1923: **El Padre Juanico,** by A. Guimerá.
1931: **Isabel de Solís,** by J. Buchs.
1934: **Patricio miró a una estrella,** by J. L. Sáenz de Heredia.
1935: **El malvado Caravel,** by E. Neville.
La hija del penal, by E. G. Maroto.
1935: **Currito de la Cruz,** by F. Delgado.
El genio alegre, by F. Delgado.
1939: **Mariquilla terremoto,** by B. Perojo.
Los cuatro robinsones, by E. G. Maroto.
1940: **La gitanilla,** by F. Delgado.
1941: **El difunto es un vivo,** by I. F. Iquino.
1947: **Serenata española,** by J. de Orduña.
1952: **Manicomio,** by L. M. Delgado y F. Fernán Gómez.

1954: **Marcelino, pan y vino,** by
L. Vajda.
1955: **Ha pasado un hombre,** by J. Setó.
La ironía del dinero, by E. Neville.
1956: **El batallón de las sombras,** by
M. Mur-Oti.
Mi tío Jacinto, by L. Vajda.
1963: **La revoltosa,** by J. Díaz Morales.
1964: **Per un pugno di dollari** (For a
Fistful of Dollars), by S. Leone.
Isidro, el labrador, by R. J. Salvia.
1965: **María Rosa,** by A. Moreno.
1966: **El arte de no casarse,** by J. Feliu
y J. Font-Espina.

INDEXES

422 **FILM INDEX**

D

E

F

G

H

I

J

K

M

N

O

P

Q

R

T

u

v

W

Y

Z

INDEX OF NAMES

A

C

D

E

G

H

I

J

K

L

M

N

O

P

Q

R

S

T

U

V

W

X

470

Y

Z